JSTOR

JSTOR

A HISTORY

ROGER C. SCHONFELD

PRINCETON UNIVERSITY PRESS   PRINCETON AND OXFORD

Library of Congress Cataloging-in-Publication Data

Schonfeld, Roger C., 1977–
JSTOR: a history / Roger C. Schonfeld.
p. cm.
Includes bibliographical references and index.
ISBN 0-691-11531-1 (acid-free paper)
1. JSTOR (Computer file).   2. Periodicals—Databases.   3. JSTOR
(Organization)—History.   I. Title.

PN4836 .S36   2003
050′.285′574—dc21
2002035907

British Library Cataloging-in-Publication Data is available

This book has been composed in Adobe Palatino by
Princeton Editorial Associates, Inc., Scottsdale, Arizona

Printed on acid-free paper. ∞

www.pupress.princeton.edu

Printed in the United States of America

1 3 5 7 9 10 8 6 4 2

Contents

Illustrations

FIGURES

TABLES

Foreword

MY FIRST encounter with JSTOR was at the University of Michigan back in 1993 or 1994 when Randy Frank showed me a demo of a very early version running on a Unix workstation.

I've been a fan ever since.

JSTOR has come a long way from those humble beginnings. As of May 2002, there were 218 journals online, accounting for 62,170 issues, 1,504,372 articles, for a total of 9,169,564 pages. At that time, JSTOR had 1,321 participating libraries from over 60 countries.

JSTOR is one of those services that makes people say "How did I ever live without it?" Indeed, now academics all over the world use JSTOR virtually daily. During the six months of 2002, 16.29 million JSTOR journal pages were accessed online and 5.54 million articles were printed.

JSTOR has not only had a huge impact on scholarship at major research universities in the United States, but it also offers even greater benefits for relatively impoverished institutions in developed and developing nations. Literature that was totally inaccessible to these institutions in the past is now just a click of the mouse away. The result should be a richer educational experience for all concerned.

Roger Schonfeld has done us all a valuable service by recording the history of JSTOR now, while it is still fresh in the participants' minds. His book is valuable not only as a historical account, but also as a compendium of lessons for those who intend to pursue similar ventures.

Academic publishing is evolving rapidly. JSTOR is one of several innovative efforts, including the HighWire Press at Stanford, Project Muse at Johns Hopkins, and the California Digital Library, to name just a few. We can expect to see many more projects in this area in the future. The history of pathbreaking efforts such as JSTOR will be hugely valuable to innovators in this area.

I draw two fundamental lessons from Roger's account for these innovators of tomorrow. First, be flexible. No matter how much planning you do, there will always be unforeseen contingencies. Be prepared to roll with the punches, and turn setbacks into opportunities.

Second, clone Bill Bowen. JSTOR was, ultimately, his vision. He not only conceived of it and funded the initial efforts, but he also went out and persuaded the core journals to come on board. With that prerequisite in place, Bill was able to persuade Kevin Guthrie to become CEO. Kevin, in turn, assembled the team that has led to JSTOR's great success.

The critical ingredient in all of this was having someone with sufficient powers of persuasion to assemble a coalition to actually change the way things are done. This is not to be taken lightly. As Machiavelli put it, "It must be considered that there is nothing more difficult to carry out nor more doubtful of success nor more dangerous to handle than to initiate a new order of things; for the reformer has enemies in all those who profit by the old order, and only lukewarm defenders in all those who would profit by the new order; this lukewarmness arising from the incredulity of mankind who does not truly believe in anything new until they actually have experience of it."

Of course, Machiavelli had it easy, living in pre-Renaissance Italy. If he had ever been president of a university, he would have been much more pessimistic about JSTOR's chances of success!

Hal Varian
Berkeley 2002

A Note on Publication

From its earliest days, the Andrew W. Mellon Foundation has taken a keen interest in the health and well-being of academic and research libraries. They were seen by my predecessor, John Sawyer, as major contributors to scholarship and teaching, and Mr. Sawyer played a key role in the founding of RLG (Research Libraries Group) and in the marshalling of foundation support for libraries. One major concern, reflected in a monograph, _University Libraries and Scholarly Communication_, authored by Anthony M. Cummings et al. soon after my appointment as president of the foundation, was to ensure that increasing numbers of academic journals and rising subscription rates did not make it impossible for libraries to continue to collect, make accessible, and preserve core scholarly materials. As more and more library resources have become available in electronic formats, the foundation's interest has evolved in these directions as a matter of course. The creation of JSTOR is an important milestone in this evolutionary process.

Within each of the foundation's areas of programmatic interest, we have had a continuing commitment to report on our activities and to publish information on lessons we think we have learned from our work. For just this reason, we have intended for some time to present an account of our experiences with JSTOR. We had in mind tracing JSTOR's history from its early days as a special project incubated within the Mellon Foundation and supported primarily through grants to its present-day status as an independent 501(c)(3) organization that is self-sustaining as a result of the revenues contributed by some 1,500 participating libraries worldwide. In the earliest days of the project, we promised to record both our achievements and our sometime frustrations. Our hope was then, and is today, that a careful, critical account of events along the way could help the scholarly community avoid at least some of our errors.

As time went on and JSTOR grew into an ever more complicated entity, it seemed impossible to capture its history in a short account, or even series of accounts, of the kind that I regularly incorporate into my annual reports. Instead, we asked Roger Schonfeld to prepare a detailed study documenting JSTOR's experiences, "warts and all." The foundation agreed to make all of its internal records available to him for this purpose, and Kevin Guthrie, president of JSTOR, also pledged his full cooperation.

There was no sense at the time that this study should necessarily become a book. As Mr. Schonfeld's work progressed, however, more and more observers of the rapidly changing world of scholarly communications expressed interest in it. Princeton University Press saw that such a study might be relevant not only to libraries, publishers, and creators of digital archives, but also to a broader audience interested in how new kinds of not-for-profit entities are created and governed. This book is the result of immense hard work, and, on behalf of the foundation, I would like to thank Mr. Schonfeld for his exceptional efforts. His work has been complicated by the fact that many "pieces" were moving at the same time, both within JSTOR itself and within the larger domain of scholarly communications as it has continued to be shaped by advances in information technology. This is a first chapter, no more than that, in ongoing efforts to understand how best to blend new technologies, viable business models, legal acumen, and an understanding of the needs of users in the creation of digital resources that will respect the age-old values of the scholarly community.

William G. Bowen
New York 2002

Introduction

IN THE past decade, technology has revolutionized scholarly communications. Ten years ago, virtually all scholars and students relied on bulky card catalogs, printed bibliographic indices, and hardcopy books and journals for their library research. Today, almost all card catalogs are fully electronic, forcing heated debate during the transition about what to do with the outdated manual behemoths.[1] Indices are widely available in electronic form. And the journals (and increasingly the books) to which these catalogs and indices point are found not only on shelves, but also online.

This revolution in scholarly communications has been accompanied and facilitated by a larger change in communications—the advent of the Internet and the accompanying boom economy. In reducing the marginal costs of information transactions, the Internet has been transformational. But some of the most advanced applications, involving video and remote operations, have been slow to develop. Of worldwide fiber-optic bandwidth, much of which was built by optimists during the boom, 91 percent went unused in 2001.[2] Despite the prognostications of many, and the efficiencies it has brought, the Internet does not yet constitute a comprehensive communications revolution.

Yet while so many of the dot.coms have failed, academia has been transformed. The Internet was born at American universities, spurring campus networking. In the early 1990s, the first step was to network with LocalTalk, which was quickly upgraded to Ethernet and fiber-optic technologies. Although the wealthiest research universities and liberal arts colleges moved first, all academia soon followed. High-capacity networking enabled all manner of new applications, many of which were unrelated to scholarship.[3]

For scholarship, the shifts enabled by networking have been profound. Traditional resources like books and journals are now available in digital form. By 1992, the few electronic journals were email-based,

---

[1] Nicholson Baker, "Discards," *The New Yorker*, April 4, 1994.

[2] Matthew Fordahl, "Market Glut May Hurt Fiber Carriers," *AP Online*, February 7, 2002, citing data from Merrill Lynch.

[3] The proliferation of online music services was almost solely enabled by high-capacity campus networks. For a journalistic account of the developments in the domain of music, see John Alderman, *Sonic Boom: Napster, MP3, and the New Pioneers of Music* (New York: Perseus, 2001).

but with the introduction in 1993 of the web, that medium became the default.[4] When published online, journal articles can link to multimedia and sometimes to raw data. And networking has led to some altogether new developments. Scholars interact via discussion lists and email, encouraging more frequent consultation. Growth of faculty email accounts between 1990 and 2000 has been astronomical.[5] In addition to formal peer review, article drafts in some disciplines are submitted to so-called preprint servers, allowing them to be shared with other scholars. In various fields of physics, 2,500 papers per month are submitted online.[6] Consequently, results are disseminated more rapidly, and in that discipline journals are necessary only for peer review, citation, and archiving. Portal sites have begun to bring together resources across a number of formats in a given discipline, allowing for significantly more convenient and effective access. Courseware is opening up new vistas for teaching within both residential and distance education. In sum, linkage and interconnection has enhanced the value and eased the use of information. All of these shifts have led to important changes in the way that scholars work on projects and in the way that they share their results with others.

At this crossroads, one of the first online scholarly communications resources to become viable was JSTOR. Publicly available since 1997, JSTOR has digitized the backfiles of about three hundred academic journals, as far back as 1665 in one case, and distributes them online to libraries around the world. Originally conceived by William G. Bowen, president of the Andrew W. Mellon Foundation, the JSTOR project was undertaken with a grant to the University of Michigan. After a year as a fledgling project, JSTOR was spun off into its own independent not-for-profit organization. With Kevin Guthrie as president, the New York–headquartered JSTOR has grown to serve nearly 1,500 library participants in over 60 countries. These are largely academic libraries but increasingly include high school, public, and government libraries. Students and scholars affiliated with any one of these institutions have access to JSTOR's collections from their local campus network and, increasingly, remotely.

JSTOR's system features were conceived in an atmosphere of early uncertainty, but they have held up well thus far. Users can access the

---

[4] Ann Okerson, "Are We There Yet? Online E-Resources Ten Years After," *Library Trends* 48, no. 4 (March 22, 2000): 671.

[5] Among language and literature faculty, for example, less than 20 percent used email in 1991. Thomas J. DeLoughry, "Humanists and Computers," *Chronicle of Higher Education,* April 20, 1993. Today, the figure approaches 100 percent.

[6] See "arXiv.org monthly submission rate statistics," available at *http://arxiv.org/show_monthly_submissions.*

journals through one of two interfaces from JSTOR's website (*http://www.jstor.org*). The first is a "browse" system, allowing a user to move through a journal's hierarchy, from the volume to the issue to individual articles (most useful when bibliographic information is already known). The second is a search interface, into which a user can input one or a number of words or phrases found in an article title, author name, or the text of every page of every journal. In either case, once a desired article has been identified, it is displayed over a standard web browser as a series of individual page images. Users can page forward or backward through the context of an entire issue, just as in the hardcopy. They seem to have been satisfied with this system; through the end of 2001, they searched it 26,811,857 times, viewed 18,147,337 articles, and printed 11,379,694 articles.

As numerous libraries participated in the initial collections of journals, JSTOR has sought and been awarded funding for new collections by a number of philanthropies. JSTOR works with a diversity of scholarly publishers, from the smallest scholarly societies to some of the largest commercial publishers, in assembling its collections. JSTOR's role is in part curatorial, bringing together the high-quality core titles of whatever discipline is being focused upon. In addition to a focus on the humanities and social sciences within the arts and sciences, JSTOR has built collections focused on ecology and botany, general science, business, and languages and literatures (this last completed after the present study), and has begun to build collections of art history and music journals. Today, JSTOR is an indisputably successful, self-sustaining organization that continues to attract journal and library participants.

JSTOR's history is necessarily complicated. The effort to build JSTOR brought together work by librarians and technologists, foundations and grantees, publishers, scanning vendors, indexing services, lawyers, the British government, and well over one thousand colleges and universities. At every point in JSTOR's development, there were many pieces in motion. To make this history readable, it has been at times necessary to privilege theme over chronology. To avoid misconceptions, a time line has been included (pp. xxvii–xxxiv).

Examining the history of an operating organization is unusual in the field of scholarly communications. To my surprise, there had been little such work on the prominent library cooperatives created in past generations, such as the Center for Research Libraries (CRL), the Online Computer Library Center (OCLC), and the Research Libraries Group (RLG).[7]

---

[7]OCLC is the exception. See Kathleen L. Maciuszko, *OCLC: A Decade of Development* (Littleton, CO: Libraries Unlimited, 1984); Albert R. Maruskin, *OCLC: Its Governance,*

Most studies of the shifts underway in the past ten years have focused on the changing information needs and expectations of the scholar.[8] There has been little study, however, of some of the most important of these new resources. HighWire Press, Project Muse, and ScienceDirect, not to mention Ebsco, ProQuest, and Lexis-Nexis, deserve attention. These resources, often so demanded by scholars, have been created or vastly expanded in a brief period, and the why and how remain unexplored.[9]

Dozens of projects, perhaps over a hundred, have created significant digital libraries. Why a book on JSTOR? Staff of the Mellon Foundation had always viewed JSTOR as an experiment to see what was possible in this domain, promising that the lessons learned would be broadly shared. JSTOR has been generally understood as a success story in the annals of scholarly communications, so a history might help to demonstrate how such success could be achieved. Despite numerous smaller-scale reports by JSTOR staff, William G. Bowen, president of the Mellon Foundation and chairman of JSTOR's Board of Trustees, believed there was an opportunity to do more. Both JSTOR and Mellon willingly made available all of their relevant files, a generous step that many others might have resisted for so contemporary a history. In addition, the staff and associates of both organizations happily submitted to far more hours of interviews than anyone could have foreseen. These factors made a study of JSTOR particularly appealing. Hence, this book is offered as an "insider's" account of the development of JSTOR—written by a member of Mellon's research staff and a former summer employee of JSTOR. My insider status notwithstanding, I have strived (and indeed been encouraged) to take the most objective, scholarly, critical approach possible.[10]

As an important new development in the field of libraries and scholarly communications, JSTOR offers some indication of the organizational relationships that technology seems to be ushering in. In this case,

---

Function, Financing, and Technology (New York: Marcel Dekker, 1980); and K. Wayne Smith, ed., *OCLC 1967–1997: Thirty Years of Furthering Access to the World's Information* (New York: Haworth Press, 1998).

[8] A fine example of this type of work is William S. Brockman, Laura Neumann, Carole L. Palmer, and Tonyia Tidline, *Scholarly Work in the Humanities and the Evolving Information Environment* (Washington, DC: Digital Library Federation, 2001).

[9] Richard E. Quandt's memoir of some of his work at the Mellon Foundation during the first half of this period is one exception, and it is therefore most valuable. See "Mellon Initiatives in Digital Libraries: 1994–1999," April 2002, unpublished manuscript on deposit at the Nathan Marsh Pusey Library of the Andrew W. Mellon Foundation.

[10] There has been some amount of debate about whether an insider can write objective history. See, for example, Michael Pinto-Duschinsky, "Selling the Past," *The Times Literary Supplement,* October 23, 1998, and subsequent discussion in the pages of *The Times Literary Supplement* through September 1999.

some libraries have willingly ceded responsibility for archiving a group of scholarly journals to an independent organization. While some form of resource-centralization has been foreseen by a number of observers, a specific case study—with the impediments, pitfalls, and diversions that necessarily occur—may be valuable. Moreover, the JSTOR example may tell us something about the broader technology-enabled shifts facing higher education.

In addition, JSTOR's story is worth telling as the case of a well-managed nonprofit. The Mellon Foundation's research staff has long had an interest in the nonprofit sector, toward which all of the foundation's grant-making work has been necessarily targeted. It sought to understand the contours of this large component of the American economy[11] and to answer specific questions about the health of some constituents of particular importance to the foundation.[12] One major publication—whose author would, not altogether coincidentally, become JSTOR's president—examined why an important research library was, despite impressive assets, continually on the verge of bankruptcy throughout the twentieth century.[13] If that study of the New-York Historical Society was the story of the pitfalls of running a nonprofit archival institution, JSTOR illustrates that, through careful management, conservative planning, and scale effects, a nonprofit scholarly archive can rapidly reach self-sufficiency.

Finally, it is possible that this study will be of interest to those concerned with the development of the Internet. JSTOR offers a case study that might be useful in considering how the Internet, as a mechanism of communications, developed. It also offers one of the few contrapositives in examining the peculiar economy that accompanied the boom of the late 1990s.[14]

[11]William G. Bowen, Thomas I. Nygren, Sarah E. Turner, and Elizabeth A. Duffy, *The Charitable Non-Profits: An Analysis of Institutional Dynamics and Characteristics* (San Francisco: Jossey-Bass Publishers, 1994).

[12]Jed I. Bergman, *Managing Change in the Nonprofit Sector: Lessons from the Evolution of Five Independent Research Libraries* (San Francisco: Jossey-Bass Publishers, 1996).

[13]Kevin M. Guthrie, *The New-York Historical Society: Lessons from One Nonprofit's Long Struggle for Survival* (San Francisco: Jossey-Bass Publishers, 1996).

[14]Unfortunately, JSTOR and other nonprofits have been omitted from the first such studies. One that otherwise offers a thoughtful and relatively comprehensive account is John Cassidy, *dot.con: The Greatest Story Ever Sold* (New York: HarperCollins Publishers, 2002). Early organizational studies are also beginning to appear. See, for example, Adam Cohen, *The Perfect Store: Inside Ebay* (New York: Little, Brown, and Company, 2002). For an amusing, if enraged, listing of so many of the failures, see Philip J. Kaplan, *F'd Companies* (New York: Simon & Schuster, 2002).

Acknowledgments

THE TASK of offering thanks is truly a pleasure for an author who has had the benefit of so much gracious counsel, enthusiasm, and assistance. A project like this could never be accomplished without the help and acquiescence of many, but the support I have received from friends and colleagues has contributed mightily to the present volume. First, I must begin by thanking William G. Bowen and the rest of the trustees, leadership, and staff of the Mellon Foundation for fostering what was, during my time there, an atmosphere of inquiry and collegiality from which so much else has flowed. Their direct support made this project possible.

There are two individuals who deserve my deepest thanks for supporting this project through all of its stages: Bill Bowen and Kevin Guthrie, the president of JSTOR. Both agreed to permit access to their colleagues and their archives, and both submitted to many hours of interviews themselves. Each read the manuscript. They afforded, and indeed encouraged, the editorial freedom necessary to this project.

At Mellon, I owe gratitude to many. My colleagues and friends Joseph Meisel and Donald Waters read the entire manuscript. Don provided much-needed context from his experience with academic libraries and the patient and thoughtful reflection that are his nature. Joe taught me, on the fly, to write history, while also being a key morale-builder. The influence of both can be found throughout the manuscript.

My colleagues on the research staff provided distractions and enthusiasm during two long years of research and writing. Sarah Levin somehow managed to leave me satisfied to have worked on the statistical aspects of one, and only one, study of college sports. Cara Nakamura's research on wealth disparities informed a number of sections of this study, and her kindness, friendship—and food—were most welcome. Susan Anderson always made me feel welcome in Princeton, and kept me focused on the big things. All three of them read a number of chapters. Although Martin Kurzweil arrived just as this book was going to press, he helped me through the stress of the finale. Having colleagues immersed in their own research projects was always a comfort.

Deanna Marcum of the Council on Library and Information Resources and Hal Varian of the University of California, Berkeley, each read the manuscript, which benefited greatly from their suggestions; I only wish I had consulted them earlier in the project. Other readers of the entire manuscript included Nancy Kopans of JSTOR and Gretchen Wagner of

Mellon. Readers of smaller sections included Charles Ellis, Saul Fisher, Ira Fuchs, Max Marmor, Lauren Meserve, Pat McPherson, Susanne Pichler, Rachel Shattuck, James Shulman, and Harriet Zuckerman. Each contributed in ways large and small to the present work.

For research assistance, I benefited from the willing labors of Susanne Pichler, who is the library director at Mellon. She provided incomparable aid with research questions that were essential to the project, but all too often turned out to be wild-goose chases. Reading large parts of the manuscript, she gave a practicing librarian's perspective on JSTOR. Lisa Bonifacic helped tremendously in locating materials of relevance from libraries around the country.

At Mellon, the grant archives are overseen by Virginia Simone, who cheerfully located information on grants, or grant requests, on numerous occasions. To Judy Mastrangelo, I must offer not only thanks, but also apologies—I drove her nearly to the edge by borrowing, and then keeping for nearly two years, all of the grant materials related to JSTOR. And nothing at Mellon is accomplished successfully without enlisting the sage counsel of the indefatigable Pat Woodford.

At JSTOR, virtually every staff member helped me locate archival information and contemporary data. These included: Ken Alexander, Gerard J. Aurigemma, Kristen Garlock, Jeffrey Hovis, Eileen G. Fenton, Nigel Kerr, Holly Kornegay, Carol MacAdam, Carmen Mocolo, Aimee E. Pyle, Nahid Rahim, Rahim S. Rajan, and Todd L. Santaniello.

Sandy Ellinger and Peggy Rector of Denison University struggled valiantly with the archives of that school's meetings of its board of trustees. Lawrence Landweber of the University of Wisconsin helped me to understand the evolution of international connectivity to the Internet. Dick Quandt offered advice on a number of critical matters, and provided free economics tutoring, while he worked on a memoir that was somewhat parallel to this study.

The many interviewees, who readily gave so many hours of time to help my study, were invaluable. Some took many hours over the course of a number of days out of their busy schedules, and I thank them for making it possible for me to capture so much of the oral history of JSTOR's development. They are listed by name in the Bibliography. Without their cheerful cooperation, only a small part of this story could have been told.

Processing these interviews was a challenge in itself. For help with transcription, I offer my deepest thanks to Bonnie Brown, Susan Dady, Deborah Longino, Diane Sintich, and Kathy Stockwell. The study's reliance on oral history would have been far more difficult to manage without their tireless help.

At a more recent stage, colleagues from Princeton University Press as well as freelancers turned a raw manuscript into the final product. My editor, Peter Dougherty, always provided good counsel and much encouragement. His judgment and sensitivity brought balance to the endeavor. Kevin McInturff identified all of the missing pieces. Debbie Tegarden stewarded the manuscript through the production process, ensuring that we held to our schedule. In addition, freelance copyeditor Jonathan Munk's careful but enthusiastic work was simply invaluable.

Finally, I would like to thank my family, Carol, Ed, and Susan Schonfeld, for all of their love, thoughtfulness, support, and exhortation. Their encouragement has had a profound effect, and for that, and so much more, my gratitude is immeasurable.

Though the support and help of so many improved this study markedly, responsibility for shortcomings and errors of course rests with me alone.

List of Abbreviations

A&I	Abstracting and Indexing
AAF	Annual Access Fee
ACA	Appalachian College Association
ACF	Archive Capital Fee
AEA	American Economic Association
AHA	American Historical Association
ALA	American Library Association
APSA	American Political Science Association
ARL	Association of Research Libraries
CPC	Cartesian Perceptual Compression
CRL	Center for Research Libraries
DDF	Database Development Fee
DEC	Digital Equipment Corporation
DIRECT	Desktop Information Resources and Collaboration Technology
DIT	Digital Imaging & Technologies
DLPS	Digital Library Production Services
EFFECT	Exchange Format for Electronic Components and Texts
ESA	Ecological Society of America
FTE	Full-Time Equivalent
FTL	Full-Text Lexiconographer
HBCU	Historically Black Colleges and Universities
HHMI	Howard Hughes Medical Institute
GALILEO	Georgia Library Learning Online
IEEE	Institute of Electrical and Electronics Engineers, Inc.
ILL	Interlibrary Loan
IP	Intellectual Property
IPL	Internet Public Library
IT	Information Technology
JHUP	Johns Hopkins University Press
JISC	Joint Information Systems Committee
MLA	Modern Language Association
NCSA	National Center for Supercomputing Applications
NERL	Northeast Research Libraries
NPC	National Periodicals Center
NYHS	New-York Historical Society
OAH	Organization of American Historians
OAI	Open Archiving Initiative

OCLC	Online Computer Library Center
OCR	Optical Character Recognition
PCI	Periodicals Contents Index
PEAK	Pricing Electronic Access to Knowledge
QC	Quality Control
RFP	Request for Proposals
RLIN	Research Libraries Information Network
RSA	Renaissance Society of America
SEF	Southern Educational Foundation
SGML	Standard Generalized Markup Language
SICI	Serial Item and Contribution Identifier
TIFF	Tagged Image File Format
TULIP	The University Licensing Project
UMI	University Microfilms, Inc.
WWW	World Wide Web

A JSTOR Time Line

1989	Origins of the DIRECT project, with principal investigator Frank and programmers Alexander and Peters (3).
March 1991	Elsevier agrees to participate in what would become TULIP (3).
1991	First WWW browser released on the Internet.
1992	The University of Michigan decides to reinvigorate, rather than close, its library school; appoints a computer scientist, Dan Atkins, dean (3).
1992	In response to the "serials spiral," Mellon research staff examines the health of research libraries, publishing *University Libraries and Scholarly Communications* (1).
September 1993	NCSA releases Mosaic browser.
November–December 1993	Bowen first conceives of digitizing scholarly journals (1).
December 1993	Mellon trustees authorize the Ekman-Quandt program on scholarly communications (1).
December 1993–February 1994	Bowen consults Ekman and Fuchs, who in turn reach out to others in an effort to understand options (1).
February 1994	Initial group of journal titles identified (2).
February 1994	Bryn Mawr and Williams agree to join Denison as test sites (2).
March 1994	Advisory Committee meets for the first time, endorses approaching UMI (2).
March 17–18, 1994	Bowen travels to Ann Arbor to meet with UMI and the University of Michigan (2, 3).

March–July 1994	Intermittant discussions with UMI (2).
Early April 1994	Outreach to journal publishers begins (2).
June 28, 1994	License agreement with first publisher, the American Historical Association, for the *American Historical Review* (2).
July 1994	Negotiations begin with Chadwyck-Healy for PCI (4).
July 1994	Negotiations begin with the University of Michigan for the DIRECT/TULIP software (3).
July 8, 1994	License agreement with Econometric Society for *Econometrica* (2).
July 12, 1994	Second advisory committee meeting (3).
July 26, 1994	License agreement with American Economic Association for *American Economic Review* (2).
August 1, 1994	License agreement with University of Chicago Press for two titles, the *Journal of Political Economy* and the *Journal of Modern History* (2).
August 5, 1994	License agreement with Institute of Early American History and Culture for *William and Mary Quarterly* (2).
August 29, 1994	License agreement with MIT Press for *Quarterly Journal of Economics* (2).
August 30, 1994	Mellon trustees award $700,000 to the University of Michigan for software development (3).
Fall 1994–Spring 1995	Michigan creates a web-based version of DIRECT, including TIFF2GIF, and begins to develop a printing application (4).
September 22, 1994	License agreement with Organization of American Historians for the *Journal of American History* (2).
October–November 1994	Decision to scan from paper rather than microfilm (4).
October 1994	Robertson alerts the ESA and the JSTOR project staff to one another's mutual interests (6).

November 8, 1994	License agreement with The Medieval Academy of America for *Speculum* (2).
November 9, 1994	License agreement with last pilot publisher, Harvard University, for *Review of Economics and Statistics* (2).
November 1994	First Netscape browser is released (1).
December 1994	Mellon trustees award $1.5 million to the University of Michigan for production work, including scanning (4).
January 1995	Journals from Harvard and Michigan are first sent to DIT (4).
January 1995	Lougee hires Aschenbrenner and Garlock as the JSTOR librarians (4).
March 1995	DIT having been asked to create metadata, PCI is no longer needed (4).
March 1995	First DIT output is received by the University of Michigan; problems are rampant (4).
March 1995	Having long put aside plans for organizational arrangements, Bowen begins to consider them in detail (5).
April 1995	Guthrie assumes increasing amounts of operating responsibility (5).
April 11, 1995	Third advisory committee meeting, discussing options for growth and organizational choices; "export" of JSTOR is envisioned within two years (5).
June–July 1995	Current issues publishing considered at length; JSTOR-C crafted (6).
June 17, 1995	Guthrie commits to leading the new independent JSTOR (5).
July 1995	Guthrie travels to Ann Arbor; finds ad hoc staffing inadequate for an operating enterprise (5).
July 31, 1995	JSTOR incorporated as an independent not-for-profit organization (5).
August 4, 1995	First meeting of the JSTOR trustees; Bowen elected chairman, Guthrie executive director (5).
September 18, 1995	Bowen speaks to the Council on Library and Information Resources,

	first major effort to publicize JSTOR (10).
Fall 1995	Michigan-based preparation arrangements are developed for the production process (7).
December 18, 1995	Mellon awards $1.5 million to JSTOR as "working capital" (5).
January 1996	Eight of the ten pilot journals are digitized, totalling nearly 600,000 pages (7).
January–February 1996	"Moving wall" in its eventual form is first proposed (6).
February 1996	Landis joins JSTOR as first production coordinator (7).
Spring 1996	Plans for current issues are put aside (6).
May 1996	AAAS expresses interest in including *Science* magazine in JSTOR (6).
June 13, 1996	Strategic and Operating Plan is presented to the board (8).
Summer 1996	Princeton programming office established; Kirchhoff and Ratliff begin to adapt software for a mirror site (9).
July 1996	Publisher license agreement is put into standard form (6).
Fall 1996	Andrews and Landis investigate and revise the production process (9).
Fall 1996–Spring 1997	As the public release gets underway, DeGennaro actively lobbies his librarian contacts (10).
October 1996	Library license agreement is finalized (10).
October 1996	Intellectual property and organizational confusions indicate the necessity of revising the JSTOR-Michigan relationship (9).
November 1996	Princeton mirror site goes online for test sites (9).
January 1997	50 journals signed; 16 online, totalling nearly 950,000 pages.
January 1997	JSTOR goes "live," as the charter period commences (10).

January 1997	At ALA, participating librarians call for usage statistics, which are implemented by Alexander and Garlock (10).
March 1997–November 1999	Regular, monthly releases of Arts & Sciences I journals.
March 17, 1997	Mellon award to the Southern Educational Foundation to encourage HBCU participation in JSTOR (10).
April 1997	Charter period comes to a close with 190 libraries participating (10).
June 9, 1997	Mellon award to the Appalachian College Association to encourage participation in JSTOR (10).
June 20, 1997	After a period of tension, Michigan and JSTOR sign an interim agreement (9).
Summer 1997	With future collections in mind, planning begins for a second production facility, in Princeton (11).
Summer 1997	Landis leaves JSTOR; Fenton becomes production coordinator (9).
July 1997	Trustees resolve that new collections should be planned (11).
August 1997	Initial planning for production of *Science* begins (11).
October 3, 1997	Michigan and JSTOR sign a final agreement (9).
October 1997	With consistent production at Michigan, JSTOR secures additional space there for expansion (11).
December 1997	Mellon awards nearly $1.5 million to the ESA to support a JSTOR Ecology & Botany Collection (11).
January 1998	Participating libraries number 243.
January 1998	69 journals signed; 33 online, totalling nearly 1.85 million pages.
Spring 1998	Production librarian position created; Kiplinger assumes it (13).
Spring 1998	JSTOR becomes available in the United Kingdom via the JISC mirror site (10).

Spring 1998	Guthrie and the trustees consider worldwide "franchising" (13).
Spring 1998	Comptroller position created; Aurigemma hired (12).
May 1998	AAAS signs license to include *Science* and *Scientific Monthly* (11).
Summer 1998	Pricing adjustment approved by trustees (12).
July 1998	Mellon awards $1.3 million for General Science Collection (11).
July 30, 1998	Trustees discuss a second major arts and sciences collection and confirm desire for business collection (13).
August 1998	HHMI awards $800,000 for General Science Collection (11).
Fall 1998	Pricing for overseas libraries is adopted, and participation soon follows (12).
November 1998	Instead of franchising, the somewhat different "consulting" business is considered (13).
Winter 1998–1999	DIT begins scanning operations for JSTOR at a second facility; the backlog is rapidly resolved (13).
January 1999	Participating libraries number 369.
January 1999	108 journals signed; 67 online, totalling nearly 3.15 million pages.
February 10, 1999	Trustees conclude that JSTOR should expand rapidly, including Arts & Sciences II and Business collections (13).
February 10, 1999	Guthrie and the trustees discuss linking in depth for the first time (14).
April 1999	Languages & Literatures added to JSTOR plans, in conjunction with MLA (13).
Summer 1999	Production operations, largely for General Science, begin at the Princeton office (14).
July 1999	Art History added to JSTOR plans (13).
Fall 1999	Michigan office initiates Ecology & Botany production work (14).

October 1999	First article-level links into JSTOR, from MathSciNet (14).
November 23, 1999	Arts & Sciences I is completed five weeks ahead of schedule—117 journals totalling nearly 5 million pages (13).
December 17, 1999	Mellon Foundation awards funds to JSTOR for humanities journals in Arts & Sciences II Collection (13).
January 2000	Pricing for community colleges is established (12).
January 2000	Participating libraries number 650.
January 2000	Sloan Foundation awards funds to JSTOR for development of linking (14).
January 2000	Niarchos Foundation awards funds to JSTOR for access to Greek institutions, and for classical-archaeological journals.
January 2000	Mellon Foundation awards funds to JSTOR for access to universities in Eastern Europe.
February 16, 2000	First General Science release (14).
June 16, 2000	Mellon awards funds to Sabinet to encourage JSTOR participation among South African university libraries (14).
June 16, 2000	Mellon Foundation awards funds to JSTOR for population and demography journals in Arts & Sciences II Collection (13).
November 30, 2000	Ecology & Botany Collection released (14).
December 15, 2000	Mellon Foundation awards funds to JSTOR for Art History Collection (14).
December 21, 2000	Last release of the General Science Collection (14).
December 31, 2000	Bennett leaves JSTOR, which reorganizes so that a single production coordinator, Fenton, manages both offices (14).
January 2001	Participating libraries number 952.
January 2001	153 journals online, totalling nearly 7 million pages.

January 2001	MacArthur Foundation awards funds to JSTOR to encourage the participation of academic libraries in the former Soviet Union (14).
March 2001	An anonymous foundation awards funds to JSTOR for the development of a consulting business (14).
June 6, 2001	First release of the Arts & Sciences II Collection, comprising 22 titles (14).
November 14, 2001	Business Collection released (14).
December 17, 2001	Mellon Foundation awards funds to JSTOR for Music Collection (14).
December 2001	218 journals online, totalling nearly 9 million pages (14).

CHAPTER 1

The Idea at Denison, the Project at Mellon

DECEMBER 1993–JANUARY 1994

WE BEGIN in late 1993, when a discussion before the Board of Trustees of Denison University alerted one trustee, William G. Bowen, to the possible demand for a digital library of scholarly journals. Shared with colleagues at the Andrew W. Mellon Foundation, of which he was president, and beyond, the initial idea matured rapidly into the basis for a major project. This chapter summarizes the influences that led Bowen to his idea, and it illustrates both how much thought went into the development of the proposed project and how rapidly the project began to congeal.

Denison University is an academically selective liberal arts college in Ohio, and Doane Library is one of the key landmarks on its beautiful campus. By the early 1990s, Doane's overcrowded and often-inaccessible stacks were no longer adequate. Denison's books, journals, and other library collections had filled all of the available space. There was no room to store new materials acquired for the collection. Responding to this need, the administration added the expansion of Doane Library to a list of capital projects on the horizon that it presented to the board of trustees in late 1993. President Michele Tolela Myers had to ask the board to find funds for a substantial and expensive library expansion.

The problems facing Denison's library had particular resonance with one of the trustees. In addition to being president of the Andrew W. Mellon Foundation, William G. Bowen was president emeritus of Princeton University and an economist specializing in nonprofit organizations. With William Baumol, he had written the definitive study of the economics of the arts, and even before becoming a university provost and president he had written on the economics of higher education. The 1966 Baumol-Bowen study had identified "cost-disease" as the core problem of nonprofit service-intensive organizations.[1] In most industries, new technology brings increases in productivity, allowing the same number of workers to produce more goods (or fewer workers to produce the same amount). A classic example is the assembly line, which

---

[1] William J. Baumol and William G. Bowen, *Performing Arts—The Economic Dilemma: A Study of Problems Common to Theater, Opera, Music and Dance* (New York: Twentieth Century Fund, 1966).

transformed industrial productivity. Baumol and Bowen showed that, because the service-intensive nonprofits are so reliant on labor, they are less able to take advantage of technology and thus they grow ever more expensive relative to the output of the economy as a whole. Indeed in some instances the amount of labor is irreducible: it will always take four musicians to perform a string quartet. Even though these socially beneficial organizations grow ever more expensive, we want them to flourish, and so a solution must be found to prevent them from becoming economically nonviable. The next year, Baumol would demonstrate that precisely the same phenomenon holds for academic libraries.[2]

ACADEMIC LIBRARIES IN THE 1970S AND 1980S

By the 1970s, with inflation rampant in the United States, the cost-disease was beginning to translate in to real problems for libraries, which began to take up some suggestions for savings. But although many libraries began to automate operations, such as circulation, the early evidence of the savings that should have resulted was uncertain at best.[3] Much technology, such as databases like Dialog, brought increased scholarly utility, but also increased costs.[4] One prior success was in cataloging, where various subscription services allowed libraries to do without scores of redundant catalog staff around the country.[5] The Online Computer Library Center (OCLC) instituted a cooperative cataloging program, allowing electronic catalogs to be developed without local cataloging.[6] The success of automation and cooperative cataloging notwithstanding,

[2]William J. Baumol and Matityahu Marcus, *On the Economics of Library Operations* (Princeton, NJ: Mathematica, for the National Advisory Commission on Libraries, 1967).

[3]William J. Baumol and Sue Anne Batey Blackmun, "Electronics, the Cost Disease, and the Operation of Libraries," *Journal of the American Society for Information Science* 34, no. 3 (1983): 181–91.

Then again, some of the automation itself began only in fits and starts. See Harrison Bryan, "American Automation in Action," *Library Journal*, January 15, 1967, 189–96.

[4]For the state of the art, a useful source is Thomas H. Martin, *A Feature Analysis of Interactive Retrieval Systems* (Springfield, VA: National Technical Information Service, 1974).

[5]Even this case is somewhat simplistic. In fact, the subscription services arose concurrently with the modern notion of cataloging. It is unlikely that, in the absence of the card catalog services, so many libraries would have offered professionally cataloged collections.

[6]The cooperative cataloging system allowed the first cataloging record, often created by a librarian at the Library of Congress, to be downloaded into the catalogs of all other libraries that accessioned the title. Thus each book would be cataloged professionally only once nationwide, rather than hundreds or thousands of times, eliminating a huge redundancy. See Arthur T. Hamlin, *The University Library in the United States: Its Origin and Devel-*

they did nothing to reduce academic libraries' voracious demand for books and journals.

Saving money by making expensive staff redundant was the only way to combat the cost disease directly—by increasing labor productivity—but it was hardly the only way to restructure libraries to save money. Thinking more radically, some librarians began to wonder if "library growth [can] be curbed or halted," moving toward a zero-growth model.[7] The "steady-state" collection model made the most sense within an efficient system of interlibrary lending (ILL) of nonlocal resources, which OCLC's national catalog helped to provide. Substantial efforts were undertaken to research the optimal balance between local and remote collections, given a variety of ILL arrangements.[8]

Other proposals, which were at least vaguely related, called for some sort of central lending library for periodicals. Two of the reasons for focusing on periodicals were the facts that their rising costs functioned as a "permanent prior lien" on the budget and that there were often local bibliographic entrance points in the form of A&I resources.[9] By the late 1970s, these ideas had coalesced into a proposal for a National Periodical Center (NPC), a central warehouse to store materials. It was predicted that the NPC would "reduce the number of back issues that each library must keep, thus relieving the pressure for expansion of library buildings"—and the vigor of one supporter's protestations to the contrary may indicate that it was intended to encourage massive subscription cancellations.[10] Indeed, some proponents were explicit about this,

---

opment (Philadelphia: University of Pennsylvania Press, 1981), 208–9. Moreover, without OCLC, e-catalogs would not have been possible, and there is no question but that electronic catalogs have increased productivity, not to mention utility, for researchers. For a somewhat preliminary analysis of the potential to save costs, see Herman H. Fussler, *Research Libraries and Technology* (Chicago: University of Chicago Press, 1973), 65–66. For a historical overview of library cooperation, see David C. Weber, "A Century of Cooperative Programs among Academic Libraries," *College & Research Libraries*, May 1976: 205–21.

[7]Daniel Gore, ed., *Farewell to Alexandria: Solutions to space, growth, and performance problems of libraries* (Westport, CT: Greenwood Press, 1976), 4.

[8]Some such studies include: [Scott Bennett], *Report on the Conoco Project in German Literature and Geology* (Stanford, CA: Research Libraries Group, 1987); T. Mackey, "Interlibrary Loan: An Acceptable Alternative to Purchase," *Wilson Library Bulletin* 63 (January 1989): 54–56; and Bruce Kingma, "The Economics of Access versus Ownership: The Costs and Benefits of Access to Scholarly Articles via Interlibrary Loan and Journal Subscriptions," in M. A. Butler and B. R. Kingma, eds., *The Economics of Information in the Networked Environment* (Washington, DC: The Association of Research Libraries, 1996).

[9]Fussler, *Research Libraries*, 37.

[10]*Scholarly Communications: The Report of the National Enquiry* (Baltimore: Johns Hopkins University Press, 1979), 13–15, 18–20, 160–64. This study received support from the federal government, the American Council of Learned Societies, and a number of foundations including the Andrew W. Mellon Foundation.

with one writing that such a library would offer "constructive encouragement to a participating institution to reduce its own acquisitions, with the knowledge that the unpurchased materials will, in fact, be available."[11] The idea was appealing because it allowed for "remote" collections while fairly apportioning the costs (and not forcing research libraries to become the "remote" collections for smaller libraries).[12] But among the librarians supporting this proposal, there is no evidence of any examination of how the cancellations engendered by the NPC might raise the costs of, or put altogether out of business, scholarly periodicals.[13]

Others thought that the remote storage of library materials in less expensive off-campus facilities would be more realistic than altogether static local collections or the ambitious but unrealized NPC. Beginning in the late 1980s, a number of libraries began to develop such remote facilities, which were in essence closed-stack warehouses for books.[14] Indeed, the consortia movement really started with libraries uniting to facilitate resource-sharing via ILL and off-campus facilities; OhioLINK, a statewide organization of academic libraries, was a prime example.[15]

Even before Bowen's arrival as president, the Mellon Foundation had also sought to find ways to offset the cost-disease for colleges and universities, and not least their libraries. In 1975, with the assistance of Mellon funds, the libraries of Columbia, Harvard, and Yale universities and the New York Public Library united to form the Research Libraries Group (RLG), a membership organization that would eventually deploy an online union catalog, that is, a collective catalog including the holdings of multiple libraries. One important aim of RLG was to find efficiencies in collections development, perhaps by coordinating the subject strengths of its constituent libraries to avoid unnecessary duplication of research materials.[16] With the savings that would result, the libraries would be better able to maintain their core mission of building robust

[11]Fussler, *Research Libraries*, 35.

[12]Ibid., 38.

[13]Other possible flaws, seen by one author as fatal, were discussed in Sheila T. Dowd, "Fee, Fie, Foe, Fum: Will the Serials Giant Eat Us?," in Sul H. Lee, ed., *The Impact of Rising Costs of Serials and Monographs on Library Services and Programs* (Binghamton, NY: The Haworth Press, 1989), 17–38.

[14]Danuta A. Nitecki and Curtis L. Kendrick, *Library Off-Site Shelving: Guide for High-Density Facilities* (Englewood, CO: Libraries Unlimited, 2001).

[15]David F. Kohl, "Cheaper by the (Almost Half) Dozen: The Ohio State-Wide Remote Storage System," in Nitecki and Kendrick, *Library Off-Site Shelving.* Glenda A. Thornton, "Impact of Electronic Resources on Collection Development, the Roles of Librarians, and Library Consortia," *Library Trends* 48, no. 4 (Spring 2000): 842–56.

[16]RLG also sought to catalog materials not represented in OCLC, and to catalog in ways that would be more useful for a research library.

research collections in the face of rising costs. Although RLG has provided many useful services for academic libraries, efforts to coordinate collections development required too many compromises to be effectively implemented.[17]

Despite the best efforts of so many, the 1980s brought only retrenchment to academic libraries. By the end of the decade, observers feared that academic libraries had reached a point of crisis.[18] The culprit was believed to be scholarly journals.

The economics of scholarly journal publishing is very similar to the economics of the creation and distribution of all sorts of information, from scholarship to entertainment. Academic journals, like movies, music, and newspapers, involve high up-front costs for creation, but low marginal costs for providing an additional copy to an additional consumer. Consequently, when a journal is sold on a fee-per-copy basis, its profit or loss is largely dependent on the number of subscribers.[19]

Beginning in the 1970s and accelerating to shocking proportions in the 1980s, the price of scholarly journals skyrocketed, especially in the sciences. Several factors, including exchange rates, paper costs, publishers' profit margins, and postage, combined to damaging effect. At the same time, new journals were constantly spawned in response to ever-increasing scholarly specialization.[20] Structural deficits at leading universities meant that library budgets were unable to keep pace with rising prices. Budget constraints forced cutbacks, first on duplicate subscriptions and then on primary ones.

As libraries canceled journal subscriptions in the face of rising prices, publishers experienced pressure on their profit margins. They were forced to raise prices even further.[21] In turn, libraries were forced to cut

[17]See Nancy Gwinn and Paul Mosher, "Coordinating Collection Development, The RLG Conspectus," *College & Research Libraries* 44 (March 1983): 128–40; and Hendrik Edelman, "The Growth of Scholarly and Scientific Libraries," in Richard E. Abel and Lyman W. Newli, eds., *Scholarly Publishing: Books, Journals, Publishers, and Libraries in the Twentieth Century* (New York: John Wiley & Sons, 2002). See also "The RLG Conspectus and the National Shelflist Count," in Thomas E. Nisonger, *Collection Evaluation in Academic Libraries: A Literature Guide and Annotated Bibliography* (Englewood, CO: Libraries Unlimited, 1992).

[18]Ann Okerson, "Of Making Many Books There Is No End," *Report of the ARL Serials Prices Project* (Washington, DC: Association of Research Libraries, 1989).

[19]See Gillian Page, Robert Campbell, and Jack Meadows, *Journal publishing* (Cambridge: Cambridge University Press, 1997), chapter 8.

[20]Roger Noll and W. E. Steinmueller, "An Economic Analysis of Scientific Journal Prices: Preliminary Results," *Serials Review* 19 (1992): 32–37.

[21]Although this phenomenon has been established most clearly for scientific, technical, and medical journals, even the most important humanities journals reported similar phenomena. The *American Historical Review*, which would be a key early component of

back further.[22] This spiral of price increases and journal cancellations plagued both libraries and publishers for many years.[23] In the aftermath, it should be noted, academic libraries spend a far greater share of their materials budgets on journals, as opposed to monographs, and on the sciences, as opposed to the humanities, than they did before. The situation as it stood was unsustainable, for both scholarship and the bottom line. The higher-education community felt it was being priced out of adequate library resources, even as college and university budgets were experiencing ever more pressure.

THE MELLON FOUNDATION CONTEXT AND BOWEN'S IDEA

The increasing pressure on academic libraries had, by the early 1990s, become a significant concern of the Mellon Foundation. Founded in 1969, The Andrew W. Mellon Foundation was always concerned with the health of higher education, the arts and humanities, and research libraries, making grants for specific projects and endowing programs in these areas.[24] Although Mellon had supported some efforts to find savings for academic libraries for a number of years, the problems were getting worse. With a mission focused on the support of higher education and the humanities most specifically, Mellon leaders felt compelled to act as scholarly resources, especially in the humanities, became increasingly endangered.

Concerned that this cycle should be definitively documented before embarking on a grants program to alleviate it, the Mellon Foundation's research staff studied both the causes and the effects of this cost-escalating spiral. One alarming finding was that academic libraries were collecting a smaller and smaller percentage of scholarly output. Published

---

JSTOR, has indicated that "with institutional subscribers, it's been a long, slow decline, and that continues," even in 2001, by some 50–100 subscriptions per year. Many of the losses were to high school libraries, small public libraries, and foreign academic libraries. Institutional prices were increased by one-third in the late 1990s as a result. Arnita Jones, interview with the author, September 20, 2001.

[22]But rather than saving costs, these cancellations often resulted, ironically, in higher costs, for ILL and document delivery rather than traditional subscriptions, according to some scholars. Carol Tenopir and Donald W. King, "Setting the Record Straight on Journal Publishing: Myth vs. Reality," *Library Journal* 121 (March 15, 1996): 32–35.

[23]Just a few years later, a Mellon Foundation senior advisor, the Princeton economist Richard E. Quandt, published a formal model to explain what had been taking place, "Simulation Model for Journal Subscription by Libraries," *Journal of the American Society for Information Science* 47:8 (1996): 66–67.

[24]See *Report of the Andrew W. Mellon Foundation, 1969–1993.*

in 1992 as *University Libraries and Scholarly Communications*, the study also contained an investigation of how developing technologies might ameliorate the problem, by "suggest[ing] a model for the library of the future that may differ sharply from the traditional one."[25] Even if it was not then possible to say with any specificity what the model should be, it was clear that new technologies might permit (or force) the adoption of better methods of distribution that could stand up to evolving economic climates. Overall, Tony Cummings and his co-authors saw some possible stumbling blocks but much potential for innovative solutions.

With renewed confidence that its staff understood the environment, the foundation altered its grant making for academic libraries. In the foreword to *University Libraries*, Bowen indicated some likely impacts:

> Specifically, we are examining the possibility of evaluating systematically some of the "natural experiments" in new modes of electronic publication and dissemination . . . and we might simultaneously encourage the development of some carefully structured experiments designed to address some of the open questions of quality, means of access to materials, convenience, and cost.[26]

Richard Ekman, the foundation's secretary (now at the Council of Independent Colleges), and Richard E. Quandt, a Princeton economist and one of the foundation's senior advisors, embarked on a systematic evaluation of preexisting natural experiments.[27] Having surveyed the terrain, Ekman and Quandt presented their findings to the Mellon board of trustees.[28] The trustees approved a program of grants, run by Ekman and Quandt, to encourage a series of "self-conscious natural experiments" on how technology could help the system of scholarly communications find efficiencies while, if possible, increasing scholarly utility. Although this program would encounter some measure of resistance,[29]

---

[25]Anthony M. Cummings, Marcia L. Witte, William G. Bowen, Laura O. Lazarus, and Richard H. Ekman, *University Libraries and Scholarly Communications* (Washington, DC: The Association of Research Libraries for the Andrew W. Mellon Foundation, November 1992), 7.

[26]Page x.

[27]This survey was eventually published as Richard H. Ekman and Richard E. Quandt, "Scholarly communication, academic libraries, and technology," *Change* 27, no. 1 (January 1995): 34–44.

[28]Richard H. Ekman and Richard E. Quandt, "Potential Uses of Technology in Scholarly Publishing and Research Libraries," discussion paper presented to the trustees of the Andrew W. Mellon Foundation, December 13, 1993 (unpublished).

[29]See, for example, Albert Henderson, "The Growth of Printed Literature in the Twentieth Century," in Richard E. Abel and Lyman W. Newlin, eds., *Scholarly Publishing: Books, Journals, Publishers, and Libraries in the Twentieth Century* (New York: John Wiley & Sons, 2002), 6–7.

it would also foster a great deal of innovation. Under their leadership until 1999, this program made awards that totaled $19 million.[30]

When Bowen was mulling the proposed library expansion at Denison in late 1993, the economic problems of academic libraries—and possible cures for their ills—had been on his mind for years. At Princeton, Bowen had seen unceasing pressure to build additions and annexes to Firestone Library, and he knew that similar pressures affected academic libraries everywhere.[31] In working on the study of academic libraries and preparing for the Ekman-Quandt program, Bowen and other staff at the foundation had been mulling the application of technology to academic libraries. As Louis Pasteur said several times, "chance only favors the prepared mind."[32] But for the foundation's work at the time and Bowen's own interest in cost-disease, Bowen might not have thought twice about the need to expand Denison's Doane Library.

The cyclical pressures to construct or expand university and college libraries as collections grew continued steadily, but only rarely had librarians and administrators acted to alleviate them. Perhaps these pressures were largely ignored because, constituting capital costs, they were often viewed as inevitable. Certainly, academic communities perceived libraries to be at their very heart, and the size of a library was often perceived as a measure of academic quality. With his mind "prepared," however, Bowen saw a special opportunity.

New technologies of the sorts that Ekman and Quandt had been studying could be used to help libraries like Doane. Specifically, Bowen thought that some of the library resources could be effectively "miniaturized" using computer technology so that they would no longer have to be held in physical form. Bowen knew that the storage problem affected many schools beyond Denison. Focused principally on teaching, most of the Doane collection would be redundantly stored at hundreds, in some cases thousands, of other college libraries across the country—

[30]Perhaps the most significant grant made under this program was to Johns Hopkins for Project Muse, but grants were also awarded in support of Project SCAN at the University of California, the *Bryn Mawr Classical Review,* and the *College Art Association Review Journal.* For a retrospective, see Richard E. Quandt, "Mellon Initatives in Digital Libraries: 1994–1999," April 2002, Unpublished manuscript on deposit at the Nathan Marsh Pusey Library, the Andrew W. Mellon Foundation. Some intermediate outcomes of the foundation's program in this area are collected in Richard Ekman and Richard E. Quandt, eds. *Technology and Scholarly Communications* (Berkeley: The University of California Press, 1999).

[31]William G. Bowen, "The Princeton Library: Report of the President March 1986," in *Ever the Teacher: William G. Bowen's Writings as President of Princeton* (Princeton: Princeton University Press, 1987), 270, 279.

[32]Louis Pasteur, *Œuvres,* ed. René Vallery-Radot (Paris, 1922–1939), vol. 7, 131.

libraries that would also benefit from the project. Even if the costs of miniaturization were far higher than the savings that accrued to Denison alone, such a digital system could be distributed nationally to several hundred institutions, taking advantage of what would presumably be its low marginal costs. The concept's scalability was particularly appealing because the low marginal costs that were anticipated meant that the savings would increase with the scope of the project.

So before Denison's board considered any action, Bowen asked library staff to determine what parts of the collection were consuming so much stack space. The study concluded that the breakdown was 64 percent books, 23 percent scholarly journals, and 13 percent government documents.[33] Earlier in 1993, President Clinton had signed a law mandating the distribution of large numbers of government documents electronically, which might reduce or eliminate the need to continue collecting such documents locally. But, as always, book and journal distribution and storage relied on the same format—print. And print materials were continuing to eat up stack space as omnivorously as ever.

Journals presented a unique opportunity, compared with other print materials, for a creative approach. In the case of books, copyrights were held by a mélange of authors, publishers, and literary estates, the negotiations for which could be difficult and costly. The backfile of an important journal, on the other hand, might stretch back a hundred years or more, and it seemed likely that the rights to each set of these volumes was held by a single publisher. Consequently, Bowen believed that a single negotiation with the publisher could secure the rights to a hundred volumes of important materials. Although not quite "one-stop shopping," a single negotiation for a hundred volumes was believed to offer the advantage of substantially reducing the cost of creating the database.[34] Bowen may also have believed at this time that the microfilm company UMI held the rights to most of the journal backfiles, which, if it had been true, would have indeed resulted in one-stop shopping for the project (a possibility that is treated at greater length in chapter 2). Journals alone occupied nearly a quarter of the total shelving in Doane Library, their ever-lengthening backfiles growing inexorably at approximately 3 percent per year, even though Doane was already

[33]"Library Space Use," unsigned memorandum, December 22, 1993, Denison University librarian's office.

[34]One prominent observer believes that this advantage in moving journals online has constituted a complementary impediment in the development of electronic books. Clifford Lynch, "The Battle to Define the Future of the Book in the Digital World," *First Monday*. Available at *http://www.firstmonday.dk/issues/issue6_6/lynch/index.html*.

filled beyond capacity.[35] And many of Doane's important journal back-files were stored in inaccessible parts of the library, which only compounded the bibliographic difficulties of accessing the journal literature.

It was not as if miniaturization strategies for containing expansion pressure at libraries were novel. Profit-seeking corporations had microfilmed extensive collections of journal backruns (and other library materials).[36] Librarians had purchased millions and millions of reels. But readers hated to use microfilm.[37] The reels were difficult to read, of varying quality, and required machines that were often in short supply, in awkward locations, and susceptible to breakdowns. The film itself was at times frustrating to use, and it could not be printed out as easily as paper could be photocopied. Responding to reader resistance, librarians were unwilling to replace paper backfiles of journals with microfilm. So even though microfilm might have saved an immense amount of space over conventional storage, the film became a supplement, and a costly one at that.[38]

Bowen thought that a digital application could miniaturize printed journal backfiles, yet bring increased access and functionality. He assumed at the time it would use CD-ROMs, then the optimal format, which could store thousands of pages on a small disc.[39] If the digitally stored backfiles could achieve greater user-satisfaction than microfilm, the paper versions could be moved to remote storage or deaccessioned altogether. With some large amount of Doane's space freed up, Denison

[35]Doane purchased 2000 journal volumes, for about 400 additional feet of shelf space, per year. This amounted to 133 new shelving units annually beyond the 4,636 then devoted to journals. "Library Space Use," unsigned memorandum, December 22, 1993, Denison University Librarian's ofice files.

[36]Probably their purpose in doing so was to allow collection building at new or growing libraries as much as it was to permit space-saving at existing collections. But savings was clearly in mind. See Peter Ashby and Robert Campbell, *Microfilm Publishing* (London: Butterworths, 1979), 129–31.

[37]Stephen R. Salmon, "User Resistance to Microforms in the Research Library," *Microform Review* 3, no. 3 (July, 1974). The industry itself explained resistance as resulting at least somewhat to microfilm's aesthetic inferiority to bound printed items. See Ashby and Campbell, *Microfilm Publishing*, 94–97.

[38]Sometimes, however, librarians deaccessioned and discarded printed materials, and microfilm did not prove to be an adequate replacement. For a passionate, if at times overstated, account of these losses, see Nicholson Baker, *Double Fold: Libraries and the Assault on Paper* (New York: Random House, 2001).

[39]In 1994, CD-ROMs were a common medium for the storage of electronic scholarly resources, largely because they could store hundreds of times more data than the previous standard, the floppy disk. Abstracting and indexing services, especially, were distributed on CD-ROMs, with regular updates. Bowen had seen and used several CD-ROM products that worked well, and as a result he envisioned using the medium as a workable, existing technology to serve the need that he had identified at Denison.

would have enough empty stacks for years of new book acquisitions. Prospectively, new journal issues could conceivably go straight to digital storage, rather than occupying shelf space. In the near term, delaying expansion of the library could allow Denison to save, or redeploy, the more than $5 million that would otherwise have been necessary for the building project.[40] By digitizing journals, Bowen saw a way to bring economic efficiency to academic libraries, a small but significant advance in battling cost-disease. This efficiency would be realized without sacrificing the quality of their intellectual resources; indeed it might enhance them. The new resource would be, as he liked to say, quoting the management mantra of the time, "better and cheaper."[41]

IMAGINING A PROJECT

On receiving the Denison report, Bowen immediately turned to colleagues. He drew in advisors from the Mellon Foundation and elsewhere to confirm that, on its face, his idea to digitize the backfiles of scholarly journals was feasible. Because there was no established market for digitized journal backfiles, Bowen had a great deal of latitude to explore options. He was largely unconstrained by prior assumptions and therefore could, as we will see, at times reverse course.

Even while seeking broad advice, Bowen was beginning the search for a grantee. It is important to keep in mind that Mellon generally works through a grantee that takes responsibility for developing a project proposal and managing all of the work of the project. At this time, Ekman and Quandt were meeting with representatives of potential grantees in beginning to develop their program in scholarly communications. In the same way, Bowen's earliest consultations, and those made by others at the foundation, were made in the hopes of identifying a grantee rather than of gaining large amounts of internal expertise with which to develop a project plan. But while they did not produce a grantee immediately, these conversations challenged, and led to the alteration of, many of Bowen's working assumptions from Denison.

We should begin with Denison's own reaction to Bowen's idea. Though scale effects were envisioned as key to the project's potential savings, it

[40]The dollar figure is from William G. Bowen, "The Foundation's Journal Storage Project (JSTOR)," in *Report of the Andrew W. Mellon Foundation 1994* (New York: Andrew W. Mellon Foundation, 1995), 26.

[41]William G. Bowen, "JSTOR and the Economics of Scholarly Communications," Speech to the Council on Library and Information Resources, Washington, DC, September 18, 1995. Revised version online at *www.mellon.org/jsesc.html*. For a critical perspective, see Baker, *Double Fold*.

had enormous appeal even with a much smaller scope. The study of Doane's stack space noted that if the Mellon Foundation opted not to pursue a journals digitization project, other options remained. Denison might even consider undertaking the project on its own or in partnership with another college, wrote University Librarian David Pilachowski (now at Williams).[42] Even though, in retrospect, such a small-scale effort would have been financially impractical, Denison's consideration illustrates the appeal of the initial idea.

To better understand the technology, Bowen's first consultation on his return from Denison was with Ira Fuchs. In 1985, President Bowen had hired Fuchs to be Princeton University's vice-president for Computing and Information Technology. When he was at the City University of New York, Fuchs was one of the founders of BITNET, a forerunner of the Internet that eventually linked together the computing systems at more than one thousand universities. Fuchs would quickly become a key player in the emerging initiative, eventually joining the foundation as a vice-president. Bowen and Fuchs met as soon as possible, on a Saturday morning, to discuss how the project could develop.

Bowen had already begun to consider the size of the project, and he was determined that it be large enough to demonstrate the feasibility of a digital library of academic journals. If it contained too few journals, it would not be useful to researchers and consequently would be received as a research project, rather than as a useful scholarly resource. Bowen believed that only with 10–20 titles—that is, 500–2000 years of journals—could a digital library of academic journal backfiles be a useful scholarly resource. Back-of-the-envelope calculations led Bowen and Fuchs to the immediate realization that an enormous digitization effort, scanning a million or more pages, would be a key component of such a pilot project. Fuchs remembers that "at this point I certainly knew Bill well and I knew that, unless I thought that the laws of physics made it impossible, you don't say that it can't be done. But no one had ever done anything like it on that order of magnitude."[43] The technical challenge and scale of such a digitization project were appealing to both Bowen and Fuchs.

In addition to the challenging digitization effort, the journals database would also require software to operate it. Fuchs believed that such software either existed or could be created, and he promised to take responsibility for investigating the options. In chapter 3, we shall see that

---

[42]David Pilachowski, "Periodical Storage Space and Mellon Idea," email to Denison President Michele Tolela Myers, December 15, 1993, in the Denison University Librarian's office files.

[43]Ira H. Fuchs, interview with author, November 2, 2000.

he would eventually lead Mellon to adopt software created for the TULIP project.

Fuchs advised Bowen that, for the purposes of distributing such a digital library, CD-ROM was an increasingly outdated technology that had limited scalability. The wealthier colleges and universities had already begun an ambitious effort to link together all computers on campus, including those in faculty offices and student dormitories. For example, under Fuchs's leadership, all Princeton's administrative and academic buildings were networked by 1989; the student dormitory network was just being completed in 1994. Campus networks like the one at Princeton were, in turn, linked to larger networks, such as BITNET and the Internet. If a CD-ROM–based project were successful, it would involve distributing thousands of CDs to each of hundreds of universities and colleges. Even if this were logistically possible, it would not eliminate the redundancy across institutions. At each college and university, stack space and reshelvers would simply be replaced with CD-ROM juke-boxes and well-paid technical staff. But, if Bowen's journals project were made available remotely over an interinstitutional network, a user with the proper software could access the journal backfiles from a dormitory room, an office, or a computer lab at any college or university in the country. Network distribution, suggested Fuchs, could thus eliminate redundancy while increasing accessibility.[44]

Bowen and Fuchs concluded their first meeting on the subject with a sense of excitement. If the project they were discussing proved successful, it would be a real demonstration that large-scale digital libraries were feasible. At the same time, their planning revolved around the premise that digital libraries could be cost-effective. Success could help libraries and administrators see the relevance of technology to their needs, both budgetary and scholarly.

With Fuchs confirming the technical promise of the journals project, Bowen discussed it with Mellon Foundation Secretary Richard Ekman, among others. In an effort to avoid unnecessary duplications of effort, Ekman agreed to see what he could learn about undertakings similar to Bowen's proposal. He then held two important conversations with Bill E. Buchanan of the International Archives Institute (IAI) and Richard DeGennaro, the Roy Larsen Librarian of Harvard College.

In late December 1993 and early January 1994, Ekman spoke with Buchanan of the IAI, which had been creating searchable indices and

---

[44]For some of the advantages of CD-ROM, most of which were largely irrelevant to the emerging project, see Page, Campbell, and Meadows, *Journal publishing*, 351–53.

tables of contents that linked to digitized page images of books.[45] Ekman and Buchanan roughed out the costs of Bowen's journal project, foreseeing the conversion of fifty-year backfiles of twenty academic journals, a total of approximately one million pages. The principal cost variable was whether the output was digitized page images or searchable text. If the former, they thought the entire conversion would cost about $80,000; if the latter, around $2 million. (These different approaches are examined with greater care in chapter 2.) In other words, the estimated cost per page ranged from $0.08 to $2. They also discussed CD-ROM, local campus networking, and the emerging Internet as distribution possibilities. Because Bowen was not so much interested in creating new technologies as in deploying them for a practical purpose, it was reassuring to find that others were undertaking somewhat similar projects.

Several weeks later, on January 19 or 20, Bowen went to the New York Public Library to learn about its experience with both journals and digitization. Bowen concluded that "not even the NYPL knows that it has everything in good order," so that a digitized journal backfile would actually make an immediate contribution to preservation. He left the library concluding that "bitmapping is everywhere now."[46]

Also on January 20, Ekman spoke with Richard DeGennaro in order to learn about Harvard's work on digital projects.[47] They spoke mainly about the Periodicals Content Index (PCI), which was an electronic bibliographic index of important arts and sciences journals. To create PCI, publisher Chadwyck-Healy was relying on copies of journal backfiles held at Harvard, inputting the tables of contents. With the tables of contents available in electronic form, Harvard hoped it could move the journal backfiles themselves off-campus to a less expensive satellite location, to be paged back to the library when needed. In essence, PCI was initially conceived with the identical purpose as Bowen's journals project—space savings—though PCI included only the bibliographic indexing as represented in tables of contents. When he heard about Bowen's idea, DeGennaro noted that, because faculty had found PCI to be an inadequate replacement to on-campus browsing of journals, Harvard had proposed to expand PCI. The proposal was strikingly sim-

[45]Richard Ekman, "Telephone Conversation with Bill Buchanan, International Archives Institute, Inc.," memorandum to William G. Bowen and Richard E. Quandt, January 4, 1994.

[46]William G. Bowen, "Scholarly Communication: Journals on CD-ROM," memorandum to file, January 20, 1994.

[47]DeGennaro had previously served in similar positions as director of libraries at the University of Pennsylvania and the Andrew W. Mellon director of the research libraries at the New York Public Library. Richard Ekman, "Telephone Conversation with Richard DeGennaro, Widener Library, Harvard University, Thursday, January 20, 1994," memorandum to file, January 25, 1994.

ilar to Bowen's idea: Harvard would digitize the page images of articles from thirty journals indexed by PCI, then link them electronically to PCI for use at Harvard. Scholars and students would have electronic access to the entire journal, which now could surely be sent off-campus. DeGennaro sent Ekman this August 1993 Harvard proposal to build out from PCI. "By improving intellectual access to crucial journals," the proposal predicted, "Harvard will be able to store the original off-site in the Harvard Depository, an archival storage facility."[48] The Harvard proposal was strikingly similar in both purpose and approach to the Mellon plan.[49]

It is worth pausing for a moment to reflect on the components of the Harvard plan and whether it could have succeeded. Its major distinctive feature was its campus-specific character, as opposed to the broad distribution envisioned by the Mellon plan. By making the journals available only at Harvard, the university seems to have believed that it could rely on the "fair-use" provision of the copyright code, which forgives certain copyright infringements that are viewed as reasonable, rather than obtaining formal permissions from journal publishers.[50] The Mellon project, in contrast, intended to seek permissions from publishers and to distribute the project widely in the hope of creating a self-sustaining business model. The Harvard plan did not appear to have had such a vision for itself.

Indeed, Ekman noted this difference from a slightly different angle. He wrote that Harvard's goal "is not to use a grant to get into a 'production' mode, but rather to familiarize Harvard's senior library staff with scanning . . . rather than microfilming."[51] Like so many projects at the time, Harvard's proposal was for learning rather than doing. Even for one of the wealthiest universities, an ongoing "production mode" was too expensive, at least when producing just for itself. Mellon's traditionally suprainstitutional approach obviated this problem and encouraged scale. Note, finally, that Harvard's lack of interest in production

---

[48]Harvard University Library, "A Proposal to Preserve and Improve Access to Periodical Literature Through Linking Digital Images to an Electronic Index," August 1993.

[49]It was impossible to find any evidence at all to indicate that Harvard's August 1993 proposal came to the attention of anyone at Mellon before this point in early 1994. Therefore, it seems that the Harvard proposal did not inform Bowen's idea to "compress" journals to save space, but was rather a remarkable coincidence.

[50]It seems to have been believed that reformatting already-owned journals for campus-specific educational use was reasonable under the guidelines of fair use.

[51]Richard Ekman, "Harvard University Library's Proposal to Preserve and Improve Access to Periodical Literature Through Linking Digital Images to an Electronic Index," memorandum to file, January 24, 1994.

in all likelihood made it inappropriate as an early partner for Mellon's journals project, which possibility was never considered after this point.

Nevertheless, the extensive discussion about PCI with DeGennaro led Ekman to contact Chadwyck-Healy to seek more information about its bibliographic index to the journal literature.[52] While Ekman's minute of the conversation did not mention the journal project explicitly, the conversation focused on the components of PCI, demand for it, and its future plans, all critical to the Mellon effort to understand the context for its emerging journals project.

SUMMATION

Making use of technology to save space and reduce costs offered a striking combination of Bowen's background, librarians' needs, Mellon's mission, and the blossoming technology of the time. Once the idea was brought back from Denison to the Mellon Foundation, the initial round of consultations involving Bowen, Ekman, and Fuchs reached several implicit conclusions. The digitized journals would be distributed widely, so that any savings that resulted could be shared broadly. Scanning and software would be important components, and the scale of scanning would be almost without precedent for academic purposes. Ekman had found that there was other work, and indeed deep interest, in digital libraries involving humanities journals.[53] As January 1994 came to a close, Bowen was convinced that the pilot project would be technically feasible.

While foundations often craft programmatic initiatives, it was most unusual for Mellon to propose a specific project on the order of JSTOR. In this case, Bowen was especially excited because, if successful, his idea would prove that technology need not be a drain on academic budgets, but could in fact be used to find new efficiencies. As a result of the internal generation of a project that fit solidly within Mellon's programmatic interests, foundation leadership—most especially Bowen—had a sense of ownership perhaps unmatched in Mellon projects. This sense of ownership would prove to be a key success factor as a number of impediments were subsequently confronted and overcome.

---

[52]Richard Ekman, "Telephone Conversation with Douglas Roseman, Executive Vice President, Chadwyck-Healy, Inc., Monday January 24, 1994," memorandum to file, January 24, 1994.

[53]Another key consultation that was a part of this initial thrust took place in February, when Bowen, along with Ekman and Quandt, met with Karen Hunter of Elsevier Science. This meeting, and Elsevier's larger role in this history, are described in chapter 3.

CHAPTER 2

In Search of a Partner, but Beginning Alone

FEBRUARY–MAY 1994

As WE HAVE SEEN, initial enquiries by Bowen, Ekman, and Fuchs produced some valuable information but no clear direction to pursue. Mellon was a grant-making, not an operating, foundation, and so any work it took on would be in partnership with a grantee. They held out hope that a suitable grantee-partner could be persuaded to participate in the project, and all signs pointed to University Microfilms, Inc. (UMI). It was hoped that UMI, about which they knew relatively little, might have the software required; the rights to reproduce the journal backfiles; and the microfilm to use as a source for scanning. Perhaps, they thought, UMI was merely feeling trepidant about combining its assets and moving them online. If so, Mellon might persuade UMI of the advantages of the online medium.

Before contacting UMI, Mellon needed more clarity in its proposed undertaking. Mellon staff worked to identify disciplines and journals that they would hope to include. In addition, they convened a very informal advisory committee before making any definite decisions. In this way, Mellon staff would begin taking on more and more responsibility for overseeing the project. Because there was still hope of working with a single grantee-partner, there was no need to appoint a Mellon project manager. Instead, several senior staffers at Mellon oversaw developments while doing their best to reach an agreement to pass along as much responsibility as possible.

CHOOSING DISCIPLINES AND TITLES

Partnering with Ekman and Quandt, in late January Bowen turned his attention to the identification of journals for the project. First, broad criteria were determined. Then, individual titles were identified as desirable. Only later would foundation staff reached out to obtain permission to include the journals in the digital library project.

It seems surprising in retrospect, but at the time there was debate over whether to include the most central, important, widely used journals or to focus on the rarely used, more specialized titles. While in 2002, huge amounts of academic literature are distributed electronically, we must not forget that, in early 1994, there was no widely shared sentiment that such a future was on the horizon. Indeed, Bowen's initial vision for the digital library did not so much depend upon increasing the ease of access to journals as the saving of prime shelf space. Following this line of reasoning, one might argue that the less important, more narrowly focused journals should be digitized and sent off-campus, since they were used least and had less need of prime campus shelf space.

But of course the technology would allow far greater functionality and easier access to the journals, best seen in comparison with the past. Libraries had long cataloged most items only at the title level—the title of a given book or journal. As a result, these catalogs were useless in a search of the journal literature. By the 1970s, many indices had begun to catalog humanities and social science journals at the article level, giving information about articles' titles, authors, and sometimes subjects. When these indices were initiated, however, they almost never retrospectively indexed the journal backfile.[1] Journal literature stretching back to the nineteenth century (and occasionally earlier) had become dark matter in the universe of scholarly communications. Perhaps largely because of their inaccessibility, journal backfiles were rarely used. Mellon was becoming aware that whatever materials its project digitized would become significantly more accessible than they had been previously.

If the proposed digital library were to shine this light—spending large sums of money to digitize a small and select group of journals—it seemed only right to include the most important, prestigious, widely held titles. For two reasons, emphasizing the backfiles of the leading journals promised the greatest potential cost-effectiveness. First, they were housed at the largest number of libraries. Second, they were likely to have the longest backruns, and therefore the most potential for space-saving.

In a sense this emphasis upon the leading journals was a key compromise: the most widely distributed titles, which presented the possibility of the greatest savings, were also the very ones that scholars and librarians would be least likely to remove from prime library locations. Staff at the foundation thus concluded that the potential for wide-scale savings was more important than the more immediate, but more limited, savings that would have resulted from concentrating on more specialized journals. This early insistence on the quality and scope of the titles to be selected was a critical leadership decision that would affect the project's mission and character in the months and years to come. The

---

[1]Concurrently with JSTOR's development, at least one publisher was planning to extend indexing back to the late-nineteenth century. See chapter 4 for more on Chadwyck-Healy's PCI product.

project would aim not only to conserve shelf space, but also to facilitate access to the core scholarly literature.

Bowen initially targeted the arts and sciences, in particular the humanities and social sciences. The liberal arts have always been central to the programmatic interests of the Mellon Foundation. An even more important consideration, however, was Bowen's belief that the greatest overlap of the teaching interests of American four-year colleges and universities was in the arts and sciences. Thus, there was a high likelihood that their libraries' journal holdings would overlap most substantially in these fields, allowing for the greatest benefits of scale and therefore cost-savings. Finally, most journals in the humanities and social sciences were less expensive than those in the sciences and professional fields. Bowen hoped the largely nonprofit publishers in these fields would therefore be more amenable to participation, compared with the big, expensive, commercial science publishers.[2]

Bowen decided to focus first on several individual disciplines, in order to attain critical mass in selected subject areas. Economics was an easy choice. It is taught, in one form or another, at virtually every college and university, so its journals are important to a great many institutions. Most economists were already very comfortable with computers, having used them in the course of their work. An economist himself, Bowen knew a large number of the leading figures in the field and was therefore more likely to win the approval of the various publishers. Economics articles, in addition to their broad interest, had the benefit, for the purposes of the experiment, of containing numerous special mathematical characters and graphs, in addition to simple text. Dealing with the complication of these nonroman characters and figures at the outset would test the system's versatility. If economics could be handled successfully, in the future the system would be better able to store mathematics and foreign language journals. Finally, economics had a group of clearly identifiable, broadly topical, core American journals. It would be relatively easy to select the most important titles.

Bowen sought a second field in addition to economics, one that would clearly mark the project as being interdisciplinary and prevent it from becoming wedded to a single set of scholars. Ideally, the field would be in the humanities, in order to locate the project solidly within Mellon's programmatic focus. At first, Bowen thought of literature, and he asked Richard Quandt to consult Alvin Kernan, the former dean of Princeton's Graduate School and Mellon's senior advisor in the humanities. Kernan

---

[2]He explained some of his decisions in a later memo, William G. Bowen, "Recent Meetings and Key Issues," memorandum to JSTOR file, July 15, 1995.

advised that the discipline was too turbulent for a simple selection of 5–10 journal titles; the boundaries of, and the terrain within, the field were in flux.[3] Kernan and others suggested that literature should be postponed in favor of a more stable discipline, such as history.

History would allow many interesting comparisons with economics. Historians were less computer-savvy, having not yet begun to use technology extensively in their work; and they used journal literature differently than did economists. Historians have long been more dependent on books, and less dependent on journals, than economists. Yet, if anything, history was a more widely taught and researched discipline, and overall could provide useful comparisons. Finally, Ekman, himself a historian, had close working relationships with several of the leading societies of historians.[4]

Within the disciplines of economics and history, then, Mellon began to identify journals of the highest quality for JSTOR. Bowen was well placed to create a list of the most important core journals in his own field of economics. Together with Quandt and Fuchs, Bowen developed a list of seven journals, six of whose backfiles were owned by university presses or not-for-profit scholarly societies. For history, Quandt consulted in early February 1994 with his Princeton colleague Lawrence Stone, who suggested ten titles, nine of them also published by not-for-profit scholarly societies or university presses.[5] Other consultations led Mellon staff to remove one title, *Annales*, from the list of history titles. On February 17, then, the proposed journal list included nine history and seven economics titles (see table 2.1), for a total of about 1,250 journal-years.[6] Later, the list was narrowed to ten pilot journals, five in economics and five in history, because "purely practical considerations" demanded the project sharpen its focus.[7]

When they first heard about JSTOR months later, several librarians were concerned that they, and the various analytical methodologies they

[3]Richard E. Quandt, "Discussion with Al Kernan," memorandum to William G. Bowen and Richard Ekman, January 27, 1994. Kernan's memoirs offer a far more thorough treatment of his sense of the changing discipline. See Alvin Kernan, *In Plato's Cave* (New Haven: Yale University Press, 1999).

[4]Bowen explained many of the reasons for the selection of these two disciplines in his public summary, "The Foundation's Journal Storage Project (JSTOR)," in *Report of the Andrew W. Mellon Foundation 1994* (New York: Andrew W. Mellon Foundation, 1995), 27–28.

[5]Richard E. Quandt, "History Journals," memorandum to William G. Bowen and Richard Ekman, February 1, 1994.

[6][Kamla Motihar], "Historical Journals," February 17, 1994; [Kamla Motihar], "Economics Journals," February 17, 1994.

[7]William G. Bowen, "Status Report," memorandum to JSTOR file, May 6, 1994.

TABLE 2.1
Journals Envisioned for the Pilot Project, February 17, 1994

Title	Copyright Holder[i]	First Published	Discipline
American Economic Review	American Economics Association	1911	Economics
American Historical Review	American Historical Association	1895	History
Econometrica	Econometric Society	1921	Economics
Economic Journal	Basil Blackwell	1891	Economics
English Historical Review	Longman Group	1886	History
Historical Journal	Cambridge University Press	1958	History
Journal of American History	Organization of American Historians	1914	History
Journal of Modern History	University of Chicago Press	1929	History
Journal of Political Economy	University of Chicago Press	1892	Economics
Past and Present	Oxford University Press	1952	History
Quarterly Journal of Economics	MIT Press	1886	Economics
Review of Economics and Statistics	Harvard University	1919	Economics
Revue Historique	Presses Universitaires de France	1876	History
Southern Economic Journal	Southern Economic Association	1933	Economics
Speculum	Medieval Academy of America	1926	History
William and Mary Quarterly	Institute of Early American History and Culture	1892	History

[i] Sometimes, other scholarly societies and/or presses are involved in the publication of journals. This column, however, lists only the holder of copyright in the journal backfile. If it turned out that UMI did not have the rights to distribute electronic versions of the full backfiles of these journals, the copyright holder was the party with which Mellon would have to negotiate for rights to include the title in JSTOR.

had developed, were not more central to this effort. The field of library studies had produced a lengthy literature on how best to determine which journals should be canceled in an age of tightening belts and so was well versed in determining journal importance. Wendy Lougee, a librarian at the University of Michigan who would later become a key player in JSTOR, remembers asking Bowen in July or August, "'How are you going to pick the content? Wouldn't you like the library to help you on that?' I can still picture Bill Bowen saying, 'I know what's needed at this point.' And, he did. . . . He knew which [journals] to go after. He was right on target."[8] Journal-cancellation programs were a complicated undertaking in which price was an important factor in addition to quality. Bowen, in consultation with a few others, would be able to determine the 5–10 most important journals in his field. (Later, as JSTOR grew, far more systematic selection procedures were put into place; see chapters 6, 9, 11, and 13.)

Quandt arranged for a quick study of the potential journals and made the important discovery that in economics, but not in history, Princeton held more than one copy of many titles. If holding multiple copies of journal backfiles was a regular library phenomenon, the potential space-savings from digitizing them would increase proportionally. By measuring the number of linear feet occupied by a given journal title in Princeton's Firestone Library, Quandt estimated the capital costs involved in housing the journals as well as the total number of pages that would need to be scanned. Combining these rough figures on capital costs (for economics, $60,000 for 215 linear feet)[9] with an estimate of the number of pages to be scanned (for economics, 445,000), the foundation could explore whether, and under what conditions, an electronic journal archive could be cost-effective.[10]

With no serious roadblocks thrown up, on Valentine's Day 1994, Bowen wrote that "all signals are positive."[11] The emerging foundation project required a name, and Bowen suggested MEG—"Mellon Electronic Group (of Journals)."[12] But that possibility came too late. Already, Bowen had created a subdirectory on Mellon's DOS computer system that he had named "JSTOR" (as an acronym for *Journal Stor*age). As hard as he and

---

[8] Wendy Lougee, interview with the author, May 30, 2001.

[9] Quandt's estimates were rough, but sought to account for all of the costs involved with new construction adding that number of linear feet to a campus library.

[10] Richard E. Quandt, "Economics journals," memorandum to William G. Bowen and Richard Ekman, February 1, 1994; Richard E. Quandt, letter to William G. Bowen, February 11, 1994.

[11] [William G. Bowen], "Notes on JSTOR Project," February 14, 1994.

[12] Ibid.

others would later try, Bowen and his colleagues were unable to find a more suitable substitute.

TEST SITES

Now that a defined project was underway, in late February Bowen spoke with Presidents Mary Patterson McPherson of Bryn Mawr College and Henry Payne of Williams College, securing their support and agreement to participate as test sites in the JSTOR undertaking.[13] McPherson reflects that the colleges were better able than the universities to "involve a significant number of students and faculty . . . in economics and history in the experiment."[14] And while the digitization of core journals could have a huge impact on a small college library, it was then impossible to conceive of a project ambitious enough to digitize anything more than a token percentage of a large research university's journal holdings. Moreover, unlike universities, colleges had long ago given up any claim to "own it all." Although the project was never intended to be exclusive to such colleges, it would remain "presently focused on small colleges" for several more months. Relative to the research universities, they had "less demand for research use of the oldest journals and fewer resources to devote to storage of little-used materials."[15]

This emphasis on colleges changed when Bowen spoke with De-Gennaro to gather some sense of research library interest. Richard DeGennaro was an extremely well-respected university librarian and had published extensively on the applications of new technologies, including networking. He was taken with the concept underlying Bowen's journals digitization project, but he thought its potential was broader. Insofar as core journals made up a far smaller percentage of the holdings of a research university library than they did at a college library, the space-saving mission of the project was of comparatively less appeal. But universities faced other journal-related challenges. Part of their mission was to hold materials for perpetuity, and it was a challenge. Volumes and issues, often those of the greatest importance, would frequently be missing from the stacks. Sometimes individual articles were pilfered. (At Harvard, for example, someone had ripped out

---

[13] William G. Bowen, "Liberal arts test sites: Bryn Mawr and Williams," memorandum to JSTOR file, February 23, 1994.

[14] Mary Patterson McPherson, personal communication, August 25, 2001.

[15] Perry van der Meer and Richard Ekman, "Summary of March 8, 1994 meeting," March 8, 1994.

every article by Einstein, presumably as souvenirs.[16]) Years of under-lining, margin notes, and environmentally inadequate storage conditions left even the remaining backfiles in sub-ideal condition. The journals project could return, virtually, all of these missing pages. And having journal backfiles available from the desktop would be a boon to re-search.[17] Eventually, several universities would be added as test sites.

The college and university test sites would prove to have intermit-tent importance to the project, as we shall see in this and the following chapters. The banner list of participants indicated that libraries were in-terested in participating, and librarians, scholars, and students at these test sites (and later, others) would offer valuable comments and advice. With Bryn Mawr, Denison, and Williams signed on, and Harvard plainly eager, the project was steaming forward.

Within a period of several weeks in early 1994, staff and advisors at the Mellon Foundation had determined that a project to digitize journal backfiles would address an important set of concerns in higher educa-tion. They had concluded that such an undertaking seemed feasible, had proceeded to assemble a title list, and had secured the support of the presidents of several prestigious liberal arts colleges. Mellon was ready to debut the project before a (slightly) broader audience.

ORGANIZING A COMMITTEE

By virtue of Bowen's presidency of Mellon, the project proceeded in a prescribed way. A key goal was to identify appropriate institutional part-ners that could undertake the actual work of building JSTOR.[18] In the course of Mellon's initiatives in early 1994, it had already become clear that the JSTOR project would be far more complicated than a traditional foundation grant. Already, as we have seen, Bowen had taken a personal interest in identifying the disciplines and titles to be digitized. In retro-spect it seems inconceivable that, even had a single grantee been will-ing and able to undertake all of the work of creating the JSTOR pilot project, Mellon would have been willing to step back. With UMI in mind as a potential partner, Mellon brought together an advisory committee in March 1994 to confirm the overall direction of the project and to give it a great deal of further definition.[19]

---

[16]Richard DeGennaro, interview with the author, March 30, 2001.

[17]Ibid.

[18][William G. Bowen], "Notes on JSTOR Project," February 14, 1994.

[19]The description of this meeting is taken largely from Perry van der Meer and Richard Ekman, "Summary of March 8, 1994 meeting," March 8, 1994.

This committee played an important role in establishing and confirming JSTOR's direction, and its composition was important. It was heavily weighted toward academic scholars, librarians, and administrators. The lack of publisher representation may have reflected the assumption, of which Mellon soon would be disabused, that UMI held rights that would make publisher solicitation unnecessary. The membership included Fuchs, by now a senior advisor to the foundation for JSTOR, but also a university administrator, as well as librarians DeGennaro and Pilachowksi. They were joined by Mary Patterson McPherson, president of Bryn Mawr College, Michael McPherson (no relation), a professor of economics at Williams College and an expert on the economics of higher education, as well as Bowen, Ekman, and Quandt. All five were scholars (three of them also administrators) in the arts and sciences (four in economics or history). Richard C. Woodbridge, the foundation's intellectual property lawyer for the JSTOR project, attended, in addition to Mellon staff member Perry van Der Meer and Financial Vice-President T. Dennis Sullivan. With the exception of these last three, the committee's composition very accurately reflected JSTOR's potential user-community of economists, historians, and librarians. Perhaps not even consciously, Mellon staff had organized a group that suggested a commitment to meeting the needs of scholars and librarians. At the same time, however, the group did not include anyone steeped in the building of a digital library. While DeGenarro was a proponent of library automation, it had been many years since he had been on the front lines; and while Fuchs was an important voice for the deployment of technology for scholarly purposes, his background at the time was strongest in IT and networking. The lack of a representative who had done something like JSTOR before is notable. It is probably best explained by one of two reasons: a sense that UMI would provide a "black-box" solution, and the lack of an obvious candidate.

At the committee's meeting in early March, Mellon staff sought advice on how to launch the JSTOR project. Some of the focus fell on whether economics and history were the optimal disciplines. Michael McPherson was convinced that economists "would be no problem." Quandt noted that historians, on the other hand, might benefit from some outreach to help them adapt to the new technology. The committee focused on technical questions at some length, including the reliability of various storage media and the nascent Internet. Fuchs continued to speak for a network-based approach, rather than CD-ROM. Pilachowski, DeGennaro, and Michael McPherson all agreed: "it has to be online to be successful." There was some uncertainty as to whether campus networks were sufficiently robust, but Mellon staff agreed to pursue this avenue further.

Perhaps the primary topic of conversation was a potential partnership with the for-profit company UMI, whose vast vaults of microfilmed journals made it particularly appealing. Its catalog contained everything from rare books held at only a few of the most prestigious research libraries to the backfiles of the *New York Times* and numerous academic journals.[20] The potential benefits for the rapid development of JSTOR were obvious: the microfilmed journals were already collected together in one place and constituted a single reproducible medium; no work would have to be done to locate backfiles or, it was believed, to ensure they were complete. In addition, in order to microfilm a journal, UMI had to obtain a license from the copyright-holder (often the publisher). In the course of negotiating with publishers for this permission, it seemed possible that UMI might have obtained the electronic distribution rights, as well. If UMI had the rights to electronic distribution and was willing to work with the foundation, Mellon believed it did not require formal permission from the copyright-holder; the paperwork and negotiation required thus could be substantially reduced. With the potential to deliver rights to the journals and to serve as a source for scanning, Bowen thought that microfilm might offer the potential to "simplify" and "reduce expenses."[21] UMI seemed like a key potential partner, or competitor.

Perhaps even more importantly, foundation staff had believed that publishers had granted UMI "full exclusivity" to reproduce the backfiles of many academic journals, exclusivity that might bar Mellon from proceeding separately.[22] UMI might have been not only a desirable partner, but indeed also a necessary one. The day before the advisory committee met, Bowen wrote that "UMI has existing contractual relationships with the copyright holders of the journals [to microfilm their publications], and the implications of these relationships need to be better understood."[23] At the advisory committee meeting, Woodbridge reported that, based on his research, "UMI does not have exclusive rights to (at least)" the journals he investigated. Consequently, the foundation would not be obligated to work through UMI: at worst, it could scan directly from the hard-copy backfiles.

---

[20]UMI has subsequently been absorbed by, and at first renamed, Bell & Howell. More recently, it adopted the name of its leading brand, ProQuest. Its electronic product ProQuest Direct offers current editions of many of the journals now included in JSTOR.

[21]William G. Bowen, interview with the author, October 31, 2000.

[22]William G. Bowen, "JSTOR Project—copyright issues," memorandum to Richard Woodbridge, February 18, 1994.

[23]William G. Bowen, "JSTOR," memorandum to JSTOR file, March 7, 1994.

Nevertheless, foundation staff continued to hope that UMI held the nonexclusive rights to digitally reproduce the backfiles, which might then be shared with Mellon. The meeting minutes reflect that the "original plan was to work with UMI on a universal contract" for all of the desired journals; but "if UMI does not have the rights to some of this material . . . we will have to go directly to each publisher," a not-unlikely possibility. We will return to the topic of UMI below, but at the meeting of the advisory committee, for the first time, it became clear that developing JSTOR might well entail negotiating one by one with journal publishers to obtain the necessary permissions.

Notwithstanding this realization, the upshot of the meeting was deep-seated enthusiasm for the JSTOR project in general, and for a partnership with UMI in particular. All members were convinced that the project would provide a valuable new resource for higher education. While in hindsight JSTOR's success may seem predestined, at the time there were doubters. Yet the committee's enthusiasm, although it was made up of friends, was taken to be representative of students and scholars. Mellon was therefore willing to put its resources toward an experiment—a risk—that could have substantial scholarly and economic advantages.

While it would be some exaggeration to suggest that this meeting was a watershed moment for the project, it was very important. Bowen had gathered a number of his most trusted colleagues in one room together, and they all agreed that Mellon should pursue the JSTOR project vigorously. Although the advice was fairly informal, Bowen had become convinced that there was value, and there would grow to be demand, for the project he envisioned.

Whereas before the meeting, little contact had been made outside the foundation and its "friends," immediately afterwards the pace of activity would pick up substantially. The committee would meet several additional times during the course of the project, until its diverse perspectives were otherwise institutionalized.

ARCHITECTURE

With the March 1994 meeting of the advisory committee, quite a few details began to fall into place. By mid-March, Mellon staff had developed a fairly clear idea of what the JSTOR project should be, from a technical perspective, and the steps that would be necessary in order to build it. It would therefore be useful to pause to spell out Mellon's plans for the JSTOR database at that point, since these plans informed so much of the work to follow.

On the most basic level, every page of every issue of every journal—the complete backfile—would have to be digitized. Even though it was believed that most usage would come from the more recent volumes, Mellon's goal was focused not on usage, but rather on saving space. To save space, the JSTOR project would digitize the full backfile of the journal, to allow volumes to move en masse off the shelves.

If these journal backfiles were to be moved off the shelves, it was clear that the project would have to offer a viable alternative to printed backfiles that would meet the highest standards for scholarly use. Thus, if it were not appealing to scholarly users of the journal literature, JSTOR would be a failure. This need had a number of specific implications.

For one thing, it was clear that JSTOR's electronic version would have to offer perfect fidelity to the original pagination and layout, as well as an accurate reproduction of the text. Scholars needed to know the page on which a sentence appeared, for their footnotes, and textual accuracy was of course imperative. A purely textual representation was ruled out early on because display would not be true to the original format and 100 percent accuracy would be laborious and exceedingly expensive to attain (not to mention impossible, due to special characters in foreign languages and mathematical equations). Had it been necessary to use text for display, it is likely that the economics would have been so prohibitive as to prevent the creation of JSTOR. To ensure fidelity and cost-effective accuracy, facsimile images of journal pages would be displayed.[24]

Basic navigability through the images would require that, at minimum, they be linked to a table of contents. Thus, metadata such as article title, author name, and page number would have to be purchased or created. This information would be interwoven to allow basic linkability from a table of contents. In this way, JSTOR could be made to replicate the features of traditional journal backfiles, allowing users to utilize the information found in references to locate a source.

Many advisory committee members were convinced that fulltext searchability was a requirement of the electronic medium. Yet the page-image architecture seemed to preclude such searchability: some scholarly resources, such as experiments being undertaken at Cornell and Yale universities, used images without searchable text. But JSTOR's commitment to be responsive to user needs pushed it to add text files that would be searchable while remaining invisible behind the images.

---

[24]A text-based system assigns a discrete electronic code to represent each letter, just like a word processor. By contrast, an image-based system consists of essentially a photograph of each page, but the computer is "unaware" of the contents of the image.

This layer of text could substantially enhance JSTOR's usefulness to scholars and students, who would be able to search the text of the journal for phrases and words in addition to its table of contents. With images in place for display, the fulltext's accuracy was of less concern—it could be, at least to some degree, "dirty." This is not to say, however, that those shaping the JSTOR concept believed the accuracy of the fulltext was unimportant. Rather, since no fulltext file could ever be a flawless rendering of the originals, the image files ensured the perfect reproduction of content that would be required for scholarly use.

Although it was seen as desirable, creating a layer of "dirty" fulltext from scanned images (the automated process was called Optical Character Recoginition, or OCR) might be expensive. In chapter 1, we saw that Ekman's preliminary investigations indicated creating searchable fulltext might add $2 to the $0.08 cost per page of scanning the images.[25] At such costs, OCR would challenge the project's cost-effectiveness. Bowen was wary.[26] In mid-March, Quandt reported to a Bryn Mawr librarian that fulltext would not be available, and the librarian was "disappointed" that the project would be "restrictive" in this way.[27] Mellon staff were growing increasingly aware of both the utility of and the demand for searchable fulltext. Subsequent investigations indicated that OCR might prove to be less expensive than feared and that its costs would fall further. In May, Bowen wrote that "we have very much in mind the question of whether it is feasible to obtain 'dirty' OCR files, as well as bitmapped files. We would like very much to make it possible for users to conduct 'dirty searches' if this is at all possible."[28] Putting the cost question out to bid to vendors through a request for proposals (RFP) would yield the final answer.

Some librarians believed that undergraduate usage would be predicated on subject-based indexing, allowing an amateur to locate a relevant article. But subject indexing did not exist for most of the proposed backfiles.[29] Crafted by skilled catalogers, it would clearly be too expensive to create. Instead of subject indexing, searchable fulltext might be a less expensive replacement. Users could search for any word or phrase

[25]Richard Ekman, "Telephone Conversation with Bill Buchanan, International Archives Institute, Inc.," memorandum to William G. Bowen and Richard E. Quandt, January 4, 1994.

[26]William G. Bowen, "The Foundation's Journal Storage Project (JSTOR)," in *Report of the Andrew W. Mellon Foundation 1994* (New York: Andrew W. Mellon Foundation, 1995), 29–30.

[27]Richard Ekman, memorandum to JSTOR file, March 16, 1994.

[28]William G. Bowen, "Status Report," memorandum to file, May 6, 1994.

[29]Ira H. Fuchs, "Meeting at Bryn Mawr April 5, 1994," memorandum to JSTOR file, April 6, 1994.

appearing anywhere in the journals. In addition to replacing subject indexing, fulltext searching would be highly useful to the research of graduate student and faculty users.

In addition to the exact format and functions to be delivered, there were also decisions to be made about the delivery mechanism. We have seen the strong endorsement by the advisory committee for a networked approach. In addition, librarians from the prospective test sites were adamant that, as a set of distributed CD-ROMs, JSTOR would "provide little advantage over either microfilm or bound copies of the periodicals."[30] Fuchs recalls that their adamancy on this point was particularly valuable in pushing Mellon to deliver JSTOR over the Internet.[31] There was as yet no specific decision as to how JSTOR could be brought online, whether via Gopher, the web, or some other application (see chapter 4).

The clear preference for Internet delivery was coupled with skepticism about whether it would be feasible. The pilot librarians worried that "even a single user printing a full article composed of bitmapped images may seriously degrade performance" on the campus Internet gateway—slowing network traffic to a halt for all campus users.[32] JSTOR was aware of these potential limitations, which might require network upgrades, and Fuchs was considering a "stress test" to determine exactly what changes might be necessary.[33] In May, Bowen would write that staff "continue to hope that it will be possible to make electronic files available online."[34]

In partnership with scholars, librarians, and university administrators, the Mellon Foundation had made important decisions about basic architectural needs for JSTOR in the late winter and early spring of 1994. This outreach represented an effort to learn what users would need if digitized versions were to replace the use of printed backfiles, even while ensuring that these needs were technically feasible and not unreasonably expensive. Since Mellon did not have the capacity to undertake the JSTOR project on its own, Bowen had long been convinced that "ultimately the project should be run by someone else."[35] It was with

---

[30] Ibid.

[31] Ira Fuchs, interview with the author, July 19, 2001.

[32] James Tanis, Michael Freeman, and Michael Durhan, "JSTOR Project," memorandum to Ira Fuchs, April 15, 1994.

[33] Ira Fuchs, "JSTOR Project," memorandum to James Tanis, Michael Freeman, and Michael Durhan, April 19, 1994.

[34] William G. Bowen, "Status Report," memorandum to principal participants, May 6, 1994.

[35] [William G. Bowen], "Notes on JSTOR Project," February 14, 1994.

these basic architectural and organizational principles that Mellon initiated its conversations with UMI.

SEEKING A PARTNER IN UMI

As we have seen, foundation staff believed that UMI had quite possibly secured the rights necessary to digitize and distribute back-issues of academic journals. Following the mantra of utilizing existing sources, Bowen looked to UMI as a possible shortcut in building the JSTOR pilot. Although at the meeting of the advisory committee Woodbridge had reported that UMI did not possess exclusive rights that necessitated partnering with it, the committee saw advantages to pursuing the relationship.

In seeking a meeting with UMI, Bowen felt that one likely connection would be through the University of Michigan, because they were both located in Ann Arbor. Gilbert Whitaker, then the provost, remembers Bowen expressing interest in UMI even before he became interested in the University's TULIP work (see chapter 3). "The thing I remember first about JSTOR was [Bowen] calling and saying that he thought maybe University Microfilms was the key to making this project work because they have all these academic journals . . . on microfilm."[36] So, Whitaker facilitated an introduction between Bowen and representatives of UMI.

At the initial UMI meeting in early March 1994, Bowen was plainly intrigued with a company so invested in an old technology (microfilm) trying to understand the implications of new developments. In terms of a potential business relationship, some possible bases for cooperation emerged. UMI had microfilmed all but one of the 10 titles then under consideration. According to Bowen's minute of the meeting, representatives of the company believed that UMI had the necessary copyright permissions for the nine titles it had microfilmed.[37] One of the UMI participants in the meeting, then-President James Roemer, recalls that the conclusion was "very easy—we had the rights to [digitize the journals] ourselves, but not to let other people do it."[38] That was precisely why Mellon was interested in a partnership. The meeting generated enough interest for the parties to agree to meet again.

At some point after this meeting, Mellon concluded that UMI's license with the journals was insufficient to permit the foundation or its

[36] Gilbert R. Whitaker, interview with the author, December 4, 2000.
[37] William G. Bowen, "Report on trip to UMI and U of Michigan, Mar. 17–18, 1994," memorandum to JSTOR file, March 19, 1994.
[38] James Roemer, interview with the author, September 26, 2001.

designee to undertake digital distribution without obtaining licenses from the publishers. Formal permission would consequently have to be obtained from each journal, even if the JSTOR database would be created by scanning from UMI's microfilm. Case-by-case negotiations would be required; and any journal could decline to participate if its publisher was dissatisfied with the terms Mellon would offer.

Even if UMI had possessed all of the necessary rights to digitize and distribute the journal backfiles without requiring the formal agreement of the publishers, it is not clear exactly how Mellon would have proceeded. Regardless of whether UMI possessed the necessary rights, Bowen had been convinced that "we need to meet with a few key publishers to get the ball rolling. . . . Momentum needs to be built."[39] Even when it was thought that UMI might possess the rights to allow Mellon to avoid formal agreements with publishers, Bowen wrote that his plan was to "test out [the] model contract on friendly publishers."[40] While it is not clear exactly what "model contract" he had in mind, it does seem that Mellon at all times intended for publishers to be actively involved. We must remember that staff of the Mellon Foundation would not have wanted to alienate the university presses and scholarly societies that published so many of the candidate journals. These presses and societies were, after all, run by and for the very scholars that Mellon existed to support. Although it is difficult to know for certain how Mellon would have proceeded had UMI possessed the necessary rights, it is possible to say what foundation staff did when they discovered UMI lacked the rights. As we shall now see, it was at this point that Mellon began developing strategies to negotiate directly with individual journal publishers. With UMI out of the picture with respect to licensing rights, Mellon staff looked to another approach.

COLLECTION DEVELOPMENT

Since no single organization held the rights to digitize and distribute the backfiles of the journals Mellon sought for JSTOR, negotiations would have to be undertaken individually with each publisher. Bowen had long been known for his powers of persuasion, and for decades Mellon supported work in the humanities and social sciences, building alliances of friends within these disciplines. Mellon as an organization, and Bowen in particular, consequently took on responsibility for nego-

---

[39] [William G. Bowen], "Notes on JSTOR Project," February 14, 1994.
[40] William G. Bowen, "JSTOR," memorandum to JSTOR file, March 7, 1994, 3.

tiations with publishers. In this domain, a number of important lessons that could not have been foreseen would be learned by experience, including the forbearance of one university press on the project.

The JSTOR project's success clearly hinged on the number and quality of journal titles that could be secured. The goal was to sign up, initially, a small group of prestigious publishers, who would in turn give the project a great deal of momentum in signing additional titles in some future phase. Before beginning to seek the agreement of journal publishers, it would be most useful to gain a better understanding of the journals and their publishers.

Bowen and Ekman began to investigate the ten target journals in history and economics, as well as their publishers. All of the publishers were nonprofits, either individual scholarly societies or university presses. Sometimes their journal publishing enterprises subsidized their other activities, but the net surplus of these enterprises was not, with a few key exceptions, very great. Of critical importance was the fact that almost no revenue was ever generated by the backfiles; in some cases, the warehousing of backfiles was a net drain on the journals program.[41] In a later speech, Bowen noted his belief that "the project offered no threat to basic revenue streams" of the publishers.[42] Consequently, he hoped that the character of the publishers—their academic mission and, in the case of the societies, scholarly leadership—would make them eager to participate in a project that would be of benefit to scholars and their institutions. It was with this sense of the "lay of the land" that Mellon Foundation staff formulated some principles for negotiation.

First, the foundation would bear the entire cost of the project, not only to create or license the software and to undertake the scanning work, but also to cover any expenses faced by publishers. The foundation would provide a promise, formally or informally, to assure the publishers that participation in the project would bring them no harm—in terms of lost revenues or other concerns.[43] This promise would prove to be absolutely critical in securing the agreement of a number of publishers, and

---

[41] A 1997 book advised publishers that sales of back-issues were being replaced by sales of microfilm. (Although it did not specify why, the plain answer was that the latter was less expensive.) It also advised that 90 percent of back-issue sales were for those volumes published in the last three years. Because of the warehousing costs and the decreasing likelihood of sales, publishers were advised to "analyze [your] holdings carefully and dispose of any surplus." Gillian Page, Robert Campbell, and Jack Meadows, *Journal publishing* (Cambridge: Cambridge University Press, 1997), 216–18.

[42] William G. Bowen, "JSTOR and the Economics of Scholarly Communications," speech to the Council on Library and Information Resources, Washington, DC, September 18, 1995; revised version available online at *www.mellon.org/jsesc.html*.

[43] William G. Bowen, interview with the author, June 26, 2001.

it is an indication of the importance of philanthropy in helping JSTOR to get off of the ground. In this original conception, not only would participation be free to the publishers, but it would be costless—and they would receive an electronic copy of the complete journal backfile.

Second, publishers would have to agree to participate, at least initially, without being paid royalties.[44] Journal backfiles sitting on library shelves did not earn publishers any money, and since these scholarly publishers were not perceived to be profit-seeking, there seemed to be no reason why they should receive a windfall. Bowen recalls that "we didn't see that there was a case for providing royalties when they weren't losing anything and were in fact gaining some things."[45] Indeed, at least one publisher would view JSTOR participation as a way to get out of the distracting business of warehousing backfiles and distributing them when requested.[46]

Finally, publishers needed to make no promise to participate exclusively in Mellon's JSTOR project. If they could find additional distribution mechanisms for their backfiles, they could pursue them. This was the first time that the foundation deployed what would become a matter of general principle: to seek only nonexclusive rights when supporting the digitization or distribution of scholarly materials.[47] For negotiations with potential publishers in mid-1994, nonexclusivity was a simple way to underscore Mellon's nonprofit motives. Mellon only wanted to succeed at its own project, rather than whip any potential competition.

With these principles in place regarding costs, replication, royalties, and nonexclusivity, Mellon staff worked with Richard Woodbridge, the foundation's attorney, to craft an initial JSTOR publisher license agreement. This agreement further provided that the foundation and the journal publisher would share joint copyright ownership of the digitized version of the journal. For the publishers, joint copyright ownership meant that they could distribute or sublicense their electronic backfile,

---

[44]Bowen noted, in early March, that if it were necessary in order to secure the participation of early risk-taking pilot publishers, he was prepared to agree to give them "claim on a pro-rata share of 'profits' (if there were any)" from an eventual distribution. But no publisher demanded such a provision at this stage and so no such agreements were made until a far later stage (see chapter 6). William G. Bowen, "JSTOR," memorandum to file, March 7, 1994.

[45]William G. Bowen, interview with the author, November 20, 2000.

[46]Richard Ekman, "Telephone Conversation with Luke Wenger, Executive Director, Medieval Academy of America, Monday, May 2, 1994," memorandum to JSTOR file, May 3, 1994.

[47]Its purpose in seeking such rights has been to bring numerous streams together in a coherent aggregation, as it would in JSTOR. For a later version of Mellon's outlook on this topic, see *http://www.mellon.org/ip.policy.2.pdf*.

created at Mellon's expense, via additional mechanisms. Although either the foundation or the publisher could cancel the agreement, the foundation would retain its half of the joint copyright in those volumes that had already been scanned, allowing Mellon or its licensee to distribute the electronic backfile in perpetuity.[48]

Based on these general principles, Bowen began to approach individual publishers.[49] Most of the scholarly societies and university presses that published the candidate titles had worked in the past with the foundation, and Mellon staff felt that their participation in the project would be relatively noncontroversial. Before approaching others, Bowen decided to target the University of Chicago Press, which published two of the desired journals. Bowen had developed a close working relationship with several senior administrators at the university, who he knew to be responsive to the scholarly and economic aims of the JSTOR project, including President Hugo Sonnenschein, President Emeritus Hanna Gray, and General Counsel Arthur Sussman. (Gray was well known to Bowen not least because she was a Mellon trustee and would subsequently assume the chairmanship of the board.) If Mellon could not convince Chicago to participate in the JSTOR project, it would have an uphill battle, indeed.

In early April 1994, Bowen sent a letter describing the project to Morris Phillipson, the well-regarded director of the press, and a meeting was arranged for the following week.[50] They spoke at length about academic publishing in general, the JSTOR project, and the two key journals that Mellon hoped to include: the *Journal of Political Economy* and the *Journal of Modern History*. Bowen was careful to secure Phillipson's agreement, in principle, with the project's goals and methods, before launching negotiations in earnest.[51] Bowen also spoke with Sonnenschein and Gray before leaving Chicago. On returning to New York, he sent Phillipson the initial version of the license for further consideration.[52]

In the next few days, Bowen reached out to a number of the economics scholarly associations, including the American Economic Association,

[48]JSTOR-A.

[49]In some cases, even the journal ownership was somewhat more complicated, a circumstance best illustrated by the *Review of Economics and Statistics*. Although Harvard retained formal editorial control over the title, and had clear ownership of current issues, Elsevier had long published the title on behalf of Harvard, which in turn was looking for a new publisher. Eventually, Elsevier agreed to relinquish whatever rights it might have had in the back-issues, allowing the *Review* to be included in the pilot project.

[50]William G. Bowen, letter to Morris Phillipson, April 7, 1994.

[51]William G. Bowen, "Meeting with Morris Phillipson of the University of Chicago Press," memorandum to JSTOR file, April 12, 1994.

[52]William G. Bowen, letter to Morris Phillipson, April 11, 1994.

publisher of the *American Economic Review*,[53] and the Econometric Association, which published *Econometrica*.[54] He knew a number of the editors of these economics titles, including Orley Aschenfelter of the *AER* and Robert Gordon of *Econometrica*, and thus it seemed there was a very high likelihood of success. These were fairly straightforward conversations.

In company with Ekman, who was a historian by training and had responsibility for Mellon's relations with the humanities in general, Bowen traveled to Washington to meet with James Gardner, the acting executive director of the American Historical Association, publisher of the *American Historical Review*. In addition to being a publisher itself, the AHA was an umbrella organization of other history scholarly societies making it an important potential ally. Gardner reported that both he and David Ransell, then the editor of the *AHR*, were enthusiastic about JSTOR and he expressed willingness to lobby other history publishers to participate.[55]

The initial agreement crafted by Bowen and Woodbridge asked a great deal of publishers, as we will see. Notwithstanding the enthusiasm of some, the model did not suit everyone. Some were more cautious. They were not in principle unwilling to participate in the Mellon undertaking, but they sought to enter into a more avowedly experimental project, with terms that would clearly state their ability to back out completely if the arrangements became problematic.[56]

Chicago, having reviewed the terms of the license, was such a case. In addition to requesting the details of which colleges would participate and under what terms, Chicago wanted a clear statement that "after the expiration of the [three-year] time limit, there should be no further use of Chicago journals in the data base."[57] Without such a guarantee, the press felt it would be ceding rights of potentially great value in perpetuity, when no one understood exactly where the market for such journals was headed or exactly how new technology might bring new value to journal backfiles. Critically, Chicago viewed the JSTOR relationship not only in relation to current revenues, but also to unknown future

---

[53] William G. Bowen, "Conversation with Elton Hinshaw," memorandum to JSTOR file, April 13, 1994; William G. Bowen, letter to C. Elton Hinshaw, April 12, 1994.

[54] William G. Bowen, letter to Robert J. Gordon, April 12, 1994.

[55] Richard Ekman, "Meeting with James Gardner, Acting Executive Director, American Historical Association, Monday, April 16, 1994," memo to JSTOR file, April 19, 1994.

[56] Bowen would reflect on some of these issues most clearly in a memo at the end of May, William G. Bowen, "JSTOR—Key Issues," memorandum to Richard Woodbridge, May 30, 1994.

[57] Estelle Stearn, letter to Richard Ekman, April 19, 1994.

revenues, a perspective that we shall see again in chapter 6. Given the volume of cancellations of journals by libraries in the preceding decade, it would be thoughtless to describe this wariness as anything other than understandable.

Even so, it was problematic for Mellon's project. In a memorandum, Bowen set out the reasons why the Chicago-proposed limit would not be possible:

> What the Foundation cannot do is invest heavily in creating a sophisticated retrospective file, linking that file to a search engine, and creating the (perhaps complicated) software needed to allow users to make ready use of such a file—and then have a publisher, some time in the future, withdraw permission to use the materials which the Foundation has created.
>
> A major reason why the Foundation cannot contemplate such a possibility is that one of the two primary purposes of this project is to allow libraries to save storage space—to avoid building as much new stack space as would otherwise be required. A decision of this kind would make sense for a library only if it could confidently remove back issues of journals, knowing that they would not be needed in the future. . . . [A library must be] confident that it has a perpetual right to [the] use of the retrospective file which it has been given.[58]

This statement is the first clear documentation of Mellon's determination that archiving was a core aspect of the JSTOR project's mission, a direct corollary of space-saving.[59] But the project's archival mission was in direct contrast with the notion that it was experimental. Bowen's plans were clearly more ambitious than that.

Finally, in a memo to Arthur Sussman of the University of Chicago two weeks later, Bowen suggested a compromise. He agreed to limit the project's scope. But rather than address the perpetual access issue, he suggested that they agree to cap the number of subscribing institutions. Although the subscribers would receive perpetual access, allowing them to make decisions about storage space, the cap would effectively

[58] William G. Bowen, "Why Perpetual (Non-Exclusive) Rights Are Necessary," memorandum to JSTOR file, April 19, 1994.

[59] In its usage here, the term "archiving" may be somewhat anachronistic. It achieved widest usage when a report distributed in 1996 drew a distinction between the principal function of a library—access—and that of an archive: permanence. This conceptual separation allowed for a discussion of the ways that archival permanence could be ensured for digital libraries. The work of safeguarding collections for the purpose of permanence has, since then at least, been known as "archiving." John Garrett and Donald J. Waters, *Preserving Digital Collections: Report of the Task Force on Archiving of Digital Information* (Washington, DC: Commission on Preservation and Access, 1996).

limit the amount of "loss" that the press could possibly suffer from JSTOR participation.[60]

The proposed compromise was accepted, and the foundation modified its publisher agreement to create a new version, the so-called JSTOR-B agreement (in contrast with the original, which was henceforth called JSTOR-A). The B agreement was similar in most respects to the A, except that Mellon could only distribute the publisher's journal to a maximum of fifty colleges and universities. Once that cap was reached, the parties would have to renegotiate. In exchange for this limitation, there would be no joint ownership of the copyright in the digitized product, but rather Mellon would own the copyright. Mellon would give the publisher a license, for the life of the agreement, to use the digitized version "as part of other electronic databases over which the publisher has direct control."[61] If the publisher were to back out of the agreement, Mellon could never distribute the product to more than those fifty sites; but in a form of mutually assured destruction, the publisher would lose the right to use and sublicense the digitized version.[62]

With this compromise acceptable to Chicago, one other significant issue had to be resolved. A lawsuit filed in federal court in New York in December 1993 claimed that databases like Nexis, which (with the permission of publishers) compiled articles from the *New York Times* and other news sources in a searchable database, violated the copyrights of freelance newspaper authors.[63] Like those freelancers, an academic journal's authors are not employees of the journal, but rather are employed by colleges and universities across the country and around the world. It was understood that the copyright code granted the newspaper or journal publisher the authority to permit another party—for instance, UMI—to produce an identical version of the entire publication in a new medium such as microfilm.[64] It was also widely believed that the publisher could not give permission for the individual articles to be separated from one another to be reproduced—for that, the permission of the underlying rights-holders would be required. The crux of the freelancers' argument was that, in the Nexis database, the articles float freely without any of the structure of the newspaper being retained. The publishers believed that although they floated freely, the database provided enough structure and retained enough of the original selection to

[60] William G. Bowen, "JSTOR—Compromises?" memorandum to Arthur Sussman, May 5, 1994.
[61] JSTOR-B.
[62] JSTOR-B.
[63] *New York Times* v. *Tasini*, 533 U.S. 483.
[64] See, for example, 17 U.S.C. 201(c).

make it the equivalent of microfilm in a new technological medium. While the disagreement may sound academic, this lawsuit would have a major impact when the U.S. Supreme Court decided it in 2001. In order for the Mellon Foundation to avoid seeking the permission of thousands of underlying rights-holders it was necessary for JSTOR to be viewed by any court as a microfilm-like rendition of the complete journals and not as a database of free-floating articles.

AEA attorney and Columbia Law School Professor John Coffey was concerned that the publisher license agreement should work to place JSTOR as firmly as possible in the "microfilm" category. As a result, he designed language that required Mellon to make only a "faithful . . . replication" of the original journals.[65] This language helped to determine the technical mechanism of the JSTOR project. Already, Mellon had been discussing a system in which the page images were visible to the user, perhaps with these images accompanied by searchable text. But the purposes of the displayed page images had been accuracy and archiving, and such a system was under consideration, though not yet adopted. Now that a faithful replication of the journal content was mandated by contract language, the JSTOR project would certainly have to display page images; any searchable text would probably have to be invisible.

While this conclusion was based on broadly solicited legal advice, it should be underscored that it was a calculated risk. Today, the Supreme Court's *Tasini* decision suggests that faithful replication of the full content of the original journals was the appropriate choice.

With substantial help from Ekman, Bowen lobbied the editors and publishers of the desired journals without pause. He felt "encouraged by the extremely positive tone" of the conversations with publishers, whom he characterized as having "genuine interest in participating actively and constructively."[66] One publisher signed on (to the A agreement) without any negotiation or indeed communication after Bowen's initial phone call and letter![67]

Even though JSTOR-A was not for the faint of heart, three of the ten publishers in the initial group eventually agreed to its terms. All three were scholarly societies, meaning that nearly half of these publishers opted for the more open-ended agreement. These scholarly societies were more concerned with information sharing than with income-generation

---

[65] William G. Bowen, "JSTOR—Key Issues," memorandum to Richard Woodbridge, May 30, 1994.

[66] William G. Bowen, "Status Report," memorandum to principal participants, May 6, 1994.

[67] Robert Gordon, letter to William G. Bowen, July 8, 1994.

and trusted the foundation's promises, so they could be more experimental. Arnita Jones, then the executive director of the OAH and now of the AHA, notes that "one thing that would be true of both organizations [is that] if there's one thing the members want out of the association, it's the journal."[68] Making it broadly available was essential.

The three university presses, on the other hand, all chose the B version, more cautious because they feared that their core business was at stake. As we saw when Chicago insisted on a compromise, it became clear that university presses had serious bottom-line concerns. They insisted on more cautious terms than did many of the societies. Arnita Jones, of the OAH, a society that eventually signed the B agreement, remembers that agreement as so trivial as to constitute "a very preliminary phase that wasn't a critical decision-making phase."[69] That would come later! The conclusion at this point, that different types of publishers had different needs based on their tolerance for risk, is in contrast to JSTOR's eventual decision to offer only one set of terms, as we shall see in chapter 6.

By July, at least five publishers had signed on, committing a total of six journals, allowing Mellon's attention to turn back to technical matters and the renewed search for a grantee (see chapter 3). In November, less than six months from the earliest work on collections development, Mellon had secured the rights to ten titles, as table 2.2 illustrates.

UMI AS SCANNING VENDOR

Even as Bowen began to develop the strategy with which to approach journals, Mellon remained interested in making use of microfilm for scanning. Although UMI's lack of electronic distribution rights in its microfilm had made publisher relations an immediate priority, Mellon had no cause to relinquish its longer-term interest in scanning from microfilm. Consequently, Fuchs continued to seek all of the information he could find about microfilm and scanning from it.

In a late-March conversation with Fuchs, Yale Associate University Librarian Donald J. Waters related his experiences with Project Open Book, a multi-institutional collaboration that used high-speed microfilm scanners to digitize microfilm editions of rare books.[70] Such high-speed microfilm scanners were then available and receiving a great deal

---

[68] Arnita Jones, Interview with the Author, September 20, 2001.

[69] Ibid.

[70] Ira Fuchs, "Discussion with Don Waters, Associate Librarian, Yale University," memorandum to JSTOR file, March 28, 1994.

TABLE 2.2

Journals Signed on to the Pilot Project, by Agreement Date

Journal Title	Discipline	Publisher	Type[i]	Version	Date
American Historical Review	History	American Historical Association	SS	A	June 28, 1994
Econometrica	Economics	Econometric Society	SS	A	July 8, 1994
American Economic Review	Economics	American Economic Association	SS	B	July 26, 1994
Journal of Political Economy	Economics	University of Chicago Press	UP	B	August 1, 1994
Journal of Modern History	History	University of Chicago Press	UP	B	August 1, 1994
William and Mary Quarterly	History	Institute of Early American History and Culture	SS	B	August 5, 1994
Quarterly Journal of Economics	Economics	MIT Press	UP	B	August 29, 1994
Journal of American History	History	Organization of American Historians	SS	B	September 22, 1994
Speculum[ii]	History	The Medieval Academy of America	SS	A	November 8, 1994
Review of Economics and Statistics	Economics	Harvard University	N/A	B	November 9, 1994

[i]University press or scholarly society.
[ii]*Speculum* published a brief report that it was participating, which has subsequently been archived in JSTOR. "Proceedings of the Annual Meeting of the Medieval Academy of America," *Speculum*, volume 70, no. 3 (July, 1995), 718–30.

of attention in the library community, and several important projects (such as Open Book) were underway to explore whether they would prove more efficient than scanning from paper. Fuchs believed that he had confirmed that microfilm was a viable source for scanning, although he did not realize that the "preservation-quality" microfilm in the Open Book project had been created with radically different standards than those used to microfilm scholarly journals.

With microfilm appearing to be advantageous from a cost perspective—recall those high-speed scanners—UMI could still serve as a possible scanning bureau. In addition, its software might also prove to be valuable. So despite the fact that UMI lacked digital reproduction rights, Fuchs traveled to Ann Arbor to meet with company executives. At this meeting in late March, UMI confirmed that the firm did not have sufficient copyright permissions to undertake the scanning work without additional permission from the journal publishers. Nevertheless, UMI was willing to work with Mellon on JSTOR if their interests could be merged.

UMI had spent millions of dollars over several decades assembling its microfilm collections, and so it was understandably reluctant to provide pieces of these collections at low cost to an outsider. One representative of UMI thought that a further distribution of microfilm would adequately achieve the goals of the journals project, which was astounding to Fuchs since librarians widely believed that microfilm impeded access to the journal literature even relative to the hard-copies. At one point, the UMI leadership discussed its own format for delivering digital content, which would eventually grow to become the ProQuest service. Roemer thought it would cost UMI approximately $5 million to create the JSTOR pilot stage and make it available to five test sites. Mellon was plainly uninterested in supporting, even implicitly, any proprietary approach, since it seemed to produce larger costs than necessary. In turn, James Roemer, then the president of UMI, has characterized the Mellon approach as "extremely naïve"—attempting to undertake negotiations without having clear expectations or goals for a project that seemed "idealistic."[71] No doubt there were stylistic differences between the academics and the businessmen. In closing the meeting, Roemer said of the JSTOR project, "I don't think sane men would do this"[72]— by which, one assumes, he meant that he could not see himself working on the project, but moreover that Mellon needed to understand more clearly its own plans and interests. Within a few days of this meeting,

[71]James Roemer, interview with the author, September 26, 2001.
[72]Ira Fuchs, "Meetings at the University of Michigan and UMI," memorandum to JSTOR file, March 30, 1994, 3–5.

reported Bowen, Fuchs wanted "to consider a range of candidates" for the scanning work.[73]

Some time passed, during which Mellon began more carefully to consider working with the University of Michigan for software (see chapter 3). Mellon continued to believe that UMI might function as scanning vendor, and Fuchs requested a price quote for that service. UMI at first asserted that it was "20–24 months away from" being effectively able to convert digitized microfilm to searchable text.[74] Although UMI was at the time developing automated OCR processes that would effectively handle microfilm's unique features, at the time all OCR software was optimized for paper.[75] But as UMI saw a potentially competitive service being created that would use its own microfilm as the raw material, it proposed a partnership at a meeting on July 22. UMI would provide scanning services for Mellon's JSTOR project. At least this way, the undertaking would yield UMI some revenues. But the price proposed for this scanning service—$3 million—seemed unreasonably high to Mellon staff.[76] (The price would eventually be set at about one-tenth that.) Perhaps the high price reflected in part UMI's effort to realize profits from the work, not realizing that its bid would have to compete with other scanning bureaus.[77] It is certain that the high price reflected UMI's belief that its microfilm could not effectively be OCR'd, but rather would need to be manually typed to create searchable text. Although this should have given pause about using microfilm as a source for scanning, Mellon could only see an expensive proposal. It was at this point that a bid process became a certainty (see chapter 4).

Thus ended several months of Mellon efforts to work, in some form or other, with UMI. Although Mellon had hoped that a partnership with UMI would provide it with the background and expertise of this major microfilm player, the interests of Mellon and UMI simply did not coincide at the time. We have already seen that Mellon began to work with individual publishers once it learned that UMI lacked the necessary licensing rights. When UMI's software proved to be suboptimal in building the database, Mellon sought to work with Elsevier and the University

[73][William G. Bowen], "Notes on JSTOR," memorandum to file, April 2, 1994.

[74]James Roemer, letter to Ira Fuchs, May 25, 1994.

[75]James Roemer, interview with the author, September 26, 2001. Had Mellon known of UMI's development work, it probably would have been unwilling to wait for its digitization technologies to be perfected, but in any event Mellon staff seem to have been unaware of it.

[76][Perry van der Meer], "Brief Summary of Contacts between the Andrew W. Mellon Foundation and UMI Regarding the Journal Storage Project," October 7, 1994.

[77]Roemer believes UMI sought only to break even. Interview with the author, September 26, 2001.

of Michigan (see chapter 3). And when UMI's scanning proposal proved to be so expensive, other scanning bureaus were sought (see chapter 4).

SUMMATION

With the exception of the formal signatures on the publisher license agreements, most everything described in this chapter was completed by June 1994. Decisions had been made about what the JSTOR project was to do and how it was to function. An advisory committee had been established and had signed off on the project, lawyers had been consulted, and UMI had been investigated carefully as a potential partner. In addition, core scholarly journals were identified in two key fields, terms had been crafted and recrafted for publisher participation, Bowen and Ekman had secured the agreement of publishers, and the formal publisher license agreements were beginning to trickle back. All of this had been accomplished in less than half a year.[78]

During this period, the primary goal of signing on a partner was not achieved, but no major errors were made. Bowen's management style had been the same as always, drawing in advisors on a generally ad hoc basis. Even though UMI would not be the partner and Mellon would have to take on a more active management role if its project were to succeed, there was no attempt yet to appoint a project manager. Indeed, there been no formal management committee, and so Bowen would tend to seek consensus with Fuchs and Ekman and sometimes others. Given this early success, it might even have seemed to foundation staff that they could continue to manage the JSTOR project successfully into the future, at least for the near term.

Having successfully developed a vision for JSTOR and secured the participation of a good number of publishers with more to come, real organizational choices remained to be made. With UMI out of the running, no potential partner was ideal. Some had the capability but not the interest; some only indexing files; some had only software to contribute; and some only scanning capacity. Certainly, none was capable of undertaking the sort of painstaking publisher relations outreach, for which personal contacts were so important, that Bowen had spearheaded. Foundation staff had, at the time, no experience whatsoever in the work

---

[78]Even while foundation staff pushed forward on all of these fronts, we should not forget that the work of administering the foundation went on.

of building a digital library, but Bowen's personal enthusiasm for the project pushed it forward. Another organization might have shied away from the challenge at this point, but Mellon had the resources, including leadership, to persevere. It is notable that under the right conditions, taking on the challenge can be the right choice for a grant maker, as subsequent chapters shall demonstrate.

Even if no organization had emerged as the perfect partner, a grantee was still critical to the project's success. Mellon surely was incapable of taking on all of the work itself! Once the JSTOR-A and -B agreements were developed, Mellon turned to Elsevier Science, and then to the University of Michigan, in the late spring and summer of 1994.

CHAPTER 3

Securing an Institutional Partner:
The University of Michigan

APRIL–AUGUST 1994

IN THE EARLY 1990s, the academic library community was rife with tension. Some librarians saw their future in developing new technologies, such as network and computer systems, that would radically alter the availability and usefulness of information resources. Others felt it their responsibility to redouble their traditional role of buying, preserving, and making available a wealth of "conventional" resources for teaching and research. At the University of Michigan, a traditional academic library and a traditional library school were being rapidly and radically transformed.

Elsewhere, there was retrenchment. The two most prominent private university library schools, Columbia and Chicago, had recently been closed.[1] The tiny faculties and student bodies at both of these schools, coupled with little external funding and a paucity of alumni giving, were seen as inadequate to justify the costs they imposed on the universities. Michigan faced much the same dilemma: radically change the character of its own library school, or shut it down.[2]

In a stunning move, a professor (and former interim dean) of engineering was put in charge of Michigan's library school in the summer of 1992. Dan Atkins began his career as a designer and builder of mainframe computers, but he had been an early advocate of distributed desktop computing, the networked connection of numerous personal computers. As a result, he had become interested in many of the behavioral aspects of such distributed computing environments. He saw distributed computing as having the potential to transform the ways in which scholars worked. He would bring this focus with him in 1992 to the subsequently rechristened School of Information.[3]

---

[1] Karen Grassmuck, "Questioning a Commitment: Columbia Treads Carefully as It Considers Closing the School of Library Service, the Last of Its Kind," *Chronicle of Higher Education,* April 25, 1990. Karen Grassmuck, "Columbia U to Phase Out Library School; Officials Hope to Move It to Another Campus," *Chronicle of Higher Education,* June 20, 1990.

[2] Gilbert R. Whitaker, interview with the author, December 4, 2000.

[3] Daniel Atkins, interview with the author, May 31, 2001.

With fresh leadership and discretionary funds from the university, the school actively built its faculty, taking in scholars from psychology, computer science, economics, business, public policy, and more. In support of such innovation, the Kellogg Foundation made a series of grants to Michigan and three other library schools to help them revamp their curricula. Michigan received more than $4 million in May 1994.[4] To Atkins, the educational mission of this changed school was clear. Administrators had been

> getting concerned that this digital revolution was going to create a technology tidal wave that was going to push the traditional library world into the background. A bunch of techie nerds were going to claim they were doing the library work but would be short on the values and the service orientation of the library world. So, they were looking to invest in a place that could prototype and then produce and propagate a new type of professional. Someone who had the heart and soul of a librarian, so to speak, with the technical promise you'd think of coming from a [computer science] department.[5]

Although in retrospect, Michigan's decision was just right, at the time it required justification. Atkins and the school had to show the profession that the change of direction would be toward good ends, and handled responsibly. In this regard, the Kellogg grant brought with it not only money but legitimacy.

While the School of Information was rapidly evolving, it was part of the university's broader commitment to become a leader in networked information. And indeed a number of digital library projects were underway throughout the university. One connected series of projects, which proved to be the earliest direct forefathers of what would become JSTOR's software, originated in the engineering school.

THE DIRECT PROJECT

Before moving to the School of Information, Atkins had been associate and then interim dean of the School of Engineering. In those roles, he worked with the school's Director of Information Technology Randall

---

[4]Beverly T. Watkins, "New Era for Library Schools: They strive to overhaul curricula to reflect the explosion in information technology," *Chronicle of Higher Education*, May 18, 1994. For a retrospective evaluation of the Kellogg grants program, see Peggy Barber, "Look up and look out—librarians are not alone," *American Libraries* 27, no. 4 (April, 1996): 65, and Deanna B. Marcum, "Transforming the curriculum; transforming the profession," *American Libraries* 28, no. 1 (January, 1997): 35.

[5]Daniel Atkins, interview with the author, May 31, 2001.

Frank (now vice-president for Technology Research and Development at Fidelity) to build what was at the time one of academia's most robust distributed computing environments, the Computer Aided Engineering Network.[6] Frank and Atkins envisioned the network as a way to drive collaboration at the university.

Local area networks were a boon to the makers of computer workstations, as funds were invested in desktop computers rather than mainframes. But there were few compelling applications to encourage the creation of these networks, and so at least one manufacturer of personal computers sought to speed their development. The Digital Equipment Corporation ([DEC]; since absorbed by the Compaq Corporation and it in turn by Hewlett-Packard) funded a project at Michigan, called Desktop Information Resources and Collaboration Technology (DIRECT), to develop useful distributed applications for academia.[7]

Working at the Engineering School in early 1991 under the general direction of Frank, programmer Greg Peters created a system that tracked lectures, seminars, and other events at the school. The system allowed users to specify types of events in which they were interested. When a new event was entered into the system, all users with matching profiles would receive an email alert.[8] It was envisioned that this could eventually be utilized with the online library catalog, to alert faculty and students of new accessions that would interest them.[9]

In a subsequent project in 1992, Peters worked with Ken Alexander to adapt the calendaring system to a Reuters-based newsfeed called ClariNet. At the time, they believed that there were no commercially available, reasonably priced search engines that could handle these massive amounts of incoming text-based news items.[10] Rather than try to

---

[6]Rather than standard personal computers, this network was a relatively tenable replacement for time-sharing use of mainframe computers. It connected engineering workstations with high-resolution monitors, significant amounts of RAM, and powerful operating systems. Randall Frank, "RE: Brief few questions on JSTOR," email to the author, January 17, 2002.

[7]See [Randall Frank], "Proposal to the Digital Equipment Corporation for Development of an Electronic Information Server," attachment to Randall Frank, "RE: Brief few questions on JSTOR," email to the author, January 17, 2002.

[8]Ken Alexander, interview with the author, June 14, 2001; Ken Alexander, "Re: Two more questions," email to the author, July 12, 2001. Greg Peters built this server-based calendaring tool around an Oracle database and search engine and users interacted with it via an X-windows client. Eventually, television listings were added, as well.

[9]See [Randall Frank], "Proposal to the Digital Equipment Corporation for Development of an Electronic Information Server," attachment to Randall Frank, "RE: Brief few questions on JSTOR," email to the author, January 17, 2002.

[10]Ken Alexander, "JSTOR software history," email to Sarah Sully and Kevin Guthrie, February 11, 1997.

negotiate for rights to an expensive commercial search engine, Frank thought Michigan should build its own, and it did.[11]

Alexander developed a proprietary search engine, called Full-Text Lexiconographer, that would be able to meet the need. Everyone called it FTL.[12] Peters built a client interface that operated on the distributed workstations, interacting with Alexander's server-based search engine. Even though its development was funded in some measure by DEC, all of the code was owned by the university, so it could be deployed without licensing constraints.[13]

The heart of the DIRECT plan was to utilize this technology to adapt a CD-ROM–based scholarly resource for network use. Even before he took the deanship at the School of Information, Atkins (and others at Michigan) were interested in testing the numerous behavioral questions of electronic scholarly resources. But CD-ROM products required a trip to the library and they were awkward to use. Once adapted for the network, the resource would be accessible simultaneously by multiple users from across the campus.

UMI had recently released a CD-ROM package containing journals published by the Institute of Electrical and Electronic Engineers (IEEE) in the disciplines of electrical engineering and computer science that was a case in point. This product could be installed on only one computer in the Michigan engineering library.[14] Frank and Atkins thought they could create a more useful application by mounting the journals— already digitized—on DIRECT. Technically, the work would be interesting, because

the system we would build would offer functionality similar to the current UMI stand-alone functionality available in a shared network environment. The requirement for dynamic, concurrent, shared access makes this project

[11]Daniel Atkins, interview with the author, May 31, 2001.

[12]Atkins nicknamed it "Faster than Light" in appreciation of its speed and versatility. Daniel Atkins, interview with the author, May 31, 2001.

[13]The general structure of intellectual property agreements between Michigan and outside funders, recalls Frank, was "Michigan retaining IP, vendors having nonexclusive access for internal use." Randall Frank, "RE: Brief few questions on JSTOR," email to the author, January 17, 2002.

[14]For more on this product, see Mary Holland, "IEEE/IEE on CD-ROM: a review from a beta test," *CD-ROM Librarian* 5:2 (February, 1990): 34. For a summary of some of the problems inherent in full-text CD-ROM products like UMI's, which suggest why DIRECT would have been a preferable interface, see Barbara Quint, "The Database Connection: Full of text; Difficulties of Full-text databases," *Document Delivery World* 9, no. 3 (April, 1993): 34.

significantly more complicated than simply providing a network interface to the current UMI product.[15]

Towards this end, DIRECT's leaders held lengthy negotiations with UMI and the IEEE. Katherine Willis, who was responsible for the project's external relations, recalls that the IEEE feared its subscription base would erode if its journals were available on the campus network (see chapter 6).[16] The upshot was that the DIRECT team met with no success. DIRECT remained "software looking for a database."[17] Atkins recalls that "we had a toy system in the sense that it functionally worked and it was scaleable but we didn't have the content, and of course we knew by that time that these things don't get used unless the collection exceeds a certain threshold of breadth and depth."[18] They would have to wait, but not long, for a publisher to become interested in working with them.

ELSEVIER AND TULIP

Elsevier Science was part of the Dutch conglomerate Reed Elsevier and it published more than one thousand scholarly journal titles, largely in the sciences. Elsevier's journals tended to be expensive, and their rapidly increasing prices in the 1980s were reflective of the broader serials spiral (see chapter 1). Because it published so many important journals, and so many expensive ones, Elsevier was a focus of librarians' ire when journal prices rose.

Elsevier Senior Vice-President Karen Hunter, by training a librarian who worked out of the New York office, was in charge of library relations and she sought to improve them. It was this desire to improve customer perceptions of Elsevier, combined with a desire to experiment in ways that might fix the underlying problems of price increases, that positioned Elsevier to take a leadership role among publishers and participate in what would come to be known as TULIP.[19]

Beginning in the late 1980s, as we have seen with Atkins and Frank at Michigan, some forward-thinking IT and library staff at a number of universities had sought to move academic content online. They hoped to prove that technology could bring benefits not only to back-office

[15][Randall Frank], "Proposal to the Digital Equipment Corporation for Development of an Electronic Information Server," attachment to Randall Frank, "RE: Brief few questions on JSTOR," email to the author, January 17, 2002.

[16]Katherine Willis, interview with the author, March 7, 2002.

[17]Randall Frank, interview with the author, July 10, 2001.

[18]Daniel Atkins, interview with the author, May 31, 2001.

[19]Karen Hunter, interview with the author, September 5, 2001.

work and library automation, but also to scholarly resources in the heart of the library. For a number of reasons, they were hoping to deploy journals, in particular, in electronic form.

It was in this context that Hunter was invited to represent Elsevier at one of the founding meetings of the Coalition for Networked Information in March 1991. The Coalition, founded by the ARL and several IT consortia, represented many of the librarians and technologists looking forward to bringing journals online. But by virtue of the librarian representation there, Hunter recalls being so unpopular that someone called her "a lion in a den of Daniels"—quite a vivid illustration of Elsevier's popularity. Nevertheless (or, more probably, as a result), Elsevier agreed to an experimental project that bundled together its impressive collection of materials science journals, distributing the page images and searchable text (but no interface or search engine) to a number of universities.[20] These universities, in turn, each committed systems-development resources to create interfaces to the Elsevier materials science collection, which was critical because Elsevier had no such capability at the time.[21]

Elsevier hoped that the experiment, called TULIP (for The University Licensing Project), would yield "sufficient market data to aid in practical product development."[22] At the meeting itself, a number of universities agreed to participate, but although Michigan "had the highest interest, in some way, they were slow in reacting," recalls Hunter. "Michigan was one of the last to come in."[23] In the end, nine universities would participate.[24]

TULIP was far more than a bold experiment in scholarly journals publishing. One publication called it, perhaps with some hyperbole, "the first attempt to make published, copyrighted material available over the Internet"[25]—well before any newspaper, magazine, or other formal

[20]For more on the technical details of Elsevier's production operation, see Paul Mostert, "TULIP at Elsevier Science," *Library Hi Tech* 13, no. 4 (1995): 25–30.

[21]Karen Hunter, "TULIP—The University Licensing Project," *Journal of Interlibrary Loan, Document Delivery, and Information Supply* 4, nos. 3–4 1994: 19.

[22]Karen Hunter, "PEAK and Elsevier Science," presentation made at the PEAK Conference, Ann Arbor, March 23, 2000, in Wendy Lougee and Jeffrey K. MacKie-Mason, eds., *Bits and Bucks: The Economics and Use of Digital Libraries* (Cambridge, MA: MIT Press, In Preparation).

[23]Karen Hunter, interview with the author, September 5, 2001.

[24]The universities involved in the project included Carnegie Mellon and Cornell universities, the universities of California, Michigan, Tennessee, and Washington, as well as Georgia Tech, MIT, and Virginia Tech.

[25]David L. Wilson, "Major Scholarly Publisher to Test Journals by Computer," *Chronicle of Higher Education*, June 3, 1992, online edition.

information source went online. At the time, it was easily the most advanced, wide-scale project to distribute digitized journal content to colleges and universities. The TULIP final report is a valuable document for understanding the development and evolution not only of electronic journals but of the Internet more broadly.[26] When Elsevier and the TULIP universities completed their project, one successor experiment was a joint project between Elsevier and Michigan called Pricing Electronic Access to Knowledge (PEAK), which approached questions of pricing in greater detail (see chapter 8 for the interaction between PEAK and JSTOR). For Elsevier's business development, TULIP was succeeded by the commercial online service ScienceDirect.[27]

For TULIP, Elsevier digitized the collection of its journals and distributed them to the universities. With each university developing its own interface(s) at no cost to Elsevier, the TULIP project could begin to understand what features of electronic journals were most useful and appealing to scholarly users.[28] Several universities developed successful implementations, including the University of California, which did so for all nine of its campuses. There, notifications were included in indexing services like INSPEC and Current Contents that article images were available through TULIP, and a user could command "display image" to receive the article electronically.[29] There was no independent entrance to TULIP, or ability to search the fulltext, which from the perspective of the University of California provided certain important advantages:

> In speaking with TULIP users, it was often apparent that only a handful of TULIP titles out of the entire set appealed to any given researcher and that the makeup of that handful varied from researcher to researcher. Since no single publisher could provide a critical mass of material for this field, it was especially important that the implementation compensate. By linking the journal images to the bibliographic records in the INSPEC and Current Contents databases, the UC TULIP implementation provides a contextual framework that does achieve critical mass. The researcher is able to search

---

[26]Elsevier Science, *TULIP Final Report* (New York: Elsevier, 1996).

[27]Karen Hunter, "PEAK and Elsevier Science."

[28]For more on the achievements and challenges of the TULIP project, an excellent source is *Library Hi Tech* 13, no. 4 (1995), edited by Nancy Gusack and Clifford A. Lynch, which was devoted entirely to the project. Lynch's contextual summary essay is especially helpful. There are also articles on each of the site implementations, which shed much light as well.

[29]Mark Needleman, "TULIP and the University of California, Part I: Implementation and the Lessons Learned," *Library Hi Tech* 13, no. 4 (1995): 69–72.

within a fuller framework and, in the course of that search, identify those items with TULIP images.[30]

California designed its implementation to compensate for a key shortcoming in the project's design. Without critical mass the resource would not be used.

As with California, Michigan's advances in digital library work and excellent Department of Materials Science made it a natural participant in TULIP. Rather than creating it as a component of an existing group, Michigan placed the central coordination in the hands of Katherine Willis (now at Cyber-State), which enabled the university library and in particular the engineering library to play key roles. Willis worked closely with Randall Frank and William Gossling, then the head of library technical services, on TULIP.[31]

Michigan developed a number of different implementations. In one case, bibliographic citations of the journal articles were integrated into the university's online catalog, allowing researchers to search or browse and then link directly to the image file, much as they could with the California implementation.[32] Most relevant for our purposes, however, was the DIRECT system, and particularly FTL, which was "expected to give the [TULIP] project improved search capability and speed."[33] The aspiration of Atkins and Frank was realized: DIRECT had found an implementation, in what was then the largest digital library project in existence. TULIP would give the DIRECT team its first significant academic "testbed" and bring with it numerous interesting challenges.

The TULIP content was sent to the participating universities as page images accompanied by searchable text. This combination of fulltext with images was the result of TULIP having been put in place before its time: Elsevier was not yet using fully digital processes to produce its printed journals. It seems in retrospect most bizarre that Elsevier would typeset and publish its printed journals, only then to scan them into a computer. This imposed both cost and delay, and was never intended to be other than a stopgap measure. The lack of standardization across Elsevier's many imprints, however, mandated such an approach, with the resulting complexity in the universities' implementations.[34]

[30] Camille Wanat, "TULIP and the University of California, Part II: The Berkeley Experience and a View Beyond," *Library Hi Tech* 13, no. 4 (1995): 73–74.

[31] Katherine Willis, interview with the author, March 7, 2002.

[32] For a summary of some of Michigan's work on TULIP, see Katherine Willis, "TULIP at the University of Michigan," *Library Hi Tech* 13, no. 4 (1995): 65–68.

[33] University of Michigan, "TULIP Status," March 30, 1994.

[34] Elsevier Science, *TULIP Final Report*, 20–24.

While the DIRECT software contained several valuable preexisting features, it also had its limits. Because the earlier DIRECT implementation was built around an "alerts" system, the TULIP implementation allowed a user to input a standing search query, which was checked against incoming journal issues; when matches were found, an email was sent to the user.[35] But, as with California's indexing-system implementation, Michigan's TULIP implementation was unable to browse through volumes and issues to reach a specific article. DIRECT had never needed to browse through hierarchically structured files, since it was only a search-based system, and the ability to browse was not seen as sufficiently valuable to expend the effort to add it for TULIP. Consequently, the only interface to Michigan's DIRECT-based TULIP implementation was through the search engine.[36] Other examples, as well, illustrate how Michigan's implementation received some of the benefits, but suffered from some of the limitations, of being built on a preexisting piece of software.[37]

This is not to suggest that a number of key modifications were not made to adapt DIRECT for TULIP. In fact, the TULIP project forced the Michigan team to undertake several improvements in the DIRECT software. Prior to TULIP, DIRECT had never dealt with images. Consequently, Alexander and Peters had to adapt the software for its new purpose.[38] The system was modified to work with Elsevier's proprietary file structure and metadata format, EFFECT (for Exchange Format for Electronic Components and Texts). On balance, the TULIP implementation functioned well, although the large size of the image files took up a great deal of bandwidth when sent to the client application.[39]

It was clear to Karen Hunter and others that TULIP's key success factor in Ann Arbor was the organizational and software experience developed under DIRECT. The TULIP Final Report concluded that "Michigan's culture of cooperation and multi-organizational activity enabled it to put together a small, functional team to implement TULIP."[40] Hunter has said in retrospect that the most successful implementations,

---

[35]Ken Alexander, "Re: Two more questions," email to the author, July 12, 2001.

[36]Elsevier Science, *TULIP Final Report*, 243.

[37]As in previous implementations of DIRECT, the client application—named TULIPView for the occasion—was a UNIX X-Windows application that operated over the campus network. Printing was accomplished by a central university print server, which routed the file to an appropriate campus printer. Ken Alexander, "JSTOR software history," email to Sarah Sully and Kevin Guthrie, February 11, 1997.

[38]For example, Alexander had to adapt FTL to search the text but then send out the images. The client application had to be modified by Peters to display those images.

[39]Elsevier Science, *TULIP Final Report*, 244–45.

[40]Ibid., 239.

including that of Michigan, had as a universal feature a sense of owner-ship of the project among its participants.

At Michigan, a core team with responsibility for the software and other services, rather than a large committee of part-time contributors, was an unquestionably important ingredient. Willis recalls that the group functioned with neither "politics" nor "friction," seeking only the opti-mal outcome for researchers.[41] It can be argued that such arrangements were important departures from the organization of most research li-braries at the time, which were rife with consensus-minded committee structures for most all decision making. Michigan's ability to move away from such structures, or more properly to avoid them by basing the effort outside the library system, was critical. That is, by creating an intramural group composed of key representatives of the information technology division, the engineering school, and the library, Michigan's TULIP implementers were able to avoid legacy organizational struc-tures. But they were equally able to avoid the library-technology rift that would elsewhere impede progress (see chapter 9 for JSTOR's experi-ences in this regard).

Perhaps most importantly, by leveraging preexisting DIRECT soft-ware, Michigan's implementation got off the ground far more rapidly than most other implementations. It soon achieved significant usage on campus and is considered in retrospect to be the most successful of the universities' implementations. Since then, Hunter has written unequiv-ocally that among the TULIP implementations, "the outstanding player was clearly the University of Michigan."[42]

MELLON AND TULIP

Many digital library projects had sought to build systems and then treat the delivery of services to a user as somewhat of an afterthought. Even DIRECT, for example, existed for some time as a digital library research project without any academic testbed, let alone providing any sort of valuable resource for researchers, until TULIP came about. Even TULIP was principally intended as a research project and a chance for systems design and development; it was only briefly made available to students and scholars.

When Bowen had approached Fuchs for technical advice, both men understood that the JSTOR project was to be just the opposite. While of

[41]Katherine Willis, interview with the author, March 7, 2002.
[42]Karen Hunter, "PEAK and Elsevier Science."

course it would utilize technology, Mellon had no desire for technological experimentation. Consequently, Fuchs explored solutions that were readily available and could easily be applied for the JSTOR project, in particular Elsevier's TULIP project. Princeton's library system, which at the time was somewhat less forward-looking than Michigan's in deploying technology, had chosen not to participate in TULIP. Nevertheless, Fuchs had actively followed Elsevier's work, and he suggested that Bowen consult Elsevier for advice. Perhaps the project, through one of the more successful campus implementations, could serve as a source of software, obviating the need to create new software.

In February 1994, Bowen, Ekman, and Quandt met with Karen Hunter of Elsevier as an extension of the initial consultations described in chapter 2. The ostensible purpose of the meeting was to talk over the Ekman-Quandt program on scholarly communications, and much of the conversation was consequently taken up with discussion of broad trends in academic publishing. Hunter also provided a description of, and status report on, TULIP. According to a Mellon-produced minute of the meeting, it "has been reasonably successful, but much slower in being developed than Hunter had hoped when the project was first set up. It is furthest along in being implemented at the University of Michigan."[43]

From the perspective of the Mellon Foundation, the notion of working with Michigan had a natural appeal beyond Hunter's endorsement of its TULIP software and library team. Bowen, Ekman, Fuchs, and others at Mellon had close working relationships with members of the Michigan faculty and administration. As a leading research university, Michigan was a major beneficiary of Mellon grants. From the foundation's first grant to the University in 1972 through the end of 1993, Michigan had received awards totaling $15.4 million. There was a pre-existing sense of trust based on compatible nonprofit educational missions. Michigan would be an ideal partner to expand JSTOR's test sites to include a research university, which had become a priority.[44] Mellon staff were comfortable that extending their working relationship to another project would be relatively low-risk. As a result, recalls Fuchs, "all other things being equal, we would have gone with Michigan. Some other school would have had to be noticeably, demonstrably better. It didn't take too long to find out there was no such school."[45]

[43]Richard Ekman, "Meeting with Karen Hunter, Vice President, Elsevier Science Publishers, Thursday, February 17, 1994," memorandum to JSTOR file, February 18, 1994.

[44]Ira Fuchs, "Meeting at Bryn Mawr April 5, 1994," memorandum to JSTOR file, April 6, 1994.

[45]Ira Fuchs, interview with the author, July 19, 2001.

Bowen traveled to Ann Arbor in mid-March to meet with representatives of Michigan's TULIP project at the same time he first met with UMI (see chapter 2). At this first meeting at the University of Michigan, the most important university spokespeople were university Chief Information Officer Doug van Houweling (now CEO of Internet2) and TULIP project chief Katherine Willis. In his memo summarizing the meeting, Bowen described the system's architecture, especially the ability to search through text and then display page images. He concluded that "the basic idea is similar to the one we are exploring" for the JSTOR project, because page images were seen as a key way to save costs rather than expensively inputting 100-percent accurate text.[46] Bowen later wrote that staff at Michigan had "already encountered—and largely solved—many, though certainly not all, of the problems involved in making literature available online."[47] He returned from Ann Arbor with enthusiasm for a potential partnership.

Shortly after Bowen convinced him to join Mellon as an advisor for the JSTOR project, Fuchs spoke with Willis and visited Michigan to follow up on Bowen's trip by learning about the technical capabilities and future directions of the DIRECT software.[48] In Ann Arbor, Fuchs met with DIRECT/TULIP staff Frank, Willis, Peters, and Alexander, and Wendy Lougee, the senior Michigan librarian managing digital work (now the director of the University of Minnesota library). They explained the project to Fuchs, including the software components and their desire to deploy them more broadly.[49] Fuchs also saw a "demo" of the software, which may have been fine for engineers but was essentially unusable for a computer novice.[50] The Michigan team assured him that they planned to migrate the system to the web soon.

Today, the decision to move to the web seems foreordained, but in 1994 the web was the most immature of a number of Internet options. In particular, Gopher was more broadly deployed than the web, as table 3.1 illustrates. But while Gopher servers had tripled in the year

---

[46] William G. Bowen, "Report on trip to UMI and U of Michigan, Mar. 17–18, 1994," memorandum to JSTOR file, March 19, 1994.

[47] William G. Bowen, "The Foundation's Journal Storage Project (JSTOR)," in *Report of the Andrew W. Mellon Foundation 1994* (New York: Andrew W. Mellon Foundation, 1995), 28.

[48] Ira Fuchs, "Telephone Conversation with Katherine Willis, U of Michigan," memorandum to JSTOR file, March 23, 1994.

[49] Ken Alexander, "Re: Time to Talk," email to the author, June 11, 2001.

[50] The software for the client implementation used the UNIX X-Windows operating system. Although not so unusual among engineers and scientists, few social scientists, and far fewer humanists, could at the time have been expected to make use of a UNIX desktop computer.

TABLE 3.1
Deployment of Internet Servers, 1993 and 1994

	Gopher	WAIS	Web
April 1993	455	113	62
April 1994	1410	137	829
Rate of Growth	210%	21%	1237%

Source: Tim Berners-Lee, Robert Cailliau, Ari Luotonen, Henrik Frystuk Nielsen, and Arthur Secret, "The world-wide web," *Communications of the ACM* 37, no. 8 (August 1994), 76.

prior to April 1994, web servers had increased by a factor of nearly 14. Clearly, the web's trajectory was steepest, in part because both the server and client applications were free but mostly because the web offered more features. In November 1994, the first Netscape browser was released publicly.[51] And in retrospect, hardly anyone remembers Gopher, WAIS, and the other options.

Fuchs concluded that Michigan's work included the essential components: page images, invisible searchable text, and network-based features. He was glad to see Michigan planning to move DIRECT in the direction of the web. On balance, he wrote, the Michigan work "fits in extremely well" with the JSTOR project.[52] Fuchs recalls that Bowen was "happy" to be able to work with a known and trusted entity like Michigan.[53]

In April, Bowen returned to visit with Hunter, this time with his assistant Perry van der Meer.[54] Bowen spoke about JSTOR to Hunter, who was enthusiastic about the project. She was pleased to hear that Mellon might work with one of the TULIP universities to develop what Bowen had taken to calling JSTOR's "software glue," the adhesive that would bind together all of the other components. TULIP was intended to be an "open" project of benefit to all academia, not only to Elsevier, said

[51]For a good narrative of the dramatic period leading up to this event, see chapter 4 of John Cassidy, *dot.con: The Greatest Story Ever Sold* (New York: HarperCollins Publishers, 2002).

[52]Ira Fuchs, "Meetings at University of Michigan and UMI," memorandum to JSTOR file, March 30, 1994, 1–3.

[53]Ira Fuchs, personal communication, August 28, 2001.

[54]Perry van der Meer, "Meeting with Karen Hunter at Elsevier," memorandum to JSTOR file," April 14, 1994.

Hunter. Each university retained the intellectual property rights to its implementation and was welcome to deploy it elsewhere. Indeed, Hunter hoped for additional deployments, to encourage more digital applications and therefore users. Other universities were creating software from scratch and most had experienced sometimes-severe organizational stresses, as contrasted with Michigan's relative harmony and already functional software. She again stated that Michigan's system was the "most advanced."

Since the TULIP digitization work had been performed centrally by Elsevier and only its final products were distributed to the universities, they did not gain any knowledge of journal-scanning processes. This was why Mellon believed, in Fuchs's words, that Elsevier's seemingly effective processes could launch JSTOR "light years ahead."[55] At the April meeting, Bowen even asked Hunter if Elsevier could take on a more active role in JSTOR. Perhaps Elsevier's successful TULIP project could be redeployed for JSTOR, with Elsevier managing the scanning process, in which it had developed what seemed externally to be great skill, while one of its university partners contributed software. But Elsevier did not want to get into the business of scanning and production for others.[56]

With such a partnership ruled out, Bowen told Hunter that Fuchs would call to seek advice on "problems you have encountered in translating ideas very similar to ours into practical forms."[57] When Fuchs and Hunter spoke, they did not explore this topic at length. Indeed, according to his minute, their conversation only "briefly" touched on the digitization process: Hunter suggested using only one vendor to produce both the images and the indexing, rather than trying to bring the two together from different vendors.[58] Although it could not have seemed so at the time, here was a clear opportunity lost for Mellon to make use of the experience Elsevier had accumulated.

After the April meeting with Hunter, there is no indication of progress on the software or scanning fronts until July, when Mellon convened the advisory committee for a second time. In the interim, the Mellon trustees endorsed the work that had been done thus far. By mid-July, the

---

[55]Ira Fuchs, "Meetings at University of Michigan and UMI," memorandum to JSTOR file, March 30, 1994, 1.

[56]Perry van der Meer, "Meeting with Karen Hunter at Elsevier," memorandum to JSTOR file, April 14, 1994.

[57]William G. Bowen, letter to Karen Hunter, April 14, 1994.

[58]Ira Fuchs, "Discussion with Karen Hunter," memorandum to JSTOR file, April 26, 1994.

AHA and the Econometric Society had signed participation agreements and the AEA and several other publishers were preparing to do so. This second advisory committee meeting therefore included the executive directors of the AHA and the AEA, the core scholarly societies for each of the two fields.

With publisher representation, the committee had an extremely technical conversation about how the JSTOR database might be built. For our purposes, the organizational implications of the meeting are most important. It seems that the committee foresaw almost two independent projects, one focused on software and one on digitization, proceeding almost altogether independently. A service bureau would be selected for scanning all of the page images, converting the images to searchable text, and merging the images and text with bibliographic indexing. While this work took place, Michigan would develop and "deliver" revamped versions of its software for use by the project. It seems that neither Mellon staff nor the committee advising them anticipated the need to coordinate and manage the work of these two subprojects beyond the normal oversight of a grant. How would the various components be brought together from different sources? Who would ensure that the scanning and text conversion were acceptable, and that the bibliographic index had been properly merged with the two? Who would be responsible for having these subprojects on schedule and in sync, being prepared to respond to any unforeseen circumstances? In other words, who was to be the project manager? On these questions, the minutes of the meeting are silent. Although Michigan would take on a nominally managerial role over the scanning vendor, it will become clear in chapter 4 that the organization of Mellon's JSTOR enterprise was not yet adequate.

Michigan was so central to Mellon planning at this point because Fuchs had researched the other TULIP participants. He consulted the recently released TULIP midterm report. He spoke on the phone with or visited several other TULIP participants. His efforts led to the conclusion that, for the purposes of Mellon rapidly securing software for JSTOR, Michigan was the optimal choice.[59] In the wake of the second advisory committee meeting, Bowen wrote that he and Fuchs "should go to Michigan as soon as possible, since they are a leading candidate" to provide the software.[60]

[59]Ira Fuchs, interview with the author, July 19, 2001.
[60]William G. Bowen, "Questions arising out of July 12 meeting," memorandum to JSTOR file, July 13, 1994.

COMING TO TERMS WITH MICHIGAN

The purpose of the Mellon-Michigan partnership that Bowen and Fuchs initially envisioned was to obtain software for the JSTOR project. Michigan's DIRECT software was, in Fuchs's estimation, "80 percent of what we needed," and Michigan staff was prepared to modify it to meet all JSTOR's needs.[61] In addition, the university would help Mellon establish processes with which a scanning vendor could merge the scanned images and text with indexing information into a database whose specifications Michigan would develop.[62]

While Bowen and Fuchs had been establishing that the software would be a useful building block for JSTOR, Michigan administrators were considering whether to participate. Many saw value in learning from the development of a major digital library, building on Michigan's growing expertise and prestige. Others were concerned over the implications for staffing and space-usage. But, Lougee recalls, "I think gradually we saw the benefit of what [Mellon] was trying to create and . . . certainly saw the benefit of having a viable project to get one's feet wet with. . . . I don't know that every institution would have seen that . . . [but] having had the investment in TULIP, I think we were kind of primed to do something."[63]

In addition to this general interest in a complementary project, the DEC monies were running out, so Mellon monies would fund software development that was, essentially, ongoing development of DIRECT.[64] Furthermore, Dean Atkins saw an opportunity for broader institutional impact. The Mellon imprimatur could be a critical asset in selling his school's new educational mission and research agenda. Atkins recalls, "I was anxious to obtain more vitality and more external dollars to get the place really moving and also in a way getting an implicit sanction from places like Kellogg, Mellon, and the National Science Foundation."[65] (As early as August 1995, Atkins began to propose other ways for Mellon to support Michigan's digital library–development work, including the creation of the "Internet Public Library."[66]) Mellon's journals project

[61]Ira Fuchs, interview with the author, November 22, 2000.
[62]Ira Fuchs, "Re: JSTOR," email to Katherine F. Willis, July 14, 1994.
[63]Wendy Lougee, interview with the author, May 30, 2001.
[64]Randall Frank, interview with the author, July 10, 2001.
[65]Daniel Atkins, interview with the author, May 31, 2001.
[66]In March 1996, Mellon awarded $200,000 for the IPL. Atkins's initial proposal was recorded in William G. Bowen, "Dan Atkins and Scholarly Communication," memorandum to Richard Ekman, Harriet Zuckerman, and Kevin Guthrie, August 30, 1995; Mellon Grant #19600690.

had the potential to both contribute to, and benefit from, DIRECT, TULIP, and the rest of the critical mass of digital library initiatives then underway in Ann Arbor.

Once Fuchs and Bowen, with the endorsement of the advisory committee, concluded that DIRECT was an appropriate platform on which to build and that the JSTOR project was sufficiently relevant to the strategic goals of the university, another trip to Michigan was arranged. The purposes of this late July Bowen-Fuchs trip was to meet with Michigan staff to begin hammering out an agreement. Michigan staff had mistakenly believed the project was to contain 250,000 pages, and Fuchs noted that Mellon was planning a pilot project thrice that size. Bowen wanted to have a "demo" he could show the Mellon trustees in early October, a mere ten weeks away, and the final product available online within six months! Although they promised to try, Michigan representatives were quite possibly shocked to find the project three times larger than expected and with such tight deadlines, as well. They "made clear several times that the database we are talking about is *vastly* larger than any database of this kind ever created—about 20 times the size of the TULIP database."[67] Having the complete database available in February would prove to be wishful thinking.

While in Ann Arbor, Bowen and Fuchs also met with Provost Gilbert Whitaker to be certain that the project would be viewed favorably at the highest administrative levels. Bowen reported back that Whitaker "was unequivocal in stating that he thought this was an exciting project and that it fit well with what Michigan is doing."[68] Bowen ensured that the highest echelons of the Michigan administration supported the project, which, as we shall see in chapter 9 most especially but also elsewhere, would prove to be a key success factor. Upon their return from Ann Arbor, Bowen summarized his conclusions:

> My overall impression of the Michigan group was extremely favorable. The individuals seemed very smart, and, in addition, they had the same view of the mission to be served and the objective of the enterprise. Ira [Fuchs] and I were both very comfortable. It is evident that we share a common "culture." I believe that we could work happily and productively together.[69]

[67] William G. Bowen, "University of Michigan Meeting/July 22, 1994," memorandum to JSTOR file, July 25, 1994, 2. Emphasis in the original.
[68] William G. Bowen, "Meeting with Gil Whitaker," memorandum to JSTOR file, July 25, 1994.
[69] William G. Bowen, "University of Michigan Meeting/July 22, 1994," memorandum to JSTOR file, July 25, 1994, 2.

The terribly ambitious schedule that Bowen had set in Ann Arbor was perhaps unrealistic, but it spurred Michigan's grant application and Mellon's own work to submit the request to its trustees.

Bowen asked to have a grant proposal in two or three days, and Frank agreed to take responsibility for writing it.[70] It was notable that a technologist, rather than a librarian, took the lead in writing the grant proposal. Software development would be Michigan's primary task, and Frank supervised the programming staff. Indeed, that the grant proposal called for library staff at all was probably only a legacy of the TULIP partnership. For the JSTOR grant, Lougee recalls lobbying to ensure funding for user support provided by two junior librarians.[71] Their function would be simply to act as liaisons with the test-site librarians.[72] The partnership between librarians and technologists would at times prove challenging (see chapters 7 and 9). But given what we know of the organizational difficulties of some other TULIP participants, it was a mark of Michigan harmony that the partnership existed at all.

Beyond these added features, Frank's draft proposal recapitulated, in formal terms, the informal agreement that the TULIP group had reached with Fuchs and Bowen to modify the DIRECT software to make it more appropriate for the JSTOR project.[73] Several improvements were required because JSTOR's initial scale was to be much greater than that of TULIP. The software would have to function effectively at remote locations and not just on a single campus. Its UNIX interface, which had been adequate for TULIP's technically advanced materials science engineers, would have to be redesigned for the web in order to give scholars in the arts and sciences an easier-to-learn and more widely familiar mechanism. Although Mellon would pay for a web interface as part of the JSTOR project, such work was particularly appealing to Michigan because it could also be applied to the ongoing TULIP project and any subsequent DIRECT implementations.

In addition to the programming work that Alexander and Peters would undertake and the liaison work of the junior librarians, Michigan would subcontract with a scanning vendor. How this decision was reached is unclear. Yet it is patently clear from the grant application that this oversight task was not viewed as a great deal of work. It seems that, on no evidence to this effect whatsoever, Frank assumed and Mellon accepted

[70]Randall Frank, interview with the author, July 10, 2001.

[71]Wendy Lougee, interview with the author, May 30, 2001.

[72]Kristen Garlock, interview with the author, May 25, 2001.

[73]See Randy Frank, grant application for JSTOR, draft of July 29, 1994; Mellon Grant #39400442.

that overseeing the work of a vendor hundreds or thousands of miles away could be accomplished by a nonexpert in free moments. As we shall see in chapters 4 and 7, the pressures to push forward rapidly prevented more careful consideration of the scanning process, a consequence that eventually proved troublesome.

We have seen several times already that Mellon, intending to be a grantor rather than a project manager, was looking for a turnkey solution. Except for negotiating with the publishers of scholarly journals and the academic libraries for which JSTOR was intended, it was planned that Michigan would provide the foundation with such a solution. It was hoped that the DIRECT system could be taken, essentially off the shelf, and applied for JSTOR purposes with little upfront effort and almost no ongoing support.[74] All this, it was proposed, could be coordinated by just 0.25 full-time–equivalent (FTE) project management staff, consisting of 15 percent of Frank's time and 10 percent of Lougee's.

To his credit, Frank was concerned with achieving the best conclusion with the least expense; Bowen had no doubt spoken at length about the project's mission to demonstrate that technology could save money. In an earlier presentation, Frank wrote that the idea was "whenever possible, [to] integrate with existing service units, for scale economy."[75] This was precisely not what Michigan had done for TULIP. The key success factor of Michigan's TULIP implementation was evading legacy organizational structures. Now, it seemed that the TULIP organization and staff, with additional outside librarian support, could take on the JSTOR project, albeit without the central coordination of Katherine Willis. This, even though JSTOR would be significantly more complicated for Michigan, most prominently in the necessity to subcontract with—and presumably manage—the work of the scanning vendor! These dreams of an incredibly lean Michigan staff, fully integrated into existing service units without significant additional local management, providing Mellon with a comprehensive package, would be quickly destroyed.

In late July, Bowen and Whitaker reached an agreement on indirect costs.[76] The development of the JSTOR project would fit in very well

---

[74] William G. Bowen, "University of Michigan Meeting/July 22, 1994," memorandum to JSTOR file, July 25, 1994, 1.

[75] [The University of Michigan], "JSTOR Preliminary Project Plan," July 22, 1994.

[76] The principle behind indirect cost charges is to support the expenses associated with the relevant physical and administrative infrastructure necessary for the work funded by the "direct" portion of a grant. Most often, indirect cost charges take the form of a specified rate—a percentage of the direct award—that varies from institution to institution. Indirect costs typically include expenses related to the maintenance of the physical plant,

with, and potentially contribute to, the broader digital library work at Michigan. Whitaker wanted to signal the university's deep institutional commitment to Mellon and its project, and he was personally enthusiastic. Consequently, he felt that Mellon's funding of the development work at the university should be seen as a partnership, rather than a purchase of services.[77] So even though Mellon might have paid indirect costs to Michigan for the grants, Michigan agreed to charge only for these expenses that could clearly be identified as direct costs.[78]

The lack of indirect costs would help to hold down the expense to Mellon of undertaking the project, which had turned out to be "affordable," from the perspective of the foundation. At a cost of $700,000 to provide all of the services noted above (other than subcontracting with a scanning vendor), Mellon's uncertainty about whether JSTOR could be created for a reasonable cost was resolved. From an expenditure perspective, at any rate, it had become clear that modifying existing software was preferable to creating it from scratch, and Bowen's and Fuchs's decision to work with existing solutions was validated.

LONGER-TERM ARRANGEMENTS

During the iterative process of writing and revising the grant proposal— standard Mellon practice—Frank made several significant modifications. In retrospect, the most critical of these involved the apportionment of intellectual property rights—the ownership of any patents or copyrights that developed—the importance of which did not become clear until late 1996 (see chapter 9). In the first draft, the proposal stated that intellectual property rights in the JSTOR software would remain "an item for negotiation" at a later stage, noting that the university was "prepared to be very flexible."[79] Earlier, however, Bowen and Whitaker had reached an informal agreement,[80] which came to be incorporated into

---

grants management and accounting, legal counsel, and general administration. Mellon's policy is generally not to pay indirect costs, although in the case of a "purchase of services" arrangement, it might have paid them.

[77] William G. Bowen, "Meeting with Gil Whitaker," memorandum to JSTOR file, July 25, 1994.

[78] The agreement to "direct cost" those services that are normally provided for via the indirect cost recovery mechanism was contained in Randy Frank, grant application for JSTOR, August 16, 1994, 6; Mellon Grant #39400442.

[79] Randy Frank, grant application for JSTOR, draft of July 29, 1994, 8; Mellon Grant #39400442.

[80] William G. Bowen, "Meeting with Gil Whitaker," memorandum to JSTOR file, July 25, 1994.

the proposal.[81] Michigan would own the software, but grant to Mellon a nonexclusive license to distribute or use the software for any non-commercial use. Mellon would be assured the right to use the software, while Michigan could continue to use it internally and distribute it to others.

With respect to real property, the arrangement was essentially the opposite: the university agreed that title to all equipment, such as servers, would reside with Mellon. This arrangement was highly un-usual for a Mellon grant, in which ordinarily any equipment becomes the property of the grantee. But although this way of proceeding was highly atypical for the foundation, it served essentially the same end as the intellectual property agreement: to retain rights to the project being developed.

Bowen reported to the Mellon trustees that he viewed these arrange-ments on intellectual and real property as one important component of long-term planning for the database that the JSTOR project would cre-ate. "At some point," he wrote, "the Foundation would almost certainly want to find an institutional partner that could take responsibility for the oversight and administration. . . . This partner might also accept some financial responsibility." The agreement to share intellectual prop-erty rights "paves the way for the Foundation to explore a wide variety of organizational options in deciding how to proceed with JSTOR after the Start-up Stage of the project has been completed."[82] It was far too early to conclude whether the University of Michigan was the right long-term partner. Accordingly, Mellon sought to keep its options as open as possible.

With this language, Bowen very clearly marked out the grant as dif-ferent from others. The foundation, rather than its grantee, would take responsibility for stewardship of the products of the grant. But Michi-gan was not, in any formal sense, a party to this vision of JSTOR's fu-ture development. It would have been highly unusual for Michigan, as the grantee, to see the foundation "docket item" (effectively, a brief to the trustees) quoted above in which Bowen was so blunt about matters; Mellon treats these documents as privileged communication between its program staff and board.

And so, despite Mellon's decisions to retain rights to the intellectual and real property funded by the grant, the Michigan grantees had a very different conception of long-term organizational arrangements. In the grant proposal, Frank wrote of a closer long-term partnership with final responsibility resting with the university:

[81]Randy Frank, grant application for JSTOR, August 16, 1994, 8; Mellon Grant #39400442.

[82]Docket Item for Mellon Grant #39400442, 5.

During the pilot project one operational goal is to transfer this technology and service to a campus organization that will operate the service beyond the pilot. This target organization within the Information Technology Division will be headed by Kitty Bridges. . . . Any further development projects to be negotiated after the pilot phase will remain within the overall University of Michigan Digital Library Project.[83]

This statement was not revised during the iterative proposal development process and was eventually included in the final grant application, which the foundation references as the grantee's contractual obligations in exchange for funding.[84] It is therefore likely that foundation staff were unaware of any disparity. Michigan had staked its own long-term claim to care for and guide the database, notwithstanding the understandings on intellectual property and Bowen's report to the Mellon trustees. These differing understandings would later cause tension in the relationship (see chapter 9).

Perhaps one reason this discrepancy went unresolved was the great pressure that Mellon felt to reach a final agreement, send funds to Ann Arbor, and push the software work forward. Although the next quarterly meeting of the Mellon trustees was only a month and a half away, the foundation's officers sought to proceed immediately via an unprecedented unanimous consent agreement. In a memorandum to the trustees, Bowen explained why extraordinary action was necessary: "It is important to maintain the momentum of JSTOR, in part to avoid any risk that the most promising people who could work on it might become committed to other projects. It is also important that the various pieces of this rather complicated jigsaw puzzle fit together at the right times."[85] Staff were pushing hard to have an initial version of JSTOR available at test institutions in early 1995.[86]

Bowen sent the docket item to the trustees, and he contacted the members individually soon after. Having been kept apprised of developments for the past six months, the board shared his enthusiasm.[87] Its

[83] Randy Frank, grant application for JSTOR, draft of July 29, 1994, p. 8; Mellon Grant #39400442.

[84] Randy Frank, grant application for JSTOR, August 16, 1994, 8; Mellon Grant #39400442.

[85] William G. Bowen, "Journal Storage Project," memorandum to Mellon board of trustees, July 26, 1994, 5; Mellon Grant #39400442.

[86] Docket Item for Mellon Grant #39400442, 2. This was written in later July or, more likely, early August of 1994.

[87] In Bowen's notes documenting these calls, words and phrases appear such as "enthusiastic" and "in full agreement." See William G. Bowen, "Calls to AWM Trustees re JSTOR," August 19, 1994; Mellon Grant #39400442.

approval was treated as an action of the finance committee, which had formal responsibility for such intermeeting actions. On August 30, 1994, an award of $700,000 was made,[88] with the understanding that a subsequent appropriation would be made for the scanning work when those costs became clearer.[89]

SUMMATION

As we have seen, the decision by Mellon to work with Michigan was not difficult. They felt that Michigan software was optimal, and that the university was an optimal partner, with which to build JSTOR. Mellon was truly fortunate that Michigan had taken such an early leadership role in developing digital libraries, for when Mellon later began to develop an interest it had a ready partner at hand.

As a result of Mellon's satisfaction, indeed excitement, at having found such a ready and inexpensive out-of-the-box solution, Bowen and Fuchs immediately began putting pressure on Michigan to rapidly deliver a proposal. At this stage in an ordinary grant, before an award is made or any actual work is undertaken, Mellon program officers have time to flag proposals that lack sufficient organizational capacity, project management, and sustainable process. These proposals are returned to the grantee for clarification and amendment before any proposal is made to the trustees. But because of the pressures to get the project underway rapidly and Mellon's conviction that Michigan would be a partner willing and able to shift course midway, the grant was rapidly approved without, as chapters 7 and 9 shall evidence, sufficient consideration of all of the relevant issues, including control over intellectual property and management responsibilities.

For most grants, once the grant check is mailed the interaction between foundation and grantees typically consists of routine reporting and occasional requests to approve minor adjustments. The grantee functions as the project manager. Although no project manager was designated at this stage in JSTOR's development—none at Michigan, none at Mellon—Bowen and Fuchs had already traveled to Michigan several times each, and they took an extremely active interest in every aspect of Michigan's work. The next chapter illustrates just how much this grant was different from others, and how these different arrangements played out.

[88] William G. Bowen, letter to James J. Duderstadt, August 30, 1994.
[89] William G. Bowen, "Conversation with Ira Fuchs, November 6," memorandum to JSTOR file, November 8, 1994.

CHAPTER 4

The Pilot Project

SEPTEMBER 1994–APRIL 1995

SECURING THE PARTNERSHIP with Michigan was a major step forward. Once it seemed certain that Michigan would agree to work with Mellon, Bowen reported to Mellon's trustees that "in almost every respect, JSTOR has turned out to be far more complex than I ever imagined it would be when I first discussed the project with the Trustees. I estimate that I have spent about one-third of my time on this project over the last five months, and others [including Fuchs, Woodbridge, and Ekman] have also been deeply involved."[1] As we saw in chapter 2, this onerous task and the "jigsaw puzzle" of partners were necessary because of Mellon's (accurate) belief that no single organization would be capable of creating JSTOR. Instead, as a project rapidly developed where previously one had not yet seemed certain, Mellon and Michigan together oversaw much of the work.

As we shall see in this chapter, the necessary oversight and management of these partners would prove to be beyond the natural abilities of the Mellon Foundation, all of whose other work involved building grantee-grantor relationships. During the six months preceding the first Mellon grant to Michigan for JSTOR, Bowen had managed every aspect of JSTOR, with all participants reporting directly to him. But once Michigan was brought in as a partner, responsibility was diffused and progress slowed, as the project turned from planning to production. Under Bowen's oversight, Frank and Fuchs—both technologists, though Fuchs had some experience at Princeton with scanning operations[2]—

---

[1]William G. Bowen, "Journal Storage Project," memorandum to members of the Mellon board of trustees, July 26, 1994.

[2]Fuchs had been involved, albeit not in a project management role, with a project to digitize Princeton University's retrospective card catalog as a collection of images. At the time, it was the largest library-related image database. See Anthony M. Cummings, Marcia L. Witte, William G. Bowen, Laura O. Lazarus, and Richard H. Ekman, *University Libraries and Scholarly Communications* (Washington, DC: Association of Research Libraries for the Andrew W. Mellon Foundation, November 1992), 116; and "VTLS Inc. teams with Princeton University to create database," *Information Today* 10, no. 6 (June 1993): 50. For more on Princeton's project, see Eileen Henthorne, "Digitization and the Creation of Virtual Libraries: The Princeton University Image Card Catalog—Reaping the Benefits of Imaging," *Information Technology and Libraries* 14, no. 1 (March 1995): 38.

made most all of the production-related decisions. In order to avoid undue delay, they made choices thought to be presumptively optimal. Michigan, however, had little experience with digital library projects invoving production. As we shall see, problems of both organization and capacity would manifest themselves everywhere from Michigan and Mellon to the scanning bureau in the Caribbean. Only after these problems were identified, could staff begin to review choices and develop production-level processes for the longer term.

DEVELOPING THE ARCHITECTURE
OF PRODUCTION

In chapter 2 we saw that Mellon lacked expertise in scanning a journal, converting the page images to searchable text, and creating necessary bibliographic information. As a result, the Foundation searched for one or more partner-grantees; it had no interest in developing its own operational expertise in such matters as scanning, OCR, indexing, and software development. But Mellon staff quickly discovered that no organization had both the ability and inclination to take on the entire project as the "prime contractor," offering a complete package of software and digitization services. Elsevier had ruled it out at once, while UMI proved unable or unwilling to take on the role. Requiring a grantee in order to proceed, the Mellon Foundation selected the University of Michigan based solely on its software proficiency.

At the time, the software development was seen as the most important contribution, perhaps in no small measure because Frank and Fuchs led the planning. Even though neither organization had any experience whatsoever in overseeing large-scale digitization operations, Mellon assigned and Michigan accepted these additional responsibilities without any documentation that such an arrangement was seriously evaluated. As a result, the digitization and other production work was viewed as a nearly black-box solution to be provided by a vendor. Michigan was not expected to provide active management, but rather only minimal oversight. As we shall see, everyone involved grossly underestimated how complex the project would prove to be—and thus how much management and oversight would be required. Many of the complexities of digital library production were not well-understood by the principal players at the time. Perhaps this was for the best—Bowen has said a number of times that, with the blinders off, JSTOR might never have happened.

Scanning from Microfilm

The fundamental production decision was how to digitize the journals' page images. Beyond this, everything else was corollary. Although the TULIP project had scanned from paper, we saw in chapter 2 that, for a number of reasons, Mellon staff believed that microfilm would be, for the JSTOR project, a more preferable choice. For one thing, it was believed that the UMI microfilm contained, in one place, all the backfiles of a given journal, which could be rapidly digitized. This presumptively optimal choice would soon prove to be problematic.

Because Elsevier scanned images of printed journals rather than producing them electronically, it had extensive experience working with scanning bureaus. Fuchs had therefore contacted Karen Hunter for a list of possible vendors, and she wrote in late April with a list of companies that had performed well in a recent Elsevier bid. She also gave a brief description of the tasks that had been requested for the scanning of the TULIP materials science journals. Since Mellon staff made the decision to delay retaining a scanning vendor until identifying a source for software and the necessary copyright permissions, it was only after the Mellon grant to Michigan that this work proceeded.

In the meantime, Mellon conversations with UMI proceeded. It had earlier become clear that a partnership was not likely (see chapter 2). In principle the scanning could be put out to bid, since the microfilm itself was held at libraries throughout the country. Mellon staff therefore began to seek other options, unsure whether UMI's nonparticipation might effectively have killed the project. So while Mellon ramped up journal negotiations with publishers, staff wondered if the foundation could contract with another vendor to scan UMI's microfilm. But could any vendor just scan from UMI's microfilm? UMI believed not; it asserted a copyright in the compilation of issues and volumes and their reformatting to its microfilm. Although earlier Richard Woodbridge had determined that UMI did not hold exclusive licenses to digitize the journals—meaning that another firm could digitize them—UMI claimed it was not permissible to use its microfilm in the process.

If UMI's claims proved true, it could bar Mellon from utilizing its microfilm as a source. But if UMI held no copyright in its microfilm versions, permission from the journal publishers would be sufficient to scan from the microfilm. The copyright in microfilm was not immediately clear, so Mellon again sought a legal opinion. Woodbridge determined that, since a microfilm version attempts to be as accurate a reproduction of the original as possible, no copyright subsists in the microfilm beyond that of the original journal.[3] Michigan staff also consulted university counsel.[4] The upshot was that, if Mellon could obtain a set of the microfilm, it could pay to have the microfilm scanned by a third party, and, barring any underlying contractual limitations, UMI had no legal recourse to prevent this. Mellon therefore began to seek microfilm editions. As publishers signed the license agreement for Mellon's JSTOR project, they ordered the microfilm copies to which they were entitled from UMI (paid for by the foundation), and passed them on to Mellon.

Over the summer, Frank and Fuchs designed an RFP (request for proposals), a formal process through which bids are solicited in an effort to select the most appropriate vendor. Although the preference was still to scan from microfilm, as a backup, bids were requested for scanning from both microfilm and from bound volumes. The RFP requested pricing for a variety of other options, including scanning at various resolutions[5] and OCR (optical character recognition) at various levels of accuracy.[6] The range of options indicated that price remained an important factor in exactly how JSTOR was to be built.[7]

Microfilm was a relatively simple source for scanning. But the alternative possibility of scanning from paper necessitated a source of paper backfiles, a far more difficult affair. Harvard librarian and advisory committee member Richard DeGennaro agreed to undertake a survey of Harvard's holdings to see if it could furnish paper copies of the journals and to provide those for which Harvard had multiple copies. This was considered to be an unlikely outcome, for at the time everyone involved seems to have thought that scanning from microfilm would prove to be preferable.[8]

The result of the RFP process was the selection of three finalists, each of which submitted samples of their work based on both hard-copy and microfilm sources. Despite (or perhaps because of) the number and

---

[3] Copyright only subsists if a work requires some creativity to produce. In the case of the microfilm under consideration, UMI's selection, coordination, and arrangement added little to that of the original hardcopy. *Feist Publications* v. *Rural Telephone*, 499 U.S. 340 (1991).

[4] Randall Frank, interview with the author, July 10, 2001.

[5] Measured in the dots per inch resolution of the scanned images. Bids were requested at 300 and 600 dpi (dots per inch).

[6] Measured as the number of inaccurate characters per thousand.

[7] "Request for Proposals: Digital Scanning of Journal Articles: The Mellon Foundation JSTOR Project," undated document of uncertain authorship (though from other evidence written by Ira Fuchs).

[8] Richard Ekman, "Conversation with Richard De Gennaro, Harvard University," memorandum to JSTOR file, October 11, 1994.

variety of options, at least one vendor, Digital Imaging & Technologies (DIT), was hesitant. In October, DIT sent a letter stating its unwillingness to bid on microfilm conversion:

> I regret to say that the quality [of the microfilm] is consistently poor. . . . There is a loss of focus on the edges of the pages. . . . There are stripes or scratches running down many of the frames. . . . The printed pages have been shot the wrong way . . . i.e. down instead of across. . . . In short we regard it as impractical to obtain images to use either as [image] files or as data for purposes of reading for OCR.[9]

This observation led to an inspection of the quality of UMI microfilm, which had never been undertaken by Mellon (or Michigan) staff.[10] The JSTOR project's archival standards demanded high-quality images. After having a close look at the film, Fuchs determined that its low quality was unacceptable not only for text-conversion, but even for imaging.[11] As a result, Fuchs became "persuaded that we will want to work from paper" rather than from microfilm.[12]

All evidence suggests this was the correct conclusion at the time. James Roemer of UMI recalls that "the technology wasn't available then." Specifically, UMI "had to work with scanner companies to make [robust microfilm] scanners. We had to develop OCR algorithms that were much different than those on the market." All of this eventually took years to do, and it was not completed until 1998.[13] Given that Mellon wanted the JSTOR database off the ground in a matter of weeks, scanning from paper was the necessary choice.

Scanning from Paper

Fortunately, because the RFP had also asked for quotes on scanning bound volumes, Mellon was more prepared to move ahead than it might

---

[9] Charles Hazell, letter to Ira Fuchs, October 31, 1994.

[10] Some librarians have since then suggested that the problems with microfilm would have been self-evident to them without having gone through this process.

[11] Some of the potential problems that could be introduced by microfilming (which foreshadow the problems that can be introduced by digitization) are documented in Peter Ashby and Robert Campbell, *Microform Publishing* (London: Butterworths, 1979), 69. Some of the problems that can be introduced by using microfilm as a source for digitization are found in Anne R. Kenney, "Digital Benchmarking for Conversion and Access," in Anne R. Kenney and Oya Y. Rieger, eds., *Moving Theory into Practice: Digital Imaging for Libraries and Archives* (Mountain View, CA: Research Libraries Group, 2000), 24–60.

[12] William G. Bowen, "Conversation with Ira Fuchs, November 6," memorandum to JSTOR file, November 8, 1994, 1.

[13] James Roemer, interview with the author, September 25, 2001.

otherwise have been. Fuchs was able to resume examining the bids, focusing on the numbers for paper scanning rather than microfilm. Although higher quality was seen as preferable, the necessity that JSTOR eventually balance its budget necessitated that quality be viewed in relation to price.

Few people knew very much about optimal scanning resolutions, especially for image files that were intended to be maintained in perpetuity (i.e., archived). So in its one major outside consultation on scanning, the JSTOR project staff consulted with Anne Kenney, a preservation librarian at Cornell University well regarded for her work on digitization standards. She pushed JSTOR to select 600 dpi.[14] Kenney made the recommendation, and Fuchs "led the charge" for this option, which turned out to add relatively little to the cost. Bowen was convinced. He recalls 600 dpi as a "critical decision made early on that was clearly right . . . if we were going to digitize all this material we needed to do it at a very high level of quality—we didn't want to have to go back and do it again."[15]

Similarly, the conversion of the page images to searchable text—OCR—was also a function of cost. If it were at all affordable, the desirability of OCR in the eyes of the librarian community was becoming increasingly clear. Given how such resources have developed since then, had JSTOR not included searchable text at the time, it might well have had to add the searchable text later.[16] The OCR cost estimates in the RFPs varied substantially. Fuchs explored at some length the option of performing the OCR work "in-house" at Michigan, which he estimated would ensure that its cost was below $1 per page.[17] He and Frank also examined the possibility of using a different type of search engine that would require searchable text of lower quality.[18] Had all of these options proved to be too expensive at the time, the database would have been created without searchable text. In this alternative, it was hoped

[14]See her "Digital Resolution Requirements for Replacing Text-Based Materials: Methods for Benchmarking Image Quality," The Commission on Preservation and Access, April 1995, and "Digital Image Quality: From Conversion to Preservation and Beyond," in Richard Ekman and Richard E. Quandt, eds., *Technology and Scholarly Communication* (Berkeley: University of California Press, 1999).

[15]William G. Bowen, interview with the author, October 31, 2000.

[16]There are a number of important dissenting voices to this view, which, while surely the majority view, is not quite settled.

[17]William G. Bowen, "Conversation with Ira Fuchs, November 6," memorandum to JSTOR file, November 8, 1994.

[18]Ira Fuchs, interview with the author, July 19, 2001.

that the high-quality scanned images would allow the fairly automated OCR process to be applied at some point in the future when OCR prices had fallen.[19]

With these decisions on scanning resolution and OCR, Mellon staff felt they understood scanning costs well enough to propose a grant to the board at its December meeting even though a vendor had not yet been selected. When all expenses were taken into account, it was expected that scanning and OCR would cost $1.30 per page, or about $1 million for the 750,000 page collection.[20] The Mellon trustees approved a grant to Michigan of $1.5 million, to pay these costs and to cover any additional contingencies.[21] With this approval in hand, Michigan would be able to sign a contract immediately once a scanning vendor was selected, rather than waiting for Mellon's next quarterly board meeting.

Soon thereafter, a vendor was chosen. Although another of the finalists delivered higher-quality output, the least expensive bidder delivered quality that was deemed acceptable. And its costs were substantially lower than those of competitors.[22] In early November, Fuchs had thought that the cost of OCR alone could be held below $1 per page; Digital Imaging & Technologies (DIT) bid to scan, OCR, and perform certain indexing work at $0.39 per page.[23] At these rates, Mellon's grants could pay for nearly four million pages! This price compared extremely favorably with the competition, allowing for both 600 dpi and high-quality OCR. But most importantly, DIT agreed that the quality of its work would meet or exceed that provided in its sample, a commitment other finalists refused to make![24] As a result, DIT—a for-profit company that conducts labor-intensive operations in Bridgetown, Barbados, and other locations—was chosen for the contract.[25] But writing the contract was a challenge. How could the level of quality delivered in the DIT sample be quantified so it could be included as a term in the contract?[26]

[19]Randall Frank, interview with the author, July 10, 2001.

[20]William G. Bowen, "Conversation with Ira Fuchs, November 6," memorandum to JSTOR file, November 8, 1994.

[21]Grant application and docket item for Mellon Grant #49400834.

[22]Ira Fuchs, interview with the author, November 2, 2000.

[23]Digital Imaging and Technology, "Proposal for Princeton University," December 8, 1994, 25. (DIT mistook Fuchs's institutional affiliation for the affiliation of the JSTOR project.)

[24]Randall Frank, interview with the author, July 10, 2001.

[25]DIT has since been subsumed by Lason, Inc., and the DIT name dropped.

[26]Randall Frank, interview with the author, July 10, 2001.

By the terms of the contact, "DIT commits that it will maintain an error rate no worse than that in the sample," which for OCR was quantified at one error per two thousand characters.[27]

In the shift from scanning microfilm to scanning bound volumes, relatively little consideration was given to how the source volumes would be obtained and assembled. Since DIT would not be scanning from microfilm, it would be necessary to take DeGennaro up on his offer that Harvard provide the journals. Bowen wrote in a memo that DeGennaro would "assume full responsibility for producing" the paper copies.[28] Bowen's language suggests he was looking for something approaching another off-the-shelf solution, perhaps with some degree of frustration that microfilm had recently proven impossible. Those journals that Harvard could not provide would be obtained from the University of Michigan.

To Buy or Not to Buy: Metadata

In addition to Michigan's software and the page images and OCR that DIT was to provide, JSTOR needed basic indexing, or metadata, to allow navigability. This information would provide the table of contents needed in order to link to each article. The alternative was unimaginable: in effect manually paging through every volume, and without the ability to search for the title of an article or an author's name. While the exact technical standards for JSTOR's metadata were not yet certain, one thing was clear. The JSTOR database required metadata, and in the same spirit that sent Mellon in search of existing solutions with Michigan's TULIP implementation and UMI's microfilm, Mellon sought out a ready-made product. If a bibliographic index existed that could be readily transformed into a metadata format, Mellon would probably be able to save both time and money in building JSTOR.

In the past, access to journal literature came principally through printed indices, such as the Reader's Guide to Periodical Literature and the Wilson indices, which could be searched by certain subjects, much like the subject index of a manual card catalog. With increasing automation, new electronic options had emerged, more powerful than the printed indices because they could be searched by many fields. In chapter 3, we saw that several of the TULIP implementations linked page images from

---

[27] "Agreement for Scanning and Optical Character Recognition Services."

[28] William G. Bowen, "Conversation with Ira Fuchs, November 6," memorandum to JSTOR file, November 8, 1994.

indexing services like INSPEC and Current Contents. Of more relevance to JSTOR, the British bibliographic company Chadwyck-Healy had developed an electronic abstracting and indexing service that focused on the humanities and social sciences.[29] Periodicals Content Index (PCI) cataloged the tables of contents of North American and European journals, allowing a user to search a CD-ROM for an unknown article by author, title, and other tags.[30] An individual library, subscribing to PCI, could customize it, so that a local user would be able to see whether the library held the journal in which the desired article was located. The PCI index was believed to be a close approximation of the metadata that JSTOR required.

In chapter 1, we saw that one of Ekman's earliest consultations in January was with a senior representative of Chadwyck-Healy. Ever since, Mellon staff had held the not-illogical assumption that purchasing an existing product would be less expensive and less complicated than creating one from scratch.[31] At any rate, using an existing product was the "presumptively optimal" choice from Mellon's perspective—the obvious, existing choice was given the chance to succeed before seemingly more complicated options were pursued. While PCI would eventually prove to be an inappropriate source for the JSTOR project, its consideration further illustrates Mellon's desire that existing solutions be used to build the JSTOR database efficiently.

The initial negotiations went remarkably well, in part because of Chadwyck-Healy's interest in the future of scholarly communications and tolerance for risk in looking to this future.[32] We saw in chapter 1 that PCI had been built in conjunction with the Harvard library system. A for-profit concern, Chadwyck-Healy had become a partner with Harvard to meet the needs of scholarly institutions. It understood Mellon's scholarly purpose and was willing to alter its own plans somewhat to accommodate Mellon's needs.

The motive behind Chadwyck-Healy's interest in discussing participation in Mellon's journals project is unknown, but the move was well timed. If it were Chadwyck-Healy's index, rather than one generated independently, that formed the spine of JSTOR, there would be guaranteed

---

[29] Chadwyck-Healy's primary line of business was originally in microfilm. In the late 1980s, however, the company repositioned itself to embrace new technologies in its offerings.

[30] "New bibliographic product from Chadwyck-Healy," *CD-ROM World* 8, no. 1 (January 1993): 19.

[31] Ira Fuchs, interview with the author, July 19, 2001.

[32] Richard Ekman, interview with the author, April 16, 2001; Richard DeGennaro, interview with the author, March 30, 2001.

revenue for PCI, whether PCI continued to be distributed independently or became nothing more than JSTOR's skeletal structure.[33] Moreover, it would demonstrate that one could build out from a bibliographic index, as librarians including Michael Keller of Stanford University had suggested, rather than thinking of a bibliographic index as a totally different product from an electronic journal.

Negotiations between representatives of Mellon and Chadwyck-Healy went well. Chadwyck-Healy agreed to change its work order, giving priority to the indexing of the journal titles of interest to Mellon.[34] In negotiating a price for the right to distribute the index as the backbone of JSTOR, Bowen was adamant that pricing should not exceed marginal costs, which is to say that Mellon should not have to pay Chadwyck-Healy an additional fee every time it included another institution, since there was no additional cost to Chadwyck-Healy. He maintained that there must be a flat value to Chadwyck-Healy in providing the index, and that would be the price that Mellon would want to pay. From the perspective of Chadwyck-Healy, since a sufficiently expanded JSTOR could, conceivably, fully replace PCI, the flat value of providing PCI to JSTOR was the total revenue from PCI's widest potential worldwide distribution. Such a fee would obviously be too large to be tenable at the outset of Mellon's untested, demonstration project. By July 1994, it was agreed that a fee would be paid to Chadwyck-Healy depending on the number of institutions to be included (not individual users), an indication of how eager Mellon was for an off-the-shelf solution.[35]

At much the same time, Mellon reached its agreement with Michigan. The decision to utilize PCI for its metadata was not reviewed with University of Michigan librarians[36]—rather, it was viewed as a technical

---

[33]Perhaps Chadwyck-Healy representatives feared that the days of indexing services like PCI were numbered. Abstracting and indexing services had provided functionality not available in the world of paper journals. Without an index like PCI, it was vastly more difficult for a user entering the stacks of a major library to locate an article by a particular author, on a particular subject, or with a particular title. With the advent of electronic versions of scholarly journals, publishers made the obvious decision to include indexing information along with the text, to allow a reader to navigate easily from the electronic table of contents to individual articles. But once indexing information was included, a sufficiently robust search engine could allow a reader to locate articles without indexing services like PCI. Later, major efforts to link together indexing information across an array of journals have sought to allow searches that are often even more powerful than those offered by journal indices. If such an environment eventually emerged, why would any library continue to pay for journal indexing services such as that offered by PCI?

[34]William G. Bowen, "Status Report," memorandum to principal participants in the JSTOR project, May 6, 1994.

[35]Sir Charles Chadwyck-Healy, letter to William G. Bowen, July 15, 1994.

[36]Wendy Lougee, interview with the author, December 13, 2001.

matter to be overseen by Frank and Fuchs. Yet as a result of the Michigan partnership, Fuchs selected as JSTOR's metadata standard the EFFECT specifications that had been used for TULIP, because EFFECT was designed to accommodate the structure of journal literature and the DIRECT software already understood it.[37] JSTOR project staff at Michigan would convert PCI into EFFECT. Elsevier gave permission to Michigan for the use of the EFFECT specifications and the overall file structure in JSTOR,[38] and hoped it would be adopted more broadly as a useful common tool.[39]

The Michigan technologists examined the PCI subset, to ensure it could be parsed into EFFECT and then merged with the image files. If there were no way to automate this process, staff somewhere, probably at the scanning vendor,[40] would have to manually merge the metadata with the images.[41] Would the combined costs of purchasing the indices from Chadwyck-Healy and then manually merging them with the scanned images prove substantially cheaper than generating the indices from scratch? It has been impossible to locate any evidence that this question was pursued aggressively. Fuchs recalls a mantra-like impulse that "having to create [it ourselves] would be horribly labor-intensive, expensive, and prone to error . . . avoid it if you can."[42]

When samples of PCI were sent to the potential scanning vendors in connection with the RFP, a number of problems were found.[43] In some cases, the indexing did not indicate the issue, but only the volume, in which an article appeared. This would complicate efforts to make JSTOR browseable. Moreover, PCI only presented what was in the printed table of contents—if there was only one entry there for book reviews, then PCI did not index each individual book review. In March, when discussing the project with UMI, Bowen had mentioned the possibility of using PCI as the metadata spine for JSTOR. At the time, both Roemer and the UMI Chairman, Joseph Fitzsimmons, "said that assembling a good index [as the source of the metadata] would be the most difficult problem we face . . . they think that there will be gaps that we will somehow

---

[37]Ira Fuchs, interview with the author, July 19, 2001.

[38]Karen Hunter, interview with the author, September 5, 2001.

[39]Elsevier Science, *TULIP Final Report* (New York: Elsevier, 1996), 26.

[40]Digital Imaging and Technology, "Proposal for Princeton University," December 8, 1994, 25.

[41]Staff at Michigan had attempted such a project for another digital library undertaking, and they were wary of its complexity. Ken Alexander, interview with the author, June 14, 2001.

[42]Ira Fuchs, interview with the author, July 19, 2001.

[43]Ira Fuchs, letter to William G. Bowen, December 8, 1994.

have to fill."[44] Despite warning that "this could be a very big problem, which deserves attention very soon," Bowen does not seem to have further acted on this information. It is clear that the October "discovery" of precisely these problems with PCI surprised Bowen, Ekman, and Fuchs, who clearly had trouble coordinating the information they were taking in from numerous sources as they pushed the project forward as rapidly as possible.

In any event, Mellon and Michigan staff now realized that if important content, not only book reviews, but also letters and advertisements, was not present in PCI, JSTOR would need to find another source for it. At first, it seemed that, at additional cost, Chadwyck-Healy might be persuaded to enlarge the scope of PCI to index these materials, but Frank recalls it "wanted a fortune for it."[45] Then, it seemed that DIT might supplement the PCI indexing, filling in the blanks for JSTOR. DIT was asked what it would charge for such a service, and it concluded that the work could be done for $0.15 per item. Although DIT had not provided any evidence of competence at what would prove to be a challenging task, Bowen was encouraged.[46]

Given the rates that Chadwyck-Healy felt compelled to charge for its index—which did not even include the expense of linking it with the digitized page images—and DIT's inexpensive quote, Mellon decided to have the index created from scratch.[47] That way, the index would meet all of JSTOR's technical and quality requirements, and would not have to be retrospectively and manually linked up with the scanned images. DIT could thus manage the range of work that was initially to be split between UMI and Chadwyck-Healy, scanning the page images, converting the images to searchable text, and indexing the bibliographic data to enable browsing. Bowen wrote with enthusiasm that if this could be brought about, "the entire effort would then be under our control."[48] This conclusion reflected Karen Hunter's April 1994 process suggestion to work with only one vendor for scanning and indexing (see chapter 2), which proved to be correct.

These considerations alone would have been sufficient to sink the Chadwyck-Healy relationship with JSTOR. But when combined with the

---

[44]William G. Bowen, "Report on trip to UMI and U of Michigan, Mar. 17–18, 1994," memorandum to JSTOR file, March 19, 1994.

[45]Randall Frank, interview with the author, July 10, 2001.

[46]William G. Bowen, "Meetings at the University of Michigan," memorandum to JSTOR file, March 20, 1995.

[47]Ira Fuchs, interview with the author, November 2, 2000.

[48]William G. Bowen, "Meetings at the University of Michigan," memorandum to JSTOR file, March 20, 1995.

evolving conclusion that JSTOR was going to be sold to many institutions and that the Chadwyck-Healy index would therefore be a costly burden, it was all the more necessary that the project create an index of its own. If nothing else, this would help to simplify the JSTOR production process. The JSTOR project and PCI parted ways in the early spring of 1995.

Why the different understandings, between Mellon and Chadwyck-Healy, of PCI's usefulness for the JSTOR project? As we saw in chapter 2, the foundation had agreed to create a "faithful replication" of the entire contents of the journal backfiles, both for copyright reasons and so that librarians and scholars would have full faith in the archive. With the publisher license agreements, Mellon's preference for "faithful replication" had become a contractual necessity. Based on Roemer's warning about gaps, it seems that this preference was clearly held as early as March since it must have been articulated to UMI. But somehow, representatives of Chadwyck-Healy did not fully appreciate that Mellon intended to create a complete replication of the entire contents of the journals. Had they understood this, they could never have proposed using PCI, as it then existed, as the spine, since for many journals PCI only indexed major academic articles. As it would develop, many services would essentially "build out" from indices of major articles. With the major scholarly articles online, these services hoped, who would need such a "faithful replication" of advertisements, letters to the editor, and so forth? Chadwyck-Healy's assumption was thus not unreasonable, but a far cry from Mellon's needs as it envisioned JSTOR. Similarly, the Mellon and Michigan staff involved in the decision never truly understood what it was that PCI covered, or their negotiations would have taken a different tack from the beginning.

There might have been some staff at Michigan who would have understood. But just as Mellon and Michigan had selected PCI for JSTOR's metadata, without library input beyond that supplied by DeGennaro, so, too, they put aside PCI without librarian input. Lougee and others who might have had a better sense of the contents of PCI, combined with a sensitivity to the JSTOR project's goals, were not yet considered integral to its success. All of that would change in due course.

Had Mellon opted to use the Chadwyck-Healy index, JSTOR's price for the ten journals for the 1,226 libraries participating in December 2001 would have been $291,200, plus an unknown additional amount to DIT for supplemental indexing.[49] As it turned out, developing its own index

---

[49]Beyond the $12,000 for the test sites (Williams, Denison, Bryn Mawr, Haverford, and Swarthmore), the charges would be $1,600 for each of the first ten sites; $800 for each of the next twenty; $400 for each of the next one hundred; and $200 for each thereafter. Sir Charles Chadwyck-Healy, letter to William G. Bowen, July 15, 1994.

for the initial ten journals cost Mellon one-fifth as much. Even with discounts from Chadwyck-Healy as JSTOR's subscription base grew, the difference in costs would have been significant. Moreover, the DIT-produced metadata allowed the JSTOR database to offer a faithful replication of all journal content, including reviews, letters, notices, advertisements, and other matter not indexed by Chadwyck-Healy, and its quality could be calibrated, from the start, to meet specifications developed for the JSTOR project.

Timing

Developing the architecture of production took some time due to changing decisions about sources for scanning and metadata. In both cases, the decision to seek out preexisting resources that could save time and money had appeal. But in both cases, on further investigation these "presumptively optimal" choices turned out to be unsatisfactory. In sum, the pursuit of microfilm cost very little time at all while the pursuit of a preexisting index probably cost several months in getting the alternative operation underway. In the case of PCI, however, we should spend a moment reflecting on why, despite warnings from two respected, well-informed people, Mellon nevertheless pursued a relationship. There was an inability or unwillingness to learn from others. It seems that, in the absence of a discrete project overseen by a single manager in early 1994, information sharing and retention was difficult. More evidence on this topic will accumulate in this and the following chapters.

Despite the time lost, the project leaders learned a great deal from the investigations that led them to abandon their initial plans. Indeed, once production work began in early 1995, Mellon staff had confidence that their choices had been the right ones, because they had so actively explored the other obvious options. This is not to say that all production efforts were flawless, as we shall see subsequently. But the broad arrangements, with a single vendor using hard-copy backfiles to produce digitized page images, searchable text, and the metadata, were at the time optimal.

While Mellon staff, in conjunction with Randy Frank, were developing the architecture of production, much work had been taking place at Michigan so that a system would be in place for the eventual vendor output. At Michigan, that work can be divided into software design and development, on the one hand, and user-interface and support on the other, topics we now take up in turn.

SOFTWARE DESIGN AND DEVELOPMENT

Once the grant was made to Michigan, software development continued uninterrupted from TULIP/DIRECT. The same team of programmers continued their work on the project, which they viewed as simply
another implementation of the same, ever improving, software. The
ability to leverage that ongoing work was a clear benefit at this point,
though in chapter 7 we shall see that it became viewed as problematic.

In Bowen's eyes, software development was to be guided by users'
needs. He and the Michigan partners agreed that "the software must be
developed in such a way that using this product will be genuinely 'pleas-
urable' for the users. And it is understood that the users will be working
with PCs and with MACs, and that the users will have varying degrees
of sophistication."[50] As the DIRECT user-base changed abruptly from
TULIP's materials science engineers to JSTOR's humanists and social
scientists, the software would require alterations to make it easier to use.
Notwithstanding these modifications, the intial deployment of the JSTOR
database would initially use a great deal of the software from DIRECT.[51]

The principal modifications involved adding a WWW interface to the
DIRECT/TULIP software. In the recent past, the web had been created
as a simple way to hyperlink through documents, and it could be used
equally by all popular computer systems. By using the web as its interface, Michigan could avoid the significant challenge of building separate "JSTORView" clients for PC, Mac, and UNIX.[52] The relatively standardized web made development efforts significantly simpler for many
services; the JSTOR project was only one example.

The decision to pursue a web interface begat other problems that
had to be resolved. The earliest web browsers (and indeed, almost all

[50] William G. Bowen, "University of Michigan Meetings/July 22, 1994," memorandum
to JSTOR file, July 25, 1994.

[51] For a more comprehensive summary of JSTOR's software design choices, see Spencer
W. Thomas, Ken Alexander, and Kevin Guthrie, "Technology Choices for the JSTOR
Online Archive," *Computer* 32, no. 2 (1999): 60–65.

[52] The existing X-Windows graphical user-interface—TULIPView—was discarded. Instead, JSTOR's principal client application was to be a web browser—at the time, Mosaic
or Netscape. So the Michigan staff installed a webserver and adapted FTL so it could interact with the webserver instead of TULIPView. Beyond this, Ken Alexander's FTL required
little substantive modification, although the program went through numerous iterations
in an effort to bring increased speed and efficiency. Ken Alexander, interview with the
author, June 14, 2001; Ken Alexander, "JSTOR software history," email to Sarah Sully and
Kevin Guthrie, February 11, 1997.

subsequent ones) did not support the display of raw TIFF images (which were important because they were something of an archival standard). Consequently, a programmer who briefly worked on the JSTOR software, Doug Orr, created a software tool known as TIFF2GIF, which provided on-the-fly translation to the GIF format for web display.[53] Frank and others praise the innovative and elegant code that Orr wrote, which was distributed freely and widely on the Internet.[54]

Another web-related adjustment related to printing. The TULIP experiment had sought, among other objectives, to understand user-behavior, and it had determined that users would print a large percentage of the articles they wanted, rather than reading them on-screen. But the Michigan-TULIP server-based printing would not scale to multi-campus distribution, and so a local printing solution was required. The GIF images that were to be sent to the web browsers for display at 72 dpi would be inadequate for local printing, however. Laser printers generally had the capability to print at 300 dpi, although some could reach 600 dpi or higher. Some software such as word processors, the primary purpose of which is printable output, can bypass the bottleneck to print at 300dpi. They do this with fonts that print differently than they display. JSTOR needed such a solution, but for images. As a result, the Michigan software team set out to create a helper application, a program that could be called upon by the webserver to bypass the web browser and bring the highest quality TIFF-based output to the local printer.[55] At first it was thought that JSTOR's academic users might be sufficiently Macintosh-based that the application could be written only for that platform.[56] That assumption proved false, so the printer application had to be designed in separate versions for each platform. Working around the web interface meant forgoing its standardization. There is evidence that,

---

[53]It was necessary to scan the pages into TIFF format since they were uncompressed and retained the most information and were therefore desirable from a preservation perspective. Beyond web display, TIFF2GIF allowed two further improvements. Computer monitors generally displayed at a resolution of 72 dpi. To reduce the demand for bandwidth, it would be preferable to send the images at 72 dpi, since a higher resolution would be wasteful. Finally, although the TIFF format only supported black and white, GIF allowed for grayscale and color, so grayscale could be used to ameliorate the low resolution of on-screen display. TIFF2GIF contained all these novel developments. Ken Alexander, interview with the author, June 14, 2001.

[54]Randall Frank, interview with the author, July 10, 2001. For the use and deployment of TIFF2GIF, see John Price-Wilkin, "Access to Digital Image Collections: System Building and Image Processing," Kenney and Rieger, *Moving Theory into Practice*, 101–18.

[55]Ken Alexander, "JSTOR software history," email to Sarah Sully and Kevin Guthrie, February 11, 1997.

[56]Spencer Thomas, interview with the author, May 29, 2001.

by March 1995, at least some printing was possible.[57] But improving the application so that it could be widely distributed took much longer. Of all the software development for the pilot, the critical printer application dragged on the longest. In late May of 1995, Frank gave this work top priority, but the complications of supporting ever increasing numbers of operating systems and printer hardware and software meant ongoing upgrades until 1999.[58]

USER-INTERFACE AND SUPPORT

In the course of developing the software, Greg Peters added a functional, though austere, web interface.[59] In this earliest version, the homepage was for DIRECT more than it was for the JSTOR project: it invited users to click on one link for the TULIP journals and on a second link for the Mellon journals. Designing web sites was not yet a science, and hardly an art—buttons on this interface were "big and blue," in a nod to the Michigan colors.[60] (Design and presentation were areas that subsequently received great attention. The professionally designed, well-received homepage that was later used is shown in figure 4.1, page 86.) There is no evidence to suggest that this particular architecture was intended to be anything other than interim or that it bothered anyone from Mellon. But the JSTOR and TULIP projects were clearly not as discrete then as they would eventually grow to be.

In addition to allowing accessibility through a web browser, this interface contained one important change from the TULIPView implementation. A user could browse through journals, once they were available, in addition to using the search interface. This would be critical, because a user interested in locating a specific article would not need to search for a keyword, but rather could navigate to a particular volume and issue.

In early January 1995, Lougee hired two recent graduates of the University of Michigan School of Information to fill the user-support positions.[61] Both Sherry Aschenbrenner and Kristen Garlock had experience developing web sites for the university. In addition to Frank, Fuchs, and Lougee, they traveled that same month to Philadelphia for the

---

[57]William G. Bowen, "Meetings at the University of Michigan," memorandum to JSTOR file, March 20, 1995.

[58]William G. Bowen, "JSTOR," memorandum to T. Dennis Sullivan, Kevin Guthrie, and Richard Ekman, May 28, 1995.

[59]Kristen Garlock, interview with the author, May 25, 2001.

[60]Ibid.

[61]William G. Bowen, "Conversation with Wendy Lougee," memorandum to JSTOR file, January 10, 1995.

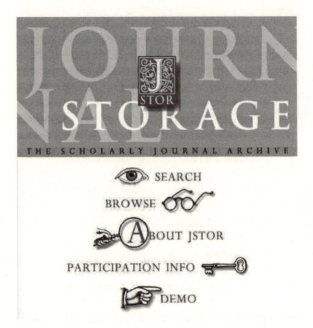

Figure 4.1. The JSTOR Homepage. Reproduced with permission of JSTOR and Michael Mabry Design.

mid-winter meeting of the American Library Association. This allowed them to meet all of the test-site librarians, with whom they would be working. They also took a side trip to visit the Pennsylvania test sites to see the equipment available there and to help install new computers and laser printers that Mellon grants provided.[62]

Back in Ann Arbor, Aschenbrenner and Garlock were stationed in the reference areas of two campus libraries, Shapiro Undergraduate and Harlan Hatcher Graduate, to provide user-support. Since JSTOR was not yet available online, their user-support required some creativity. At first they helped teach classes on how to use the web, which was still a novelty to many students and faculty. When the first scanned journals became available on JSTOR, they gave instruction to anyone who was interested. Because they were paid via the Mellon grant, their official term of appointment was short, so being stationed in public areas of campus libraries had an advantage, recalls Aschenbrenner: "We thought we were only there for a year, so we were going to learn all the reference skills that we could" to prepare for their next jobs.[63]

[62]Kristen Garlock, interview with the author, May 25, 2001.
[63]Sherry Aschenbrenner, interview with the author, May 30, 2001.

PRODUCTION PROGRESS AND PROBLEMS

With arrangements made for DIT's work, the journals were sent from the Harvard and Michigan libraries directly to the scanning vendor in Barbados. There, given the constraints imposed on them, DIT employees tackled the project as best they could (see below). A few weeks later, in early March, discs with the digitized titles began to be shipped back to Michigan. Alexander and Peters attempted to load the first datasets into the system, running a proprietary "checker" program they had developed for incoming TULIP datasets.[64] At once, it became clear that there were numerous shortcomings in the digitized materials that would delay the project substantially.

Alexander, Aschenbrenner, Garlock, and Peters made more detailed manual inspections of the datasets. They discovered still more problems that the checker program had missed. "The checker program was enhanced to do many more checks," recalled Alexander, "but in the beginning we were discovering new types of mistakes faster than we could improve the checker to check for the old ones."[65] The indexing file had missing entries, incorrect links with image and text files, inconsistent capitalization, mistagging of fields, and other errors. The page images themselves were often not properly aligned or otherwise inadequate. The OCR accuracy was below expectations (although much better than initially had been assumed).

On March 13, 1995, Randy Frank wrote to the DIT president to alert him that, per the terms of their contract, the first five datasets would be rejected for indexing, scanning, OCR, and packaging problems.[66] In total, about twenty datasets were rejected before the first was accepted.[67] Although DIT clearly had serious problems with the quality it was delivering, many of the flaws in these first scanning attempts were more process-related, including incomplete journal backruns and insufficient indexing guidelines sent by the JSTOR project to DIT.

Indexing Problems

As we have seen, DIT had agreed to take on the preparation of the entire index, and was eager to step up to the challenge. And, we saw that

[64]Ken Alexander, interview with the author, June 14, 2001.
[65]Ken Alexander, "JSTOR software history," email to Sarah Sully and Kevin Guthrie, February 11, 1997.
[66]Randall L. Frank, letter to Richard Coleman, March 13, 1995.
[67]Ken Alexander, interview with the author, June 14, 2001.

when Michigan decided, in conjunction with Fuchs, to retain the metadata standard Elsevier had used for TULIP, Elsevier was glad to share it. There was no librarian input on this decision or its initial implementation. Without any consideration of how the standards might be adapted for the humanities and social science backfiles of JSTOR rather than the materials science current issues of TULIP, the existing EFFECT specifications were forwarded to DIT.

Its enthusiasm notwithstanding, DIT was largely unfamiliar with the work necessary to create such metadata. Although DIT had a great deal of experience with scanning, OCR, and data input, these processes were largely automatic or, conversely, purely manual. The work of creating the metadata demanded a skilled person who could understand, on some level, the content of the journals, and then make the intellectual determination of how best to structure that content for search and retrieval. For example, what constitutes an article? Although in most cases there might be an obvious answer to such a question, some journal issues were not organized in the typical structure of five to ten major articles, but rather had one or two major articles, each with sections by different authors, for perhaps a total of twenty subarticles. Should such a journal issue be indexed as if it had two articles or as if it had twenty?[68] Such decisions could not be effectively made without understanding, to some degree, the nature of the articles. DIT was unprepared to undertake the intellectual components of such work. Chadwyck-Healy had looked to tables of contents for the answer, but there was little consistency there. After Chadwyck-Healy was dropped from the JSTOR plans, DIT had been asked to create metadata without having demonstrated any capacity for doing so competently—metadata had not been one of the tests of the RFP. Mellon staff were relieved to find what sounded like a better alternative than Chadwyck-Healy's PCI, and they did not adequately investigate what would be required to use that alternative effectively.

Not surprisingly, when the indexing data were returned to Michigan, staff were displeased with the work that had been done. Problems fell generally into two categories. For one, there were simple errors in data entry, which resulted in not only spelling mistakes, but also "very rampant" broken links between the metadata and the articles they represented.[69] But the greater concern was DIT's inability to make the intellectual determinations required to implement EFFECT properly.

Beyond these problems at the level of production, there were also shortcomings in the EFFECT specifications, often related to its original

---

[68]Wendy Lougee, interview with the author, May 30, 2001.
[69]Sherry Aschenbrenner, interview with the author, May 30, 2001.

purpose. Custom-designed for the indexing of the fairly straightforward content in materials science current issues, EFFECT was unable to handle the complexities of old humanities and social science backfiles. Its structure could not accommodate a journal whose volume number was reset to one due to the creation of a "new series," or in which unnumbered supplement issues were included in a journal on an irregular basis.[70] EFFECT, and the software that would implement it for the JSTOR archive, had to be modified to allow for such irregularities, rather than making a priori assumptions about the structure of journals.[71] In chapter 7, we shall see some of the solutions that were found to these indexing problems, including bringing skilled catalog librarians into the production process.

Source Backruns

Another impediment to the early production work was that the Harvard and Michigan backruns were incomplete. DIT staff in Barbados processed what they received. Much was missing. With the decision to scan from paper rather than from microfilm, no one at either Mellon or Michigan had thought to implement a process for identifying complete backruns. As a result, whole volumes were absent, issues were missing, or articles were ripped out, with alarming frequency. Only sometimes had Harvard or Michigan librarians inserted copied pages, inadequate for digitization, in place of the missing originals for their readers. Frequently, margin notes or underlining obscured the text sufficiently as to make it inadequate for display and OCR. It should be noted that this state of affairs was diagnostic of the journal backruns present in most academic libraries and suggests how useful JSTOR would prove to be— far superior as a comprehensive archive to anything that could be found on the shelves of even the best library. But, at this juncture, DIT was returning only a "checkerboard" of digitized backruns.[72]

Michigan staff made an effort to fill in the numerous holes that had been discovered. Lougee, her assistant Pat Hodges, and user-services librarians Aschenbrenner and Garlock were all pressed into service in an ad hoc effort to track down missing volumes, issues, and pages. Many other libraries, including especially those at Cornell, were helpful in

---

[70] Wendy Lougee, interview with the author, May 30, 2001.

[71] Spencer Thomas, interview with the author, May 29, 2001.

[72] Kevin Guthrie, interview with the author, December 13, 2000; Kevin Guthrie, "Journal Storage Project Meeting, Tuesday, April 11, 1995," memorandum to JSTOR file, William G. Bowen, and Richard Ekman, April 18, 1995.

sharing their own journal backruns. But as they called various libraries to track down these materials, the Michigan staff realized the enormity of the task at hand.[73]

Due in part to the length of their publication histories, some of the titles had very complicated and even erratic backfiles. Several ceased publication during World War II, others had seemed to change their publication frequencies from quarterly to monthly, and so forth, essentially at random. Publishers often lacked the complete backrun, and sometimes did not even have a record of the journal's publishing history. Garlock sought out a definitive reference source listing all of these variations, just the sort of scholarly tool a serials librarian might have been expected to create. No such record existed.[74] The effort to track down regularly published backruns would have been difficult enough, but the variability of the histories was an impossible complication. The ad hoc group would try, essentially by "triangulation," to determine whether they had identified a complete backrun. Even after the process improvements that were put into place in late 1995, this would still prove to be a key challenge for JSTOR as late as 2000 (see chapters 7 and 9). By early 1995, Lougee recalls, "it was getting absolutely untenable—as a process—to try to do this cleanup."[75]

The Bigger Picture: An Absent Process

The real problem, however, was that this increasingly untenable "process" had not, in reality, ever been designed. After the initial "presumptively optimal" choices of scanning from microfilm and using PCI as metadata fell through, Mellon and Michigan staff had not regrouped to design a real process. Instead, they made a new iteration of presumptively optimal choices. As a result, it had been assumed that backruns could be sent directly from library shelf to scanning vendor without any preparation. It had been assumed that the scanning vendor could take on the complicated indexing work with little training, supervision, or quality control. It had been assumed that Michigan could receive the vendor's work product without designating a person or structure to evaluate it, decide to accept or reject it, and load it onto servers. All of these assumptions had now proved to be wrong. It is actually surprising how much was accomplished under this arrangement! While a pe-

[73] Wendy Lougee, interview with the author, May 30, 2001.
[74] Kristen Garlock, interview with the author, May 25, 2001.
[75] Wendy Lougee, interview with the author, May 30, 2001.

riod of experimentation was understandable, natural even, an active reappraisal might have led to some of these problems being fixed sooner than they were.

For instance, while TULIP's work was not identical to that of JSTOR, it did confront challenges from which JSTOR might have learned.[76] In one small example of a lesson that had already been learned, Elsevier was befuddled in trying to expedite the shipment of journal issues from each of its various imprints to its scanning vendor. The coordination of several sources of hard-copies with a scanning vendor was very difficult. A key shortcoming of TULIP was the lack of a system to track items through the digitization process, so that the project manager knew where they were. The extent to which such a lesson might have been available to Mellon, or to Michigan, remains unclear. Michigan staff were surely aware of many of the TULIP shortcomings, even if Bowen and Fuchs were not.

Exactly why the JSTOR project did not act on the instinct—expressed by Bowen in chapter 2—to borrow process from Elsevier remains unclear. Frank has suggested that Elsevier's process focused on new, clean issues, and so would have had little to offer JSTOR's need to track down backfiles. He has also pointed out that JSTOR's monthly production rate was many times that of TULIP.[77] But Elsevier had learned important lessons about how to manage the work of a scanning and indexing vendor and coordinate it with multiple sources. It is also possible that Elsevier, widely perceived as a vigorously competitive corporation, would have been unwilling to consult extensively with Mellon, as Bowen and Fuchs have suggested.[78] But competitive as Elsevier was believed to be, it shared its metadata and file-structure standards with JSTOR, its Senior Vice-President Karen Hunter made suggestions to Mellon about scanning vendors, and it later published the *TULIP Final Report,* all of which suggest an interest in contributing its knowledge to other efforts. Today, Hunter is adamant that Elsevier "would have been happy to" consult with Mellon, and she says, regretfully, "they would have learned a lot."[79] Although the *TULIP Final Report* would not be published until 1996, a conversation with TULIP's project manager might have led Mellon or Michigan staff to anticipate more of their problems.

---

[76]Some broader conclusions less relevant to the operational advice needed for the JSTOR project were collected in Karen Hunter, "Publishing for a Digital Library—What Did TULIP Teach Us?," *Journal of Academic Librarianship,* May 1996: 209–11.

[77]Randall Frank, interview with the author, July 10, 2001.

[78]William G. Bowen, interview with the author, June 26, 2001; Ira Fuchs, interview with the author, July 19, 2001.

[79]Karen Hunter, interview with the author, September 5, 2001.

SUMMATION

As we have seen, the failure to design a process for production stemmed largely from the evolution of the JSTOR project away from certain initial plans, such as using microfilm as the source for scanning and PCI as the source for indexing. When these options proved not to be viable, the JSTOR colleagues regrouped and assigned the Harvard and Michigan libraries the responsibility to serve as the source for paper backfiles, while the scanning vendor would create the indexing files. While at its core this arrangement would be used for years to come, in its immediate implementation there still remained insufficient involvement of skilled librarians to achieve what was intended in both processes. In chapters 7 and 9, we shall see how it was revamped.

In addition to the altered procedures, the JSTOR project suffered from some degree of organizational uncertainty created by designating Michigan as the paymaster, but never really the active manager, of the scanning vendor. Michigan lacked the authority, if not the skills, to oversee the work of production, and in any case initially viewed its principal responsibility as software development. Uncertain about precisely what roles Michigan could play in the production work beyond paymaster, Bowen and Fuchs were in any event not positioned to oversee the production process themselves. Mellon was used to grants management, which is to say evaluating the work of the grant, rather than operational management of day-to-day tasks. The foundation was totally unsuited to provide any kind of day-to-day management and had no intention of playing any such role.

Just days after Frank wrote to DIT outlining the many problems that had been detected, Bowen arrived in Ann Arbor. In his minute, Bowen reported that Frank was "guardedly optimistic that DIT will come through." It seemed that at least DIT-specific problems of image and OCR quality could be ameliorated fairly rapidly.[80] Rather than drawing broader conclusions about management and process, it seemed that the existing arrangements might be made to work.

Although the Mellon grant had only called for Michigan to function as the paymaster for DIT, it had of necessity begun to take on a larger role. As the digitization of the *American Economic Review* was nearing completion, the Michigan group began to prepare it to be stamped on a CD-ROM for the publisher, to fulfill one term of the pilot license agreement. In so doing, they realized the enormity of the quality-control task at hand. A more professionalized QC operation was sorely needed.[81]

---

[80] William G. Bowen, "Meetings at the University of Michigan," memorandum to JSTOR file, March 20, 1995.

[81] Sherry Aschenbrenner, interview with the author, May 30, 2001.

In April 1995, Frank wrote to Fuchs with a proposal. By the terms of its agreement with the scanning vendor, Michigan had retained the option to reject, within three business days of receipt, any dataset that did not meet the agreed-upon standards. But to examine every CD-ROM that quickly required more staff. As he envisioned it, the quality-control operation would examine all of the digitized materials returned by DIT. He estimated this work, about twelve seconds per page, would add about 8 percent on top of the price paid to DIT for scanning, indexing, and OCR.[82] Although Bowen was very pleased that Michigan was taking on this task, it did not get underway as quickly as had been expected, as we shall see in chapter 7.

Even as Frank responded to the poor quality of the materials being returned from the scanning vendor, the lessons of the pilot to date were unmistakable. The Mellon managers, Bowen, Ekman, and Fuchs, had worked together as an extremely nimble committee. Because they had no formal organization in place, they were able to experiment, keeping what worked and modifying the rest. They added the B agreement with publishers, replaced Chadwyck-Healy, and began to scan from paper rather than microfilm. By early 1995, the pieces were in place for the creation of an important archive of academic journals. But the task of managing these pieces was far larger than anyone had foreseen.

The seeming appeal of a JSTOR was also greater than anyone had foreseen, and Bowen was eager to move forward. While in Ann Arbor in March, Bowen shared with Atkins, Frank, and Lougee a draft of the Mellon Foundation's 1994 *Annual Report*. In it he had written,

> It is evident that the Foundation itself cannot manage the project indefinitely, and careful thought must be given to the identification of suitable institutional partners. Are there existing organizations that could take over the project or should some new entity, perhaps a consortium, be created for this purpose?[83]

As Atkins would later reflect,

> At the point when Bill decided that [JSTOR] was really a go, and he wanted to launch this as a sustainable robust enterprise, that was the period of adjustment and changing the structure of the organization. . . . So, it went from a feasibility research project to a real serious product development very quickly, and universities are not really set up for that.[84]

---

[82]Randall Frank, "Funding for QC function," email to Ira Fuchs, April 19, 1995.

[83]William G. Bowen, "The Foundation's Journal Storage Project (JSTOR)," in *Report of the Andrew W. Mellon Foundation 1994* (New York: Andrew W. Mellon Foundation, 1995), 32.

[84]Dan Atkins, interview with the author, May 31, 2001.

CHAPTER 5

Evolving Organizational
Decisions—and Independence

FEBRUARY–DECEMBER 1995

IN THE AFTERMATH of his March 1995 trip to Ann Arbor, Bowen became determined that JSTOR's operations had to be rationalized. Although the JSTOR project was not stagnating, Mellon staff felt that its development had outpaced its organizational capacity. Michigan's research and development structure had been invaluable in exploring options for the creation of the JSTOR database, turning a project outline into a working, if insufficient, prototype. Yet now, Mellon's expectations had changed. Expansion—adding journals and library test sites—was on everyone's near-term horizon. A production-level intensity would be necessary to bring such an expansion to fruition. To scale up JSTOR's capacities while keeping it nimble, it was clear that the operation would have to be re-thought. Eventually, it would become an independent organization.

By March of 1995, Bowen had been considering, at least informally, organizational possibilities for JSTOR for quite some time. In February 1994, Bowen had noted that it should be determined, "later, how to move forward on the organizational front. It is possible that OCLC could be a useful player."[1] In March, he had wondered, "What enterprise should run this show, presuming [the pilot] works?"[2] Four months later, when DeGennaro had also suggested OCLC as a possible organizational home, Bowen wrote that while "we need to think ahead about a partner for the longer run operation of JSTOR . . . this question is much less pressing than the others."[3] Until Mellon had some sense of whether JSTOR could be built affordably, or at all, it made little sense to pursue these questions.[4] Once all of the plans for the pilot were at least tentatively in

---

[1] [William G. Bowen], "Notes on JSTOR Project," February 14, 1994.

[2] William G. Bowen, "JSTOR: Confidential Memorandum," memorandum to file, March 7, 1994.

[3] William G. Bowen, "Questions arising out of July 12 meeting," memorandum to JSTOR file, July 13, 1994.

[4] Thomas Hughes and others have pointed out that, in reference to Edison's methods of invention, "he clearly realized . . . that his system would have to be economically competitive, and thus he conceived of the problem to be solved by invention as inseparably technical and economic." Although Mellon staff were not interested in actually "inventing"

place, around March 1995, and Michigan and DIT were struggling with the first scanned pages, the question of independence had become more pressing, enough so that Bowen publicly posed it in the 1994 Mellon Foundation, written in February 1995.[5] At some point during the winter of 1994–1995, Bowen had concluded that it was time to push JSTOR toward independence.

A LINE OF REASONING

Even though the database was not yet available at the test sites, all of the experience that had been gained through early 1995 suggested that the pilot should be only the beginning of a far larger project. But even in its pilot phase, JSTOR had become an enormous management task for Mellon Foundation staff. JSTOR's future leader, Kevin Guthrie, would later write that the project "was both too promising and too complex to continue to be managed as a grant program of the Foundation."[6] He recalled that if it "didn't get more attention it was going to be severely handicapped. . . . I remember Bill [Bowen] saying quite a lot that [as a Mellon project] it had become too complex."[7] Of course it was understood to be conceptually possible to set up a permanent "JSTOR Department" of the foundation, essentially building an operating unit into the Mellon organization.[8] But such an arrangement would be in direct contrast with Mellon's style of operating—with as small a staff as possible that aggressively sought partner-grantees. Pilachowksi recalls Bowen later explaining his reasoning to the advisory committee that "Mellon is not a production unit, we can't be doing" JSTOR on an ongoing basis.[9] As we saw in chapter 4, JSTOR had proven to be a much more complicated undertaking than had been expected. It was clear that the JSTOR project could not continue to be managed effectively into the future with the limited institutional infrastructure that Mellon's grant-making mission provided. Beyond the need for a better organizational home for

---

something new, much the same could be said of their perception of their challenges. Thomas Parke Hughes, *Networks of Power: Electrification in Western Society, 1880–1930* (Baltimore: Johns Hopkins University Press), 29.

[5] William G. Bowen, "The Foundation's Journal Storage Project (JSTOR)," in *Report of the Andrew W. Mellon Foundation 1994* (New York: Andrew W. Mellon Foundation, 1995), 32.

[6] Kevin M. Guthrie, "JSTOR: From Project to Independent Organization," *D-Lib Magazine* July/August 1997, available online at *http://www.dlib.org/dlib/july97/07guthrie.html.*

[7] Kevin Guthrie, interview with the author, December 13, 2000.

[8] William G. Bowen, interview with the author, June 26, 2001.

[9] David Pilachowski, interview with the author, June 22, 2001.

JSTOR, Bowen had other important reasons for thinking about JSTOR's future.

First, as an economist, Bowen was convinced that JSTOR's growing success—its "value"—would be demonstrated best by users' willingness to pay for the service. Otherwise, he wrote, "one should wonder about the utility of the enterprise."[10] Thus, JSTOR would have to find support beyond foundation subvention. Although the ability to generate revenues would be a mark of JSTOR's value, it also posed a fundamental problem because the federal tax code impedes grant-making foundations like Mellon from selling services and generating operating revenues.[11] It was no great leap to conclude that the nascent JSTOR, rather than all of Mellon, should be restructured.[12] Bowen believes in retrospect that "the decision to pursue independence was driven by a single fact, which was that libraries needed to pay and Mellon couldn't take their money."[13]

Second, the project could not live indefinitely on foundation subvention without binding a future generation of Mellon trustees with the grant-making preferences of the moment and limiting the resources available to address new needs. An institution whose mission is potentially as broad as Mellon's could not commit to any project indefinitely. "Perpetual subsidy," wrote Bowen of the foundation's role, "is both unrealistic and unwise."[14] This proposition was in Bowen's mind even as the first grant to Michigan was being made, nearly a year earlier.

Third, it was becoming increasingly clear to Bowen and others that a major part of JSTOR's task would be to assure libraries that its electronic collection of academic journals would be preserved in perpetuity. If it could provide such an archiving assurance as a self-supporting organization, it could serve as a model for others considering applications of information technology to libraries and scholarship. But if it were a permanently subsidized arm of a wealthy foundation, its successes would be viewed as nonreplicable.

---

[10]William G. Bowen, "JSTOR and the Economics of Scholarly Communications," speech to the Council on Library and Information Resources, Washington, DC, September 18, 1995; revised version online at *www.mellon.org/jsesc.html.*

[11]See, for example, Bruce R. Hopkins and Jody Blazek, *Private Foundations: Tax Law and Compliance* (New York: John Wiley and Sons, 1997), chapter 11.

[12]The clearest documentary evidence of revenue being an important near-term reason to restructure the JSTOR operation is a record of Bowen's June 1995 trip to Ann Arbor, by which point he was considering the relationship between the journal backfiles and their current issues, about which much more can be found in chapter 6. See William G. Bowen, "Meetings in Michigan on Tuesday, June 6th," memorandum to JSTOR file, June 7, 1995.

[13]William G. Bowen, interview with the author, June 26, 2001.

[14]William G. Bowen, "JSTOR and the Economics of Scholarly Communications."

Finally, Mellon had been integral in establishing credibility for its JSTOR project within the higher-education community, but JSTOR's audience was clearly going to be much broader than the academically selective colleges and universities that are the bulk of Mellon's traditional constituencies. For this reason alone, it made sense to house the JSTOR project under a governing structure more suited to its own mission and audience. With an independent governing structure, JSTOR's constituency could be broadened beyond Mellon's universe of selective American colleges and universities.[15]

Although JSTOR might eventually have left Mellon for any of these reasons, and while revenue concerns would have eventually driven them apart, the bulk of evidence from the time points toward management and organizational needs as the driving factors. By early 1995, it was clear that JSTOR's long-term success required signing a stream of new journals; digitizing them; and eventually selling or licensing the collection to subscribers. Yet with the first ten journals licensed, the technical work of production and software development was increasingly becoming JSTOR's principal focus. Production in particular was threatening to become a quagmire, and, as we saw in chapter 4, the Mellon-Michigan organization lacked the capacity to bring order to the chaos. Altering JSTOR's organizational infrastructure had of necessity become a high priority for Mellon staff. Bowen began a lengthy set of consultations to confirm that that reorganization was appropriate and, if so, to determine what form it should take.

ORGANIZATIONAL CHOICES AND RECONVENING THE ADVISORY COMMITTEE

Just after his return from Michigan, Bowen turned for a third time to the advisory committee, which had not met for nine months. Previously, the committee had provided helpful advice and measured enthusiasm. Its last meeting launched a number of developments: the Michigan relationship had been established, a scanning vendor secured, and all manner of software, interface, and scanning decisions made. Now that an entirely new set of organizational questions had to be addressed, it made sense to reconvene the committee. The meeting, held on April 11, 1995, focused on a number of issues relating to JSTOR's expansion and independence.[16]

---

[15]Kevin Guthrie, interview with the author, December 13, 2000.

[16]This section is based on Kevin Guthrie, "Journal Storage Project Meeting, Tuesday, April 11, 1995," memorandum to JSTOR file, William G. Bowen, and Richard Ekman, April 18, 1995.

First, even though the pilot journals were not completely online, Mellon was already receiving noticeable pressure, especially from the library community, to expand the pilot project to encompass more journals. If it went beyond the first ten, should JSTOR continue to expand its holdings of core journals, or should it instead digitize more specialized and less commonly collected journals? The core journals had by far the greatest overlap among academic libraries and therefore the greatest potential for cost savings, but the electronic backfiles of more specialized journals could be made available to institutions that never subscribed to the hard-copy. Although this was a strong argument, the advisory committee demurred and recommended continued focus on the original mission: core journals that had the greatest institutional overlap. JSTOR's project leadership at the Mellon Foundation, and Bowen in particular, was especially resistant to proposals for JSTOR to provide access to extremely low-circulation journals, proposals that would dilute its mission of saving space for libraries.

Second, if an eventual expansion of the database's core journal holdings were to add breadth, what new disciplines should be included? Were there disciplines that were particularly amenable to electronic access, or that would particularly benefit from such access? There was no clear answer to this. Most arts and sciences disciplines have core journals with lengthy backfiles, and in theory all scholars in these disciplines could benefit from improved access to the core journal literature. The path ahead could lead the JSTOR project far beyond economics and history.

Third, what libraries, beyond the initial test sites, should be allowed access? The JSTOR-B publisher licenses permitted more than forty additions. Mellon staff were particularly aware that the benefits of access would be immediate to researchers and students served by libraries, particularly abroad, but also poorer libraries in the United States, which lacked the backfiles. For example, Mellon had grants programs to serve universities in Eastern Europe and South Africa and the historically black institutions in the United States. Although all members of the committee wanted to see the JSTOR database available at such institutions eventually, the committee concluded that connectivity problems at many of these schools would be a significant near-term impediment. In chapters 10 and 12 we shall see how JSTOR outreach and foundation grants allowed the database to reach all of these institutions and many more like them.

The range of needs and priorities among enthusiastic library and scholarly communities had the potential to pull the nascent JSTOR project in many different directions. Aware of this possibility even before the meeting, Mellon did not want the committee to become directly caught up in these debates. Instead, the meeting invitation had asked the committee to broaden the question: "When and how" should the project "be handed over to another institution or organization that is capable of managing it"?[17]

Several existing library cooperative organizations were briefly discussed, but each met with some form of negative comment. The criticism that one of the most successful of these had begun operating in too much of a revenue-hungry manner led DeGennaro to speak up. He bristled that criticism "was inevitable for these kinds of groups and worried that the Foundation might be looking for an entity that could not survive," because its altruism would obscure its responsibility to self-sustenance.[18] Bowen was adamant that it would be possible for a not-for-profit to be both self-sufficient and also perceived by the library community as fair in its business practices.

The minutes of the meeting record one additional criterion for the future of the JSTOR project, to which everyone agreed. It would be "desirable for the Foundation to continue to be involved." Innocuous as this conclusion seems, it effectively eliminated any possibility that JSTOR would be linked with an existing entity. But whatever its organizational home, the JSTOR project would be "exported," in Bowen's eyes, in the next twelve to twenty-four months.[19]

In fact, the export process would occur much more rapidly. The advisory committee was enthusiastic and had directed him toward an independent organization, and Bowen's initial supposition was to establish a not-for-profit, since JSTOR would want to work largely with colleges and universities. But this was a decision that would be largely irreversible. That is, the "presumptively optimal" choice would not be sufficient; careful planning was required. Since there were other possibilities, the options had to be weighed, with some caution, before any decision was made. We will turn now to an examination of several of the principal options that Bowen and others at Mellon, Michigan, and elsewhere considered and some of the context for each of these considerations.

A University Satellite?

Some of the Michigan principals involved in the JSTOR project were convinced that the new organization, whatever form it might take, should be housed in Ann Arbor, in all likelihood as an administrative satellite

[17]Ibid., 3.
[18]Ibid., 6.
[19]Ibid., 4.

of the university. They thought that situating JSTOR at Michigan would help build on the important digital library projects underway at Ann Arbor. Bowen spoke about this possibility with several senior Michigan administrators, including Atkins[20] and then-President James Duderstadt.[21] It appears that at some point, the operating assumption was for JSTOR to be housed in such a joint Mellon-Michigan–founded organization, located in Ann Arbor.

The "satellite" idea was never defined with a great deal of precision, but it seems likely that the idea was to create some sort of enterprise unit in affiliation with the university. In other words, the satellite would be akin to a university press, especially on those campuses where the press was a separately incorporated organization. Such an arrangement might have brought a number of advantages over the existing set-up, including greater flexibility in the realms of budget, personnel, and administration.

But despite its leadership in software development for digital libraries, Michigan was not especially well positioned to undertake the non-technical work, such as licensing journals from publishers and licensing the database to libraries. These activities were an increasing concern to those overseeing the JSTOR enterprise, and indeed soon would be central to the organization's work. And even among the responsibilities set out in the Mellon grant, it was too early for Michigan's successes, if they were to come, to be evident. We saw in chapter 4 how great the production challenges were. If Michigan staff thought they would have until the grant expired before their work was evaluated, they were to be disappointed. Bowen was frustrated by the slow progress, especially in the digitization work.

Given this frustration, Bowen would have been likely to move in a different direction. And, although several Michigan leaders were interested in bringing JSTOR into their growing cache of digital library projects, there is no evidence that the university or any of its staff made a serious proposal for the radical restructuring and business planning this would necessarily have entailed. Without such a formal proposal, it was straightforward for Bowen to sidestep the idea.

The foundation also feared that there were broader structural problems with a satellite organization that would leave JSTOR's mission and focus muddled. In seeking external support, for example, would the host university focus more on a JSTOR-related service mission, or on its own

---

[20]William G. Bowen, "Meetings at the University of Michigan," memorandum to JSTOR file, March 20, 1995.

[21]William G. Bowen, "Conversation with James Duderstadt," memorandum to JSTOR file, March 21, 1995.

core institutional and academic needs? Also, in the good-natured competitive spirit that has elsewhere served American higher education so well, if JSTOR belonged to one university library, would other libraries resist paying fees to subscribe? If JSTOR resided with a university press, would other presses resist licensing their journal titles to it? These potential conflicts led Mellon to avoid establishing JSTOR at a university library or a university press or to otherwise house it as a university satellite.

Despite Bowen's concerns at the time, in retrospect we can see several successful implementations of precisely this option. When these revenue-generating enterprise units have been sufficiently insulated from the rest of the university, there has been a chance for success. When there has been a means for enterprising leaders to cut through bureaucracy to push an independent vision, they have produced noteworthy results. Projects hosted by Johns Hopkins and Stanford universities illustrate success stories.

Stanford's HighWire Press was created in 1994 and 1995 as a service-provider to nonprofit publishers. For a fee, HighWire would digitize the current issues of a given publication, mounting them on a publication-specific website. HighWire was founded by Michael A. Keller, a strong leader with a clear vision who had been afforded budgetary flexibility. It was organized as an enterprise unit, separate from the university library and the university press. In part because of this organizational autonomy, and in part because of its good vision and clear lines of leadership, HighWire encountered few if any of the problems that had interfered with the JSTOR project, would continue to do so, and had soured Mellon on giving more autonomy to JSTOR-Michigan.

The Johns Hopkins example offers somewhat less clarity but a similar conclusion. Its university press had long been a principal publisher of academic journals, and in 1994 it announced a program to begin posting the current issues of its journals online.[22] This daring move, taken in conjunction with the university library and information technology group, would make the JHUP one of the first journal publishers to create a commercial, online, current-issues service. Funded by the National Endowment for the Humanities in addition to the Mellon Foundation, the online journals initiative was known as Project Muse. It was not at first an enterprise unit of its own, but rather an operating division of the press. As a result, Muse's business plan depended on initial subsidies from other press operations and so did not appear to be self-sustaining

[22] Thomas J. DeLoughry, "Scholarly Journals Via the Computer," *Chronicle of Higher Education,* March 9, 1994.

in the long run.[23] But Muse continued to expand, by the summer of 2001 distributing the online version of the current issues of nearly two hundred journals from about ten publishers. Over 1,100 libraries subscribed to one or more of the various packages of journals that Muse distributed. Both HighWire and Muse have demonstrated the ability of a university to manage a production-scale enterprise that distributes the online versions of academic journals from a variety of copyright holders to a variety of libraries.

There is, however, one critical difference between HighWire and Muse, on the one hand, and what would become JSTOR, on the other. JSTOR has always paid all of the costs of the work, bringing its own collections to the library marketplace, whereas Muse and HighWire operate as subcontractors for the journal publishers, charging them a fee for services. Both are essentially service bureaus to publishers. Consequently, Muse and HighWire "work for" the journal publishers, rather than for the publishers and the libraries at once. More than once, JSTOR has forgone the option of taking a large number of its journals from an interested publisher, instead focusing its energies on a hesitant publisher with only one (key) title. (Chapters 6, 9, 11, and 13 contain fuller descriptions of JSTOR's publisher-relations practices.) JSTOR may have had a greater ability to accumulate the capital necessary for this role by avoiding satellite status.

While the examples of Muse and HighWire suggest that universities have played a successful role in online work not altogether dissimilar from that of JSTOR, their operations are distinguishable from JSTOR in critical ways. While their organizational choices may be optimal for their purposes, in the coming chapters we shall see the importance to JSTOR of its selectively curated collections. It is unclear that as a service provider to publishers, such careful collection development could have been undertaken. It is certainly an open question. And even if such an arrangement might have been workable in the abstract, Bowen was skeptical at the time that Michigan could rapidly create such an organization.

Library Cooperatives?

To some in the library community, it made sense that JSTOR be transferred to OCLC, RLG, or CRL,[24] three nonprofit organizations that, in

[23]See Richard E. Quandt, "Mellon Initiatives in Digital Libraries: 1994–1999," April 2002, Unpublished manuscript on deposit at the Nathan Marsh Pusey Library, the Andrew W. Mellon Foundation, chapter 2, 14–19.

[24]See chapter 1 for more on OCLC, RLG, and CRL, cooperative nonprofits that have sought to reduce cataloging costs for libraries.

one form or another, seek to centralize library functions and thereby reduce costs while improving services. JSTOR advisory committee members and other leaders in the library profession had trepidations, and so the foundation shied away from such partnerships. For one reason or another, each of these organizations was viewed as lacking in key elements needed to support JSTOR's mission.

Numerous librarians have long perceived OCLC to have reached such a scale (due to its successful cooperative cataloging program) that it ceased to behave as a nonprofit. Although DeGennaro had expressed enthusiasm—he had long been involved in several other library cooperatives—Pilachowski remembers feeling that negative perceptions in the library community made OCLC a "non-starter."[25]

For RLG and CRL, membership organizations governed directly by their constituent libraries, the complexities of governance increased with the addition of each new member. Some suggested that these structures would confound the rapid and determined leadership that JSTOR would require for success. Moreover, both CRL and RLG included only major research libraries in their membership, and JSTOR was intended (from its Denison roots) to reach a larger audience.

More important than any perceived shortcomings in these cooperatives' organizational structure was their very mission. As library cooperatives, they were appropriately charged with representing—solely—the interests of libraries. JSTOR's success, it was clear, would rest on its ability to find a balance between the interests of libraries, publishers, scholars, and others involved in journal-based scholarly communications. RLG, CRL, and OCLC were not constituted to achieve such a balance.

An Umbrella Organization

When Bowen visited Ann Arbor in June 1995, after the planning work for a new organization had proceeded significantly, Dean Atkins suggested that Mellon consider establishing an umbrella organization to include any of the nonprofit digital initiatives that sought to come under it. Referring to the umbrella organization as "Scholarship, Inc.," his idea was to consolidate the burgeoning number of such projects to find efficiencies and to build critical mass. In Bowen's abbreviated minute of the conversation, he sounded skeptical, perhaps in part because Atkins did not propose any specific organizational structure. Presumably, such

---

[25]David Pilachowski, interview with the author, June 22, 2001.

an organization, if not planned with extreme care, would tend to suffer many of the same faults identified with a university satellite or a library cooperative. How would it achieve the laser-sharp focus that Bowen had perceived as a prerequisite for success? Not even one of these digital projects was self-sufficient at the time, and putting them all under one roof might have seemed to threaten the ability of any of them to achieve self-sufficiency. Although Bowen does not seem to have considered Atkins's proposal at any length at the time, in later years various similar options would gain some amount of appeal, to JSTOR, to Mellon, and to others.

An Independent Organization and the Question of Profit

Between universities and library cooperatives, Bowen was convinced of the difficulty of reprioritizing or reorganizing an existing organization. The motivation to create JSTOR stemmed from Bowen and infused the foundation; how, then, to institutionalize this sense of enthusiasm and ownership in an improved organizational structure?

Bowen began to perceive significant advantages in creating a new entity to house the project. A new entity could be forged with the mission and priorities most appropriate for JSTOR. For example, if archiving were to be a core part of the mission, the new organization could be created with that expectation, without other distractions and with undiluted responsibility. For a mission-driven entity like the JSTOR project, Bowen decided an individual organization was the best option. He quickly settled on a board-run, rather than a membership, organization, because of the problems of governance noted above.

The most critical resulting question was whether to organize it as a for-profit or a not-for-profit? Bowen discussed with the Mellon trustees the possibility of creating a new entity at the board's June meeting. At that point, the board authorized Trustees John Whitehead and Taylor Reveley to explore further the question of whether to create a for-profit or a nonprofit.

Some observers were so convinced of the potential for JSTOR's success that they thought it should be a for-profit corporation. As a for-profit, JSTOR could raise large sums of capital and expand far more rapidly. Mellon Trustee John Whitehead was particularly concerned that JSTOR not overlook such substantial advantages of a for-profit structure.[26] It must also be noted that the history of small not-for-profits contained a

---

[26] William G. Bowen, "JSTOR," memorandum to members of the board of trustees, July 31, 1995.

number of alarming precedents, including the near bankruptcy of the New-York Historical Society, that must have given pause to many observers. At the time, for-profits were viewed with a great deal of respect for their professional management.

It would not have been entirely novel for creative projects initiated by nonprofits, such as Mellon and Michigan, to be broadly distributed to the public by commercial concerns.[27] In 1994, the developers of Mosaic, an early web browser, were leaving the University of Illinois, Urbana-Champaign, for Silicon Valley. Transplanted to Silicon Valley, the nonprofit, government-funded Mosaic blossomed into what was, by mid-1995, the commercially successful Netscape Navigator. Only with market intervention did the web become broadly available to American (and worldwide) households. The option of JSTOR becoming a for-profit thus held some promise.[28]

Generally, though, JSTOR's leadership at Mellon and its external audience, did not see many advantages to this model of the well-capitalized for-profit startup. Guthrie, for one, did not believe that there was something fundamental to not-for-profits that enabled poor management to flourish. The main advantage to a for-profit structure would be to provide for large capital needs, if such needs were substantial. But this was not believed to be the case for JSTOR; its capital needs seemed relatively modest. Its plan would probably be to learn by doing, gradu-

---

[27]Examples abound. Indeed, the federal Bayh-Dole Act encourages universities to seek patents and licensing fees from discoveries and inventions that are made with federal grant support. Its purpose was not so much to return licensing revenues to higher education, though that has been a happy outcome, but rather stemmed from the belief that nonprofit universities had no incentive to make important discoveries and inventions available to the general public if they could not profit from them. A National Research Council study, chaired by President Richard Levin of Yale University and Mark Myers of Xerox Corporation is, in 2002, attempting to document the outcome of this, and other, recent intellectual property developments.

[28]Later examples of online databases of library materials that pursued a "dot.com" business model include Questia. By early 2001, this service had obtained some $135 million in venture capital funding in support of an ambitious program to digitize some 300,000 books. If successful, Questia would be larger by an order of magnitude, both in dollars and in pages, than JSTOR. But so far it seems to have failed to create a compellingly curated collection of titles, and it has enacted pricing policies that have met with widespread criticism in university and library circles. At this point, Questia does not seem to be meeting its ambitious goals. In mid- and late 2001, it was cutting staff precipitously. See Paula J. Hane, "*IT Interview:* Questia Provides Digital Library, Research Tools: Company president and CEO Troy Williams discusses details of the new research service," *Information Today* 18, no. 2 (February 2001); Tom Fowler, "Online college library and research firm slows pace, reduces staff by almost half," *Houston Chronicle,* May 9, 2001; Tom Fowler, "Questia again cuts its workforce 50% on low growth rate," *Houston Chronicle,* November 30, 2001.

ally increasing its scope rather than seeking to make a major impact, as did Questia, from day one. As a nonprofit, it could obtain these relatively modest amounts of capital via foundation grants. (Later in this chapter, we shall see that Mellon would elect to be the sole funder at this stage.) Moreover, JSTOR's key clientele would be nonprofit libraries and publishers, which could be expected to feel more comfortable working with another nonprofit. A nonprofit structure could best allow JSTOR to navigate the terrain between funders, libraries, and publishers.

Largely in retrospect, there was another important reason for JSTOR to be organized as a nonprofit: its archiving commitment. As libraries seeking to save space and deaccession journals considered participating in JSTOR, it would be most important that they view JSTOR as a trusted archive. Guthrie believes that its nonprofit motives offered significant reassurance to the library community.[29] Beyond perceptions, it is also the case that a mission-driven, rather than profit-maximizing, perspective would allow JSTOR to commit itself to archiving in a way that would have been difficult for many others. But there is little indication that the importance of archiving and the notion of a third-party archive were, as organizational matters, fully understood at the time of JSTOR's spin-off.

Bowen was convinced that a nonprofit organization was preferable. Michigan President James Duderstadt had earlier reminded Bowen of precedents for founding a nonprofit, which was then "transformed into a for-profit company when the market made that feasible."[30] Duderstadt's familiarity with the development of the nonprofit Advanced Network Services, later sold to AOL, probably provided reassuring flexibility. As a not-for-profit, JSTOR could bring these often-divergent communities together without feeling constrained by investors' demands and appearing to pursue its own self-interests. Proceeding at a deliberate pace, guided by a well-defined mission, and having only modest capital needs, a nonprofit JSTOR could grow and develop according to educational priorities rather than those of equity holders. Whitehead and Reveley gave their assent to Bowen's conclusions.[31]

To explore the contrapositive for a moment, we should recall that, had it pursued the for-profit option, JSTOR would have been among the first of the so-called "dot.coms." These corporations, established in the late

[29]Kevin Guthrie, personal communication, January 8, 2002.

[30]William G. Bowen, "Conversation with James Duderstadt," memorandum to JSTOR file, March 21, 1995.

[31]Bowen later reported that assent in a memorandum to the full Mellon board of trustees. William G. Bowen, "JSTOR," memorandum to members of the board of trustees, July 31, 1995.

1990s to commercialize the Internet, almost unanimously developed along very different lines than did JSTOR. Uncaring about the long-term and convinced that market principles would change to accommodate them, these firms followed a more ballistic trajectory. Few of the dot.coms founded in this period remained in business by 2002. It is difficult to imagine JSTOR, as a "dot.com," even with Guthrie as president, successfully pursuing an archiving mission.

DEVOLVING RESPONSIBILITY

In late May, Bowen and Fuchs had a conversation that may have been the tipping point pushing JSTOR to near-term independence. They had met to review JSTOR's operations and status but were troubled by several developments. The software was not yet completed; JSTOR still could not print to a PC-Windows machine. The scanning vendor had made substantially less progress than expected, in some measure because of quality problems in the source materials (see chapter 4). Organizations of ecologists and mathematicians had expressed interest in bringing their journals into JSTOR; would the vendor be up to the task? Could quality be improved without radically increasing the cost? Would the software move along quickly enough? In his memo summarizing the conversation with Fuchs, Bowen wrote, "We need to continue to think about organizational issues. It may now be timely to take the first steps in exploring the legal issues that would be associated with the Foundation setting up a separate nonprofit corporation in order to roll JSTOR out. . . . We don't want to be assuming things are feasible which are not."[32] Bowen had clearly set on independence, via a new organization, and he was ready to move forward. Mellon staff began to consult with Sullivan & Cromwell, the foundation's outside counsel, to determine exactly what arrangements could be made and what would be in the project's best interest.

While lawyers worked on the mechanisms by which this could be accomplished, in the late spring of 1995 Bowen had begun to turn day-to-day operations over to a single deputy, so that lines of responsibility would become clearer and more professionalized. It might have been possible to put this improved organizational structure into place earlier, with the effect of avoiding some of the problems we saw in chapter 4. But only now, in Bowen's mind, was the JSTOR project sufficiently mature to ask someone to devote himself to it. And only recently was an

---

[32]William G. Bowen, "JSTOR," memorandum to T. Dennis Sullivan, Kevin Guthrie, and Richard Ekman, May 28, 1995.

obvious leader sufficiently free of other Mellon responsibilities to take on this new role.

Kevin Guthrie was a member of Mellon's research staff who was just completing a major study of the New-York Historical Society, a landmark museum and research library that had struggled financially for decades.[33] In addition, Guthrie held an undergraduate engineering degree from Princeton and a Columbia M.B.A., and he had experience as an entrepreneurial software developer and thorough inculcation into Mellon's core values.

All of this combined to make Guthrie an ideal candidate to take some responsibility for JSTOR. Software development and complicated production work constituted much of JSTOR's day-to-day operations. And for long-term preservation of the database, it was clear that JSTOR's archive would share many key policy questions with the New-York Historical Society: How can an organization ensure that, tens and hundreds of years later, its archive will still be in good condition and accessible? While the technical answer would lie in the software, Guthrie's book on the New-York Historical Society was almost obsessively focused on the financial and organizational answers.

As he completed the New-York Historical Society study in the Spring of 1995, Guthrie had become increasingly involved in JSTOR, taking on a number of tasks that began to focus responsibility on him. In June Guthrie formally took over as Mellon's coordinator for JSTOR, with a mandate to bring JSTOR forward to independence.[34]

THE TRANSITION TO INDEPENDENCE

With Guthrie beginning to take on various responsibilities, Bowen tersely reported to some key Mellon staff: "Decision to push ahead aggressively

---

[33]Kevin M. Guthrie, *The New-York Historical Society: Lessons from One Nonprofit's Long Struggle for Survival* (San Francisco: Jossey-Bass Publishers, 1996). Although it was not yet published when Guthrie took up his JSTOR duties, his book was to have an important impact on the understanding of a unique group of not-for-profit organizations—the independent research libraries. Like museums, these libraries are trusted with storing and preserving cultural heritage and making their collections available to students, scholars, and the public. Under weak leadership, the New-York Historical Society had long struggled financially, exhausting its endowment without bringing in other revenues. Guthrie diagnosed the diseases of management that had plagued the New-York Historical Society. Since then, with new leadership, the society has found itself in improved financial health.

[34]At a breakfast meeting with Bowen on June 17, 1995, Guthrie committed to leading JSTOR only until the end of the calendar year, at which point they agreed to reconsider the needs of the organization and Guthrie's own plans.

seems made. Project has great potential."[35] Before formal legal work could begin, the name of this new organization had to be determined. Among the possibilities considered were Journalex, Sco-Com, and Mr. Miles. But "JSTOR is not bad . . . so in the interests of time and simplicity," wrote Bowen with optimism that a replacement name would in time be found, "I vote for moving ahead by incorporating [it as] 'JSTOR.'"[36]

Guthrie began researching existing JSTOR-Mellon relationships, attempting to see which could be passed along to a new organization and how. Luckily, Mellon had carefully structured most all agreements—with, for example, the publishers—so that they could be passed on to another organization. Soon, the foundation decided to transfer all of its JSTOR-related rights and licenses to the new organization, at no cost.[37]

Guthrie traveled to Ann Arbor in July to introduce himself to staff at Michigan and to better understand the operations there and the costs involved. Although he was disappointed that he was unable to get a better handle on costs, his trip resulted in some crucial discoveries, principally that "there was not as much 'infrastructure' as I had expected there would be." By this he meant people. When the programmers, Alexander and Peters, were away for a week, incoming data from DIT went unattended, awaiting their return. Another part of the production process clearly had to be improved. Guthrie also wondered whether the management and organization in place were appropriate for JSTOR's goals.[38]

Guthrie also sought to understand particular software needs. The printer application was far from done, and Frank had determined it would be best to bring in someone to focus on this particular task.[39] Bugs remained in the search engine,[40] including one in which searching in the author field was hampered by middle initials.[41] Finally, because a search of the fulltext identified only a relevant article and could not

---

[35] William G. Bowen, "Thoughts on JSTOR and Issues to Consider," memorandum to T. Dennis Sullivan, Ira Fuchs, Kevin Guthrie, and Richard Ekman, draft of June 18, 1995.

[36] Ibid.

[37] William G. Bowen, "Recent meetings and key issues," memorandum to JSTOR file, July 15, 1995.

[38] Kevin Guthrie, "Meetings at the University of Michigan, July 10, 1995," memorandum to William G. Bowen, Richard Ekman, Ira Fuchs, T. Dennis Sullivan, and the JSTOR file, July 12, 1995, 7.

[39] Randall Frank, interview with the author, July 10, 2001.

[40] Kevin Guthrie, "Meetings at the University of Michigan, July 10, 1995," memorandum to William G. Bowen, Richard Ekman, Ira Fuchs, T. Dennis Sullivan, and the JSTOR file, July 12, 1995.

[41] William G. Bowen, "Recent meetings and key issues," memorandum to JSTOR file, July 15, 1995.

highlight the word being searched for, everyone wanted a mechanism that would at least take the user to the page with the word on it. Although Frank thought the feature was largely completed, Alexander and Peters told Guthrie it would take at least another month. In addition to the delays, Guthrie was frustrated by clearly imperfect communications.[42]

Guthrie's trip to Ann Arbor differed from previous Mellon attempts at oversight. Most importantly, Guthrie traveled to Ann Arbor with an understanding that the responsibility for improving the operations there would fall, in the last analysis, to him. He was not thinking solely of barriers to progress, which was largely Bowen's focus, or on technology questions, which was Fuchs's. Rather, Guthrie viewed the work at Michigan as requiring a sustainable organizational structure and production process. He was led to this approach by a combination of the responsibility placed squarely on him and his temperament; it was precisely why Bowen selected him. We shall see more clearly in chapters 7 and 9 the ongoing advantage of this new approach.

THE FOUNDING BOARD

Once Bowen determined that JSTOR should be organized as a nonprofit, the immediate organizational step was to secure a provisional board of trustees for the new organization. Bowen sought the Mellon trustees' consent to serve as founding chairman of JSTOR's board, because of "my knowledge of some of the publishers and other key institutional players, and the need for considerable hands-on involvement at this point in the evolution of JSTOR; also, I am strongly committed to the project and am willing to make the commitment of time that is required."[43] It is doubtful that, even at that late date, Bowen knew exactly how large a commitment he was making.

As the JSTOR board's provisional chair, Bowen began assembling the rest of the founding trustees. By coincidence, he had recently published a book of reflections and recommendations for the constitution and operation of governing boards.[44] In creating the initial governance structure for JSTOR, he followed his own recommendations by seeking a small

---

[42]Kevin Guthrie, "Meetings at the University of Michigan, July 10, 1995," memorandum to William G. Bowen, Richard Ekman, Ira Fuchs, T. Dennis Sullivan, and the JSTOR file, July 12, 1995.

[43]William G. Bowen, "JSTOR," memorandum to members of the board of trustees, July 31, 1995.

[44]William G. Bowen, *Inside the Boardroom: Governance by Directors and Trustees* (New York: John Wiley and Sons, 1994).

and agile group appropriate for a service-providing (rather than money-raising) not-for-profit. He wanted a group that could provide the consultation and advice, in addition to oversight, that Guthrie would need. Bowen earlier had sought and received assurance from Mellon outside counsel "that there could be overlap with [the Mellon board], if the overlap were not too great and other tests of non-control were met."[45] This way, Mellon could ensure that the new organization would adequately represent its values.

The board's founding membership was notable for its breadth—especially compared to the likely nature of oversight in a different organizational model. Its membership was remarkably broader than that of the original advisory committee (see chapter 2). All evidence indicates the care with which Bowen assembled individuals who, while representing JSTOR's several constituencies, would keep the new organization true to mission. Librarians were surprised, and in some cases dismayed, to find that JSTOR's board had only one librarian; but JSTOR was not a library project. And JSTOR was not a publishing project; the closest it came to a publisher representative was Cathleen Synge Morawetz, past president of the American Mathematical Society (though Bowen had also sought, and later was able to attract, Charles Ellis, chief executive officer of John Wiley). Rather, in addition to the librarian, JSTOR's founding board consisted of college and university administrators, two technology executives, a lawyer, and a working scholar.

Mary Patterson McPherson, then-president of Bryn Mawr College, and Gilbert Whitaker, then just stepping down as Michigan's provost, had long experience with the colleges and universities that would be JSTOR's principal initial audience. Both had a broad understanding of the costs and benefits of higher education, with particular concern for system-wide effects. Whitaker knew the ins and outs of Michigan, and it was hoped he could continue to help solve any problems there. Taylor Reveley, then the managing partner of a major law firm, brought his vast legal background as well as a link to Mellon through his role as a foundation trustee. His legal perspective was important not least because copyright and licensing provisions were central to JSTOR's work. Cathleen Synge Morawetz, a mathematician and former director of New York University's Courant Institute, provided the perspective of a faculty member, a researcher, a teacher, and a scholarly society publisher. Richard DeGennaro, recently retired as director of the Harvard College Library, had served on the advisory committee. Elton White, the former

---

[45] William G. Bowen, "Thoughts on JSTOR and Issues to Consider," memorandum to T. Dennis Sullivan, Ira Fuchs, Kevin Guthrie, and Richard Ekman, draft of June 18, 1995.

president of NCR, added a keen sense of the challenges and workings of managing a technology business. In addition, Ira Fuchs joined the board, offering his university experience and important technical expertise.

The board's breadth was indicative of JSTOR's complicated work and audience. Unlike the advisory committee, it was not just a collection of scholars and librarians. That group was important in defining user needs and the infrastructure necessary to meet them, but now JSTOR was leaving its experimental stage. Effective management and business savvy were of comparatively more importance, a point that cannot be overstated. Bowen could have put together a vastly different board with vastly different results, but instead he made the conscious decision to assemble a more market-driven group. JSTOR's board remained representative of scholars and librarians, and it should be noted that all of its members had extraordinary sensitivity to its scholarly mission, but they were not working without a sense of the important technological, legal, and business questions that such an enterprise necessarily required.[46]

INCUBATION

With only one journal substantially completed, JSTOR was formally incorporated on July 31, 1995. The organizational meeting of its board of trustees was held, by telephone, on August 4, 1995. Bowen was elected as chairman, Guthrie executive director, and Fuchs chief scientist. The board charged Guthrie with preparing a preliminary business plan, in part so that JSTOR could consider applying for an initial grant from the Mellon Foundation. And JSTOR assumed all relevant responsibilities from Mellon.[47]

Even though formally independent, JSTOR was for several months nurtured at the foundation. Bowen's vision was for JSTOR to use "borrowed supporting services and staff of other kinds so that [it will not] have to incur big, duplicative infra-structure expenses up front. . . . For

---

[46] As JSTOR has grown since that time, the board's base has broadened somewhat, but it has continued to stay small and focused. Additions have included Laura N. Brown, president of Oxford University Press in America; Nancy M. Cline, DeGennaro's successor as the librarian of Harvard College; Richard C. Levin, Beinecke Professor of Economics and the president of Yale University; Michele Tolela Myers, the president of Sarah Lawrence College, who had been the president of Denison when Bowen's idea for JSTOR was developed; James Carmichael Renick, the chancellor of North Carolina Agricultural and Technical State University; Ruth Simmons, then president of Smith College; and Stephen M. Stigler, the Ernest DeWitt Burton Distinguished Service Professor of Statistics at the University of Chicago.

[47] Minutes of the JSTOR board of trustees meeting of August 4, 1995.

a time, could [Mellon] 'incubate' an entity of this kind in our present offices"?[48] This incubation period allowed JSTOR to grow a bit, administratively and organizationally, before setting up its own offices.[49]

Michigan Relations

During this initial phase, JSTOR's New York staff consisted of only Guthrie and an assistant. A third person would not be employed in New York until mid-1996. In the meantime, the rest of its tiny staff—two programmers and two user-services librarians—were located in Michigan, on the university's payroll, undertaking the work of the two Mellon grants to Michigan. Several staff at Michigan had assured Mellon that the university was committed to providing production operations for digital libraries. But these arrangements were somewhat more complicated (see, in particular, chapters 7 and 9).

As Bowen had thought through the needs of the new JSTOR organization, he looked for ways to clarify organizational relationships. Principally, he searched for a means to increase the amount of JSTOR's leverage on the university to demand particular outcomes, or as Bowen put it, "clarify and define" their relationship. He thought about retracting the grant from Michigan, either formally or in effect, and giving it directly to JSTOR, which in turn could subcontract with Michigan. Organizationally, any such expansion of JSTOR's authority in its relations with the university would have been helpful. It has been impossible to determine why such a rearrangement did not take place.[50] But

---

[48] William G. Bowen, "Thoughts on JSTOR and Issues to Consider," memorandum to T. Dennis Sullivan, Ira Fuchs, Kevin Guthrie, and Richard Ekman, draft of June 18, 1995.

[49] Kevin Guthrie, interview with the author, December 13, 2000.

[50] One possibility may relate to the IRS regulations that impede foundations like Mellon from simply funding organizations like JSTOR. These regulations demand that certain types of nonprofits demonstrate a diversity of funding in order to qualify for extremely desirable 509(a)(2) status. Any Mellon monies that passed through JSTOR unnecessarily would make it more difficult for JSTOR to demonstrate a diversity of funding.

When Sullivan & Cromwell began the work that would be necessary to spin JSTOR off as a separate nonprofit, it believed that JSTOR would initially have to be set up as a "private operating foundation," since 100 percent of its to-date revenues came from a single source, Mellon. Later, when revenues from libraries were received, the balance of support would shift and JSTOR could convert to a "public charity" under the terms of section 509(a)(2) of the federal tax code. Such public charity status was preferable from a tax perspective, but it required a broad base of revenues. The IRS believed broad-based revenues were soon to come. Consequently, it made an "advance ruling" that allowed JSTOR to assume public charity status immediately, on condition that it met the 509(a)(2) requirements by the close of 1999. That gave JSTOR four-and-one-half years to broaden its stream

instead, by early August 1995 it had been decided that the Mellon grants to Michigan would be spent down before JSTOR could assume direct control.[51] JSTOR would begin to manage the Michigan operations, while Mellon would continue to manage the finances.

Hindsight suggests that more attention should have been paid to Michigan's relationship with the new JSTOR. By mid-1996, it would become clear that the digital library production services provided through the Mellon grants to Michigan were no longer adequate. Both the organizational and intellectual property arrangements were flawed, as we will see in chapters 7 and 9. A renegotiation in the summer of 1995 might have speeded JSTOR's production and software development work and prevented tensions that were later to arise. But Michigan remained interested in providing production services directly to digital library projects. The new JSTOR had not developed the ability to take on the work itself, and Bowen and Guthrie saw no need to do so when Michigan was a willing partner. The Mellon grants functioned without pause; and at the time it seems no one felt compelled to adjust them in any way.

"Working Capital"

Even while the new JSTOR began to incubate at Mellon, it was desirable for it to separate as soon as possible. But JSTOR was not ready to begin licensing access to paying participants; too few journals were online or even signed up, and those journals that were scanned were not yet ready for public release. Even though JSTOR was independent, it did not want to begin commercial operations until it had reached critical mass. While the earlier Mellon awards to the university funded Michigan expenses (including scanning), the new JSTOR organization had expenses of its own. To pay for initial operations after the incubation period, JSTOR sought a Mellon grant.

At first, it had been unclear whether the law would permit Mellon to issue a grant to such a young offspring.[52] If a grant were impossible, the incubation period of direct support might simply have to be continued.[53]

---

of revenues, which it would have to do in any case since the Mellon grant was designed to pay for only about a year of operations. See James I. Black III and Elaine Waterhouse Wilson of Sullivan & Cromwell, letter to Kevin Guthrie, February 14, 1996.

[51] William G. Bowen, "JSTOR: Michigan Trip," memorandum, August 7, 1995.

[52] William G. Bowen, "Recent meetings and key issues," memorandum to JSTOR file, July 15, 1995.

[53] William G. Bowen, "JSTOR," memorandum to members of the board of trustees, July 31, 1995.

Bowen preferred a grant, however, so that JSTOR could "maintain its own books from the outset, if this is possible,"[54] and thereby establish the economics of the organization.[55] Legal research confirmed that a grant could be made, and an "officer's grant" of $50,000 was approved in early November 1995, allowing JSTOR to pay office expenses and salaries for the first weeks.[56] Under the foundation's rules, this was the largest grant that could be awarded without requiring formal approval from the board of trustees. The grant supported JSTOR until Mellon's next board meeting. Guthrie then prepared a more formal request to Mellon for a larger grant.

In his grant request, Guthrie wrote that with "most of the initial organizational work near completion, it is now time for JSTOR to venture out on its own."[57] The brief but intense incubation period had allowed him to create an extremely preliminary business plan. This bare-bones budget would also be submitted to the IRS for tax purposes, without which the Foundation could not have made a grant. Although this budget was probably intended more as a placeholder than for the purposes of serious planning, it is the only documentation suggesting that Guthrie carefully considered the size of his grant request.

Guthrie projected that the overwhelming majority of JSTOR's work would continue to be subcontracted to Michigan. He foresaw significant revenues beginning during the 1996 calendar year, during which JSTOR nevertheless expected to lose over $1 million, with its ledger reaching near-balance in 1997. JSTOR requested $1.5 million from Mellon, essentially to pay for the shortfall anticipated from 1996 operations. It is notable that JSTOR did not request more than this amount, but rather identified what Guthrie believed to be a realistic but not generous startup fund, to make up the shortfall until JSTOR's database was publicly accessible and revenues exceeded expenses.

On December 18, the Mellon trustees approved a grant of $1.5 million for JSTOR's "working capital."[58] There is no chance that Mellon would have given just any newborn organization a $1.5 million grant, precisely because any financial planning at that stage in its development was mere conjecture. For an ordinary grantee, financial conjecture of this scale is generally a fatal disease. But rather than continuing to incubate JSTOR for another year or more, Mellon made a wise exception to its usual policy (although it is important to note that the two organizations remained

---

[54] Ibid.

[55] William G. Bowen, interview with the author, June 26, 2001.

[56] Grant application and docket item are for Mellon Grant #49500605.

[57] Kevin Guthrie, letter to William G. Bowen, November 25, 1995.

[58] Grant application and docket item are for Mellon Grant #49500617.

extremely close with the president of the one serving as the chairman of the board of the other). Guthrie developed financial plans, even while recognizing that they were estimates derived from guesses based on insufficient experience with software and a markedly inadequate production process. These projections were the basis of the $1.5 million grant. Although JSTOR continued to be housed at Mellon's New York offices for several additional months, by the end of 1995 it would be a financially independent organization.

SUMMATION

The changes that Bowen oversaw for JSTOR in 1995, culminating in its independence from Mellon, would play an enormous role in its eventual success. As we will see in the chapters to follow, both JSTOR's organizational structure and its leadership were radical departures from the Mellon grant project that we have observed in the last several chapters. Not least of these critical changes was Bowen's selection of a single responsible leader, and Guthrie in particular, to oversee the growth of JSTOR. In identifying a single leader, Bowen created a mechanism in which responsibility for success or failure could be vested. With Guthrie as chief, there could be no one else to blame; he would have to make JSTOR work, and if it did not, the new JSTOR board would hold him responsible.

In turn, a combination of responsibility and temperament led Guthrie to begin seeking solutions in process changes and organizational improvements. Imagine being in Guthrie's position at this point. With a wealthy foundation subsidizing his work, another person might not have felt the pressure to push forward, but Guthrie recognized that JSTOR needed a challenge if it were to succeed. The specifics of Guthrie's impact will become more evident in the chapters that follow, but even in his first few months at the helm of JSTOR, they were clear. On the one hand, in partnership with Bowen, Guthrie began planning the mechanisms necessary for an ongoing enterprise, including a refocusing of its mission. But he also felt no compunctions about "getting his hands dirty" in the operations.

During the first months of JSTOR's incubatory independence, Guthrie began more and more to exercise his authority. While at first he worked daily with Bowen on a whole host of matters, it would not be long before Guthrie began to take primacy in overseeing the relationship with Michigan. While Bowen and Guthrie would always maintain a remarkably close and successful chairman-CEO partnership, Guthrie, with Bowen's encouragement, took increasingly more responsibility. It was in this role, as the project manager, that Guthrie played the most critical role in the beginning, leading JSTOR and feeling responsible for its success, rather than administering it from afar and only mourning its shortcomings. We see more on this theme in the chapters that follow.

With undistracted, high-quality leadership, JSTOR as its own organization could push forward with software and digitization while beginning to find its exact position in the market and articulating a focused mission. A year earlier, the lack of an existing organization with both the ability and inclination to undertake the JSTOR project had forced Mellon into the awkward managerial role that constrained its development. Now, with independence, Bowen and others at Mellon had created precisely the organization of which they had earlier been in search (even if this was not fully evident at the time).

With JSTOR in receipt of a Mellon grant of its own, responsibility for performance fell on Guthrie alone. Without the pressure that this brought, it is difficult to say whether there would have been success. If JSTOR had an open tap to the Mellon kitty, it is likely that far more funds would have been expended in creating what would become the Arts & Sciences I Collection. Guthrie's willingness to take a risk, both personally and on behalf of the JSTOR organization, is notable. It is surely a key success factor in JSTOR's development. In the following chapter, we shall see the work that was ongoing concurrently to identify JSTOR's mission and specific goals, which in turn would allow it to expand and refine its business planning.

CHAPTER 6

Defining a Mission in
Partnership with Publishers

SEPTEMBER 1995–AUGUST 1996

WHEN IT BECAME INDEPENDENT in the summer of 1995, JSTOR inherited a project and a mission from the Mellon Foundation. In the year that followed, it faced myriad challenges as it moved to consolidate the work of Mellon and Michigan into a viable business entity. For one thing, the production arrangements that we observed in chapter 4 were substantially flawed and would have to be revamped (see chapter 7). But more broadly, the new organization had the singular opportunity to consider its mission. While it had been defined broadly at first—"to help the scholarly community benefit from advances in information technology"—for over six months, Bowen and Guthrie would wrestle with questions of the basic services that JSTOR would provide. In this way, the strategic events of this first year were foundational to both the organization and the business model that would result.

CURRENT ISSUES AND THE
ECOLOGICAL SOCIETY OF AMERICA

Well before production began on the pilot journals, or JSTOR's independence was seriously contemplated, staff at the Mellon Foundation had begun speaking with several scholarly societies outside history and economics about the possibility of participating in JSTOR. Indeed, the need to focus more attention on cultivating such relationships was an important reason to seek independence. A number of societies had expressed an active interest in participating, and the Ecological Society of America (ESA) was by far the foremost enthusiast.[1]

William Robertson IV, Mellon's long-serving program officer for Conservation and the Environment, heard details of the pilot's rapid progress at a Mellon staff meeting in October 1994, well before JSTOR's

---

[1] Much of this section treating the interactions between Mellon, JSTOR, and the ESA is based on Katherine McCarter and Mary Barber, interview with the author, September 20, 2001 and William Robertson, interview with the author, January 17, 2001.

independence.[2] Robertson perceived the advantages of backfile access for the ecology community and told Bowen that "the Ecological Society would be a good partner for the beginning of the experiment because it had three journals, they were financially stable, we knew the leadership very well, and the leadership was very good."[3] Financial stability and well-known high-quality leadership had come to be prerequisites for Mellon in considering potential grantees, certainly.

In addition, there were three other critical advantages that the ESA brought to a relationship with JSTOR. First, whereas many societies included subscriptions to their flagship journals with the basic membership fee, the ESA separated subscription from membership. That meant the ESA was confident that it would lose no society members, or their annual dues, if its journals lost subscribers. This unusual feature meant that it could treat its journals division as a separate tub floating on its own bottom. The ESA's concerns about lost revenues were thus restricted to its journals division. Serious though this may have been, at least they posed no threat to the larger organization. The second advantage was that the ESA, according to Robertson, had "figured out that the back issues weren't worth much" economically. By contrast, other scholarly publishers might have been (and would subsequently prove to be) holding out for significant revenues from backfiles. The ESA's principal interest was in the broadest possible availability of its publications. Finally, the ESA was far more technologically savvy than many other scholarly societies. It was then in the process of developing an online-only journal, *Conservation Ecology.* The society had given serious consideration to distributing scholarship online and was aware of, but undeterred by, the uncertainties of online publication.

In addition to the advantages that the ESA as an institution would bring to what was then Mellon's JSTOR project, ecology as a discipline had appeal. First and foremost, it was a natural science and would therefore bring opportunities to test the JSTOR concept beyond economics and history. As with economics and history, ecology had a strong core scholarly society (the ESA), a clearly academic orientation, and a substantial accumulation of journal-based scholarship that remained relevant for current researchers. But unlike most economists and historians, ecologists can spend years at a time researching in remote areas, often in developing countries, where adequate library resources are frequently unavailable. Finally, ecological articles often contain images, which would present new and appealing challenges for the project.

[2] William Robertson, "Ecological Society journals," memorandum to Richard Ekman and William G. Bowen, October 12, 1994.

[3] William Robertson, interview with the author, January 17, 2001.

After the staff meeting, Robertson contacted Professor Robert Colwell of the University of Connecticut, who also served as vice-president of the ESA and headed its committee on electronic publishing. Colwell confirmed Robertson's memory that the ESA was actively exploring how to begin electronic dissemination of its three print journals, *Ecology*, *Ecological Monographs*, and *Ecological Applications*. Robertson put Colwell in contact with the JSTOR project, and Bowen and Colwell exchanged several emails discussing the shape of a partnership.

Of particular note was the ESA's primary interest not in backfiles alone, but in current issues as well. Colwell wrote to Bowen, "Your commitment to making both historical and future issues of professional journals available electronically on an economically sustainable basis is just what we have been envisioning. . . . the possibility that [you] would fund the process of digitizing our past opus, as well, makes the prospect truly tantalizing."[4] Contained here was a clear statement of the root of the ESA's enthusiasm. For one thing, the mere identification of a committed partner in these matters was probably exciting. Plus, it was impressed by the commitment to system-wide savings that would help to ameliorate the trend toward unsustainable pricing. But, perhaps most importantly, no capital would have to be contributed by scholarly societies that were, and are, notoriously capital-poor. As other organizations subsequently would move to digitize backfiles, these latter two factors would be among the most significant that distinguished JSTOR.

Also contained in this email was the first documentary evidence that the JSTOR project might be ready to expand its role to include current issues. Previous to this, there is evidence that Bowen had been interested in how the JSTOR archive could be linked to current issues.[5] While it had not been viewed as being integral to JSTOR's success, linking was thought to have both scholarly and economic value. Nevertheless, the pilot project had focused on the backfiles alone. But the ESA's enthusiasm for the idea had traction now in large part because Bowen was considering how to create a new organizational home for JSTOR. Such organizational change might make it the right time to expand JSTOR's operations in a significant new direction. Robertson's instinct to bring together the ESA and the JSTOR project would seem to have brought about major new opportunities.

As conversations proceeded between the ESA and Mellon, the appeal of a partnership became evident. In an April 1995 letter to Bowen, ESA

---

[4]Robert K. Colwell, "Ecological Society of American electronic publishing," email to William G. Bowen, January 19, 1995.

[5]William G. Bowen, "Notes on JSTOR," memorandum to file, April 2, 1994. William G. Bowen, notes for a presentation, October 6, 1994.

President and University of Georgia Professor Judy Meyer summarized the ESA's views on participating in JSTOR: "The Society has four broad goals in this effort: to assure that the ecological research published in our journals has the widest dissemination possible, that future scholars have access to our journals, that the intellectual property rights of the authors publishing in our journals be protected, and that Society finances not be jeopardized by electronic participation."[6] The ESA's priorities, and especially the order in which Meyer had listed them, were just what Mellon believed to be appropriate for a fruitful partnership.

System-wide Savings

The online publication of scholarly journals was appealing to Mellon because it would have clear and concrete benefits, both to the JSTOR project itself and to the academic world in general. The scholarly benefits were most obvious. Available online via the campus network, current issues would be far more widely accessible than in display racks in the campus library. Furthermore, if current issues were to be available online, it made sense for them to be available through the same interface as the backfile. That way, a user could search across all of a journal's volumes—beginning with volume 1 in the JSTOR backfiles and moving into this year's current issue.

Online current issues also held out the possibility of substantial savings on back-office functions within academic libraries.[7] The work of receiving and routing the journals, a manual process that delayed new issues from reaching their readers, would not be needed, leading to net savings in staff. Libraries typically bound several issues together to create a sturdier volume, with multiple volumes per title in many cases. Binding, plus preparation and handling costs, added at least $20–$30 in costs per year.[8] Stack and display shelves could be freed up for other purposes. Although no one took account of the expense that license negotiations would impose on both libraries and publishers,[9] enthusiasts

[6] Judy L. Meyer, letter to William G. Bowen, April 12, 1995.

[7] William G. Bowen, "JSTOR and the Economics of Scholarly Communications," speech to the Council on Library and Information Resources, Washington, DC, September 18, 1995; revised version online at *www.mellon.org/jsesc.html*.

[8] There are a number of relevant studies in James R. Coffey, ed., *Operational Costs in Acquisitions* (New York: Haworth Press, 1991).

[9] One article reporting on the development of generic licenses noted that, in general, a library's "legal counsel is required to review each license—a time-consuming and expensive process." John Cox, "Model Generic Licenses: Cooperation and Competition," *Serials Review* 26, no. 1 (2000): 3.

had long predicted that online current issues would cost significantly less to publish, given the efficiencies that technology might bring.[10] Conventional wisdom held that libraries stood to save at least some costs by replacing print subscriptions with online current issues.

Even if publishing current issues online proved to be more expensive than print, it was believed that JSTOR's involvement could nevertheless reduce system-wide costs. In Bowen's words, online current issues would allow JSTOR to expand its own archive "annually and automatically," without maintaining an ongoing scanning and production operation.[11] It was believed that this would make the backfile operation far less costly.[12] In other words, more space could be saved at less expense, thereby reducing, perhaps substantially, the overall system-wide costs of creating, disseminating, and storing scholarly journals. Thus there was a clear advantage to JSTOR becoming involved in current issues publishing, if it alone could internalize these positive externalities.

System-wide savings was the positive side. The obverse was the defensive sense that commercial players would soon enter the online current issues market. If so, they might well adopt pricing models thought to bring "enormous profit opportunities."[13] Librarians were alarmed by Elsevier's model, then only recently announced, which initially charged 135 percent of the print price for a print and electronic combination package.[14] Although libraries found this pricing unreasonable, we should keep in mind that searchable text and network-wide desktop

[10] Their predictions have yet to be proven, at least for scholarly journals. In fact, published studies have since indicated that, although there are opportunities to save money, online journals rarely use the opportunity to save money, but rather add useful features not present in print. Willis Regier, "Electronic Publishing Is Cheaper," in Richard Ekman and Richard E. Quandt, eds., *Technology and Scholarly Communication* (Berkeley: University of California Press, 1999), 158–67.

[11] William G. Bowen, "JSTOR and the Economics of Scholarly Communications."

[12] Although these savings seemed obvious at the time, they have subsequently proven to be far less concrete. If a journal has both a print and an online edition, will librarians consider the former or the latter to be "of record"? This is critical, because JSTOR promised to be the trusted archive for these journals and a system under which it archives both would result in less system-wide savings. On the other hand, it is not clear that it would be desirable, at least not yet, for the edition of record to pass to the electronic version, which often lacks the pagination, advertisements, and lengthy backfile of the print. There might, of course, be advantages to having both the print and electronic version archived. And finally, the automatic updates of the archive have proved to be far from automatic, imposing nontrivial costs of their own. This problem will manifest itself again in chapter 14.

[13] Kevin Guthrie, "Journal Storage Project Meeting, Tuesday, April 11, 1995," memorandum to JSTOR file, April 18, 1995.

[14] Kevin Guthrie, "Conversation with Wendy Lougee," memorandum to William G. Bowen, Richard Ekman, Ira Fuchs, T. Dennis Sullivan, and the JSTOR file, June 29, 1995.

availability may well have increased the "value" of the journals by even more than 35 percent. Moreover, publishers were investing substantially in their shift to online publication. But even if the value of the journals rose, the "demand," measured by libraries' willingness to pay, did not. If new technology led to unsustainable pricing increases, scholarly information would grow to be less accessible and the system of scholarly communications would be further damaged. It seemed quite plausible that technology might result not in the panacea of cost savings envisioned by the backfiles project, but rather in a deep destabilization of the system.

Bowen and Guthrie thought that an alternative was needed, a nonprofit service that would offer both online access and restrained pricing to libraries. A new JSTOR service would harness the cost-saving advantages without exploiting new profit opportunities. In the system of journal editing, publication, acquisition, and storage, the JSTOR backfiles pilot sought to address only the last of these four stages. But additional savings would naturally make the JSTOR system even more appealing to participants. The JSTOR project and its publishing partners could address the overall system of journal publishing, clearing away the underbrush of redundancies and inefficiencies while increasing the utility of these journal backfiles. Bowen's vision of a service that would be "better and cheaper" could encompass work to encourage the transition to online publication of current issues, if there were willing partners.

An Important Detail:
Availability on the Campus Network or in the Library Only?

With the ESA's enthusiasm dovetailing well with what appeared to be an obvious future step for the JSTOR project, Bowen and Guthrie began detailed consideration of how the new service would operate. While in principle they were committed to pursuing current issues, even with a willing partner there were complications. Initially, Bowen assumed that online current issues would have to be restricted to the library building and not made available throughout the campus network. The JSTOR pilot had dealt mainly with scholarly societies, many of which believed that availability of current issues on a campus network would eliminate the need for individual subscriptions and, therefore, society memberships.[15] By June 1995, Bowen endorsed this view, noting that "to make

[15]At a JSTOR Advisory Committee meeting, for example, AEA Secretary-Treasurer Elton Hinshaw wondered, "If the journals were on-line . . . why would anyone want to become a member of the association?" While the minutes of the meeting may overstate

electronic access to current issues more widely available, say by putting [them] on a campus network, could kill individual subscriptions and thus should not be allowed."[16] This strong statement was but one indication of the balancing of interests embraced by the JSTOR project and later by the independent organization.

In addition to this fear about the hemorrhaging of scholarly societies' membership, there was a worry more generic to journal publishing. The business model for core journals had long depended on selling numerous copies to the same campus, sometimes to multiple campus branch libraries, sometimes to individual faculty members and graduate students, and often a combination of both.[17] There was often one price for libraries and a lower one for individuals to account for the multiple readers who could access a journal at a library. Multiple per-campus subscriptions had the effect of broadly distributing the one-time cost and therefore of lowering, sometimes substantially, the per-copy price.[18] Publishing current issues online could upset this arrangement if a site-wide license were offered.[19] In the online environment, publishers wanted to maintain the system of numerous per-campus subscriptions. To do this, many publishers believed (and some have continued to believe)[20] that they would have to restrict online access to their journals to a specific computer workstation, say in a library or faculty office, thus encouraging the continuation of existing multiple per-campus subscriptions.

---

his fears, many societies were deeply uncertain whether their members had demand, in economic terms, for their activities beyond journals publishing. At the same meeting, Hinshaw's AHA colleague James Gardner suggested that scholarly societies "need to re-think their basic mission and . . . provide different kinds of services to their membership in the future." Kevin Guthrie, "Journal Storage Project Meeting, Tuesday, April 11, 1995," memorandum to JSTOR file, April 18, 1995.

[16] William G. Bowen, "Thoughts on JSTOR and Issues to Consider," memorandum to T. Dennis Sullivan, Ira Fuchs, Kevin Guthrie, Richard Ekman, June 18, 1995.

[17] See Gillian Page, Robert Campbell, and Jack Meadows, *Journal publishing* (Cambridge: Cambridge University Press, 1997), chapter 8.

[18] See *Scholarly Communication: The Report of the National Enquiry* (Baltimore: John Hopkins University Press, 1979), 65–68.

[19] Usage pricing is often contrasted with site licensing. As it is popularly used, however, the site licensing regime consists of two distinct features: first, the resource can be used anywhere at a given site (e.g., a college or university campus), and second the resource can be used an unlimited amount. Because these two features are conceptually different, they have been separated here. The term "unlimited-use pricing" is used in contrast with usage-based pricing, whereas the term "site licensing" is used in contrast with library, computer, or password licensing. From its earliest days, JSTOR was planning to offer site-wide access for its backfiles service.

[20] Elizabeth Lorbeer, "NEJM," email to Lib-License discussion list, August 24, 2001; available at *http://www.library.yale.edu/~llicense/ListArchives/0108/msg00041.html*, and the responses that followed.

On the other hand, since a major advantage of online publication is its network-wide availability, librarians had begun imagining the "library without walls." In this vision, librarians wanted to be rid of the very usage restrictions that publishers believed were their lifeblood. Librarians rightly saw the restrictions as nothing but an artifact of subscription pricing for hard-copy journals.

Rather, librarians preferred site licensing, to provide access to all students and scholars at a given institution, without regard to a specific workstation or building. Coupled with an unlimited-usage pricing plan, site licensing would obviate the need for a large share of current issues subscriptions to core journals: libraries could cancel copies at other campus branches, and faculty and graduate students could cancel their personal copies. Clearly, unlimited-usage site licensing would require a new financial model to offset the lost revenues to publishers from cancelled subscriptions.[21] Yet despite their interest in making scholarly information so much more broadly available on campus, librarians did not have the funds—squeezed as they were by the ongoing serials spiral—to pay its costs.[22] And so, paradoxically, even if online current issues were less expensive to produce, there was a substantial possibility that journals' revenues might fall at a far greater rate than their expenses. The serials spiral would be accelerated by additional downward pressure, driving the journals themselves to extinction.[23]

If online at all, it seemed current issues would have to be marketed on a library-restricted basis rather than via unlimited-usage site licensing, to preserve multiple subscriptions. This was only sensible if JSTOR were to continue working largely with the small society publishers that depended on a bundled membership-subscription and were believed to

[21]In addition to these concerns about cost shifting from individual subscribers to libraries—the very organizations that the JSTOR project was hoping to protect with monetary savings—there was another worrisome potential cost shift. Site licenses might have the counterproductive effect of eliminating price distinctions between small and large institutional subscribers. Smaller institutions that had subscribed to only one copy of a journal might find themselves paying the same price for access to a site license as a very large research university like Harvard, which could save a great deal of money compared with its five institutional subscriptions to, for example, *Ecology*.

[22]Some observers and publishers had long touted online publication as far cheaper than print, cutting out expensive manual steps. It made sense that librarians would be unwilling to pay more for an ostensibly cheaper publication system.

[23]See Page, Campbell, and Meadows, *Journal publishing*, 362. From the publishers' perspective, another important concern was that online publication eliminates many of the practical barriers to copyright violations. Rather than being forced to use a photocopier, now a researcher could just email an article to a nonsubscriber. Of course, licensing and technological barriers would be utilized with increasing frequency; however, these present their own challenges and have at times been ignored or outsmarted.

publish a large share of the journals most reliant on multiple per-campus subscriptions. While Bowen's reasoning was sound, the conclusion he proposed would have been unfortunate.

By July, he had studied the question further and changed his mind. He had begun to realize that it would be impossible for JSTOR to build a carefully selected, curated collection without considering the world beyond scholarly society publishing. While the societies would remain important, they themselves were diverse, less uniformly dependent on individual subscriptions than he had previously believed.[24] Moreover, some of the work on the economics of information by Hal Varian and others was beginning to have an impact on the way the field was perceived: it might be possible for some journals to retain individual subscribers precisely by offering them additional value.[25]

There was a good deal of emerging context for JSTOR's consideration, including two projects in journal publishing that we encountered before. Elsevier had digested its lessons from the TULIP experiment and had announced its intentions to disseminate its corpus of over one thousand scientific journals online (at a substantial price increase).[26] Most of Elsevier's journals were highly specialized and therefore tended not to have multiple per-campus library subscriptions; they were consequently less likely to suffer substantial revenue decreases under a site-licensing regimen. The Johns Hopkins University Press's Project Muse would eventually contain the current issues of all of Hopkins's forty journals, most of which were very well regarded, several of which were

---

[24]After examining financial statements provided by several friendly publishers, Guthrie concluded that many journals depended little if at all on individual subscriptions. In some disciplines, such as mathematics, the number of individual subscriptions was low enough to be essentially irrelevant. William G. Bowen, "Recent meetings and key issues," memorandum to JSTOR file, July 15, 1995. In others cases, the price of a subscription to an individual was so much lower than the library price as barely to exceed, if at all, the marginal cost of printing the copy. At one of the advisory committee meetings, one member reported that "individual subscriptions represented a marginal cost = marginal revenue operation." Kevin Guthrie, "Journal Storage Project Meeting, Tuesday, April 11, 1995," memorandum to JSTOR file, April 18, 1995. For a similar argument, see George A. Cressanthis and June D. Cressanthis, "Publisher Monopoly Power and Third-Degree Price Discrimination of Scholarly Journals," *Technical Services Quarterly* 11(2): 13–36, at 17.

[25]Varian's efforts at the time were widely discussed and disseminated and have since been collected in an excellent source for a broad view of this terrain: Carl Shapiro and Hal R. Varian, *Information Rules* (Cambridge, MA: Harvard Business School Press, 1999). A more economic approach to many of the same concepts is found in Brian Kahin and Hal R. Varian, eds., *Internet Publishing and Beyond: The Economics of Digital Information and Intellectual Property* (Cambridge, MA: MIT Press, 2000).

[26]For the history of Elsevier's post-TULIP work, see Karen Hunter, "PEAK and Elsevier Science," in Wendy Lougee and Jeffrey Mackie-Mason, eds., *Bits and Bucks: Economics and Usage of Digital Collections* (Cambridge, MA: MIT Press, In Preparation).

core to their fields, and many of which had multiple per-campus library subscriptions. Muse was also to be provided on the Internet via site license. In the case of Muse, principal investigators Scott Bennett and Jack Goellner planned to study both the effects on scholarly practice and the economic feasibility of online current issues.

Although both Muse and what would become Elsevier's Science-Direct were at least somewhat experimental in character, they represented business decisions that could prove to be difficult to reverse. Reputable, savvy publishers perceived the benefits to exceed the risks, and their conclusion that online current issues could prove economically viable was a step forward. Memos clearly reflect that Bowen saw Muse and Elsevier as important trailblazers, whose leadership in the field would nevertheless constitute an important "push" for others.[27] With Elsevier and Hopkins moving solidly in that direction, Bowen worried that "if JSTOR is perceived as standing in the way of the apparently obvious path to the future, the entire project may lose some credibility." If the advantages exceeded the costs, which was beginning to seem probable, Bowen believed that JSTOR should encourage partner publishers to make their own decisions about access to current issues.[28]

Thus the plans for publication of current issues shifted from being an extremely uniform and relatively conservative proposal to one that was more responsive to the uncertain and rapidly changing environment. Yet at the same time, by introducing the opportunity for publishers to make their own choices, the proposal no longer shielded publishers with its own conservatism. Making their own decisions and taking their own risks—both economic and perceptual—may have had more appeal to some publishers, but rather less to others. The broader issue of offering a more standard model versus multiple options to its partners was one that JSTOR would only later resolve.

The ESA Agreement

Emboldened by the ESA's strong enthusiasm, Guthrie and Bowen spent several intense days together writing the JSTOR-C proposal, so-called because it followed sequentially the two versions of the pilot publisher agreements A and B, to summarize their thinking on current issues.[29]

---

[27] William G. Bowen, "Recent meetings and key issues," memorandum to JSTOR file, July 15, 1995.

[28] Ibid.

[29] William G. Bowen and Kevin M. Guthrie, "Electronic Access to Scholarly Literature: JSTOR-C Project," June 14, 1995, unpublished memorandum.

The C proposal was meant to be a working document that would set out the basic terms of a current issues relationship, providing a basis for consideration by publishers. It was essentially another case of working toward the "presumptively optimal" outcome. In addition to laying out many of the advantages of publishing online (discussed above), the proposal discussed the role that JSTOR would assume.

The vision was for JSTOR to be something of a service provider for online services to its publisher partners on the backfiles project. All editorial work would remain with scholars and their societies, which would also retain control over pricing, marketing, and licensing the journals' current issues. JSTOR would contribute infrastructure such as servers and software. Presumably, it would offer production and distribution services. The proposal was intentionally vague on many of the technical issues of exactly how such an enterprise would operate. The goal was to move current issues distribution online without imposing new costs or efforts on small scholarly societies. The rest could be worked out later.

Although JSTOR's idea seems to have been developed independently, it was resonant with other proposals. A 1979 publication suggested the need for a nonprofit organization to take on much of the work of scholarly society publishing, an organization "that provides services but that leaves publishing decisions to the sponsoring group."[30] Both were similar to the business model that was independently adopted by Stanford's HighWire Press. HighWire, it will be remembered, is a well-regarded vendor that provides online services for nonprofit publishers of scholarly journals. HighWire's success indicates that JSTOR's eventual retreat from such a business model resulted not from a problem with the business per se, but from a challenge unique to JSTOR.

The ESA agreement was signed October 2, 1995, bringing to a close the initial period of planning for these new responsibilities. Thus the agreement, and the planning, was concluded almost concurrent with JSTOR's own independence.

PUSHING PUBLISHERS TO PARTICIPATE

With the ESA agreement, JSTOR's mission had come to encompass more than just the backfile. It perceived an opportunity for more than just a single experiment. With a number of scholarly societies lobbying for JSTOR to play a role in the online publication of current issues, which would be linked to its archive, the time seemed right for broader action.

---

[30]*Scholarly Communication: The Report of the National Enquiry,* 71–72.

A potentially complicating factor was JSTOR's transition to independence. Although the transition provided an opportunity for creativity, was the newborn organization's mission becoming overbroad, its attentions diverted? Lougee suggested demonstrating success with the backfiles project before moving along to current issues, and Fuchs seems to have shared this sentiment.[31] But Guthrie believed that "we need to wade in if we're going to discover what the true complications are and whether they can be overcome."[32] In his September speech, just after JSTOR's independence, Bowen noted that it wanted to address all of online journal publishing, and in particular the economic concerns of publishers and libraries, for both back and current issues, together and one time only.[33] A piecemeal approach would leave inefficiencies in place. Both Bowen and Guthrie clearly perceived an opportunity to make a major impact.

In this way, JSTOR rapidly came to the conclusion that all core arts and sciences journals could benefit from publishing current issues online. In August 1995, Bowen noted for the benefit of the advisory committee that "it could well make sense to explore similar arrangements with some of our other ten [pilot] journals, and also with associations and journals outside our initial set."[34] By his September speech, there was no doubt that the enthusiasm that he and Guthrie felt was significantly greater.

After independence, JSTOR attempted to offer the ESA experiment as a model for several subsequent publisher agreements, especially in renegotiating its pilot agreements. It was hoped that JSTOR's aggressive outreach would lead many scholarly societies and other publishers to see the advantages of online current issues.[35]

In some cases, such as with the American Economic Association, the experiment had appeal. Indeed, at one point Bowen reported that if JSTOR did not make the current issues of economics journals available online, "I would anticipate rebellion on the part of economists who could not understand why they should be denied access to this material."[36] Although the AEA's executive committee viewed JSTOR's involvement in its current issues "with favor," the devil was in the details. Substantial concern was expressed about the impact of the scheme on

---

[31]Kevin Guthrie, "Conversation with Wendy Lougee," memorandum to William G. Bowen, Richard Ekman, Ira Fuchs, T. Dennis Sullivan, and the JSTOR file, June 29, 1995.

[32]Ibid.

[33]William G. Bowen, "JSTOR and the Economics of Scholarly Communications."

[34]William G. Bowen, memorandum to members of the JSTOR Advisory Committee, August 8, 1995.

[35]Kevin Guthrie, interview with the author, February 1, 2001.

[36]William G. Bowen, "UChicago Press," email to Kevin Guthrie, January 16, 1996.

membership in the association, not just on its revenues.[37] A publications committee, led by Hal Varian, was empowered to study the matter further and was innately sympathetic to arguments about system-wide costs and benefits. JSTOR and the AEA readily reached agreement for online current issues.[38]

In other cases, though, publishers felt great anxiety about the current issues proposal. In some cases, there were strategic reasons that made them hesitant to cede online current issues to JSTOR. In other cases, there was just a broad trepidation about online publication in general. Thinking through the JSTOR proposal, a number of JSTOR's pilot publishers, including the American Historical Association (AHA) and the Organization of American Historians (OAH), were uncomfortable. Both were very dependent on current issues, since society membership was linked to subscriptions.[39] Jones recalls that the principal fear was that online access would have serious detrimental effects on individual subscriptions—that is, memberships in the society.[40] As a result, they were far more cautious than had been anticipated. With JSTOR having recently resolved its concerns about current issues on campus networks, it probably presented a less cautious, and less sympathetic, outlook than the societies sought. Around this time, Bowen first realized that, even if university presses were hesitant to embrace online current issues publishing because they were more business-oriented (see below), society publishers had membership reasons to be worried.[41]

Even in terms of the back issues, Jones believes that the JSTOR proposal was not trivial. Although backfiles had not previously generated significant revenues,

> there was a sense that royalties could get to be important because we might lose current income [from memberships]. It was the loss of income, the fear

---

[37]"Proceedings of the Hundred and Eighth Meeting," *American Economic Review* 86, no. 2 (May 1996): 470.

[38]For a useful summary of the AEA's decision to publish online, see Hal R. Varian, "The AEA's Electronic Publishing Plans: A Progress Report," *Journal of Economic Perspectives* 11, no. 3 (Summer 1997): 95–104.

[39]For a brief overview of the practice of linking the two, see Page, Campbell, and Meadows, *Journal publishing*, 142–44 and 283–84.

[40]Arnita Jones, interview with the author, September 20, 2001.

[41]William G. Bowen, "University of Chicago," memorandum to JSTOR file, November 28, 1995.
   And these were not the societies' only concerns. Many scholarly associations had organizational arrangements that are ambiguous about the relationship between the staff executive director and the journal editor. Although ordinarily each covered a different domain, a project like JSTOR, requiring the endorsement of both, could expose tensions. Arnita Jones, interview with the author, September 20, 2001.

of the unknown out there. . . . you're signing away something that could become valuable economic property. . . . That's asking a lot. The cause was clearly a good one—if you value scholarship, you're going to value libraries. [But] I think there was a sense that [JSTOR] was not worrying too much about the long-term health of these scholarly associations.[42]

If some existing sources of revenue were to disappear (say, as a result of further library cancellations or online current issues), it made sense for the publishers to protect potential sources of revenue. Although Bowen and Guthrie believed they were looking after the best interests of both libraries and publishers in arguing that backfiles had always generated little revenue and should not begin to do so, Jones and others were looking toward the possibility of a bleaker future. Their concerns about revenue-loss from online current issues thereby magnified concerns about committing to the backfiles component.

More broadly, says Jones, some of the editorial staff was not well versed in the advantages of moving online.[43] Guthrie recalls that during this period in mid- to late 1995, many academics were upset when he shared his belief that scholarship was—inevitably—moving online.[44] The resistance of a journal editor would surely have lessened any enthusiasm, or confirmed all the concerns, held by the other society leadership. In general, reports Jones, the scholarly societies in history were not yet prepared to make decisions about online current issues publishing; they did not yet have any sense of the breadth of options available. Only later did they feel confident, founding the History Cooperative to publish the current issues of a number of journals online. Eventually, the AHA and the OAH signed on to JSTOR's backfiles archive, but not the current issues proposal.

Similarly, the University of Chicago Press was deeply troubled by the proposition of JSTOR publishing its current issues online. This was to be the future of its business! Chicago was investing major resources of its own in online distribution of current issues, not unlike many of the commercial publishers and university presses with large journals programs. It had little interest in the services that JSTOR was offering.

Resistance from the AHA, OAH, Chicago, and others indicated that current issues would fragment JSTOR's support among publishers, leading to at best a subset of publishers agreeing to the current issues proposal. And a business in current issues would also cause certain publishers to perceive JSTOR's backfiles project as a competitive threat,

---

[42] Arnita Jones, interview with the author, September 20, 2001.
[43] Ibid.
[44] Kevin Guthrie, interview with the author, February 1, 2001.

dissuading support for that, as well.[45] JSTOR wanted its expanding database of backfiles to be as complete as possible, which had to be achieved, recalls Fuchs, "without blood in the streets and without carnage and without taking forever."[46] By extending its mission, would JSTOR threaten its core?

After hearing some of Chicago's resistance, Bowen wrote to Guthrie that "my assessment is that we will get the backfile agreement, and I only hope that not too much work is required. . . . Re current issues, it may be easiest all around (easiest for us), if we put the University of Chicago people on the backburner as far as this Q is concerned, at least for the time being."[47] It was apparent that, by this time in early January 1996, Bowen and Guthrie had begun to view current issues as less integral to JSTOR's core mission than they did the backfiles project. While this should not be altogether surprising, given the fundamental mission of saving space, it positioned them to begin making some difficult decisions about priorities.

This was further confirmed by Guthrie's concerns about technical difficulties. The work necessary to publish current issues online was radically different from that of JSTOR's pilot, and Guthrie visited several presses, including that of the University of Chicago, to get some sense of the magnitude of the task.[48] One such difficulty related to mathematical formulae—no problem in the image-based backfiles, but how could they be properly rendered in text-based current issues? There were also questions about standards; if JSTOR's publishers all adopted different mechanisms, JSTOR would have to take on the burden of ensuring interoperability. Additional staff with new capabilities would be required, but at this point JSTOR was far from mastering the digitization of backfiles, as we will see in chapter 7. Guthrie and Bowen feared the new line of work could not only fragment support for its backfiles initiative but, additionally, distract it from a sharp organizational focus at this critical early stage.[49]

As a result of these uncertainties, both strategic and technical, Bowen and Guthrie refocused JSTOR on backfiles. By mid-1996 JSTOR began "emphasizing its archival role; it does not endeavor to become a

[45]Kevin Guthrie, "The Development of a Cost-Driven, Value-Based Pricing Model," in Richard Ekman and Richard E. Quandt, eds., *Technology and Scholarly Communications.*

[46]Ira Fuchs, interview with the author, November 2, 2000.

[47]William G. Bowen, "UChicago Press," email to Kevin Guthrie, January 16, 1996. Bowen conceded as much to Chicago soon after. William G. Bowen, letter to Hugo Sonnenschein, March 6, 1996.

[48]Kevin Guthrie, "Meeting to discuss JSTOR and the University of Chicago Press," memorandum to William G. Bowen and the JSTOR file, February 29, 1996.

[49]Kevin Guthrie, interview with the author, February 1, 2000.

'publisher' of current issues."[50] For a young organization to retreat from an ambitious component of its initial plans is often difficult indeed. But pride of that sort would not have been helpful.

Despite this decision to focus attention on backfiles alone, JSTOR had signed agreements for current issues with the ESA, AEA, and APSA, yet it had not then developed the technology necessary to publish current issues for these organizations. According to William Robertson, during the period of time during which JSTOR had an appetite for experimentation, internal ESA problems prevented that organization from pushing JSTOR to act.[51] Then, each of the publishers developed online current issue strategies of its own, and their agreements with JSTOR consequently would lie dormant indefinitely. At some point in the future, if the market structure or JSTOR's place in it changed, these agreements could be brought back to life. But for the meantime, current issues would be connected with JSTOR only through external links that would not be operational for several years. (See chapter 14 for more on linking.)

Probably the main lesson to be drawn from JSTOR's experience with current issues in this period is the difficulty faced by a newborn organization attempting to take on two complementary, but not mutually dependent, projects. It may not have been possible to foresee that the goal of curating collections for libraries tends to cut against providing services to publishers. A more established organization might have developed the means to balance both.

If the young entity was reaching beyond its means in its detailed consideration of current issues publishing, the potential for savings and increased accessibility was great had its plans succeeded. Ultimately, by exploring this terrain, JSTOR reemerged with a far clearer sense of its mission. Moreover, the young organization learned more about its market and the publishers with whom it would have to work than it otherwise could have. By understanding the opportunities and challenges of the current issues business and the broader market structure, JSTOR was in a significantly better position to create a viable business based on the backfiles, as the next section, as well as chapter 8, will indicate.

CLOSURE, AND THE MOVING WALL

Stepping back from the ambitious plans for current issues was a gradual process. As JSTOR confronted publishers that were not interested, it continued to pursue them exclusively for the backfiles project, as we

---

[50]Packet for the JSTOR board of trustees meeting of June 20, 1996.

[51]William Robertson, interview with the author, January 17, 2001.

saw with Chicago and the history societies. Guthrie and Bowen worked to develop terms that could be offered to publishers with or without an additional agreement on current issues.

The plan for current issues had been for the JSTOR archive to expand annually by taking in the year's current issues. Bowen had referred to the separation between the current and the archival as the "moving wall" at least since mid-1995.[52] The notion that current issues would move into the archival database after some set period of time was not particularly controversial; if such concerns existed, they were subsumed within broader publisher concerns about online current issues.

But if at least some publishers were to participate only in the backfiles endeavor, would JSTOR end up being only a static database terminating in 1989? The pursuit of current issues had served to moot this question, but now it was back on the table. Would a database running only as far forward as 1989, growing increasingly stale each year, prove to be sufficient? JSTOR believed not, for both archival and business-model reasons.

With respect to the archival, we have seen time and again that JSTOR was determined to save shelf space for libraries. Bowen understood as early as the spring of 1994 that this implied an archival commitment: if libraries were to deaccession their journal backfiles, they would require a rock-solid guarantee from JSTOR that the intellectual content of the journal would be safe-guarded and accessible in perpetuity. (In chapter 2, we saw this concern for the first time, when Bowen insisted on perpetual rights and agreed to the JSTOR-B compromise that guaranteed them.) The JSTOR database would be ridiculous if it offered libraries the prospect of deaccessioning the old backfile, but required them to continue archiving the hard-copies going forward. To avoid an incomplete solution, JSTOR had somehow to ensure that each journal was archived electronically prospectively, as well. This was clearly a corollary of its core mission. JSTOR was beginning to search for a solution to what can be called "prospective archiving." In Guthrie's words,

> if you were going to address the [stack space] problem that JSTOR was supposed to address, you had to move the wall. Otherwise, libraries were just starting over and in twenty years they would have twenty years of content that a "JSTOR 2" would have to come along and take care of, and if you didn't address this on an ongoing basis, you weren't dealing with archiving at all.[53]

---

[52]William G. Bowen, "Thoughts on JSTOR and Issues to Consider," memorandum to T. Dennis Sullivan, Ira Fuchs, Kevin Guthrie, Richard Ekman, June 18, 1995.

[53]Kevin Guthrie, interview with the author, February 20, 2001.

This mission-driven concern synergized well with JSTOR's business-model needs. It had become clear, for reasons that are discussed in chapter 8, that it would be desirable for JSTOR to charge an annual fee in support of the ongoing work to keep its archive accessible online. But an archive that ended in 1989 and thenceforth became a year further out of date every year could never be judged to be compelling by libraries with scarce resources. Only if it were brought forward could it avoid becoming stale. Initially, adding current issues at the time of their publication had been the obvious fix. But with current issues put aside, at least for some publishers, how, then, to solve this dilemma?

The solution, which continued to be known as the moving wall but was rather different in effect, was novel. When the pilot agreements were negotiated in 1994, keeping the most recent five years offline seemed fair, to reassure publishers that JSTOR would not threaten their current issues subscriptions. Now, to maintain JSTOR's ongoing archival function, Guthrie and Bowen proposed that a year of each journal be added to the archive annually. This lag would allow JSTOR to expand its archive prospectively while clearly separating its archival responsibilities from the publisher's current issues responsibilities. This licensing provision, called the moving wall, allowed JSTOR to digitize journal issues going forward, so long as the publisher continued to participate, but without, JSTOR believed, posing a threat. Some publishers were not so sure.

While viewed as being significantly preferable to JSTOR becoming involved in the publication of current issues, the moving wall itself experienced publisher resistance. Conversations with the University of Chicago Press are, once again, unusually well documented, and illustrative of broader publisher resistance. We must keep in mind that, less than two years before, Chicago's resistance prompted the creation of the JSTOR-B agreement and, in late 1995, Chicago was deeply unhappy about the prospect of JSTOR undertaking online current issues. While this context is important, Chicago's arguments were logical and deserve attention.

At the end of February 1996, Guthrie and Fuchs traveled to Chicago, to meet with representatives of the press, including director Morris Philipson, journals manager Robert Shirrell, and technical coordinator Evan Owens. Probably because of all the prior interaction between Mellon, then JSTOR, and the university—including conversations between Bowen and University of Chicago President Hugo Sonnenschein—the University General Counsel, Art Sussman, was included in the meeting. According to Guthrie's minutes, the meeting largely "came down to pretty much a single point: the UCP wanted no part of the 'moving wall.'

They regarded this as moving into their territory."[54] And for good reason: in the increasingly inevitable shift to publishing current issues online, the press regarded current issues not only as its territory, but as exclusively so. Since JSTOR would pay to digitize the press's backfile, participation made sense. But going forward, since the press would eventually be creating the current issues itself, and since keeping the journals online indefinitely seemed to be only a marginal expense, why provide this content at no cost to JSTOR, when it might displace sales of the press's current issues? There seemed to be no incentive for Chicago to participate.

At this meeting, Guthrie faced a dynamic with which he would grow increasingly familiar: trying to distinguish commercial from scholarly incentives. He explained that the purpose of the moving wall was not so much to "control" prospectively but to take "responsibility" for archiving. He said that "libraries are very worried about the long-term archiving and protection of this information," which begat a small debate about whether a press or a third-party like JSTOR was the more appropriate repository. The press believed its long and prestigious history was more relevant; JSTOR believed that a mission-driven organization like itself was more appropriate. But most importantly, Guthrie moved the conversation away from commercial incentives and toward scholarly needs.

Today, third-party archiving is widely believed to offer the most assurance of perpetuity. Even large commercial publishers are working with mission-driven nonprofits to create archives, recognizing that the search for revenue can cut against an archiving mission. A number of universities have given consideration to whether they would be willing to become the third-party custodian for commercial electronic publications. Yet in 1996, JSTOR was blazing new ground in claiming not only to save space, but to constitute the most appropriate archival institution for this set of material.

In the end, the meeting with Chicago did not result in precisely the agreement Guthrie sought. Two options were left on the table. First, to leave things as they currently were, with 1989 being the fixed wall of JSTOR's archive. Second, to allow JSTOR to update its moving wall only until the University of Chicago Press began to publish current issues online. This second option gave JSTOR a moving wall, but only in the near-term. It was better than nothing but really not sufficient if JSTOR were to offer libraries a comprehensive archiving solution.

[54]Kevin Guthrie, "Meeting to discuss JSTOR and the University of Chicago Press," memorandum to William G. Bowen and the JSTOR file, February 29, 1996.

Reaching an agreement with Chicago was important. It was JSTOR's most important pilot publisher, if only because it contributed two journals, and it would be a waste of time if those journals—by now already digitized—were not included in JSTOR's public release. In addition, JSTOR could see that, in the future, many of Chicago's other journals could be key participants, and their absence would have negative consequences to the quality of the collection. Finally, Chicago was an extremely prestigious publisher whose participation would signal positively to others. So the very next week, Bowen traveled to Chicago to firm up the agreement. Philipson agreed to the second option, a temporary moving wall, in place until Chicago began its own online publishing program.[55] Trusting that Chicago would eventually come to share his view on the need for third-party archiving, Guthrie signed the license agreement.

Although a few publishers were unwilling to participate without some sort of fixed wall, these agreements included a guarantee that JSTOR would offer a backup archive if the publisher were no longer distributing recent materials online. Obviously, the specific form of the moving wall was less important than the inclusion of some sort of archival commitment. And the overwhelming majority of publishers willingly accepted the moving wall itself, recognizing that libraries benefited from the type of archival guarantee that JSTOR sought to offer. Several years later, the majority of the few fixed-wall agreements would be shifted to the standard moving-wall format. Without its willingness to offer this initial flexibility, JSTOR might have been unable to secure the participation of several key journals.

The moving wall was a key compromise, allowing JSTOR to provide prospective archiving services and thereby permitting libraries to become less dependent on their own archiving of paper journal issues. Although JSTOR was not to become a player in the provision of online current issues, the moving wall allowed its content to avoid becoming stale without putting competitive pressures on its publisher partners.

CRAFTING PUBLISHER AGREEMENTS

In the year after independence, the conversations between JSTOR and publishers were far from restricted to current issues and the moving wall, and they led to a far broader set of conclusions. At first, Bowen had imagined JSTOR focusing primarily on scholarly associations, to a lesser

[55] William G. Bowen, "University of Chicago Press," memorandum to JSTOR file/ publishers, March 6, 1996.

degree on other nonprofits like university presses, and not at all on commercial publishers.[56] His reasoning had been that the scholarly associations "generally publish the journal of record, and are in some sense
less profit-seeking than the university presses."[57] This was the model
under which JSTOR publishing current issues made most sense: unlike
the others, societies generally lacked the resources or expertise to embark on online publication themselves.

During the course of the 1995–1996 academic year, as Bowen and
Guthrie explored and then put aside current issues, JSTOR's plans came
to encompass many publishers beyond scholarly societies. In this time,
JSTOR worked with a limited number of friendly disciplines and publishers that, through negotiations for participation, could help JSTOR develop a standard set of appealing terms. But during this period, studies
of specific disciplines made clear the importance of journals published
by commercial and university presses, even in the arts and sciences.
Blackwell, Cambridge, Chicago, Johns Hopkins, and Oxford were some
of the most important players. To build a truly curated collection, it
would be critical to find a set of terms that would also appeal to these
and other university and commercial presses. And so in the give-and-
take of negotiations, JSTOR would attempt to develop the most appealing standard set of terms that would allow it to work with all publishers,
or at least the widest range possible. Rather than current issues, which,
if anything, would limit JSTOR's potential publishers, it sought the most
inclusive terms possible.

Later, negotiations with new journals became somewhat more routine, in part because JSTOR shifted into a mode of sustained effort to
sign specifically targeted journals for participation under a standard set
of terms. But at first, everything about JSTOR's relationship with publishers had to be carefully examined.

Basis for the New Agreements

The Mellon project had successfully assembled ten pilot journals, but
independence brought with it new complications for JSTOR. To reach
a sufficient breadth of arts and sciences disciplines, JSTOR would now
have to approach journals in disciplines outside of Mellon's core programmatic interests, disciplines for which it could not rely on Mellon's
long-standing partnerships with universities, their presses, and societies

[56] William G. Bowen, "JSTOR: Michigan Trip," memorandum, August 7, 1995.
[57] William G. Bowen, "Understanding of Things," memorandum to JSTOR file, November 28, 1995.

of their scholars. And there was no longer any uncertainty in the negotiations as to whether JSTOR's database would be made broadly available; for that was the new organization's entire purpose. To reflect these new realities, JSTOR created a new publisher agreement, completed in July 1996, that was different in many respects from those negotiated by Mellon for the pilot.[58]

There was never any reconsideration of the decision made in 1994 to digitize the complete backfile of each journal. As had been the case previously, the determination to save the most space with the smallest administrative effort meant that JSTOR intended to digitize the full run of a journal, rather than the most recent portion of the backfile, presumed to have the greatest utility to many researchers. This decision was largely noncontroversial; as was seen in the negotiations over the moving wall, publishers valued the most recent period of the journal backfile most highly. While many publishers might themselves not have chosen to digitize the full backfile, JSTOR's belief that its model saved money made the expense a moot point.

Under the pilot, Mellon paid for all the digitization through grants, and JSTOR intended to continue to absorb these costs. Participation would continue to be free to publishers. This principle was key in establishing JSTOR's position as the distributor of the titles of a carefully selected, curated collection, rather than as a service-provider for publishers seeking to bring their backfiles online. There might have been a place for a fee-based service provider (and some publishers would request such services from JSTOR), but curation was deemed to be an important part of JSTOR's mission.

But while publishers paid nothing, they would not receive any royalty fees from JSTOR. Mellon had not offered any royalties to the pilot journal publishers, a move that they accepted in the spirit of experimentation. With independence, JSTOR continued to oppose revenue-based publisher royalties. It continued to be the case that backfile sales generated relatively little revenue, and permissions revenues were also not great.[59] Its mission was to enable institutions to save money on their preexisting journal collections, which had been sitting in stacks that had generated no ongoing revenues for publishers. From this perspective, a royalty to publishers for JSTOR participation would give them ongoing revenues merely for allowing libraries to continue storing existing journals at lower cost. But JSTOR would eventually give access to its

---

[58]A copy of the license agreement, which is the principal source for this section, appears in the packet for the JSTOR board of trustees meeting of October 29, 1996.

[59]For publishers' sources of nonsubscription revenue (but little in the way of hard numbers), see Page, Campbell, and Meadows, *Journal publishing*, 205–39.

database to numerous libraries that subscribed to relatively few of the journals—libraries that, as a result, were getting access to these titles for the first time. And since some publishers did not have revenue streams resulting from subscription sales to such libraries, a legitimate argument could clearly be made that JSTOR should pay royalties for at least some of its participants to at least some of its publishers. But since paying royalties to publishers would add to JSTOR's expenditure-base and put upward pressure on its own fees to libraries, its leaders worried that they would diminish the possibility that the venture could, in the long term, break even. While JSTOR would retain its formal stance against paying royalties—a percentage of gross revenues—eventually it would offer payments to publishers once a certain revenue threshold was reached, as we shall see later in this chapter and again in chapter 14.

Another complication was that JSTOR now wanted to distribute its journals database to a much larger number of subscribers than during the pilot. In chapter 2, we saw how the JSTOR-B agreement was crafted to include the fifty-institution compromise intended to prevent the pilot journals from being used as anything more than an experiment. With JSTOR hoping to license its database to hundreds of American academic institutions, the cap had to be removed.

Asking publishers to accept no fees for the unlimited distribution of their backfiles, including a moving wall, was bold. There was no question but that some publisher revenues would be sacrificed, however small, perhaps even displacing some current issues sales to libraries that were willing to wait for an issue to cross the moving wall. Publishers' tolerance for risk would have to be rather high. The reason that the request made sense at all was that JSTOR's intentions were purely nonprofit in nature. Its primary audience was to be academic and other not-for-profit libraries. And it tried, in a number of ways, to request only the minimum rights required.

One example of reducing its needs was JSTOR's conclusion that it did not need to be assigned the copyright in the image files and searchable text that it created for each journal. In a departure from the pilot licenses, these rights could remain with the publisher, with JSTOR only receiving a license for their use.

Another example of offering flexibility to publishers was withdrawal procedures. If JSTOR were to save stack space for libraries, we have already seen that its archival commitments would have to include perpetual access to its journals. Yet it was impossible to obtain perpetual licenses from publishers. Consequently, the license explicitly permitted publishers to withdraw from JSTOR, but only under a predefined arrangement. If the publisher were to withdraw its journals from the archive, JSTOR could not license the electronic archive to additional libraries. But the most basic principles of archiving necessitated that JSTOR continue to distribute the backfile in its archive to each currently participating library in perpetuity. So even if the publisher were to terminate its participation, the license mandated that "JSTOR shall continue to have a royalty-free, non-exclusive, perpetual license to continue to distribute any information or images that it had previously captured, stored or distributed as part of a database prior to the termination."[60] In other words, a fixed wall would be put into place. But once a title was digitized, JSTOR could, within rigorously circumscribed limits, distribute it perpetually to its current user-base.

It is inconceivable that JSTOR could have been launched without perpetual rights from journal owners. An unlimited number of library participants might not have been absolutely necessary, though the ability to serve all of American higher education surely was. An expansion of the number of sites and perpetual rights to include the journals in its archive constituted the minimum changes that would be necessary for JSTOR to move beyond its pilot phase and establish itself as a going concern. But other provisions, such as the stand against paying publisher royalties, were very important and also carefully negotiated with publishers.

Sweetening the Terms

With independence, JSTOR could no longer rely on the leverage that the Mellon Foundation had brought to bear on the pilot titles and their publishers. While JSTOR was confident that it would play a positive role in the system of scholarly communications without hurting the business of publishers, it would have to convince them of this. And JSTOR was no longer offering an experiment, but an ongoing business relationship. In its earliest probes, some publishers were very enthusiastic, while others fell into a range between indifferent and in need of convincing to afraid and bordering on hostile. While JSTOR preferred to work with publishers who were ready to work with it, assembling only the lowest-hanging fruits would leave its archive an embarrassing disarray of uncurated titles.

To avoid such an outcome, Guthrie began testing a set of contractual terms that might be offered to those publishers most willing to join soon, as enticement for their participation. These terms were eventually packaged as the "Charter Publisher Rider," an agreement that was attached

---

[60]Packet for the JSTOR board of trustees meeting of October 29, 1996.

to the standard license. It contained two broad provisions, one to guard against negative effects and the other to share in any positive outcomes, which together were to guarantee that the effect on publishers of participating would be quite possibly rewarding, but at worst benign.

DOWNSIDE GUARANTEE

The first provision was the "downside guarantee," effectively a replacement of the broad promises that the Mellon Foundation had offered the pilot journals. As JSTOR transitioned to independence, Bowen had written of the need to "provide a safety net of some kind under the first few publishers for some limited period of time."[61] In the first half of 1996, responding to publishers' perceived needs, JSTOR's downside guarantee was developed to make amends for any canceled subscriptions or lost permissions revenue.

Many of the publishers did not have detailed revenue data, and they had no sense of the amount of permissions and backfiles revenue by year of publication. In the absence of such knowledge, the publishers had real fears that libraries' JSTOR participation would lead to subscription cancellations and other lost revenues. JSTOR could provide the guarantee because, as Guthrie wrote at the time, "we are not terribly concerned about the loss of subscriptions to current issues due to libraries' participation in JSTOR."[62] They did not believe that interlibrary loan would be an adequate substitute for subscriptions in the years before the moving wall brought new issues into the archive. From JSTOR's perspective, the improbability of canceled subscriptions made such a guarantee a risk well worth taking.

Consequently, JSTOR committed to paying publishers the value of any subscription cancellations attributable to their participation. In September 1995, Bowen envisioned the guarantee as focusing on individual, rather than library, journal subscriptions, though in the end it applied solely to library subscriptions.[63] (This shift may have come as a result of JSTOR's belief that individual subscriptions were often priced at marginal costs.) The formula calculated the rate of cancellation among nonparticipating libraries of JSTOR, contrasting this figure with the rate among JSTOR participants. If the latter were larger than the former, JSTOR would be liable for this difference. Bowen says that "it was maybe too complex, but the principle was right—that we were willing to hold

---

[61]William G. Bowen, "Thoughts on JSTOR and Issues to Consider," memorandum to T. Dennis Sullivan, Ira Fuchs, Kevin Guthrie, Richard Ekman, June 18, 1995.

[62]Packet for the JSTOR board of trustees meeting of October 29, 1996.

[63]William G. Bowen, "JSTOR and the Economics of Scholarly Communications."

people harmless for problems that we caused, but not for other problems."[64] By calculating the difference, rather than an absolute loss, JSTOR made an effort to separate its effects from broader market forces. Although the provision did not do this perfectly, it was a sufficiently good proxy. JSTOR smartly refused to insulate publishers from those broader market forces.

It would, however, insulate them from whatever effects it caused. If JSTOR participation harmed publishers, then JSTOR itself would suffer, in effect yoking its own interests to those of its publishers. By virtue of having been created to help libraries, there was some danger that JSTOR would consider their interests foremost. But with this provision, JSTOR did much to solidify its position between publishers and libraries in the scholarly community, making more concrete its claim to serve both sets of needs.

Compared with cancelled subscriptions, other revenue declines—such as the income that publishers received from ongoing sales of old journal issues—seemed more likely. These revenues amounted to a trivial source of funds for most potential publisher participants and may often have constituted a net cost.[65] Based on strong anecdotal evidence, JSTOR's leadership believed that backfiles never generated much money, and whatever they did bring in was most likely to be applied to warehousing fees. Although permissions revenues were nontrivial, they were not all that significant. The *William and Mary Quarterly*, for example, earned about $10,000 per year.[66] The University of Chicago Press had probably the most to lose (which may help to explain its caution). All seven of its journals that would eventually participate in the Arts & Sciences I Collection generated $63,038 in FY 1998,[67] with one particularly important title generating about $20,000 per year, of which about 90 percent was for articles older than five years.[68] Because the amounts were in general not great, JSTOR promised simply to make up any declines in these revenue streams, rather than attempt to determine the amounts specifically attributable to JSTOR.

In retrospect, the two components of the guarantee were extremely useful. They were very helpful in getting around a principal cause of publisher hesitance. And perhaps even more important, publishers rarely found it necessary to request payments. Indeed, only two publishers ever

[64] William G. Bowen, interview with the author, October 31, 2000.

[65] See Page, Campbell, and Meadows. *Journal publishing*, 216–18.

[66] Packet for the JSTOR board of trustees meeting of October 29, 1996.

[67] Richard E. Quandt, "Mellon Initiatives in Digital Libraries: 1994–1999," April 2002, Unpublished manuscript on deposit at the Nathan Pusey Library, the Andrew W. Mellon Foundation.

[68] Julia E. Noblitt, letter to Sarah Sully, May 22, 1998.

initiated the process, and of these two only one had losses that led to payment based on the agreed-upon terms.[69]

More long-term, Guthrie recognized that JSTOR might have, inadvertently, "facilitated this revenue loss" even while achieving its important goals. In what ways, he wondered, could JSTOR "help publishers move into other revenue producing possibilities and to move away from reliance on course pack revenue?" One thought was to allow publishers to use JSTOR to perform fee-based document delivery to libraries and scholars lacking JSTOR access. "It is our hope," he wrote, "that this will replace [interlibrary loans] to a large extent."[70] Another idea was individual access, in which publishers would offer subscriptions to their titles in JSTOR to their members (see chapter 12). Clearly, the leadership understood the importance of helping publishers find benefits from participating.

RETURNING ANY SURPLUS

Even the downside guarantee and related sweeteners were not enough for some publishers. They insisted that, even though their print backfiles were generating very little income at the moment, they could not sacrifice future revenues. JSTOR participation should therefore bring with it material gain. To balance JSTOR's hesitance to pay publisher royalties with the need for publisher participation, JSTOR decided in principle that some amount of its surplus, if any were ever generated, should be returned to publishers.

In JSTOR's earliest postindependence agreements, a simple mechanism termed "Net Funds Available" was utilized. After paying out all of its expenses, JSTOR would promise to return one half of the net to publishers and one quarter to libraries, retaining one quarter for its own further development.[71] Its remunerative responsibility only came into effect if there were any net funds available, effectively eliminating any risk from the provision. JSTOR was to take responsibility for the accounting work to determine the net. Guthrie explained to the board that this provision had been "difficult for publishers to accept," presumably because of uncertainties that the "net" would be properly determined.[72]

---

[69] Heidi McGregor, interview with the author, April 9, 2002.

[70] Packet for the JSTOR board of trustees meeting of October 29, 1996.

[71] William G. Bowen, "JSTOR and the Economics of Scholarly Communications."

[72] Minutes of the board of trustees meeting of June 20, 1996. Guthrie refers to such accounting maneuvers as the "classical Hollywood contract problem," in which a star is promised a certain percentage of the profits, and then the producer loads the expense side of the ledger so there appears to be no profit. Kevin Guthrie, interview with the author, April 11, 2001.

Once the business plan was put into place, JSTOR had a working break-even number, approximately $3.6 million in ongoing annual expenditures (see chapter 8). Revenues in excess of this figure were foreseen as surplus, and so once revenues grew toward this goal, some could be returned to publishers. JSTOR therefore created a "publisher pool," which would come into effect when annual revenues from libraries exceeded $2.5 million, or roughly two-thirds of the $3.6 milion in annual expenditures. At that point, JSTOR would begin paying out 15 percent of its annual operating revenues in a pool to publishers. This pool would be shared among the publishers in rough proportion to the number of journals that they contributed, and their length. The basic point remained that if JSTOR "makes a lot of money, the publisher gets a goodly share" for helping to support its mission.[73]

Generally, neither publishers nor JSTOR could see the point at which the publisher pool would actually deliver significant returns to the publishers. It was constructed more as a good-faith proposition to show that JSTOR would share any excess revenues than in the conviction that JSTOR would ever generate annual revenues at this level. As Guthrie would explain to publishers, there would be no enormous profit opportunities, for anyone, through JSTOR participation. If they chose to allow their journals to participate, it should be principally for nonfinancial reasons.[74]

Later on, JSTOR's break-even number was substantially revised (see the Conclusion). As a result, it would begin paying out "surplus" to publishers before its break-even had been achieved. Although for a number of reasons this circumstance did not cause major problems, it indicates that this "sharing" provision involved a real risk for JSTOR.

The publisher pool was later renamed "revenue sharing," and it was expanded from Arts & Sciences I to include subsequent collections as well (see chapter 14). But the downside guarantee was only offered to publishers for the first seventy-five titles. After that point, JSTOR had accumulated enough evidence that its effects would be, on balance, benign that it no longer continued this charter provision.

LIMITED COLLECTIONS GROWTH

In the year after independence, the current issues dilemma and the development of the moving wall and other standard license terms led

---

[73] William G. Bowen, "Thoughts on JSTOR and Issues to Consider," memorandum to T. Dennis Sullivan, Ira Fuchs, Kevin Guthrie, Richard Ekman, June 18, 1995.

[74] Kevin Guthrie, personal communication, September 24, 2001.

JSTOR to a clear articulation of its mission and its relationship with publishers. It is almost miraculous that, given everything else that Bowen and Guthrie accomplished during this first year, an additional eight journals (beyond the ESA's three) agreed to participate. These would form the nuclei of three new subject clusters—mathematics, political science, and population studies—in addition to strengthening the existing history cluster.

The strategy for signing these titles combined shrewd opportunism with a determined focus on high-quality, core journals. First, JSTOR approached those journals with sympathetic editors and publishers or via champions. JSTOR Board Member Cathleen Synge Morawetz was a professor of mathematics, and she pushed the organization to focus on this discipline. The mathematics journal that was signed in this first year, *Annals of Mathematics,* was published at Princeton, where Bowen had critical contacts. Mellon's Program Officer for Population, Carolyn Makinson, observed the ecology cluster that Robertson had been able to assemble, and she encouraged JSTOR to establish such a cluster for Population Studies. She championed titles published by the Population Council (a long-time Mellon grantee) and her alma mater, the Office of Population Research at Princeton. Finally, Hanna Holborn Gray was by this time chairman of the Mellon board of trustees and a prominent and passionate historian of the Renaissance. She was also a past president of the Renaissance Society of America, which published a major journal in the field, *Renaissance Quarterly*. Gray urged the RSA to participate in JSTOR. Later, Executive Director John Monfansi would describe JSTOR as having "enormous possibilities not only as a marvelous research tool and search file but also as a new form of publication of *RQ* and as a source of revenue."[75]

Each of these titles was an important core journal in its field and could be proudly considered to be a part of a carefully curated collection. It is clear, however, that the initial group of journals was selected because of introductions that were facilitated by these influential champions. But the strategy was not as ad hoc as it might have appeared. Bowen believed that every prestigious journal added made JSTOR more appealing to other publishers. Additionally, the introductions allowed Bowen and Guthrie to test its novel terms on friendly publishers, negotiating around any problems, rather than potentially causing unnecessary confrontations with relatively unknown publishers.

In addition to fresh negotiations with new journals, the JSTOR organization had to sign new agreements with the publishers of the ten

---

[75]Laura Schwartz and Sarah Covington, "Renaissance Society of America Council Meeting," *Renaissance Quarterly* 49, no. 4 (Winter 1996): 918.

pilot titles. These pilot publishers were also offered various drafts of the experimental agreements discussed above, and they helped JSTOR to work through possible problems. Most of these new agreements with pilot publishers were fairly straightforward, because the publishers were familiar with JSTOR and supportive of its broad goals.

SUMMATION

This chapter has covered the most important developments in the year following independence. By focusing JSTOR's mission on backfiles, creating the moving wall, and developing standard licensing terms, Bowen and Guthrie had put the new organization in motion. The obvious next step would be to write a formal business plan (see chapter 8). For some, the temptation to dawdle, to seek additional grant funding for further study and consideration, would have been irresistible, but Bowen and Guthrie had together avoided it. Less than two-and-one-half years after Bowen had his idea for journals digitization, and despite a number of setbacks, not only was JSTOR an independent organization with a pilot database available at a number of test sites, but it had carefully considered its mission and was preparing to embark on it in earnest.

Amid these major developments with long-lasting implications, the duo also signed another eleven journals. Progress here was less than desired and only came about with major help from outsiders. For JSTOR's publisher relations, the first year after independence was a period of experimentation and negotiation with publishers to develop strategy, rather than the production-level operation it would soon become. This first year, as will become even more clear in the next chapter, was a period of substantial strategic progress but of virtual stagnation in terms of operations.

CHAPTER 7

Operational Changes at Michigan

SEPTEMBER 1995–AUGUST 1996

IN NEW YORK, Bowen and Guthrie worked together, with only one JSTOR-specific assistant, on strategy and collections development. Guthrie took more responsibility for the operations at Michigan, where work was continuing on software developments, production, and user-services. With his engineering and software-development background, Guthrie was well positioned for this area of responsibility. But it was not yet clear how JSTOR and the university would work together, and as a result there were numerous problems in this period.

With independence, JSTOR would gradually begin to take owner-ship of the Michigan operation in a way that Mellon had consciously avoided. For Mellon, production and software development had been something for which a grantee—Michigan—had to take responsibility. But while Mellon was not focused on the specifics of the Michigan op-eration, independence brought changing responsibilities. Developing software and digitizing journals were two of JSTOR's core operations. As we shall see, the grantor-grantee relationship with Michigan, which JSTOR inherited from Mellon without modifications, proved to be prob-lematic for early efforts to expand its database.

But while examining a number of real flaws in this section, we should keep in mind the context. Guthrie and Bowen were working hard dur-ing the 1995–1996 year to determine exactly what JSTOR's focus should be: backfiles alone, or current issues, as well. Had JSTOR pursued the current issues strategy, it would have required a significantly different set of technology and production services than it eventually developed. As a result, Guthrie likely spent less time working with Michigan to de-velop its capabilities, since he could not yet be certain precisely what capabilties were needed.

THE IMMEDIATE EFFECTS OF INDEPENDENCE

When JSTOR was becoming independent, one obvious option was for it to internalize the functions that Mellon had outsourced to Michigan and DIT. But no one wanted to see an end to Michigan's role. Bowen had written of his presumption that "we [the new JSTOR organization] would continue to contract out most complex and expensive undertakings, such as bitmapping and scanning and software development and maintenance, to Michigan."[1] Although the pilot project had been making slow progress on digitization, Michigan's software worked well with the first scanned journals. Scanning quality was improving, and the university had agreed in principle to create a production operation. The partnership remained viable.

With JSTOR's independence, Bowen and Guthrie had begun discussing a goal of digitizing one hundred journals (although the deadline and plan for such an ambition would not be set until mid-1996, as we shall see in chapter 8). To reach such a goal, by whatever deadline, the operations at Michigan for software development and journal digitization would have to be scaled up. To do so, it was clear to Bowen and Guthrie that some changes would have to be made. During the spin-off, Bowen alerted the Mellon board to several "blips" at Michigan and of his plan to speak frankly about "their interests and our needs."[2]

Some of these "blips" were organizational in nature. Michigan continued to view JSTOR in relation to its strategic interests in digital libraries. Daniel Atkins, the dean of the School of Information, told Bowen that he hoped the university would offer digital library production services to a host of projects.[3] Eventually, Michigan would undertake a formal service, but for now it was useful for the university to learn more about digital library production services. Wendy Lougee, the co-director of the JSTOR-Michigan operation, recalls that she and Atkins and others were "looking for whatever would be useful in the way of [digital library] projects to ive us both experience and things we could leverage."[4] Randall Frank, the other co-director, did not believe that "if it succeeded, [JSTOR] should necessarily leave the university environment."[5] Despite these visions of offering a black-box solution to JSTOR, none of the staff or infrastructure was in place to do so. JSTOR needed a production-level operation imminently if it were to transform rapidly into an ongoing concern. Clearly, the university's long-term vision and JSTOR's near-term needs were in conflict.

Since the university did not have a production-level enterprise, but only grant-funded research staff, how, then, to achieve the desired re-

---

[1] William G. Bowen, "Thoughts on JSTOR and Issues to Consider," memorandum to T. Dennis Sullivan, Ira Fuchs, Kevin Guthrie, and Richard Ekman, draft of June 18, 1995.

[2] William G. Bowen, "JSTOR," memorandum to the Mellon Foundation board of trustees, July 31, 1995.

[3] William G. Bowen, "Meetings with Spencer Thomas, Gil Whitaker, Randy Frank, and Dan Atkins in Michigan," memorandum to JSTOR file, August 16, 1995.

[4] Wendy Lougee, interview with the author, December 13, 2001.

[5] Randall Frank, interview with the author, July 10, 2001.

sults? Guthrie wanted to end the grant-like system of "principal investigators," with the distance and hierarchy it tended to impose. Instead, he began to give more responsibility to Michigan staff such as Alexander, Aschenbrenner, Garlock, and others, supervising their work directly. The staff would have to transition from research and development to production. This made all sorts of sense for JSTOR, but direct interactions between JSTOR and the Michigan staff were problematic in at least two ways. First, it cut against the black-box production service that Michigan was working to establish. Second, it contradicted the understanding of the Mellon grants to the university. Just after the spin-off, Bowen had noted that "Michigan understandably views Mellon's support as a 'grant' not a 'contract.' As a consequence, they may resent our efforts to provide direction and make decisions."[6] It was only natural that feathers were ruffled. Bowen traveled with Guthrie to Ann Arbor in August 1995 to gauge the University's interest in working with a JSTOR it did not control.

At that point, he spoke directly with Atkins and Frank (Lougee was out of town). According to Bowen's trip reports, both were enthusiastic about continuing Michigan's work, albeit in a new role.[7] But their enthusiasm notwithstanding, the operations had to be improved. Both the production and the software-development arrangements were too ad hoc for a marketplace enterprise.

Production

In chapter 4, we saw that production was not proceeding with the high quality and efficiency hoped for by all. In April, Frank had proposed a quality-control operation, previously not believed to be necessary, but little progress had since then been made on setting it up. In mid-July, Bowen wrote that "we have some real reasons to be dissatisfied" with Michigan. He noted, among other things, that "no one seems to have a clear idea of what is being done by [the scanning vendor], on what schedule, how OCR is to be checked, what priorities should prevail, etc."[8] At any rate, the quality-control function had not yet been established. A month later, in an indication that these problems remained

---

[6] William G. Bowen, "Recent meetings and key issues," memorandum to JSTOR file, July 15, 1995.

[7] William G. Bowen, "Meetings with Spencer Thomas, Gil Whitaker, Randy Frank, and Dan Atkins in Michigan," memorandum to JSTOR file, August 16, 1995.

[8] William G. Bowen, "Recent meetings and key issues," memorandum to JSTOR file, July 15, 1995.

unresolved, he wrote that the quality-control work "absolutely must be" undertaken, "since our expectations for quality are and should be very high."[9] It was not until later, after Guthrie pushed Michigan to do so, that the QC operation was finally activated; other pieces would similarly take time.

In terms of expectations and accomplishments, Michigan staff believed that the scanning vendor had been the principal bottleneck. With DIT seemingly back on track, in early August Michigan staff informed Bowen that the vendor could digitize 50,000 pages per *week,* completing the ten pilot journals by the third week of September. DIT reported that it might be possible to accelerate even this schedule.[10] These projections were not just overly optimistic; they were simply unrealistic. For one thing, it would be discoverd that the number of pages in the remaining pilot journals far exceeded the 350,000 pages that Michigan and the vendor believed them to include. And it would be nearly four years before the scanning vendor's throughput for JSTOR even neared a 50,000-page-per-week rate. As we shall see later in this chapter and in chapter 9, major shifts in operating procedure (and an incredible amount of patience) would be required for these journals to be completely digitized—about six months later.

No one had any idea how to create a production process from the scattered (though heroic) work being done by the user-services librarians and the software developers. The proper structure to manage this nascent production process clearly had to be created. In July, Bowen had concluded that "there needs to be a single Project Manager for JSTOR at Michigan, if Michigan is going to continue to be a major partner."[11] This project manager would give Guthrie a contact at Michigan who was dedicated to JSTOR, someone to coordinate the work of the others and provide updates on their progress. During the August trip to Ann Arbor, Bowen and Frank concluded that the enterprise "had made [a] bad mistake in underestimating the difficulties involved in building the electronic file and indexing it properly. It has turned out to be a much more complex task" than expected.[12]

At that point, Frank selected his long-term colleague Spencer Thomas to take on the "project manager" function. Bizarrely, Thomas was not

---

[9] William G. Bowen, "Meetings with Spencer Thomas, Gil Whitaker, Randy Frank, and Dan Atkins in Michigan," memorandum to JSTOR file, August 16, 1995.

[10] William G. Bowen, "JSTOR: Michigan Trip," memorandum, August 7, 1995.

[11] William G. Bowen, "Recent meetings and key issues," memorandum to JSTOR file, July 15, 1995.

[12] William G. Bowen, "Meetings with Spencer Thomas, Gil Whitaker, Randy Frank, and Dan Atkins in Michigan," memorandum to JSTOR file, August 16, 1995.

solely focused on JSTOR, but continued to have half his time assigned to existing projects.[13] He was an experienced technologist who had taught computer graphics at Michigan, and his technical skills allowed him to begin working on the printer application and other programming challenges.[14] He would manage the technology staff and coordinate their work with that of JSTOR's nascent production staff and user-services librarians. He also oversaw Michigan's day-to-day interactions with the scanning vendor.

Aschenbrenner recalls that when she and Garlock showed JSTOR to Thomas for the first time, he examined the interface and carefully looked through the scanned materials. At last he said, "'There are lots of problems'. . . . It made us feel really good because we'd been telling people there were lots of problems. . . . not knowing if anybody was going to do anything about them."[15] Although Frank's suggestion of the need for a QC function had been in response to their concerns, its implementation had not followed. It was only after Guthrie and Thomas took on their JSTOR responsibilities that the quality-control group was established. First students, and then temporary workers, were hired to take on the tedious work under the loose supervision of Aschenbrenner and Garlock. Thomas worked with DIT and the quality-control group to try to improve the quality of the digitized journals.

Software Development

The production and digitization that Michigan undertook for JSTOR was started from scratch. It did not use existing organizational structures or processes. While initiating these structures and processes was difficult, at least JSTOR had the advantage of avoiding legacy arrangements. With software development, it was a different matter. Existing programmers working in existing organizational structures took on the task of modifying existing software for JSTOR. As a result, with JSTOR's independence, Guthrie treaded much more carefully in beginning to manage software development than he did with production.[16]

An early and obvious problem was Michigan's overdependence on part-time software developers for its JSTOR operations. Guthrie recalls the split time as being particularly difficult, especially since he was

[13]Ibid.

[14]Kevin Guthrie, "Meetings with Spencer Thomas and Gil Whitaker," memorandum to William G. Bowen, Ira Fuchs, and JSTOR-University of Michigan, August 16, 1995.

[15]Sherry Aschenbrenner, interview with the author, May 30, 2001.

[16]Kevin Guthrie, interview with the author, December 6, 2001.

remote.[17] Alexander and Peters only worked for JSTOR for 50 percent of their time, for a total of just one FTE of programmer time.[18] This was very little programmer support to begin with, and they were in fact spending much of their limited time on receiving datasets, quality control, and other nonprogramming tasks. Before Thomas arrived, these factors contributed to communications problems between Frank and programmers Alexander and Peters.

The organizational arrangements put into place after JSTOR's independence involved Frank and Thomas coordinating the software development in conjunction with Ira Fuchs. Guthrie was not involved and indeed recalls that "there wasn't clear direction from New York."[19] It would be over a year after JSTOR's independence—only after a group of programmers was hired at Princeton University—before Guthrie began to participate actively in technology management (see chapter 9). In a sense, leaving this to others was a relief to Guthrie, who was stretched beyond the breaking point focusing on current issues strategy and overseeing collection development and production. But it also frustrated him. He recalls that the list of near-term programming tasks never seemed to get shorter.[20] Scheduled deadlines for specific projects, such as a Windows-based printer application and the ability to locate the specific page on which a search term appeared, were frequently not met. (Deadlines, which are probably fated always to be problematic for creative work, are discussed again in chapter 9.) It was sometimes difficult for the programmers to work with other Michigan-JSTOR staff, who had JSTOR as their full-time agenda.

The presence of Thomas as project manager to coordinate both the librarians and the technologists was a major improvement. But it was only during the August trip that Bowen discovered a more fundamental problem. Frank "thought that we had only a one-year commitment to this project. . . . One has to give full-time people at least a two-year commitment [at Michigan]. I told [Frank] that we were committed to this project for the longrun."[21] Although JSTOR's assumptions had changed radically with independence, these changes had not been sufficiently communicated to Michigan, whose staff continued, understandably, to use the terms of the Mellon grants as the basis for decisions.

[17] Ibid.

[18] Kevin Guthrie, "Meetings at the University of Michigan, July 10, 1995," memorandum to William G. Bowen, Richard Ekman, Ira Fuchs, T. Dennis Sullivan, and the JSTOR file, July 12, 1995.

[19] Kevin Guthrie, interview with the author, December 6, 2001.

[20] Ibid.

[21] William G. Bowen, "Meetings with Spencer Thomas, Gil Whitaker, Randy Frank, and Dan Atkins in Michigan," memorandum to JSTOR file, August 16, 1995.

This affected all parts of the JSTOR-Michigan operation. Even Thomas, the project manager, only worked half his day for JSTOR. The programmers' inability to focus full-time on JSTOR made it difficult to set goals and deadlines. People were being "pulled in many different directions," splitting time between TULIP, the National Science Foundation's Digital Library Initiative, and other digital library projects, in addition to JSTOR.[22] Michigan had even built common office space for programmers working on all of its digital library projects. Were its mandate to conduct research, JSTOR could have viewed such arrangements as offering synergistic opportunities.

To an emerging marketplace operation, however, such arrangements were worrisomely inefficient. JSTOR needed committed staff if it were to thrive in the marketplace, a point of view that Guthrie and Bowen made clear to Michigan. Frank soon wrote a letter to Bowen outlining a budget and staffing plan through mid-1998, reflecting a shift to full-time staff.[23] In the fall, again on JSTOR's request, Thomas became its first full-time programmer.[24]

Overall

In the quarter-year following JSTOR's independence, Bowen and Guthrie had effectively altered the relationship between JSTOR and the university. Rather than making grants to Michigan and ceding operational responsibility, JSTOR was beginning to assemble a dedicated, if not completely full-time, staff of its own. It seems that this development was less by design than by default. Had the grant-like arrangements succeeded, they would have been retained. Had a black-box digital library service been available, it might have been utilized. But since they did not, and since it was not, a full-time dedicated operation was gradually established.

Similarly, although they were formally mentoring and supervising JSTOR's Michigan staff, Frank and Lougee became more sporadically involved. Guthrie worked on a day-to-day basis with the librarians and technologists, and he was their de facto supervisor. Although Atkins, Frank, and Lougee had all been enthusiastic for the university to provide production infrastructure for digital libraries, there was no existing capacity. Instead, JSTOR built capacity of its own at Michigan with the help of Frank and Lougee, building out from their initial

[22]Ken Alexander, interview with the author, June 14, 2001.
[23]Randall L. Frank, letter to William G. Bowen, September 14, 1995.
[24]Randall L. Frank, letter to Kevin Guthrie, October 10, 1995.

arrangements. Eventually, Michigan would create a Digital Library Production Service, but not in time for JSTOR to consider using it.

Instead of being part of a shared university digital library capacity, JSTOR's Michigan staff began to identify more and more with JSTOR, even though their paychecks came from a University bank account. This change in attitude did not result in a complementary change in organization. Consequently, as we shall see in chapter 9, the solutions we have seen here were imperfect. Instead, they were the minimum necessary for JSTOR to be comfortable in continuing its activities at Michigan.

MICHIGAN-BASED PRODUCTION

In the shift, by far the most significant change was the introduction of a formal production process. The quality-control staff was not a perfect solution, because it was only working with the digitized journals after the fact. Nevertheless, it was a major improvement. It allowed JSTOR to begin to fix problems in the database.

Guthrie was not alone in feeling frustrated that the initial digitization of pilot journals was a "checkerboard" of missing content. "Nobody knew what was what," recalls Guthrie, who saw no system in place to correct this confusion.[25] During one of his earliest trips to Michigan, in the summer of 1995, Guthrie's naïveté allowed him to ask a simple question: Wouldn't it make more sense to collect all of the journals in Ann Arbor before sending them to DIT? This, he thought, would allow Michigan to take count of what was being sent to DIT so that afterwards quality-control staff could ensure completeness.[26] Michigan staff and others immediately recognized that such a procedure would radically improve the production process. Indeed, it would allow them to develop a process for the first time—even if it would increase costs. Marshaling the journals in Ann Arbor allowed JSTOR to ensure that volumes sent to DIT for scanning would be adequate.[27]

A librarian, Debbie Woo-Ming, was added to the Michigan group and began this work. The examination of the hard-copies before shipment to DIT led to the end of the default practice of using surplus library

[25]Kevin Guthrie, interview with the author, October 30, 2001.

[26]Kevin Guthrie, "Meetings with Spencer Thomas and Gil Whitaker," memorandum to William G. Bowen, Ira Fuchs, and JSTOR-University of Michigan, August 16, 1995.

[27]For a subsequent overview of this component of production work, see Paul Conway, "Production Tracking," in Anne R. Kenney and Oya Y. Rieger, eds., *Moving Theory into Practice: Digital Imaging for Libraries and Archives* (Mountain View, CA: Research Libraries Group, 2000).

copies, because of their poor condition. Instead, JSTOR began to seek clean copies directly from the publishers. Even so, Bowen recalls the shared belief that publishers had detailed information about the publishing history of their journals as being a "simple-minded, naïve assumption."[28] If library copies were inadequate and publishers' warehouse copies insufficient, then a professional effort to ensure completeness was required. Although mint hard-copies were preferred, often library copies were the only ones available.

Even once the complete journal backfiles were obtained, Lougee wrote, "we would benefit from the type of volume preparation common in the preservation microfilming community—that is, checking on the quality of the physical volume beforehand."[29] Woo-Ming checked for pages that were missing, stained, or underlined, or which had writing in the margins. When she found inadequate pages, clean ones were scanned from a library copy at Michigan or elsewhere. In addition, Woo-Ming used special notations to alert the scanning vendor to the presence of images, fold-out pages, and other unusual contents that required special attention. She created a template to list all of the content of a journal, both to assist DIT in its own work and to speed Michigan's postdigitization quality-control.[30] This would come to be known as the "collation" process. As a result of these efforts, JSTOR's backfile of any given journal was more complete than probably any set of hard-copies on a library shelf.

Beyond this important physical preparation, JSTOR-Michigan began to undertake what became known as "intellectual" preparation. To alleviate DIT's problems with indexing, Lougee retained a skilled serials cataloger from the university library system, Tom Champagne, in the summer of 1995 to develop general indexing guidelines that would aid DIT in implementing EFFECT for the pilot titles that had not yet been digitized.[31] For each title, Champagne supplemented these general guidelines with specific rules for how EFFECT was to take account of journal-specific features. The goal was consistency across all of JSTOR's journals, but this consistency had to be responsive to journal variances. While Champagne's work did not solve all of the indexing problems, this preindexing work was a necessary step that produced substantial improvement.[32]

[28]William G. Bowen, interview with the author, June 26, 2001.

[29]Wendy Lougee, "JSTOR; Bowen Visit Background," memorandum to Dan Atkins, August 10, 1995.

[30]Ibid.

[31]Wendy Lougee, "Re: JSTOR help," email to Kristen Garlock and Sherry Piontek [Aschenbrenner], August 27, 1995.

[32]Wendy Lougee, interview with the author, May 30, 2001.

These preparation processes were put into place gradually, as procedural shortcomings were discovered. The process as described above was completely in place by February 1996, when it was presented to the board.[33] Developing the process was made substantially easier as a result of being located at a university library. At first, skilled Michigan librarians were hired on a part-time basis to handle the physical and intellectual preparation work. Although this led to some of the typical complications that part-time staff can bring, there was not yet sufficient throughput to justify full-time staff. It was this group, working with Lougee, Aschenbrenner, Garlock, and others, that developed many of the initial production procedures.

Although none of this Michigan-based production work was envisioned by the terms of the initial Mellon grants, Lougee recalls being eager for Michigan to take responsibility for it "as good experience for the university's burgeoning expertise in building digital libraries."[34] But despite the university's strategic involvement in such work, no one was monitoring the day-to-day operations of this developing team, with Spencer Thomas loosely involved from another location and Lougee receiving, at best, weekly progress reports. If DIT's datasets were delayed, there was rarely, if ever, an immediate JSTOR response. And in reality, very little had been digitized.

By January 1996—about a year since digitization work began, during very little of which was the production process in place—JSTOR had converted a total of about 600,000 pages, or around 50,000 pages per month. Only eight of the ten of the pilot journals were scanned.[35] These digitized journals were riddled with problems, as we shall see in chapter 9. And with a newly focused mission and increasing outreach, Guthrie and the JSTOR Board of Trustees expected a stream of journals to be signed in the near future. The group that had been assembled at Michigan to coordinate the digitization process, prepare the journals for it, and perform quality control on the digitized files, had completed work on most of the pilot titles, but its ability to expand significantly with limited coordination was dubious.

With this in mind, Bowen and Guthrie decided that this emerging "production" function at Michigan should operate coherently under one full-time leader, someone who could turn a group of individual processes into a goal-oriented, deadline-conscious operation and who would take responsibility for its success. Bowen, still actively involved as JSTOR Board of Trustees chairman, told Lougee that he would be in

---

[33]Minutes of the JSTOR board of trustees meeting of February 20, 1996.

[34]Wendy Lougee, interview with the author, December 13, 2001.

[35]Packet of the JSTOR board of trustees meeting of February 20, 1996.

Ann Arbor in a few weeks, so they could interview candidates together. Here is an indication of how centrally involved Bowen remained at this point—only after he interviewed candidates did Guthrie meet them. Lougee recalls the challenge of writing the job description for this position: "It wasn't clear in my mind whether we needed a librarian or whether we needed somebody who could understand workflow processes, a detail-oriented kind of person. Part of me said you needed a librarian because you needed someone who understood journals [and] their structure."[36] Ideally, they would identify someone with the background of a librarian but who was adept at operational management, an atypical combination of education and experience. Bill Landis, an archivist and a recent University of Michigan library school alumnus, was hired in February 1996 to begin the formidable work of turning the ad hoc assemblage of preparation and quality control into a streamlined process.

It is clear, with the pilot journals still incomplete, that JSTOR wanted to professionalize its production operation. Guthrie and the board were sufficiently concerned about it that they discussed accountability in the new unit. They concluded that Landis "reports to JSTOR" rather than through other Michigan staff.[37] Guthrie recalls distinctly that "he was hired with the understanding that JSTOR was directing his activities."[38] More so than software development, production and digitization was being brought directly under JSTOR's aegis.

Landis began to put into place a formal and consistent production operation. One component of this was to give much more attention to identifying potential scanning problems in advance. In June, Landis reported on some of the challenges of digitizing the *American Political Science Review*, the first title he supervised from start to finish.[39] First, the backfile set obtained by JSTOR was bound with programs from the society's annual meeting; a decision was made that these were not to be scanned. Second, Landis had to decide how to handle a related publication, *Proceedings of the American Political Science Association;* it would be scanned, but as a separate title. Third, the set of backfiles included some later reprints from which some advertisements had been excised; JSTOR would seek the original versions with the original advertisements. These challenges proved altogether typical of JSTOR's later experience, and they would eventually be treated as routine.

---

[36] Wendy Lougee, interview with the author, May 30, 2001.

[37] Minutes of the JSTOR board of trustees meeting of February 20, 1996.

[38] Kevin Guthrie, interview with the author, December 6, 2001.

[39] Bill Landis, "Report on production progress," memorandum to the JSTOR board of trustees, June 20, 1996.

Beyond this integral work to ensure that JSTOR met its promise to offer a "faithful replication" of each journal, Landis also took on the day-to-day relationship with DIT. Scanning operations became part of the production group's responsibility, allowing Spencer Thomas to be relieved of this duty so he could focus instead on JSTOR's technology needs. Coordination with the scanning vendor was especially critical for the quality-control group, which was in frequent contact with DIT about concerns and solutions.[40] Landis pushed for timelier quality control, examining incoming datasets without delay. Nevertheless, the 100 percent quality control on the *American Political Science Review* would take three months to complete.[41] Landis's frustration with quality control will be taken up at greater length in chapter 9.

SGML: AN EARLY QUESTION OF MIGRATION

In 1995, Mellon's decision for JSTOR to utilize a page-image format came under question. Although identified the year before as the optimal solution to the "faithful replication" and archiving concerns (see chapter 2), its efficiencies were largely limited to retrospective work. Although for some time, the page-image approach had been relatively common, digitization projects were beginning to take on prospective work. These prospective projects often adopted standards most appropriate for fulltext, such as SGML. With this newer technology more readily available, a number of JSTOR's partners began to question if the page-image format were truly necessary.

SGML would have brought a number of advantages. It would have permitted more robust searching than did page images combined with EFFECT. In addition, if both the JSTOR archive and the current issues were formatted in SGML, it would be far simpler to create a seamless and standard interface for the two. Because it is text-based, SGML could have reduced by a factor of fifty, compared with page images, the data to be transmitted from JSTOR's server to the user.[42]

On balance, many librarians would have preferred an SGML or other fulltext system. For those primarily concerned about intellectual access to collections, and less so about the necessity of faithful archiving of the

---

[40] Ibid.

[41] Kevin Guthrie, "Michigan Report (Part One)," email to Sarah Sully, William G. Bowen, Ira Fuchs, and Gilbert Whitaker, October 14, 1996.

[42] Kevin Guthrie, "Meetings at the University of Michigan, July 10, 1995," memorandum to William G. Bowen, Richard Ekman, Ira Fuchs, and T. Dennis Sullivan, July 12, 1995.

precise original page images, a fulltext solution would have been substantially preferable. Robert Kieft of Haverford told Guthrie just this in March 1996.[43]

At Michigan, the Humanities Text Initiative, led by John Price-Wilkin, proposed some use of SGML for JSTOR as early as March 1995. As prospective projects made greater use of SGML, it made sense to test its applicability on retrospective digitization. The quality of the searchable fulltext planned for JSTOR—at most one error in two thousand characters—made its archive a useful testbed for such work. And because of JSTOR's interest at that point in publishing current issues and bringing them together with its archive, an experiment seemed desirable. Price-Wilkin proposed applying SGML to the most recent five years of the backfiles of the pilot journals. For this test and the usage that would result, he hoped to learn about the cost of applying SGML as well as about usage differences between a page-image resource and the more robust searching enabled by SGML.[44]

In the wake of the test, Guthrie concluded that migrating JSTOR's archive to SGML would be too expensive to consider. In addition to the costs of applying tagging, there would have been increased digitization costs, since a higher accuracy rate would probably have been necessary—perhaps as high as one error in twenty thousand characters. JSTOR concluded that page images remained optimal.[45] Even had SGML not been costly to implement, it is difficult to imagine how SGML could be utilized to deliver the "faithful replication" promised to the journal publishers. But, Guthrie reflects, perhaps librarians' desire for SGML would have outweighed their desire for a faithful replication. Given JSTOR's subsequent emphasis as an archive, it is impossible to test the proposition. The expense mooted the question.[46]

Despite concerns at the time, the page images themselves seem not to have caused great concern to users subsequent to the public release. Dale Flecker of Harvard calls it "a reasonable solution given the nature of the problem" and a number of other librarians seem to concur.[47] But

[43]Kevin Guthrie, "Meeting with Librarians and Faculty from the Bryn Mawr-Haverford-Swarthmore Test Site," memorandum to JSTOR file, Library Services, March 5, 1996.

[44][John Price-Wilkin,] "Supplemental Proposal to the Andrew W. Mellon Foundation: Standard Generalized Markup Language Tagging," undated but given to William G. Bowen in March 1995. Kevin Guthrie, "Journal Storage Project Meeting," memorandum to JSTOR file, April 18, 1995.

[45]Kevin Guthrie, "Meetings at the University of Michigan, July 10, 1995," memorandum to William G. Bowen, Richard Ekman, Ira Fuchs, and T. Dennis Sullivan, July 12, 1995.

[46]Kevin Guthrie, interview with the author, March 25, 2002.

[47]Dale Flecker, interview with the author, March 13, 2002; Frank Conaway, interview with the author, March 22, 2002.

one downside was that the page-image architecture made certain types of article linking much more difficult, if not impossible. Even by the end of 2001, it continued to inhibit all planning to link dynamically from the articles in the JSTOR archive out to other sources. And some librarians viewed such linking as a key feature that remained lacking (and seemed unlikely to be implemented).[48] Librarians' calls for features that were certainly appealing, but sometimes mutually incompatible—quick download times, robust linking, low cost, unassailable archiving—led JSTOR to seek appropriate trade-offs.

INTERFACE DEVELOPMENT

During the 1995–1996 academic year, JSTOR and Michigan staff tried to anticipate user needs in improving the software and interface. Only toward the end of this period did JSTOR staff begin more actively to solicit the opinions of users at the test sites for the valuable perspective they could bring.

Before JSTOR's independence, almost all of the software development was for JSTOR and TULIP together. Mellon funds paid for the development of the web version and the "page of first match" feature for searches, both of which were incorporated into the JSTOR-TULIP software. Some additional Mellon-motivated priorities during the summer of 1995 were more challenging. A request to modify the treatment of abstracts—believed to be an important user concern—did not fit clearly within Michigan's plans for FTL development. And the suggestion that Michigan begin to test search engines other than FTL to see if they were more appropriate for the JSTOR database did not, understandably, meet with a great deal of enthusiasm.[49] This decision seems to have contributed, at least indirectly, to the decision, discussed in chapter 9, to establish a second location for software developement.

User-services librarians Aschenbrenner and Garlock began to work in conjunction with Guthrie and Thomas to design the interface. The four had a lengthy meeting in Ann Arbor during which they designed the essential blueprint of the JSTOR website and interface, a blueprint that would remain in place at least for the next five years.[50] Of significant importance, JSTOR retained a graphic design firm, Michael Mabry, to create a logo and other design elements that would be built into the

---

[48]Dale Flecker, interview with the author, March 13, 2002; Michael Keller, interview with the author, May 21, 2002.

[49]Randy Frank, "Re: JSTOR Technical Agenda," email to Ira Fuchs, July 25, 1995.

[50]Kristen Garlock, interview with the author, August 14, 2001.

interface. By the fall of 1996, JSTOR had one of the more visually appealing sites on the web, certainly of those with scholarly content.

JSTOR was, as expected, made available to the test sites, Bryn Mawr, Harvard, Haverford, Michigan, Swarthmore, and Williams. At Michigan, JSTOR's own user-services librarians could publicize the availability of the new database, while at the other sites local librarians publicized it in a number of different ways, such as library newsletters, instruction groups, handouts, and web pages. But despite the clear opportunity for JSTOR to receive significant feedback as it was revising its software and interface, in fact very little was spontaneously contributed.

In March 1996, when Guthrie traveled to Bryn Mawr, Haverford, and Swarthmore, he received months of pent-up comments and criticism. Perhaps most significantly, Guthrie spoke with several faculty members, most notably David Ross of Bryn Mawr, about their use of the database. Ross, an economist, would search the abstracting and indexing database EconLit to find articles of interest. He would not search JSTOR, because its list of economics journals was so much smaller (five versus about seven hundred). With a list of citations in hand, he would obtain articles from JSTOR or from hard-copy back files as appropriate. If in JSTOR, he browsed from the journal to the volume, issue, and table of contents to locate the article, rather than simply typing in the title and bringing it up automatically. At the time, Guthrie was surprised both by the use of EconLit and by the browsing approach. He noted that "this is the kind of feedback that is invaluable if we are going to have a system that truly understands the approach of the users."[51] In this case, Ross' method might have suggested linking EconLit to JSTOR, as the University of California had done with TULIP in order to achieve critical mass (see chapter 14).

Having discovered that some of the most important feedback at this prerelease juncture would not come if unsolicited, JSTOR began more actively to speak with its test-site contacts. Another nine test sites were added in the spring of 1996, and efforts were made to be more proactive. Aschenbrenner and Garlock were responsible for communication with the librarians and users, and they analyzed research needs and user habits so that software and interface design could better respond to real experience.[52]

<hr />

[51]Kevin Guthrie, "Meeting with Librarians and Faculty from the Bryn Mawr-Haverford-Swarthmore Test Site," memorandum to JSTOR file, Library Services, March 5, 1996.

[52]Sherry Pionteck [Aschenbrenner] and Kristen Garlock, "Report on User Services and Interface Development," memorandum to JSTOR board of trustees, June 20, 1996, included in packet for the JSTOR board of trustees meeting of June 20, 1996.

Although the design of JSTOR's front-end increasingly responded to user needs, there is little evidence that identified needs resulted in specific alterations in that period of time. They would be clearly responsive in the period after release, as will be seen in chapter 10.

SUMMATION

In this chapter and the previous one, we have witnessed JSTOR's significant progress in the key period between independence and the adoption of a business plan. Although JSTOR was not to publish current issues online, the moving wall provision would allow the database to grow every year and provide a comprehensive archiving service. JSTOR's identity as an archive of the backfiles of academic journals was established. With this strategic progress, Guthrie was in position to write up a thoughtful business plan, as we shall see in the following chapter.

While so much strategic progress was completed, tactical advance was of necessity held at bay during the critical first year of JSTOR's independent existence. The Michigan operation was, in some ways, struggling. It was something of a historical artifact, continuing to be managed at least formally as a Mellon grant to the University of Michigan even as JSTOR had increasing marketplace needs for a robust enterprise of its own. The digitization work had only just begun to represent a process, Mellon and Michigan having earlier failed to appreciate its complexity. And with a growing process, it seemed there was no one at Michigan, and in New York certainly neither Guthrie nor Bowen was, capable of managing its complex day-to-day operations. In this early period the operation made relatively little tangible progress, and so Bill Landis was hired to bring discipline to the process. Even under his leadership, there were struggles to complete the digitization of the *American Political Science Review* and a number of other titles, struggles that only confirmed the difficulties of scaling up the production operation to meet even the limited progress being made in publisher relations.

Progress in other areas was if anything more stunted. Certainly in the first months after independence, JSTOR did not make sufficiently clear that it was committed to a long-term, full-time staff. It also had difficulty indicating that it no longer viewed software development as a grant project to find new uses for DIRECT/FTL. While Thomas would help to focus the group on JSTOR's own needs, this was a gradual shift. Finally, the user-services librarians were not granted sufficient authority to do their work until mid-1996. The evolution of these groups had clearly begun, but only just.

The conclusion of strategic planning for publisher relations put JSTOR in position to commence production-level operations. But before doing so, the JSTOR board of trustees would begin to consider how to distribute the database commercially. Even as it would settle on JSTOR public availability by the beginning of 1997 (as we shall see in the following chapter), it could not help but be concerned whether the production operation would be capable of rising to the challenge. With the publisher-relations operation picking up speed and the production team under a new and unproven leader, we will now turn to Guthrie and the board, who were working to develop a business plan that could enable the developing organization to become self-sustaining.

CHAPTER 8

Developing a Business Plan

JANUARY–DECEMBER 1996

IN THE EARLY SPRING of 1994, JSTOR had been little more than an idea in Bowen's mind. None of the pilot journals had yet been approached, let alone signed, and major strategic and organizational choices were only just being considered. Nevertheless, Bowen was already thinking about how JSTOR, once fully deployed, could become self-sustaining. The attention given to this principle, and the care taken in its implementation, were inextricably linked to the archiving mission and led directly to JSTOR's initial success and future growth.

Over the course of the year that JSTOR was a Mellon grant project, Bowen developed several principles. For example, pricing should not exceed marginal cost to any substantial degree;[1] and, if possible, JSTOR should be available everywhere on the campus network of a subscribing institution.[2] But in addition to such principles (discussed below in greater detail), Bowen was most concerned to find revenues. JSTOR's promised cost savings notwithstanding, would any library holding these journals be willing to pay an ongoing fee for backfiles that it already owned in print form and that seemed to cost nothing once deposited in library stacks? The decision to spin JSTOR off from Mellon, in the summer of 1995, reflected the belief that they would.

Why were such revenues required? It was not always recognized that the economics of a digital archive must be fairly similar to the economics of a traditional library. "Information wants to be free" was only the foremost of the mindless aphorisms suggesting that one need not budget for ongoing costs.[3] In reality, both traditional libraries and digital archives

---

[1] William G. Bowen, "JSTOR," confidential memorandum to JSTOR file, March 7, 1994, 2.

[2] William G. Bowen, "Thoughts on JSTOR and Issues to Consider," memorandum to T. Dennis Sullivan, Ira Fuchs, Kevin Guthrie, Richard Ekman, draft of June 18, 1995.

[3] Fred Shapiro traces this phrase to Stewart Brand, who reportedly said it at a 1984 Hackers Conference. Reported in Katie Hafner, "A New Way of Verifying Old and Familiar Sayings," *New York Times*, February 1, 2001, G8.

Although the phrase itself may often have been used with an understanding of the challenges it brought, others have clearly embraced the notion that permanence can always be later assured. One example among many is the case of Stephan Harnad, who has asserted that "tomorrow will take care of itself" in urging authors to post their scholarly

entail substantial ongoing costs for maintenance and preservation.[4] Clearly, an ongoing operation, even if it added no new materials, would require an ongoing stream of revenue to keep it accessible online. Where would JSTOR find the revenues to pay these ongoing costs?

PROBLEMS AND PLANNING

In chapter 1, we saw that by the early 1990s, libraries were pressed for funds and unable to support historic levels of collecting. At libraries that already owned the journal backfiles in print form—those that stood to save space—JSTOR's archive would surely seem duplicative. In 1995, Bowen suggested that, if the backfiles to be digitized were linked to current issues, "libraries might subscribe regularly [to the package], with a stream of annuity income, since there will be new issues each year."[5] In these early days, Bowen envisioned a JSTOR packaged by title, with backfiles bundled in "for free" (really for a modest charge) with a subscription. Subscribers would perceive the fee as paying for the current issues. With the pricing structure somewhat obscured, libraries would continue to subscribe to journals and JSTOR would have a steady revenue stream. This cannot have been far from anyone's mind while pursuing current issues.

More than a year later, on a trip to Ann Arbor just as JSTOR was gaining its independence, Bowen met Michael Lesk, who was directing the National Science Foundation's digital library work. Lesk asserted that libraries would want to "own" the electronic files that made up JSTOR, since that was how they had traditionally taken on their archiving role. Bowen agreed with Lesk's logic. In writing up the minutes of his trip to Ann Arbor, Bowen wondered "How to reflect such an arrangement in charges?" He reflected that

> one thought would be to charge libraries a basic one-time cost for obtaining permanent access to a basic file from, say, 1990 back to inception. These files could be made available to them on CD-ROMs [as a backup, in addition to Internet availability], if necessary. Then, we would be able to add

---

articles online and put aside "needless worries about permanence and preservation." Stephan Harnad, "Re: PostGutenberg Copyrights and Wrongs for Give-Away Research," email to CNI-COPYRIGHT Listserv, June 22, 2001, online at *http://www.cni.org/Hforums/cni-copyright/2001–02/0598.html*.

[4]Donald Waters and John Garrett, *Preserving Digital Information: Report of the Task Force on Archiving of Digital Information* (Washington, DC: The Commission on Preservation and Access, 1996).

[5]William G. Bowen, "Notes on JSTOR," memorandum, April 2, 1994.

"units" to this owned back file in, say, five or ten-year units. Meanwhile, they would pay a current fee, in effect a license fee, for access to the current issues.[6]

This is the earliest documentation of what would become the split fee, more about which below. But just days later, Bowen had changed his mind, perhaps after speaking with some publishers. It would be best, he now wrote, for current issues pricing to be entirely distinct from the archive pricing.[7] Under this new approach, which of course was not pursued, Bowen did not explain how to get libraries to pay an ongoing fee for the archive.

As late as the end of 1995, JSTOR considered offering libraries the choice between acquiring "permanent" rights to the archive with an associated upfront fee and in essence leasing it.[8] One advantage of such a plan would have been to allow libraries to pay for archiving—or not—depending on their mission. In the print world, probably about one hundred of the major research universities plus a handful of the wealthiest liberal arts colleges enumerated archiving as part of their mission. While it was not a far stretch to view the others as receiving many of the benefits of archiving without paying for them ("free-riding"), there were few calls to change this system.[9] Under this first JSTOR proposal, the archivers could have obtained permanent rights to the JSTOR archive, while all other libraries could have leased it, roughly maintaining the existing system.

But JSTOR's leadership believed, accurately, that a far broader cross-section of academic libraries held its journal titles and therefore stood to save space from an electronic archive of them. Surely, it seemed, they should be compelled to contribute toward those costs. So the lease option was eliminated. In other words, all participants would contribute in some measure to the costs of archiving, even when their missions had previously focussed on building ever-changing working collections. While there is no evidence that the broader effects of this decision were

[6] William G. Bowen, "Meetings in Michigan on Tuesday, June 6th," memorandum to JSTOR file, June 7, 1995.

[7] William G. Bowen, "Thoughts on JSTOR and Issues to Consider," memorandum to T. Dennis Sullivan, Ira Fuchs, Kevin Guthrie, Richard Ekman, June 18, 1995.

[8] William G. Bowen, "JSTOR and the Economics of Scholarly Communications," speech to the Council on Library and Information Resources, Washington DC, September 18, 1995; revised version online at *www.mellon.org/jsesc.html*.

[9] Many academic libraries, as well as virtually all public libraries, have benefited greatly from the archivers. Even though they do not maintain their holdings perpetually, the non-archivers can ILL virtually anything from the archivers at any time. To do so, they pay only the direct cost of the loan (sometimes not even that), and contribute nothing toward the cost of acquisition or the capital and operating costs of archiving.

understood at the time, we can see in retrospect that this constituted a cost shift from those libraries that traditionally were archivers to those that would be contributing to the costs of archiving for the first time. Preliminary evidence indicates that, by making available only the "archive" licensing model, JSTOR may have been able to reduce the free-rider problem with relatively little pain even to the non-archiving libraries (see Conclusion).

These memos illustrate how tenaciously JSTOR's leadership sought to develop a business model. Whether through current issues or, as we shall see, other arrangements, viability was a major topic of consideration. The challenge of bringing JSTOR to sustainability was never far from Bowen's, and later Guthrie's, mind.

The challenge of viability became only more pronounced as the evidence continued to mount (incorrectly, as it turned out) that researchers would not use JSTOR very much. Evidence from the multicampus University of California system indicated that the TULIP database had not been used all that much.[10] From its earliest days as a pilot project, some critics thought that JSTOR was focused on the wrong library materials. It had always been assumed that the backfiles of print journals received only a trivial amount of use, and so perhaps scarce digitization funds should instead be directed at library collections that were in higher demand. In response to the skeptics, Bowen wrote, "We shall see. In any event, even if usage is modest, JSTOR should have major implications for library storage."[11] Clearly, however, it was critical to obtain good usage statistics to answer a key question: were journal backfiles sufficiently well used that libraries would want to pay money for online access to them? There was also the longer-term, but highly related, question, does online access lead to increasing levels of usage?

In their hard-copy format, there was a dearth of good information on the usage of the backfiles of core journals. Although citation analysis documented that the value of such backfiles to scholarly research was enormous, anecdotal evidence suggested there was very little usage in the aggregate. For one thing, there were few access points for the student or new researcher. Indexing services generally dated back only a few decades, providing no point of entrance to the earliest literature. Another possible access point was by following footnotes, an incredibly useful but onerous affair most readily available to experienced

---

[10] Only 2,447 views and 929 prints were reported. Mark Needleman, "TULIP at the University of California, Part I: Implementation and the Lessons Learned," *Library Hi Tech* 12, no. 4 (1995): 70.

[11] William G. Bowen, "The Foundation's Journal Storage Project (JSTOR)," in *Report of the Andrew W. Mellon Foundation 1994* (New York: Andrew W. Mellon Foundation, 1995), 30.

researchers. In general, the anecdotal evidence of low usage was over-whelming.

To document these anecdotes, Michigan implemented a study at the test sites.[12] Aschenbrenner, Garlock, and Lougee designed a simple survey of hard-copy journal usage. Slips were placed in each bound volume, asking readers to note that they had consulted the volume. Although their system inevitably resulted in undercounts, it was seen as more effective than any alternative. Circulation records or even hand-counts by reshelvers would certainly have resulted in undercounts of their own.[13]

Of the five test-site libraries that were studied, it was unsurprising that Michigan, a huge research university, tended to have more uses per journal than the liberal arts colleges, Bryn Mawr, Denison, Haverford, Swarthmore, and Williams. During the months of the study, the journal receiving the most use was the *American Economic Review*, which showed a total of 132 uses of its entire backfile, nearly half of which were recorded at Michigan (57). These data were broadly indicative of use as it would eventually be manifested in electronic form, although not to scale: the *AER* would be used more than other pilot journals, and research universities would account for a very high percentage of use. But the scale of usage indicated by this survey was shocking, and perhaps a bit disconcerting, for those trying to predict revenues. Even if the survey had failed to count 75 percent of uses, journal backfiles were not used very much.[14]

The indications that arts and sciences journal backfiles were little-used probably underscored JSTOR's attention to the ability of a participating library to free up space and eventually save money. Yet in the early transition to independence, Gilbert Whitaker shared an important, sobering concern with Bowen and Guthrie about JSTOR's ability to generate revenues under this model. As Michigan's provost, Whitaker strongly endorsed the application of technology to find efficiencies, but he worried that it would prove difficult to turn JSTOR's value into a viable business model. In many academic budgets, including Michigan's,

---

[12] William G. Bowen, "Meetings at the University of Michigan," memorandum to JSTOR file, March 20, 1995.

[13] [Sherry Aschenbrenner, Kristen Garlock, and Wendy Lougee,] "Recommended Methodologies for Measuring Use of the JSTOR Target Journals in Print Format" [undated].

[14] Especially for the economics journals at Michigan, there is reason to think that the undercounting may have been serious. Most of the economics faculty members and graduate students would most likely have used a separate departmental library for their research in these journals.

the money saved in construction would accrue to a capital fund, and general budgeting practice suggested that it would therefore save no money for the library budget. But the participation fees would in all likelihood come from the library budget, leading to the following question. If the collections budget would accrue none of the savings that JSTOR generated, why would a librarian spend from that budget to save money for another part of the university? For economists, this was the classic problem of externalities. For JSTOR, this meant that it might be difficult to convince libraries, especially at state universities with less flexibility in their capital budgeting, to participate. In his memo of the meeting, Guthrie agreed that he did "not think these sales are going to be easy."[15]

Between this concern and the exploration of current issues, Bowen and Guthrie did not pursue the development of a business plan immediately after independence. By early 1996, the initial ten pilot titles were finally online, and costly production work was beginning on subsequent titles, with the grants from the Mellon Foundation to Michigan funding the work. With Mellon grants to JSTOR and to Michigan paying all of the costs, there was no immediate need for JSTOR to focus on other sources of revenue. And until current issues strategy was set, there was no way to do so.

Guthrie's study of the New York Historical Society had demonstrated, if nothing else, the importance of establishing a realistic financial plan before undertaking any new work, even as a nonprofit. "During the planning process," wrote Guthrie, "nonprofit leaders need to think less in terms of what their organization *must* do and more in terms of what they realistically *can* do."[16] With this in mind, current issues had been ruled out of scope, and the mission was focused on backfiles (see chapter 6). Now it was appropriate to undertake a planning process for backfiles, to put into place a viable business plan to focus, clarify, and rationalize their efforts to digitize and then distribute them publicly.

Guthrie presented initial thoughts to the JSTOR Board of Trustees in February 1996, and then took the board's reactions into account as he developed the Strategic and Operating Plan.[17] Thus, Guthrie spent months in the first half of 1996 working with Bowen to craft the details of such a business plan, with DeGennaro ensuring that library assumptions were reasonable. Guthrie submitted the Strategic and Operating Plan to the board on June 13, 1996. It is probably JSTOR's most important

---

[15]Kevin Guthrie, "Meetings with Spencer Thomas and Gil Whitaker," memorandum to William G. Bowen, Ira Fuchs, and JSTOR-University of Michigan, August 16, 1995.

[16]Guthrie, *The New-York Historical Society: Lessons from One Nonprofit's Long Struggle for Survival* (San Francisco: Jossey-Bass Publications, 1996), 176 (emphasis in original).

[17]Packet for and minutes of the JSTOR board of trustees meeting of February 20, 1996.

document, and the time of its creation was a critical defining period for the newborn entity. It came right on the heels of the decision to focus on backfiles, when it became clear that self-sustainability would have to be achieved based on that business alone, without using current issues as a crutch. The plan eloquently set forth how a self-sustaining organization could be created from such a seemingly obscure product. Although the financial projections focused exclusively on the Arts & Sciences I Collection, the basic model would later function well for subsequent collections (see chapter 14). The board would take an active role in refining the document, but left in place all of its basic principles. And while the model has, as a matter of course, been refined somewhat, most of its assumptions and principles would prove to be remarkably robust.

FOCUSING THE MARKET

An early and critical decision was to choose the organization that would take responsibility for marketing the database and licensing it to subscribers. At JSTOR's independence, Bowen assumed individual publishers would take on this responsibility, just as they were responsible for selling current issues.[18] This was yet another example of searching for preexisting solutions, in the form of marketing and sales. Such an arrangement would have allowed current issues and the backfile to be available from the same source. JSTOR would have focused on software and production as a vendor to publishers, a fairly passive service-provider instead of an active agent in crafting a product.

Several times, the JSTOR Board of Trustees gave consideration to arrangements by which publishers would market the backfiles of their own titles, but such proposals would always be successfully resisted (see chapter 11 for the analogous case regarding *Science*). In this case, JSTOR decided that it preferred one organization—itself—represent the entire collection to the library world. There are many reasons why this makes good sense. Imagine if libraries subscribed to the *American Economic Review* and received access to a package of every issue from volume one to this month's. In that case, for a library to obtain the backfiles of every Arts & Sciences I title would, we can see in retrospect, have required arrangements with each of sixty-eight publishers. Even if all of these backfiles sat on JSTOR's server in JSTOR's format—and it is by no means clear that they would—the price to libraries would likely have been much higher. Prices would have been higher as publishers tried to

[18] William G. Bowen, "Thoughts on JSTOR and Issues to Consider," memorandum to T. Dennis Sullivan, Ira Fuchs, Kevin Guthrie, and Richard Ekman, draft of June 18, 1995.

recoup their investments in the digitization, for which they would not likely have received grant funding. Three shortcomings would have resulted. First, the backfiles would have been distributed to a smaller selection of libraries. Second, libraries might not have viewed such an arrangement as having archival potential. Third, the ability to search across a massive database of arts and sciences journals might well have been lost.

Instead of such a seemingly sensible but hopelessly fragmented situation, Guthrie, Bowen, and the rest of the JSTOR Board of Trustees took a calculated risk. They marketed all of the titles under the JSTOR "brand name." This key decision had a number of important effects.

First, it enabled all of the journals to be licensed by a large number of libraries at a smaller overall price. Grant funding, the majority of which came from Mellon but a not insubstantial amount of which would eventually come from other sources, paid for a significant percentage of digitization costs. It would probably not have been possible for hundreds of publishers to attract grant funding, and in any event scale-effects would have been lost.

Second, JSTOR's decision to work for libraries rather than for publishers has allowed the system of scholarly communications to prioritize more effectively those backfiles to digitize. Rather than publishers making their own impulsive decisions as to whether their backfiles should be digitized, collections were carefully curated. JSTOR, attempting to represent the choices of libraries and scholars, targeted the most sought-after disciplines and titles. Of course sometimes there were challenges in collections development, but JSTOR rejected more journals requesting to participate than it wooed unsuccessfully. The large number of libraries that would eventually participate is an indication of overall satisfaction with a resource that was curated.

Finally, in building a curated collection that is agnostic toward individual publishers, JSTOR allows for cross-searching by discipline rather than by publisher. The need to structure scholarly resources in this way was identified as key in the *TULIP Final Report*. There, Elsevier reflected that its impressive selection of materials science titles was nevertheless insufficiently deep for research purposes.[19] JSTOR's coherent collections were one answer.

Although JSTOR's pilot phase had been observed with interest beyond America, and indeed beyond academia, it was initially created with the purpose of serving American academic libraries. With only Guthrie and one other central office staff member, even addressing the

---

[19]Elsevier Science, *TULIP Final Report* (New York: Elsevier, 1996).

U.S. market was an ambitious goal. And it seemed best to demonstrate success in the United States before testing more uncertain waters. If revenues from the U.S. market could recover all costs, markets later added would allow prices to be effectively lowered for American libraries (see chapter 14). This conservative approach was intended to guarantee, to the extent possible, JSTOR's financial health and long-term viability.

Part and parcel of its initial focus on American academia was JSTOR's choice to license its database only to libraries, and not to individuals. Initially, Guthrie had been skeptical that there would be sufficient library demand to recover costs.[20] He made calculations suggesting that focusing on individual, rather than library, subscribers could yield a great deal more revenue.[21] Others entering this market, such as Questia, seem to have reached similar conclusions. But that involves predicting demand for fee-based resources that continue to be available at no charge to individuals in print format in libraries. This may have led both Guthrie and Questia to estimate demand by individuals in ways that were overly optimistic. Besides, JSTOR was not attempting to maximize revenues, only to break even. And if JSTOR was intended to save money for academic libraries, it made most sense that they should shoulder the costs.[22] Fuchs and other members of the board were, for a combination of reasons, led to dispute Guthrie's reasoning. This was one of the first of many cases—the organization was less than a year old—in which a board meeting provided for carefully working through a problem. Whereas many other boards function more as a rubber stamp, JSTOR's trustees constituted a working, as well as a governing, group. In this case, the conclusion pushed JSTOR away from individual subscribers and toward libraries. In focusing on under one thousand potential customers rather than millions, JSTOR was able to direct its marketing toward professional purchasers of scholarly information, rather than having to devise strategies to appeal to an underinformed audience of millions.[23]

---

[20] Kevin Guthrie, interview with the author, March 25, 2002.

[21] The idea would be to limit accessibility to the building itself, rather than making it available throughout the campus network. That way, faculty and students who wanted desktop access would pay an additional fee. While such an arrangement would have made JSTOR less convenient for many researchers, it would have lowered the fee to libraries. Kevin Guthrie, interview with the author, March 25, 2002.

[22] Of course, had Guthrie successfully implemented this type of individual access, costs would have been shifted away from library budgets—no small accomplishment.

[23] By contrast, Questia spent millions of dollars to market its database in television and radio advertisements and in personal outreach on college campuses. These modes

"BY-THE-DRINK" PRICING?

Although, in retrospect, JSTOR's leadership views the decision as obvious, their rejection of usage-based rates was also a critical move. In their first incarnations, many digital academic resources utilized a fee structure that varied directly with usage. Compared with unlimited pricing, usage-based rates have the inevitable effect of limiting use of the resource. In the electronic world, usage pricing can have variants, including "connect time," which made the most sense when, before the widespread availability of the Internet, a modem connected a user directly to the resource. With each resource having a limited number of modem ports, charging for connection time was an effective way to ration this scarce resource. Sometimes, libraries passed along these usage fees to their readers, but often they simply accepted the budgetary uncertainty as to how much, say, Lexis-Nexis would be used. At times, this posed problems for library budgets.

This was precisely the way document delivery operated. Several players had entered the field of document delivery, believing that they could offer on-demand journal articles when institutions lacked the journal locally. As the serials spiral forced increasing journal cancellations, this industry seemed poised for major success. Its limitation, though, was its business model. Although, like JSTOR, a document-delivery company could provide speedy (overnight) access to a desired journal article, it might cost $30 per article. As a result, every use of document delivery had to be weighed against the cost. In scholarly research, when much of the reason for seeking any given article is not the certainty that it *will* be useful, but rather the sense that it *might* be so, the prices were prohibitively high. That is, the value to a scholar or student of receiving an as-yet unread article was rarely, if ever, $30. As a result, higher education generally shunned the document-delivery firms, preferring the lengthy wait of inefficient interlibrary loan procedures in which the costs were often absorbed by the institutions (even though the cost, when teased out of each transaction, was shown to be about the same).

From the very beginning, JSTOR's leaders were adamant that they would not charge individuals on a per-use basis. Bowen's dismay at the commodification of scholarly communications was one of his driving concerns from JSTOR's earliest days. In several 1994 conversations, with Doug van Houweling of Michigan and Jim Roemer of UMI among others, Bowen confirmed that "transactional, or time-based, pricing

---

of marketing may have worked against its desire to be perceived as a serious scholarly resource.

[was] the traditional model, and subscription [i.e., unlimited usage] pricing the way to go."[24] Bowen has since then written that "to charge for journal literature 'by the drink' can lead to results that are far from optimal socially. . . . It would be undesirable, from the standpoint of resource allocation, to discourage an impecunious student from using JSTOR because of a per-use pricing model."[25] Usage-based pricing for libraries placed librarians in the counterintuitive (and undesirable) position of hoping that resources would not be used too much, even though they were selected precisely for reader use![26] If paper backfiles could be used seemingly without limit, while each additional use of JSTOR cost more, librarians might feel that replacing the one with the other was irresponsible.

Rather, to have the most socially efficient outcome, economists apply the principle that no usage fee should exceed "marginal cost"—the cost of providing one additional use. It was generally believed that JSTOR's marginal costs would be approximately zero.[27] Consequently, by-the-drink pricing would be untenable.

Instead, JSTOR offered unlimited use of its database in exchange for a flat fee, permitting access at every Internet-accessible computer on the campus. An arrangement for unlimited usage, sometimes called "country-club pricing," contains the implicit presumption that value does not derive purely from use. Both membership in the country club, and participation in JSTOR, have value of their own: a club membership confers prestige, and JSTOR allowed a library to free up shelf space or offer titles and searchability never before available. Because of this, JSTOR had value to the institution as a whole independent of how much it was used. The unlimited usage provision was one way for JSTOR and its library participants to acknowledge this critical point.[28]

Later, after JSTOR was widely available at colleges and universities, the marginal costs of providing access became clearer. And while it proved true that the single marginal use of JSTOR—one additional search, one

[24] William G. Bowen, "Report on trip to UMI and U of Michigan, Mar. 17–18, 1994," memorandum to JSTOR file, March 19, 1994, 6, 10.

[25] William G. Bowen, "JSTOR and the Economics of Scholarly Communications."

[26] Or, as the chairman of the Securities and Exchange Commission put it in 1995 when that organization was placing huge amounts of corporate information on its websites, "a library that charges people by the page, or by the minute, is no longer a library." "Internet EDGAR snatched from death!" *Searcher* 3, no. 9 (October 1995): 18.

[27] For JSTOR's planning, however, "approximately zero" could not equal zero. As JSTOR would anticipate and demonstrate, the negligible cost of any one additional use compounds very quickly as millions of uses during peak periods take an enormous toll on even the most robust server infrastructure.

[28] There are also, it would later be discovered, economic benefits to unlimited usage pricing. See Yannis Bakos, Erik Brynjolfsson, and Yu (Jeffrey) Hu, "Site Licensing Information Goods," unpublished paper, May 2002.

additional article viewed—imposed an altogether trivial cost, when these uses were aggregated by hundreds of campuses, there was a clear necessity for JSTOR to continually purchase additional servers to maintain acceptable performance. In late 1997, with JSTOR publicly available for nearly a year and usage skyrocketing (see chapter 10), Fuchs wondered if there might not be some way to "pursue a pricing strategy where usage was limited in some way at given price levels or where revenues would increase with usage."[29] Although such an arrangement could have been a throwback to by-the-drink pricing, it also would have been reasonable to cut off usage during peak periods for any individual participant. In essence, he was proposing that just as any one copy of a journal backfile has implicit usage restrictions, so should JSTOR. But JSTOR did not pursue this option.[30]

Unlimited usage pricing is often called "site licensing," but that term has been intentionally avoided here for a specific reason. In addition to his determination that JSTOR set a flat fee for unlimited usage, Bowen was far less certain that JSTOR should be available site-wide. Most particularly for current issues (see chapter 6), but also in the very early days of the archive, Bowen believed it might make the most sense if unlimited usage was restricted to computers in the physical library. That way, JSTOR could lessen the amount it would charge libraries by also charging individual subscribers for access outside of the library. But by mid-1995, he conceded that site-wide licensing was inevitable.[31]

THE COST BASIS

JSTOR's goal was to set a price for a service that had never before existed, for an entity that sought no profit but had a bottom line. One resource that provided some useful guidance was a University of California, Berkeley, dissertation on the costs of a digitized document collection, which Bowen, Guthrie, and Lougee all consulted. It concluded that many nonunique library holdings could be digitized to save money.[32] But Guthrie had to focus on JSTOR's own costs, not the usefully hypothesized costs of such a resource. Logically, Guthrie began with what JSTOR had so far learned about its costs, to ensure that the eventual pricing scheme would allow them to be met. Tracking down these costs was

[29] Minutes of the JSTOR board of trustees meeting of November 6, 1997.

[30] Ibid.

[31] William G. Bowen, "JSTOR and the Economics of Scholarly Communications."

[32] William Richard Lemberg, "A Life-Cycle Cost Analysis for the Creation, Storage and Dissemination of a Digitized Document Collection," Ph.D. diss., University of California, Berkeley, 1995.

more difficult than one might have thought.[33] What part of the Michigan operations' work was essentially one-time—initial software development, equipment purchases, and early inefficient systems that would be improved? What part would continue into the future as production increased and new features were added? And what new costs would arise as a result of JSTOR's broad public availability?

JSTOR's own variable costs depended largely on the growth of its database. Most of those costs could not be calculated by journal title, because titles varied radically by age, length per year, and complexity. Because the production costs depended largely on the number of pages, and hardly at all on the number of subscribers, it was most convenient to think of JSTOR's costs on a per-page basis. Using this model, Guthrie began to calculate the anticipated expenses associated with JSTOR operations, separating the capital costs of production and the ongoing costs of operations.[34]

Guthrie's initial production-related estimates were based on the experiences of the past year's production work. DIT, the scanning bureau, charged about $0.55 per page for scanning, OCRing, and indexing by the terms of its original contract with the University of Michigan. Production-related expenses at the University of Michigan, including prep and quality control work, added about a quarter dollar, according to the Strategic and Operating Plan. Both estimates, for the scanning vendor and for Michigan-based production, would soon rise. When JSTOR negotiated its own agreement with DIT in autumn 1997 (see chapter 9), the price rose to an estimated $0.75 to $1 per page. And although DIT's prices did not relate directly to other production costs, these also rose, largely as a result of the professionalization of the operation under Bill Landis and Eileen Fenton, to an estimated $0.75 to $1 per page.[35] These digitization expenses would be incurred not only for the initial creation of the archive, but also to include an average of one thousand pages per journal annually as the moving wall advanced. In addition to digitization expenses, there were also upfront costs for software development and servers.

Beyond these expenses, JSTOR's archival commitment led it to hold funds in reserve, for two purposes. First, Guthrie was convinced from

[33] Guthrie recounted his earliest attempt in "Meetings at the University of Michigan, July 10, 1995," memorandum to William G. Bowen, Richard Ekman, Ira Fuchs, T. Dennis Sullivan, and the JSTOR file, July 12, 1995.

[34] All of the figures for the cost basis in this section derive from the Strategic and Operating Plan.

[35] Kevin Guthrie, "The Development of a Cost-Driven, Value-Based Pricing Model," in Richard Ekman and Richard E. Quandt, eds., *Technology and Scholarly Communications* (Berkeley: University of California Press, 1999).

his research on the New-York Historical Society that endowments were critical to the long-term success of collections-based institutions.[36] For JSTOR, an endowment would provide a reliable base of annual spendable income to supplement ongoing revenues and thereby ensure institutional stability. In addition to this endowment, JSTOR promised that if it were to fail, each subscribing library would receive the database on CD-ROM; to guarantee this arrangement, it would hold sufficient reserve funds in "escrow." The endowment and the escrow were two legs of JSTOR's archival commitment.[37]

There were also costs associated with maintaining ongoing accessibility. User-services librarians based in Michigan would educate other university and college librarians, remotely assist users and ensure that their experiences were positive. In 1996, it was still too early to have any sense of the demand for user services, which Guthrie estimated at one full-time librarian per seventy-five participating libraries. Technical staff would update hardware and software as necessary to keep JSTOR readily available as technology evolved. Projections for technology costs were, and still remain, an educated guess. For example, if the web is eventually replaced with some other standard interface, much work will likely be required for the migration; but it is impossible to predict whether, or how often, a change of such magnitude will occur and what it might cost. As a placeholder, the business plan assumed these costs would average $357,000 per year, which would also include incremental software and interface upgrades as well as the programmers writing code. Central office costs, including library and publisher relations,

---

[36] Guthrie illustrated the problem of donations to museums with an anecdote. If a person with a modest income wins a Jaguar on a game show, he will be forced to pay taxes, insurance, gas, and maintenance on that car. In the long run, it may be in his interest not to take the car, or to sell it immediately.

Any collection imposes the same costs, whether housed in a university library, a public museum, or JSTOR. Although acquired as though they are assets, such collections must be budgeted for as imposing a long-term liability. For this reason, every new collection added to JSTOR must be accompanied by adequate financial resources to ensure its long-term survival.

As Guthrie wrote of the New-York Historical Society, "If an institution somehow falls out of favor, contributions can decline precipitously. . . . Obviously, other things being equal, all nonprofit managers would like to have a large endowment base to support their operations" (*The New-York Historical Society*, 165).

[37] Another leg, though more technical in nature, was an agreement for OCLC to house an offline copy of the JSTOR archive, which Guthrie anticipated would "send a positive message to the library community that we have redundant and fail-safe protection for the database in multiple technological media." Packet for the JSTOR board of trustees meeting of October 29, 1996.

would total $600,000, growing with the number of subscriber and publisher partners to $1.6 million by the close of 1999.

THE DUAL FEE

Guthrie and DeGenarro looked carefully at a list of American academic libraries and identified those institutions with the greatest number of journal subscriptions and the most research-oriented missions. Data had been obtained from OCLC on the journals to which the most small colleges subscribed (the "overlap" of their subscriptions). This data was used not only to select journal titles and disciplines (as we shall see in chapter 9), but also to identify institutions that were likely, based on a high number of journal subscriptions, to participate in JSTOR. Even more important than the OCLC data was the Carnegie Foundation for the Advancement of Teaching classifications of American colleges and universities, which are organized by objective measures such as number of students, types of degrees awarded, and research funding.[38] Using the Carnegie classifications and the OCLC overlap data, Guthrie and DeGennaro estimated that 1,400 American academic libraries were potential participants. They made the bold estimate that, of these, 750 might subscribe within the first four years.[39] With this scale in mind, Guthrie used the cost estimates, split into capital and operating, to develop some initial plans for prices.

All libraries that chose to participate in JSTOR would do so by paying both upfront and ongoing charges in exchange for "permanent" rights. The upfront charge, which was called the Database Development Fee (DDF), was to cover most of the expensive initial costs of production, including scanning. The fee would allow JSTOR both to include the Arts & Sciences I journals that were not paid for by the Mellon Foundation's early grants and to accumulate a modest endowment.[40]

In calculating the DDF, Guthrie at first projected that $0.01 per page would be sufficient. If 750 libraries subscribed at once, this fee would

---

[38] *A Classification of Institutions of Higher Education: 1994 Edition* (Princeton, NJ: Carnegie Foundation for the Advancement of Teaching, 1994).

[39] This projection was a substantial increase over a previous estimate that was made when Guthrie foresaw individual access to the database playing a key role. In that model, he saw under four hundred libraries participating. Thus, there was anticipated to be some elasticity of library demand depending on whether researchers had other access points to JSTOR.

[40] In the end, roughly one-quarter of the total upfront cost of Arts & Sciences I would be paid for by Mellon, first in the grants to Michigan and then in the working capital grant to JSTOR. The rest of the collection was built using revenues from the Database Development Fee.

yield $7.50 per page, of which JSTOR would direct more than two-thirds to an endowment fund. As additional pages were added to the archive, whether from another journal being signed or the moving wall pushing forward another year, the subscribing libraries would need to contribute correspondingly more. This way, they would pay only for what they received and the libraries were not at risk if JSTOR did not succeed in recruiting sufficient journals. The pricing structure would thereby help to build subscribing libraries' confidence in the new organization, without forcing them to assume risk.[41]

The second charge, the Annual Access Fee (AAF), was to make JSTOR self-sustaining. The plan was for the AAF revenues (combined with modest endowment income) to give JSTOR the funds necessary to ensure long-term survival, even if no further journals were added after the initial one hundred that JSTOR had tentatively set as its goal a year earlier. So, the AAF was intended to ensure that technological migration and user services would be provided so long as institutions remained willing to subscribe. It was designed to keep the archive updated and accessible to users throughout the world. This fee was also to be calculated per page, to be set at only one-tenth of the Database Development Fee, but it would be annual.

Charging both an upfront and an ongoing fee had compelling advantages. A much larger upfront fee without an annual charge, with ongoing expenses paid for by endowment income, would force JSTOR to assume the (perhaps high) risk for any unexpected inflation. More imminently, a large upfront fee might limit the number of libraries willing to participate. On the other hand, amortizing the upfront costs via increased ongoing fees would force JSTOR to borrow to cover its initial capital costs. Finally, the two fees allowed a close analogy with traditional archiving, in which a large capital cost is associated with building the library, but then ongoing fees are necessary to ensure maintenance and access. The split fee was an optimal solution, funding the database-creation work while ensuring an ongoing annuity stream that could be adjusted to some degree if necessary.[42]

These cost-based data led to the creation of the split fee and would be critical to build a balanced budget. But there was more to be done. Board member Elton White was convinced that, in setting prices, JSTOR should follow the principles of value-based pricing and avoid the trap of focusing too vigorously on matching costs with revenues. The rest of the leadership readily assented.

---

[41]Kevin Guthrie, interview with the author, February 20, 2001.
[42]Ibid. Elton White, interview with the author, February 6, 2001.

VALUE-BASED PRICING

Briefly, value-based pricing is most clearly understood in contrast with cost-based pricing. Cost-based pricing relates revenues to the cost of producing the product. JSTOR could have divided costs by the expected number of subscribers to reach such a pricing plan (and a for-profit would have added a percentage to that). Value-based pricing recognizes that customers will pay no more for a good than what they perceive to be its value. Since different customers will assign different values to the same product, they will be willing to pay different amounts. These differences in perceived value can allow for "price discrimination," maximizing potential revenue by charging more to certain customers.[43]

In following the principle of value-based pricing, the Strategic and Operating Plan included consideration of the value of JSTOR in reducing shelving costs for academic libraries. Bowen had long been interested in JSTOR's potential for generating savings in this area, and by 1995 he was estimating them publicly.[44] His estimates have since then been confirmed by other observers.[45] Capital costs to libraries for shelving and space were estimated at approximately $0.024–$0.041 per journal page, or $1,800–$3,100 per journal title. Annual operating costs were estimated at $0.60–$2.00 per journal retrieval, or anywhere between $27–$360 per year, depending on use.[46] With these estimates, JSTOR had a ceiling above which the database would not have value as a cost-saver.

Whitaker's sobering comments in 1995 about the difficulties of a transaction structured around cost savings did not lead Bowen, Guthrie, or, it seems, Whitaker to question whether cost savings was the appropriate value measure. As a result, space-saving (rather than *realizable* cost savings) was used as essentially the sole quantifiable measure of value.

A key feature of Guthrie's estimates at this stage was the (unconscious) choice to conflate space-savings and archiving as values to libraries. JSTOR had long believed, based on conversations with librarians at research universities and selective liberal arts colleges, that it would be impossible to offer space-saving without making an archival commit-

---

[43] See, for example, Hal R. Varian, "Differential Pricing and Efficiency," *First Monday* 2 (1996), online at *http://www.firstmonday.dk/issues/issue2/different.*

[44] William G. Bowen, "JSTOR and the Economics of Scholarly Communications."

[45] See Brian L. Hawkins, "The Unsustainability of the Traditional Library and the Threat to Higher Education," in Brian L. Hawkins and Patricia Battin, eds., *The Mirage of Continuity* (Washington, DC: Council on Library and Information Resources and Association of American Universities, 1998).

[46] Use was particularly difficult to estimate, and it seems that the original pricing policy radically underestimated it for some broad categories of libraries.

ment. No doubt for these schools, the two were paired. But at many other schools, as later chapters shall suggest, it might be possible to achieve savings without an archival promise—especially at schools that had not traditionally included archiving in their mission. The calculations made at this stage, however, did not allow for pricing that varied by these two distinct sources of value.

Of course, Guthrie was aware that there would be sources of value other than space-saving. For example, users would have access to complete backfiles of dozens of journals, from their dormitory, office, or library, with every word of the journals fully searchable. But how could this value be quantified? All evidence suggested that hard-copy backfiles of JSTOR's journals were used rarely, and then mostly at the largest research universities. There was no way to predict how this would have been different in digital form, and, even if it were identical, there was no way to monetize it with the data then available. If the value from access were expected to be low, and if there were no way to quantify it in any case, JSTOR would continue to focus on space-saving for the value basis of its pricing.

Combining estimates of JSTOR's costs with estimates of its value to libraries suggested that JSTOR could be provided at a price that libraries would find appealing, if the key challenge of scale were overcome. For the price they paid to be at or below the value they received, JSTOR would have to take advantage of significant economies of scale in order to spread its costs across enough libraries. It was clear that if JSTOR could find only one hundred subscribers, its ongoing costs could not be covered. Only with a larger library base, on the order of the Guthrie-DeGennaro estimate of 750, would the economics work.

The JSTOR board recognized that the database's value would vary from one institution to another. Libraries at the largest research institutions held complete copies of all of the core academic journals, and indeed often held several copies of key JSTOR titles. For example, the *American Economic Review* might be held in the main library, the undergraduate library, the social science library, the law library, and elsewhere. Libraries at small colleges, on the other hand, rarely held more than one copy of a JSTOR title, and some held only a moderate percentage of the JSTOR titles. The large libraries would receive the most value from space-saving. But the smallest libraries would receive the most value from access to backfiles not currently in their stacks. Economically speaking, the largest research libraries actually stood to save more money from participation. Some small libraries would be asked to pay for a resource that, in paper form, they had not felt was worth purchasing. Consequently, the value-based pricing framework used by JSTOR indicated that the largest participants should pay more.

TABLE 8.1
Proposed Participation Fees, per Page

Library Size	DDF	AAF
Large	$0.015	$0.0015
Medium	$0.01	$0.001
Small	$0.0075	$0.00075

Guthrie and Bowen therefore hoped to divide American academic libraries into the categories of small, medium, and large, with the understanding that the small received the least value (in terms of space-savings) and the large the most. In the Strategic and Operating Plan, these per-page prices were proposed to cluster around a penny per page for the Database Development Fee and about a tenth of a cent per page for the Annual Access Fee (see table 8.1). At these rates, the cumulative DDF for JSTOR's Arts and Sciences I collection, as it eventually developed, would have cost $87,000 for a large school and $43,000 for a small school like Macalester College.[47] But in fact, these fees were developed without any clear notion of which libraries would fall into which category. While they were convinced that objective standards could be found with which to make the categorization, the prices themselves as proposed in this document did not attempt to link specific prices with specific values.

JSTOR's use of value-based pricing was not its first deployment in the library community. In 1909, the H.W. Wilson Company instituted a "service-basis" policy for pricing its periodical indices. A library subscribing to very few of the indexed periodicals might be charged as little as 3 percent of the price charged to a library subscribing to all of the indexed titles. Although many of the major research libraries found this approach to be unfair—since they paid so much more for the same "product"—in the end, they supported using value-based pricing to take advantage of scale effects.[48]

---

[47] These calculations freeze JSTOR's Phase I database—subsequently renamed "Arts and Sciences I"—in 2001, by which time it included several years of annual updates to its 117 journals.

[48] Frank M. McGowan, "The Association of Research Libraries: 1932–1962," Ph.D. diss., University of Pittsburgh, 1972, 88–98.

Assumptions: In first year, JSTOR acquires and loads 1.2 million pages in 25 titles.

Invoice for 1/1/97
Presented Semi-Annually

JSTOR Database Page Count	
Opening Balance (7/1/96)	0
New pages added this year:	
New journals	1,200,000
Journal 1: 48,000	
Journal 2: 48,000	
Journal 3: 48,000	
...	
Journal 25: 48,000	
Updates to existing journals (moving wall)	0
Sub-total new pages added	1,200,000
Closing Balance (12/31/96)	1,200,000
One-time Capital Payments:	
Your capital price per page	$0.0075
Capital charge	$9,000.00
Subscription Service	
Your access price per page	$0.00075
Access fee (1/1/97 - 12/31/97)	$900.00
Updates to existing journals (moving wall)	$0.00
Subscription Service charge	$900.00
Total	$9,900.00
Discount for taking entire database (10%)	($990.00)
TOTAL FOR THIS INVOICE	**$8,910.00**
Note: Capital cost per journal	$360
Note: Annual subscription cost per journal	$36

Assumption: During second year, negotiations are easier, and back runs are shorter, so JSTOR acquires and loads 1.2 million pages in 40 titles.

Invoice for 7/1/97
Presented Semi-Annually

JSTOR Database Page Count	
Opening Balance (1/1/97)	1,200,000
New pages added January through June:	
New journals	600,000
Journal 1: 30,000	
Journal 2: 30,000	
Journal 3: 30,000	
...	
Journal 40: 30,000	
Updates to existing journals (annual basis)	0
Sub-total new pages added	600,000
Closing Balance (6/30/97)	1,800,000
One-time Capital Payments:	
Your capital price per page	$0.0075
Capital cost of new pages	$4,500.00
Subscription Service	
Your access price per page	$0.00075
Access fee (charged annually)	$0.00
Updates to existing journals (moving wall)	$0.00
Subscription Service charge	$0.00
Total	$4,500.00
Discount for taking entire database (10%)	($450.00)
TOTAL FOR THIS INVOICE	**$4,050.00**
Note: Capital cost per new journal	$113

Figure 8.1. Sample Typical Invoice—Small-size Library

REFINING THE PLAN: A FLAT RATE FOR A STANDARD BUNDLE

The business plan was thought out in meticulous detail, but it was also much too complicated, which the board recognized immediately when it formally considered the plan on June 20, 1996. Its very merit—of taking money from libraries only in exchange for pages of real content—meant that JSTOR would be unable to predict accurately what its database would cost for a potential subscriber. The problems of library budgets were too well documented for JSTOR to add further uncertainty to them. It seemed only reasonable for JSTOR to assume some of the risk itself.

One important shortcoming, which Guthrie realized when the Strategic and Operating Plan was created, was its dependence on one-time fees. These fees were charged whenever new pages were added and therefore were not "one-time" at all.[49] This threatened the simplicity with which the plan could be explained to potential subscribers. Figure 8.1,

[49]Kevin Guthrie, interview with the author, February 20, 2001.

which is a sample invoice that Guthrie created for the board, reflects this impossible degree of complexity.

Perhaps even more importantly, the title-by-title arrangement would have required hundreds of participants for each individual title before JSTOR would have accumulated the funds to pay for their digitization. Because it was not likely that hundreds of libraries would immediately participate, JSTOR would have to find a way to front the bulk of these capital costs itself. With only about $500,000 of cash on hand, it would have been looking at some sort of capital call.

As they continued to consider the Strategic and Operating Plan, JSTOR's leadership took another look at the pricing structure. In consultation with additional librarians, they became convinced that institutions would be willing to subscribe to the entire JSTOR package. This would mean, as we shall see in chapter 10, that libraries would be asked to pay in advance for a collection of uncertain scope by an unproven nonprofit. Yet JSTOR believed that librarians would buy its promise, and so it could bundle all of its journals together and charge a flat fee for them. The bundled arrangement would allow JSTOR to accumulate capital up front from the early participants. Other advantages lay in reducing the administrative burdens for the small organization and its forthcoming participants.[50]

Bundling was not seen by all of JSTOR's trustees as being the necessarily preferable choice. As an experienced technology executive, White had become "a strong believer in unbundling, giving people a choice, trying to make everything stand on its own." But he saw that the case of JSTOR was different. There were real values to the aggregation of JSTOR journals, such as the ability to search across titles. It would later become apparent that the curated collection is one of the foremost values that JSTOR adds to the journals, whereas bundling expensive software with a personal computer only decreased options. We shall see further in subsequent chapters how important a value this really was. White and the rest of the board recognized that bundling would be simpler to implement and preferable for libraries, and so it was adopted.[51]

JSTOR opted for the round number of one hundred journals in its initial collection. This target seemed achievable based on the pace of publisher negotiations thus far. JSTOR would promise delivery of these one hundred journals, or an anticipated 2.4 million new pages beyond the pilot journals, within three years, or by the close of 1999. This seemed

[50]Ibid. March 25, 2002.

[51]Elton White, interview with the author, February 6, 2001. Kevin Guthrie, interview with the author, March 25, 2002.

like a conservative estimate, since it implied throughput of 60,000 pages per month when JSTOR's capacity appeared to be on the order of 100,000 pages per month. JSTOR did not want to overpromise on the production side, however, because many aspects of the process had yet to be tested.

Guthrie was keenly aware of the unrealistic goals that were set and then missed during JSTOR's pilot phase. Processes in Michigan were only just being improved, while publisher and library relations had not yet scaled up for a major push. As the leader of a newborn organization, Guthrie did not want to "promise and then fail as the first thing we did."[52] JSTOR wanted to be positioned to deliver on whatever promises it made.

The effects of the decision to create a bundle are substantial. No significant academic library could simply ignore JSTOR's huge database, which would appeal not merely to any one department, but to professors and students across a broad cross-section of arts and sciences disciplines. In other words, JSTOR was a resource that would not fall solely under the aegis of individual subject librarians, but rather would be a resource for the entire library system. Also, the bundle of journals would appeal broadly to faculty and student users, minimizing the chances that a library might subsequently cancel JSTOR access and thereby threaten the economics of the archive.

The breadth of the collection would not only have appeal within disciplines, but would also facilitate research across disciplines at a time when cross-disciplinary research was growing in prominence. Even in its pilot stage, economists and historians could without additional effort extend their searches to one another's journals, potentially broadening the scope of their work. In other words, as a collection, the journals themselves took on added value, a value proposition that JSTOR created by deciding to license only its curated bundle of core journals.

Finally, the decision to create a substantial bundle of titles allowed JSTOR to avoid the transaction costs that would have been associated with providing different sets of journals to different subscribers. It allowed JSTOR to curate a collection as a whole, rather than feeling pressure to choose the journals that would be most popular. Most importantly, the bundle would constitute a "critical mass" of scholarly materials.

Since JSTOR's adoption of a bundle-based business plan in 1996, economists Yannis Bakos and Erik Brynjolfsson have made significant contributions to the field of bundling, developing a new methodology that allows them to consider the effect of bundling on information

---

[52]Kevin Guthrie, interview with the author, February 20, 2001.

goods. They have found that low marginal costs of information goods combine with low transaction costs of bundling to make the combination frequently attractive. They conclude that it is "much easier to predict consumers' valuations for a bundle of goods than their valuations for the individual goods when sold separately." Bundling can have the effect of making "traditional price discrimination strategies more powerful by reducing the role of unpredictable idiosyncratic components of valuations."[53]

JSTOR would benefit from both of these features of bundling its archive, even if it was not aware of the scholarship that had been developing concurrently. With the concept of a bundle of one hundred journals in place, JSTOR could more reasonably set a DDF for the entire collection. In this revised pricing structure, JSTOR would accept the uncertainty as to the costs of creating the full archive. Taking this risk upon itself, JSTOR would give libraries a pricing guarantee.

But there were also potential problems with bundling. Librarians were accustomed to selecting the specific materials needed for their libraries. JSTOR would diminish the independence of individual selectors, a downside that could be mitigated only by the high quality of the package as a whole. As it turned out, however, JSTOR's bundled approach generated little controversy, although enough to constitute one factor, as we shall see in chapter 11, in JSTOR's decision to begin creating smaller discipline-specific bundles.

CALIBRATING FEES

Following the value-based decision to divide libraries into small, medium, and large categories, JSTOR had to identify a mechanism for the division. Obvious choices such as the number of students or faculty would fail to take account of the space that the journals took up in the library stacks, the amount of money that the libraries could save, and, JSTOR believed, the value that libraries would receive from participation. In essence, JSTOR needed a system that would allow it to distinguish the largest, most research-intensive universities from the smaller, more teaching-intensive schools. (Also, JSTOR's licenses were to be signed and paid for by an institutional subscriber, a structure that seems deceivingly simple to identify, so the system would ideally help JSTOR determine whether, say, a multicampus state university constituted one,

---

[53] Yannis Bakos and Erik Brynjolfsson, "Bundling Information Goods: Pricing, Profits, and Efficiency," *Management Science* 45, no. 12 (December 1999): 1613.

TABLE 8.2
Carnegie *Classification* Groupings and
JSTOR Pricing Classes as Initially Proposed

Carnegie Classification Grouping	JSTOR Pricing Class	Database Development Fee	Annual Access Fee	# of Each Kind
Research I	Large	$40,000	$5,000	88
Research II	Large	$40,000	$5,000	37
Doctoral I	Large	$40,000	$5,000	51
Doctoral II	Medium	$30,000	$4,000	60
Master's I	Medium	$30,000	$4,000	435
Master's II	Medium	$30,000	$4,000	94
Baccalaureate I	Small	$20,000	$3,000	166
Baccalaureate II	Small	$20,000	$3,000	471

or several, institutions.)[54] Bowen realized that JSTOR could make use of the Carnegie *Classification* as the primary criterion of value, using it to place institutions in JSTOR's Small, Medium, and Large pricing classes.[55] The Carnegie *Classification* groups schools into two types each of Research universities, Doctoral universities, Master's-granting universities (Master's hereafter), and Baccalaureate colleges, which seemed at once to be a fairly good proxy for the value distinctions that JSTOR intended. By using the Carnegie proxy, pricing was not based on the actual amount of shelf space occupied, but rather by institutions' research intensity. The use of this proxy would, thereby, lessen to some degree the focus on space-savings.

With the decision to make use of the Carnegie *Classification*, Guthrie was quickly able to categorize academic libraries. Table 8.2 shows how, under his initial rubric, each group in the Carnegie *Classification* was assigned to a pricing class. Note that the one-time and annual fees were remarkably round numbers. Guthrie recalls the calibration of these fees

---

[54]In fact, one of the versions of the pilot license (JSTOR-B), in attempting to define a "site" without reference to Carnegie, stated: "shall mean any institution or cluster of institutions (e.g., grouped colleges are one [1] site) which share a common source of information (e.g., a tape or CD-ROM jukebox or equivalent)." Once JSTOR opted to serve information centrally, even this complicated definition became inadequate.

[55]*A Classification of Institutions of Higher Education: 1994 Edition.*

as being relatively unscientific, with their linear simplicity clearly appealing. "We didn't work real hard about what the comparative prices should be. . . . we knew that the larges would value it more than the smalls, but we didn't think carefully about whether it was twice as much or four times as much. What would be the determinant of that?"[56] While it might have been possible to research the average size of the libraries, the number of current subscriptions, or something similar to derive a sense of scale, JSTOR did not do so.[57] With little data on which to base a pricing scale, JSTOR simply sought to distinguish, roughly, the value that the various types of academic institutions would receive from participating.

Unlike JSTOR, some commercial vendors followed the practice of negotiating special deals with almost every subscriber, deals that as a result had to be kept secret. If JSTOR followed suit, a great deal of negotiation would be required for every new license agreement, imposing significant transaction costs, and librarians could never be certain they were getting the best deal. JSTOR's Carnegie-based pricing classes, on the other hand, were predetermined and fixed, so they could be posted right on its website. In this way, the Carnegie *Classification* brought to JSTOR's pricing system added objectivity, transparency, and therefore legitimacy. As we shall see, this transparency had the effect of making relations with consortia nearly impossible.

To correct for what was, for JSTOR's purposes, an overemphasis in the *Classification* on research interest, Guthrie proposed adjusting the categories for full-time–equivalent enrollment. This allowed it to take some account of (in)ability to pay. Here was a nod to the fact that value was derived not only from the holdings of the library and the savings that could result, but also, in a way, from access.

In soliciting feedback on the pricing plans from librarians such as David Pilachowksi, Guthrie gave additional consideration to the significant number of Baccalaureate colleges, in particular the Baccalaureate II colleges, with under one thousand students.[58] Despite their tiny size and exclusive focus on teaching, there was evidence that they, as well as foundations and research centers, would want to participate.[59] The Baccalaureate II colleges grant the bachelor's degree exclusively and are

[56]Kevin Guthrie, interview with the author, October 30, 2001.

[57]Other resources, such as indexing services, sometimes based pricing on the number of indexed journals to which a library subscribed. JSTOR clearly could have done just the same thing; however, what had at one point been an innovative approach admittedly made less sense in the era of the faxed interlibrary loan of literature.

[58]David Pilachowski, interview with the author, June 22, 2001.

[59]Kevin Guthrie, interview with the author, February 20, 2001.

TABLE 8.3

Carnegie *Classification* Groupings and JSTOR Pricing Classes as Revised

Carnegie Classification Grouping	JSTOR Pricing Class	Database Development Fee	Annual Access Fee
Research I	Large	$40,000	$5,000
Research II	Large	$40,000	$5,000
Doctoral I	Large	$40,000	$5,000
Doctoral II	Medium	$30,000	$4,000
Master's I	Medium	$30,000	$4,000
Master's II	Medium	$30,000	$4,000
Baccalaureate I	Small	$20,000	$3,000
Baccalaureate II	Very Small	$10,000	$2,000

either less restrictive in admissions or not as focused on the liberal arts, compared with the Baccalaureate I schools.

By default, JSTOR had placed all of these smallest institutions in the Small class, but without really expecting significant participation. The $20,000 DDF for the Small institutions was not matched with the value that schools with so few of the journals and such small enrollments could be expected to receive. With interest much greater than expected, but their characteristics very different from those of the other schools in the Small class, JSTOR sought to accommodate these smallest schools and encourage their nascent interest. It did so by creating a Very Small category for Baccalaureate schools with enrollment under one thousand (which included a large number of the Baccalaureate II colleges), as well as for foundations and research centers.[60] The Very Small class would be charged $10,000 up front and $2,000 on an ongoing basis, (see table 8.3). These colleges would benefit from having access to journal titles to which they had rarely subscribed, and because they were unexpected participants, their payments would only add to JSTOR's bottom line.[61]

[60] William G. Bowen, "DU-Pilachowski," email to Kevin Guthrie, October 20, 1996.

[61] The use of the Carnegie *Classification* and the addition of the Very Small class were both summarized for the board in the packet for its meeting of October 29, 1996.

If the admittedly unscientific estimate of library take-up proved accurate, and the cost estimates realistic, the various points of this fee structure would put JSTOR on a strong financial footing. (See chapter 10 for an analysis of how libraries actually responded.) And in comparison with the per-page system, it would prove to be substantially simpler to offer JSTOR to libraries at, say, $20,000 up front and $2,000 per year for one hundred journals. In the end, this simpler structure, which limited budgetary risk to libraries, doubtless made the archive easier to sell than would have been the case had it adopted page-based pricing.

CONSORTIA

Also included in the Strategic and Operating Plan, but eventually modified, was JSTOR's consideration of consortia. Bowen and Guthrie appear initially to have been influenced by their experience at the Mellon Foundation, which had supported library collaboration both in the United States and abroad. For example, consortia of American liberal arts colleges seemed like an ideal model for bringing greater efficiency to certain operations that might not otherwise remain tenable, with discussions in this period leading to the eventual creation of the Virtual Classics Department among the Associated Colleges of the South.[62] In Eastern Europe, especially, it became clear that more centralized, or "tight," consortia could yield substantial savings coupled with vastly improved services.[63] But Mellon had only sponsored collaborative consortia.

In the early 1990s, American academic libraries realized that they could use their market power to negotiate with publishers for lower prices. Digital publications had relatively low marginal costs compared with printed materials, but publishers generally made no effort to adjust pricing to take this into account. Instead, prices continued to rise. Librarians felt that publishers had increased flexibility in setting prices for digital materials. As a result, the consortia movement boomed, as individual libraries came together to negotiate deals.[64]

[62] The Virtual Classics Department was an ideal solution because there was not enough interest in a classics major at any given college, but when several colleges were "virtually" linked via computer network and videoconferencing facilities, sufficient students and faculty could be combined. Grant #10100659 awarded March 2001.

[63] For example, Mellon funding had created online library and union catalogs through implementing consortia. For a fascinating and valuable history of Mellon's work in Eastern Europe (and its library work in South Africa), see the history by Senior Advisor Richard E. Quandt, *The Changing Landscape in Eastern Europe: A Personal Perspective on Philanthropy and Technology Transfer* (New York: Oxford University Press, 2002).

[64] Glenda A. Thornton, "Impact of Electronic Resources on Collection Development, the Roles of Librarians, and Library Consortia," *Library Trends* 48, no. 4 (Spring 2000): 842–56.

Perhaps as a result of Mellon's consortia-related experiences, along with the attention consortia were attracting at the time, the Strategic and Operating Plan initially imagined JSTOR following the lead of virtually all other electronic data providers. JSTOR would license access to consortia of academic libraries at discounted rates. It envisioned a sliding scale of discounts based on the number of members in the consortium.[65] Guthrie recalls this sliding scale as more of a placeholder for discussion purposes than as an intended outcome.[66]

Had JSTOR sold its content title by title, consortia might have served a valuable purpose by selecting a preset number of titles for its entire membership, a function that was now irrelevant. But with the business model altered to eliminate many of the uncertainties in sales—so that any subscribing library would have to take the entire collection at a flat rate—it became much more difficult to understand the role of the consortium. One remaining benefit would be to encourage the participation of libraries unlikely to join. Another would be to speed the licensing process, which would bring increased operating revenues in the near term, decreasing the need to "burn" capital. But JSTOR's value-based pricing was specifically designed to reflect the value to an institution of participating. Giving further discounts to consortia could only have the effect of upsetting the value-based calibrations in JSTOR's business model and possibly even threatening its long-term viability.

Moreover, when he was beginning to discuss the JSTOR pricing structure, Guthrie began to hear from enthusiastic librarians. One in particular warned him, "We're going to be in from the start, but I don't want to learn later that everyone else got a cheaper price than us because we came in first." Guthrie recalls this comment clarifying for him the fairness issues implicit in pricing cooperatives; is it fair for two libraries, which value JSTOR the same and fall into the same pricing category, to pay different amounts, simply because one belongs to a consortium?[67]

Instead of dealing with buying cooperatives in this fashion, board member Elton White suggested in June that consortia be thought of in terms of their "value to us"—that is, the real savings or revenue they offered to JSTOR.[68] In the board packet for October, Guthrie would suggest that "there is no way that we alone are going to buck this trend and

---

Another good source on the development of consortia is Adrian W. Alexander, "Towards the 'Perfection of Work': Library Consortia in the Digital Age," *Journal of Library Administration* 28, no. 2 (1999): 1–14.

[65] Strategic and Operating Plan.

[66] Kevin Guthrie, personal communication, September 24, 2001.

[67] Ibid., interview with the author, February 20, 2001.

[68] Minutes of the JSTOR board of trustees meeting of June 20, 1996.

not deal with consortia," and he agreed with White's suggestion that (the extremely small amount of) system-wide savings be passed along. But he was not sure if an additional rebate, on the order being proposed by some consortia (see chapter 10), would prove necessary.[69] DeGennaro and Guthrie concluded that it was not,[70] and the board accepted this conclusion.[71] The Charter Library discount (see below) would have to suffice.

The upshot was that JSTOR would make special arrangements with consortia under certain circumstances. Foreign institutions sometimes joined via consortia, saving JSTOR the significant expense of marketing its database in non-English-speaking countries. JSTOR also allowed state university systems to join as a group, when the funding came from a central source and the work of selling to numerous institutions could thereby be reduced.[72]

Most other publishers provided discounts to consortia for their online products.[73] Many librarians consequently expected the same or better from JSTOR. With the smallest libraries being asked to pay more than could, as a general rule, be reasonably expected, a number of them looked to consortia as a way to participate. Because this was not permitted, JSTOR's policy on consortia became the most controversial aspect of its pricing plan, as we shall see in chapter 10.

JSTOR was well aware of the challenges that this decision would bring. At the October meeting of trustees, Bowen stated that "these decisions may slow the pace of incoming revenues [and he] indicated that it would be a mistake to make important strategic choices solely because of cash flow reasons at this early stage."[74] While, as a matter of general principle, this was undoubtedly true, most infant nonprofits nevertheless must face up to their cash-flow needs. The trustees endorsed an evaluation of "possibilities for shoring up JSTOR's cash position, in case that proves necessary." And these were not just empty possibilities. Less than a week earlier, Bowen had wondered whether it might make sense for Mellon to grant (or somehow loan) further funds to JSTOR to "provide cash flow while JSTOR waits patiently for libraries to make their payments and simultaneously continues to add to the database by

---

[69] Packet for the JSTOR board of trustees meeting of October 29, 1996.

[70] Kevin Guthrie, personal communication, January 8, 2002.

[71] Minutes of the JSTOR board of trustees meeting of October 29, 1996.

[72] Packet for the JSTOR board of trustees meeting of October 29, 1996.

[73] It is interesting to note that when HighWire does so, it is "not so much [for] price reduction as [for] the ease of implementing and activating the sites . . . we do provide some price breaks, but they're not huge." Michael A. Keller, interview with the author, May 21, 2002.

[74] Minutes of the JSTOR board of trustees meeting of October 29, 1996.

scanning."[75] While Bowen's intentions were good, librarians would likely have viewed any grant from Mellon to JSTOR at that point as an indication that JSTOR was struggling. In the end, no grant or loan was ever made for such purposes. The JSTOR Board of Trustees' consideration of cash-flow options in the event of revenue shortfalls is, however, ample evidence of the degree of commitment it felt to what it perceived to be an important principle: pricing the database fairly even in the face of consortia-related pressures.

THE CHARTER PERIOD

Plans called for the Arts & Sciences I Collection to take some three years to create. In mid-1996, only one-third of the titles were secured and only fourteen titles were digitized.[76] Clearly, at this point, JSTOR was offering a vision more than a tangible product. Nevertheless, it was not possible to wait three years to begin distributing JSTOR. On the one hand, JSTOR's production operation had an appetite for capital, while on the other there was no sense in delaying the benefits of access to scholarly users. Indeed, had every library opted to delay licensing until the entire database was completed, JSTOR would have run out of funds with only half of its journals digitized, surely discouraging any library from ever participating![77]

In order to encourage libraries to join what, at that point, could only be described as an experiment, some inducement would have to be offered. Such an inducement could be consistent with value-based pricing, since an early subscriber, joining at some risk that the project would fail, can only estimate the project's potential. Elton White explained that "they were buying a promise and so they were taking a risk. [The charter period discount] was one way of compensating them for that risk."[78] And an early participant is of greater value to a nascent enterprise than a later one.

The board consequently approved the so-called Charter Library status, for those institutions joining during the first four months. Along with this status came a fee reduction of 25 percent for both the Database Development Fee and the Annual Access Fee, in addition to promised

---

[75] William G. Bowen, "JSTOR on December docket," email to T. Dennis Sullivan, October 24, 1996.

[76] Packet for the JSTOR board of trustees meeting of June 20, 1996.

[77] The Archive Capital Fee paid for, in a very real way, nearly all of JSTOR operations in 1998 and 1999. Without this revenue, JSTOR could not have completed Arts & Sciences I.

[78] Elton White, interview with the author, February 6, 2001.

discounts for any future JSTOR products. Clearly, the new organization wanted to encourage as many libraries as possible to participate early.

SUMMATION

By mid-fall of 1996, the business plan was finalized. Guthrie was following his own conviction that planning was critical, a lesson he learned while writing about the New-York Historical Society. Whatever shortcomings the plan may have contained, it was a thoughtful overview of the work ahead, the risks it entailed, and how success could be achieved. It included what was believed to be a sustainable ongoing business model, including an annuity fee and provisions to build an endowment. Such careful, realistic planning was hardly typical of technology start-ups in this period.

With the sole exception of its position on consortia, JSTOR's leadership was convinced that its business plan was well crafted. On the consortia issue, analysis and discussion led Guthrie to revise his belief that it would be necessary for JSTOR to work through numerous consortia. Surely Karen Hunter's question in early 1997 about whether consortia were "just the flavor of the month" may have been indicative of the mood at the time.[79] At a time when many others were embracing consortia, JSTOR decided against standard discounts for consortia out of a sense of fairness, but only really as an interim conclusion. It seems plausible that, had market conditions later indicated the necessity of working through consortia, JSTOR would have done so. Had more libraries insisted on joining through consortia, it would have had no choice. In this way, the position against consortia was one of the more speculative, and probably flexible, elements of the plan.

One relatively inflexible aspect was the adoption of Elton White's recommendation that the pricing be value-based. In practice this meant that the prices reflected the value received from space-saving rather than from access. As we shall see in chapter 12, it would become clear that the relative pricing of the largest and smallest schools was insufficiently differentiated. Participation rates would indicate that the Research universities received far more value for their price, while the Master's and some of the Baccalaureate schools received less value for the price they

---

[79]Karen Hunter, "Things That Keep Me Awake At Night," *Against the Grain* February 1997: 40–42.

were asked to pay. Guthrie himself has since observed on a number of occasions that JSTOR's pricing differentials were inadequate. He notes that there was a degree of insecurity whether it would be possible to "charge the 'big guys' more for such a speculative product."[80] His efforts to correct for this inadequacy are dealt with in chapters 12 and 14.

With the business model approved by the board, Guthrie had key commitments to meet. The Michigan staff working on software development and journal production would take on a renewed importance, for Guthrie was determined that JSTOR would fulfill its promises and achieve success. The increased importance of the work at Michigan would cause Guthrie to give greater attention to, and grow increasingly frustrated with, the university's ability to deliver production-level services. The next chapter focuses on how JSTOR's database grew, in part with the help of a changing relationship with the University of Michigan.

[80]Kevin Guthrie, personal communication, January 8, 2002.

CHAPTER 9

A More Thoroughly Professionalized Operation

SEPTEMBER 1996–DECEMBER 1997

THE LAST SEVERAL CHAPTERS have followed the gradual evolution of JSTOR away from its Mellon origins. In chapter 6, we saw that Bowen and Guthrie explored the terrain of scholarly communications and focused JSTOR's mission, while, at the same time, as detailed in chapter 7, the Michigan production operation was somewhat reorganized. In the last chapter, the board of trustees adopted an innovative pricing plan while setting down ambitious goals for growth in the number of both journals and participants. In partnership with Bowen and the rest of the board, Guthrie was pushing JSTOR to ready itself for the marketplace, and, if much had changed since its Mellon days, that was the point. This chapter examines JSTOR's development following the creation of the business plan. In all domains, JSTOR's pace increased. During this time, the loosely coordinated remnants of the Mellon project were finally excised, a professional organization emerging in their place.

LICENSING THE REMAINING JOURNALS
FOR ARTS & SCIENCES I

With the adoption of the aggressive business plan, the JSTOR organization—no longer an infant—was under a great deal of pressure. JSTOR needed to sign many prestigious journals rapidly, put them into the production pipeline, and move them online if it was to begin generating revenues before its initial funds ran out. Publisher relations were therefore key, and the clearly defined terms for license agreements that were established in 1995–1996 put JSTOR in position to begin a major push to sign journals.

In the last chapter, we saw the board charge JSTOR with completing the digitization of one hundred journals by the close of 1999, a little more than three years off. Given the time necessary to digitize a title after securing the necessary license, all of the journals would have to be licensed by very early in 1999. In other words, another eighty journals would have to be signed on to participate in a little more than two years. The rate of journal signing would have to increase from the eleven that were signed in the 1995–1996 academic year to approximately forty titles per year.

At the same time, the work was becoming more complex. JSTOR moved from the low-hanging fruit of the enthusiasts to titles with rights-holders who would be more reluctant. Although settled licensing terms would increase the speed of negotiations, it was clear that Bowen and Guthrie could not hope to sign forty journals per year without help.[1]

During previous negotiations with publishers, Guthrie teamed with outside counsel Richard Woodbridge, who had originally been selected by Mellon for journal negotiations in 1994. By 1996, a significant amount of Woodbridge's time was occupied by these journal negotiations, as he became involved throughout the process. Guthrie realized that, for about the same amount as JSTOR was paying for outside legal counsel, it could hire its own counsel, who could be directly responsible for journal negotiations. That way, the negotiations would be handled by someone who could easily articulate the complicated licensing arrangements to another attorney.[2] Soon, JSTOR hired Sarah Sully, an intellectual property associate at the firm Skadden, Arps. As general counsel and director of Publisher Relations, she combined negotiating savvy with her knowledge of licensing to work effectively with publishers to sign on their titles. (She also had responsibility to oversee production work.) Over the next two years, working in close partnership with Guthrie, Bowen, and "champions," Sully successfully recruited over eighty additional journals to complete the Arts and Sciences I Collection.

Selecting New Disciplines and Titles

The journals that had, by the middle of 1996, already agreed to participate formed the core of several disciplinary clusters. The pilot titles, all of which would participate in the full release, formed strong collections in economics and history. In addition, there were groups in ecology, mathematics, and population studies, fields with which Mellon had very strong connections.

JSTOR's goal for Arts & Sciences I was about fifteen disciplinary clusters, each with a "critical mass" of journals (see table 9.1). Although this concept of critical mass was entirely subjective, there was reason to believe that 5–10 similar journals "clustered" together would have much more value to a scholar than the combination of 5 strong, but more random, titles. So, in addition to filling out the fields in which it already

---

[1] William G. Bowen, "Recent Developments," memorandum to the JSTOR board of trustees, May 1, 1996.

[2] Kevin Guthrie, interview with the author, February 1, 2001.

TABLE 9.1
Proposed Fields and Number of Titles, Arts & Sciences I

Discipline	Proposed Number of Titles, March 1998	Actual Number of Titles[i]
African-American Studies	6	7
Anthropology	4	6
Asian Studies	5	5
Ecology	6	6
Economics	12	13
Education	1	4
Finance	4	5
History	15	15
Literature	9	13
Mathematics	9	11
Philosophy	8	10
Political Science	10	9
Population	8	8
Sociology	6	9
Statistics	7	11
Total	110	117

[i]Some titles are included in more than one discipline, so the total is not additive.

had participants, JSTOR would begin to focus on fields with a reasonable expectation of signing 5–10 of the most important core titles.

As a result of this initiative, JSTOR's approach changed. In the first year after independence, JSTOR worked with Mellon staff and associates to recruit the candidate journals that were most likely to participate. This worked well when JSTOR started off and had to build up a list of publisher participants that could help convince others of JSTOR's merit. But then, in 1996–1997 and onward, publisher relations grew far less opportunistic, with JSTOR more often approaching publishers on its own and without the help of friends. JSTOR's collections development became strategic and curatorial. Clusters that already had a small number of titles were filled out, and new disciplinary clusters were designed and created.

Further disciplines would be chosen only from the arts and sciences, and within the arts and sciences almost entirely from disciplines without large nonacademic constituencies. This principle reflected JSTOR's sense that publishers in more profit-oriented fields would be more reluctant to license their journal backfiles without substantial financial compensation. In addition, they were more likely to have the resources to digitize their backfiles if it seemed economically feasible. Disciplines were ranked by the degree to which the backfiles of journals were important to ongoing scholarship. Fields that directly fostered interdisciplinary work, most notably statistics, were considered to be especially important in an interdisciplinary database. As a result of these principles, JSTOR began to set aside certain fields, such as chemistry, that fell outside of its focus.

In other cases, disciplines were of interest, but could not yet be added. Art history was originally slated for inclusion in Arts & Sciences I, but eventually it was put aside for possible future inclusion. A number of especially acute concerns, including complicated technical issues related to reproducing images, made art history too difficult. Technology to digitize images with sufficiently high quality and yet sufficiently affordable cost was not available. Even if it were, high-quality color art images might take far too long to download. For an effort that was feeling serious time pressures to grow significantly but rapidly, art history required too many problems to be overcome for its journals to be incorporated. Art history would later be included as a subsequent collection.

In still other cases, fields had principal publishers that were unwilling or unable to participate. If the primary publishing society—for example, the American Anthropological Association, which in April 1997 was still a target but by March 1998 was not—were unwilling to participate, the cluster could not be viable. Bowen and Guthrie used publisher willingness to join as a factor in narrowing the list of disciplines to include in JSTOR. Fields lacking enthusiasm were postponed, in case the publisher later changed its decision.[3]

In several cases when it was not possible to include a discipline for one reason or another, it was replaced with another field of interest. Generally, this led JSTOR to concentrate more titles in the fields that were eventually selected, rather than include fewer titles in each of a larger number of fields. When several fields had been put aside, Sully

---

[3] Both classics and anthropology were eliminated as target fields sometime in second half of 1997 or early 1998. [Kevin Guthrie], "JSTOR Phase I—Proposed Titles and Fields," April 3, 1997; [Kevin Guthrie], "Phase I: Proposed Fields and Number of Titles," March 4, 1998. Both were subsequently included in the Arts & Sciences II Collection (see chapter 11).

played an important role in advocating for the inclusion of African-American studies, a field that was both interdisciplinary and growing.

Within these disciplines, it was necessary to select the core journals. Richard Ekman had previously obtained from OCLC a listing of the "overlap" in journals subscriptions among liberal arts colleges. Those titles with the greatest overlap were seen to be of most appeal. At this stage, JSTOR focused on journals with over one thousand institutional subscriptions, according to this overlap list, although some modest exceptions were made. This focus tacitly imposed the requirement that the journal still be published. For certain fields, JSTOR created committees of scholars to recommend journals for inclusion. In the case of philosophy, for example, Princeton Professor Paul Benacerraf led a group of scholars that evaluated potential titles. In other cases, JSTOR itself consulted practicing scholars. Although citation statistics were consulted, they were not considered to be determinative because JSTOR wanted to build balanced groups of core titles with significant publishing histories.

Soliciting Publisher Participation

Reaching out to publishers was often complicated, and on this task Bowen and Guthrie often worked in partnership with Sully. Sometimes, they worked through "champions," as we saw in chapter 6. Sully always took on the nitty-gritty of the negotiations, after publishers agreed in principle to participate. Often, she carried these conversations from start to finish. It seems that a very high percentage—probably well over three-quarters—of those publishers that JSTOR pursued eventually signed on to participate.[4]

There were several features that seem to have held appeal for publishers. First, although most publishers were not yet actively seeking to publish current issues online, those with foresight could surely appreciate the value of having all of the volumes of the backfile online and linked to their current issues, at no cost whatsoever to them. Also, as we have seen several times, a number of academic libraries held publishers in less than high esteem. Participation in the nonprofit JSTOR could be seen as a low-cost way for them, especially the for-profits, to improve their images among the JSTOR-enthusiast library community.

Once JSTOR put aside its plans for current issues (see chapter 6), it was better able to secure agreements with some publishers. For ex-

---

[4] It has not been possible to reconstruct the rate of publisher participation, because conversations progressed to varying stages and, in some cases, continue to progress.

ample, it was not until this point that JSTOR's first pilot publisher, the American Historical Association, agreed to participate in the full-scale deployment. At the time, leadership of the AHA had judged the threat of online current issues to be so great—it "gave everybody nightmares"— as to question the wisdom of dealing with JSTOR at all.[5] While concern about current issues was not always the sole deal-breaker in negotiations with publishers in that period, once JSTOR's hope to publish current issues had faded, a key bone of contention was no longer present. Had JSTOR not put aside its plans for current issues, negotiations at later stages would certainly have been more complicated and would, in some cases, have led to a dead end. On the other hand, no publisher refused to participate in JSTOR because it did *not* store and distribute digital current issues. Thus, JSTOR's decision to focus on backfiles only allowed it to achieve that mission far better than had it also been attempting to store and distribute current issues online.

Even so, negotiations almost never were simple, and some publishers were simply unwilling to participate. As a vigorously competitive company that had alienated many of its customers, Elsevier engaged in efforts to improve its public perception, not least of which was the creation of TULIP (see chapter 3). It was inevitable that JSTOR would want to include at least a few of the one thousand academic journals that Elsevier published at the time, even if they were largely in the sciences. JSTOR's leaders hoped that Elsevier would agree to participate, perhaps in part to positively influence its customers. Initially, Elsevier was fearful about JSTOR's plans to publish current issues, which would thereby threaten its own core business. By the time JSTOR abandoned its consideration of current issues, Elsevier had begun considering digitizing its own backfiles. Elsevier executive Karen Hunter recalls promising the academic community that "if we weren't going to digitize [the backfiles], I would be sure that [they] were released to [JSTOR] or to anybody else who wanted to digitize them."[6] Eventually, despite Elsevier's claims that digitizing backfiles would generate little revenue, it began to do so and to mount them exclusively on its ScienceDirect website.[7]

On the other hand, the nonprofit American Mathematical Society, representing a noncommercial discipline, was an enthusiastic participant. Allyn Jackson, a staff member, wrote an article for *Notices of the AMS* in which he described why a publisher like the AMS might choose to participate in JSTOR. The publishers "are unlikely to obtain further revenue

---

[5] Arnita Jones, interview with the author, September 20, 2001.

[6] Karen Hunter, interview with the author, September 5, 2001.

[7] Scott Carlson, "JSTOR's Journal-Archiving Service Makes Fans of Librarians and Scholars," *Chronicle of Higher Education*, July 27, 2001.

from older back issues of journals and . . . storage on JSTOR helps to make their publications more widely accessible."[8]

As the license agreements were signed, virtually all terms were standard. The major variable was the length of the moving wall. This divider delayed current issues from being included in the JSTOR archive. Publishers were allowed to choose a number that made them comfortable, generally up to five years. In a consistent demonstration of caution, most selected this maximum figure. In one notable exception, almost all of the Population and Demography titles chose shorter moving walls. This discipline's commitment to public service led it to rank broad distribution of knowledge above business-related worries. As it turned out, the Population and Demography titles did not show any evidence of suffering from their shorter moving walls, and several other titles subsequently reduced their moving walls. Indeed the *American Journal of International Law* reduced its moving wall to zero, effectively allowing JSTOR to digitize and distribute its current issues. It is somewhat surprising that more publishers have not opted to reduce the size of the moving wall for their titles, given that JSTOR's effects on the journals seem to have been benign at worst. But then, JSTOR has never really pushed publishers to reconsider initial decisions on the moving wall.

Science *and Serendipity*

Well before 1997, quite a few publishers had expressed interest in participating in JSTOR without even being solicited.[9] While sometimes these journals were successfully accommodated within the planned collection, it was more often the case that journals were only appropriate for some future collection. Before 1997, the prospect of journals beyond Arts & Sciences I is best understood as JSTOR's caution in the face of pressure to expand. This caution generally led JSTOR to continue focusing on Arts & Sciences I, although the interest of one publisher tempted Guthrie to deviate.

Guthrie attended the 1996 annual meeting of the Ecological Society of America, where he met Jane Lubchenco, president-elect of the American Association for the Advancement of Science (AAAS), which published the weekly magazine *Science*. Guthrie explained to her the database that JSTOR was creating, and Lubchenco was impressed. She suggested considering *Science*.

---

[8] Allyn Jackson, "JSTOR, A Great Leap Forward in Electronic Journal Access," *Notices of the AMS* June/July 1998, 713.

[9] Packet for the board of trustees meeting of October 29, 1996.

With some 140,000 individual and 15,000 library subscriptions (of which high school and public libraries were a significant component), each issue of the magazine included several broadly important peer-reviewed scientific articles, shorter research reports, and a wealth of news on relevant current events. *Science* was unlike any of the journals in Arts & Sciences I, both because of its massive subscriber base and its topical news content. Its backfile, stretching back well into the nineteenth century, was also twice the size of that of the largest journal targeted for Arts & Sciences I and it was heavily laden with graphics and complicated page layouts. Guthrie recalls thinking at the time that JSTOR was not prepared to take on such a project. And yet it was difficult to imagine a more useful title for the study of the history of science.

In May, Guthrie and Bowen met with the editor-in-chief and the managing editor of *Science*. In cooperation with HighWire Press, *Science's* current issues were already being mounted online. This was a vivid demonstration that the magazine lacked, in Guthrie's words, "the basic fears of technology" that other publishers often felt. Instead, they discussed digitizing the *Science* backfile and how JSTOR's work would relate to the current issues of HighWire Press. The meeting ended positively, but Guthrie was somewhat concerned about JSTOR's ability to take on the massive project. His minute of the meeting concluded, "*Science* is an important title and JSTOR should take it on if it can, but if it does, it will require a production line all its own and will probably be a very long project. Before making any commitments, we have to think very hard about just how big a project *Science* would be, how much it would cost, and whether it would be worth it."[10]

In the face of considerable enthusiasm for the opportunity to take on a journal like *Science*, Guthrie appealed for caution and planning. After all, not one journal from Arts & Sciences I had been made publicly available, yet JSTOR was already facing the question of how to treat such a prospective participant. The board discussed *Science* at its October 1996 meeting, when Cathleen Morawetz suggested that *Nature* could be "a valuable complement" to *Science*. The board agreed that any project focused on *Science* would have to seek external funding, perhaps from the federal government's science-funding agencies.[11] Despite the tantalizing opportunity, the task at hand in 1996 was not the development of further collections, but rather the completion of the first one. As we will see below, only seventeen journals were available online at the close of 1996, and much work had to be done to improve the production

[10]Kevin Guthrie, "Meeting with Floyd Bloom and Monica Bradford, *SCIENCE*," email to Bill Landis, William G. Bowen, and Ira Fuchs, May 22, 1996.

[11]Minutes of the board of trustees meeting of October 29, 1996, 5.

**Cumulative
Journals Signed**

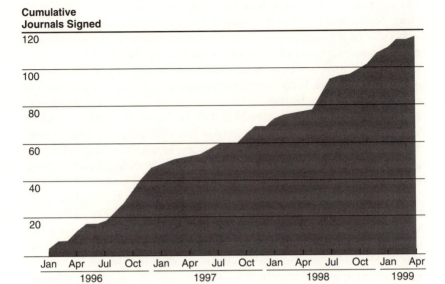

Figure 9.1. Cumulative Journals Signed for JSTOR's Arts & Sciences I
Collection

operations if that collection was to be completed before the December 31,
1999, deadline. With this focus in mind, JSTOR put off conversations
with the AAAS. As we shall see in chapter 11, this would turn out to be
only a temporary postponement.

Overall Progress

The steady licensing of journals for Arts & Sciences I resulted in well
over one hundred journals signed (see figure 9.1). In October 1998,
JSTOR signed its hundredth journal, the *Journal of Finance,* but it did not
stop there. Even though JSTOR had fulfilled its formal goal for the Arts
& Sciences I Collection, it had been working toward a curated collection
with "critical mass" in certain disciplines. Offers had to be extended for
more than one hundred titles, on the assumption that some number
would no doubt decline or delay participation. Thus while one hundred
was the target, it was treated by JSTOR staff as a minimum. Arts &
Sciences I contained the complete backfiles of 117 journal titles (see ap-
pendix A for the complete title list). Its fees, however, remained as originally promised libraries for one hundred titles. Participating libraries

received a "dividend" of extra journals that would make many librarians happy.

JSTOR used citation analysis to examine retrospectively the quality of its collection. Although citation data has its limits, and was missing for about twenty of JSTOR's titles, the results for the others were remarkable. Of the fifteen disciplines making up Arts & Sciences I, in two of them JSTOR titles constituted about 75 percent of the citations; in another four, over 40 percent of the citations; and in another four, over 25 percent of the citations. In most disciplines, JSTOR had the majority of the most-used titles. This was quite an achievement, one that could be built on still further.[12]

CREATING THE PRINCETON MIRROR SITE

Another important development in the wake of the business plan, as JSTOR prepared to go live, was the need for a mirror site. That is, JSTOR's website could not be solely dependent on any one connection to the Internet, but rather needed multiple physical connections to limit downtime in case of a server or network failure. Because of the constraints of international networking at the time, recalls Guthrie, "We had it in our mind that we wanted to do 5, 6, or 8 mirror sites, we wanted to create a kind of 'JSTOR in a box' that you could then put in different places around the world."[13] A U.S. mirror would be only the beginning.

Although in concept, setting up a mirror site could be as simple as duplicating the hard drives of a server and installing them elsewhere, a number of factors complicated matters. For one thing, the JSTOR server at Michigan was operationally dependent on other University of Michigan servers, and the programmers had lost track of all of the many interdependencies. So several programmers would have to be assigned the task of unpacking exactly what software was needed for JSTOR, and then organizing that software efficiently on a new server. In addition, a user would have to interact with only one server through an entire session, which would not be simple.[14]

For a number of reasons, it made sense to hire new programmers at the mirror site, rather than try to do the work at Michigan. First, the JSTOR programmers at Michigan were overburdened as it was, and, as we shall see, they were at this point operating fairly independently of

---

[12]Packet for the JSTOR board of trustees meeting of February 10, 1999.

[13]Kevin Guthrie, interview with the author, December 6, 2001.

[14]Kevin Guthrie, "Conference Calls/Technology Issues," email to JSTOR staff, August 15, 1996.

the New York office. Second, it was deemed to be important that there be JSTOR-assigned staff at the mirror site itself, to manage and oversee its operation. Finally, as JSTOR sought to professionalize itself and become less dependent on Michigan, it wanted to have an independent look at some of the Michigan-built software. Natural ownership interests at Michigan were preventing an objective evaluation of existing systems. New programmers at a new mirror site could also undertake such an analysis to determine whether better solutions existed.

With Ira Fuchs still overseeing much of the technical work of software development, it made sense to establish the mirror site, and hire several new programmers, at Princeton. As vice-president for Computing and Information Technology, Fuchs could ensure that the JSTOR presence at Princeton would be welcome and, at least conceptually, could advise and oversee staff there. Bowen's honorary title of president emeritus of the university was also an asset in maintaining harmony.

An agreement between JSTOR and Princeton was soon reached, and Fuchs charged Serge Goldstein, a manager in his department, with recruiting two software developers. Goldstein soon hired Amy Kirchhoff and Mark Ratliff. There was initially some strain between staff at Michigan and Princeton. The DIRECT programmers at Michigan were "losing" their exclusivity, and the distance between Michigan and Princeton made initial problems more difficult to overcome. Yet, by November, the user-services librarians were able to announce that the mirror was operational and JSTOR access being supplied redundantly.[15] With redundancy, JSTOR maintained remarkably low levels of downtime once it was released publicly in January 1997. Kirchhoff and Ratliff soon turned to other important JSTOR-related projects, but because many of these were undertaken in response to the public release, they will be discussed in chapter 10.

MICHIGAN:
RESEARCH UNIVERSITY AS DIGITAL LIBRARY CONTRACTOR

As JSTOR prepared itself for the marketplace, the continuing stream of journal participants burdened the Michigan production operation. Despite the gradual, steady improvements that had been introduced (see chapter 7), it became increasingly clear that JSTOR's production operation remained severely challenged. In January 1996, the ten pilot jour-

---

[15] Sherry Piontek [Aschenbrenner], "JSTOR URL Pointing to Princeton," email to JSTOR test site library contacts, November 5, 1996.

nals, totalling nearly 725,000 pages, were online; but it would not be until the middle of 1997 that the number rose to twenty. Although at the time, JSTOR could not have known how slow the progress would be, it was soon evident that this pace was inadequate for market deployment. To correct this, important changes were made. Although they caused a great deal of stress to the relationship with the university, in the end they left JSTOR's Michigan operation more nimble and poised for success as the Arts & Sciences I Collection was being released to the public.

The Andrews-Landis Process Redesign

As was seen in chapter 7, JSTOR hired a production coordinator, Bill Landis, to bring order to the process. While this broad challenge would outlast his own tenure at JSTOR, Landis made substantial inroads in rationalizing what had been a slowly congealing, ad hoc group. Under his leadership, the work of physical preparation by technicians, indexing preparation by a librarian, scanning by the vendor, and quality control began to congeal into a process. In mid-1996, after having been with JSTOR for about six months, Landis gave thought to a more thorough revamping of the production operation.

Landis developed two principal concerns. First, it was difficult to negotiate for the programmer support necessary to create software tools for the production staff. As described in chapter 7, bringing together discrete pieces of JSTOR's Michigan operation in the first year after independence had been a challenge. Below, we shall see that this challenge had not yet been resolved. Landis's second concern was that the quality of the DIT content continued to be inadequate, forcing his quality-control staff to ameliorate files that, he believed, probably should never have left Barbados.[16]

Nearly a year before, Guthrie had suggested some sort of Michigan-based preproduction process, which Lougee had helped to put into place. The goal of this preparation was to reduce the amount of remediation needed after digitization. But despite this preparation process, the quality of the vendor's datasets continued to be lacking. As a result, Landis felt compelled to continue quality control of 100 percent of incoming datasets—tedious and expensive. The 100 percent quality-control operation ate up huge amounts of staff time, which could have been spent instead on pushing additional journals through the preparation processes.

---

[16] Bill Landis, "JSTOR Production Operation at U-M," fax to Kevin Guthrie, August 13, 1996.

JSTOR's hope to increase its production rate was not being achieved. Landis was convinced that "the current process is fundamentally flawed . . . pieced together on the fly."[17]

Surely, he thought, there must be ways to improve DIT's work, so it would deliver better quality material to Michigan. One tactic he suggested was for DIT to digitize a sample issue for each journal backfile. Michigan staff could quickly check this sample to ascertain whether DIT was properly implementing Champagne's indexing system before it indexed one hundred years of a title incorrectly. This would soon be implemented, with great success.[18]

More fundamentally, Landis wanted to shift the burden for quality to the scanning vendor. The problem with 100 percent quality control was that it took so long to complete. By the time it was finished, the window in which JSTOR could just reject a dataset had long passed. As a consequence the quality-control staff had to fix the problems itself. Landis suggested instead that JSTOR should quality control for only a small percentage of each dataset, which would be done expeditiously. If that sample passed an appropriate threshold, it would be accepted. If not, JSTOR would reject it and DIT would have to repair the entire dataset. The result would be that the burden for fixing errors would fall on DIT, as the contract stipulated, rather than on JSTOR-Michigan.[19]

Bowen and Guthrie immediately agreed, and the very next day Bowen suggested that JSTOR find a statistical process consultant, who could revamp the entire system.[20] To examine only a small percentage of the datasets, some process for statistical sampling had to be put into place, but this process required careful study and development. Whitaker recommended they consult R. W. ("Andy") Andrews, a professor at Michigan's business school who had worked principally with the automobile industry on quality control.

Andrews and Landis traveled to Barbados to visit the DIT operation. Andrews needed to understand DIT's processes, so he would learn how errors could be introduced into the digitization work. Understanding where errors tended to develop allowed him to determine the appropriate rates of sampling for various pieces of the product that DIT delivered to JSTOR. With this basic information, Andrews helped Landis design a new quality-control process. JSTOR programmers developed

[17]Ibid.

[18]Eileen G. Fenton, interview with the author, May 29, 2001.

[19]Bill Landis, "JSTOR Production Operation at U-M," fax to Kevin Guthrie, August 13, 1996.

[20]William G. Bowen, "Statistical process control (sampling) consultant for JSTOR," email to Gilbert R. Whitaker, August 14, 1996.

software that allowed quality-control staff automatically to check the appropriate sample of a dataset. With this software, JSTOR staff began to sample a small subset of the contents of a given CD, and accepted or rejected it based on that sample. Rather than repairing problems in the datasets, quality-control staff made rapid binary decisions.[21]

This process redesign brought several added advantages. First, since DIT was not paid until JSTOR accepted the dataset, it added significant incentive for the dataset quality to be improved. Second, for the datasets that were accepted, it radically increased the speed with which they could be put online. Third, it increased the capacity of the quality-control team, which spent significantly less time on each dataset. Although costs increased, productivity increased far more.[22] The process redesign was one of several developments that enabled JSTOR to begin increasing the pace of production in early 1997. Other critical developments around this time included redefining the relationship with Michigan and the growing pressure from the burgeoning queue of signed journals.

Production Progress, Early 1996 to Mid-1997

The Andrews-Landis process redesign created the basis for more coherent and efficient operations. At the same time, a Michigan-JSTOR reorganization, about which more below, also brough new efficiences. Fed by the rapid pace of journal participation shepherded by Sarah Sully in New York and aided by new software and processes, production progress increased.

The first ten journals had taken about a year to digitize, from the winter of 1994–1995. A second ten titles were not completed until April 1997, another fifteen months. At this point, the new Andrews-Landis production processes were put in place. The newfound efficiency that this brought was reflected in the monthly releases. By May 1997, production staff had begun to release approximately 100,000 pages per month. While the data were not collected with precision until later, table 9.2 provides the best estimates available of the number of pages released from the production process per month.

---

[21]A useful perspective on quality-control proceses may be found in Oya Y. Rieger, "Establishing a Quality Control Program," in Anne R. Kenney and Oya Y. Rieger, *Moving Theory into Practice: Digital Imaging for Libraries and Archives* (Mountain View, CA: Research Libraries Group, 2000).

[22]Production expenses exclusive of vendor services in 1997 were more than twice the projection, which was developed before the process redesign. Packet for the JSTOR board of trustees meeting of March 5, 1998.

TABLE 9.2
New Pages Released,
January to August 1997

Month	Pages Released
January	0
February	0
March	10,209
April	41,482
May	98,079
June	132,424
July	224,383
August	53,227

Landis had been particularly attuned to the need for documenting both the production process itself and all operational decisions that were made in implementing it. This documentation was critical in later allowing JSTOR to expand dramatically its production capacity (see chapter 11). It also was critical for the large-scale process improvements that Landis would spearhead. In the summer of 1997, Landis left JSTOR and his newly hired deputy Eileen Fenton took over his responsibilities. Fenton proved to be an unusually able manager. She was able to take the guidelines and processes that Andrews and Landis had developed and apply them to the production line. This entailed coordinating the pre- and post-scanning teams with the vendor, no small organizational task since the workflow of each was dependent on the other. In particular, Fenton began battling with the vendor to develop realistic production schedules and greater fealty to deadlines and to reduce the worrisome backlog of journals to be scanned that had accumulated at the vendor. With Fenton at the helm of production, and the reorganization that we shall see below, the pace of digitization work continued to increase throughout 1997.

DIT agreed to implement its side of the Andrews-Landis production redesign, conceding things had been "a little easy" because there had in practice been very little quality control.[23] JSTOR's needs for increased quality had in turn imposed higher costs on DIT. So long as a higher

---

[23]Kevin Guthrie, "Dinner with Digital Imaging," email to William G. Bowen, Ira Fuchs, Bill Landis, Sarah Sully, and Gilbert Whitaker, December 8, 1996.

level of quality could be maintained, JSTOR was willing to contribute toward these costs. In early 1997, JSTOR and DIT began to renegotiate their relationship. One substantive change in the agreement was that JSTOR would no longer pay a flat rate per page, but rather on a sliding scale depending on complexity. Thus, the vendor no longer assumed the risk from JSTOR's variably complex journals. Also, the agreement specified that JSTOR would have ten working days to accept or reject a dataset; under the previous agreement, a dataset could only be rejected in the first three days, unrealistic even under the Andrews-Landis sampling procedures. If the dataset were to be rejected now, DIT would in turn have ten days to fix it. Thus, in twenty days, JSTOR could receive a dataset, reject it, and receive a corrected version, rather than putting it in a lengthy queue for repairs. As a result, it was possible for the first time to set realistic production and content-release goals.[24]

With the process for digitization finally satisfactory, JSTOR had to confront problems with the titles that had already been completed and put online. These journals would have to be brought into compliance with the new standards for quality. In part, this entailed simple QC of the journals already in the JSTOR database. But it also involved additional work to take account of new digitization methods that had been adopted. For example, JSTOR had begun to scan images individually, to capture color or grayscale, in addition to the black and white images of the journal pages.[25] All of this work was undertaken for the first seventeen journals, and it took a long time. More than a year later, in the summer of 1998, retrospective quality control was finally completed.[26]

Because it was generally smooth and successful, we will not dwell further on production in 1997 and 1998. Under Fenton, progress was steady.[27] But because the improvements in production were so successful, at this point in mid-1997 Guthrie and the board turned to thinking about future collections that would follow Arts & Sciences I, a subject dealt with in chapter 11.

Organizational Challenges

The organization of the Michigan operation had evolved in certain ways during the year between JSTOR's independence and mid-1996, although

[24]Kevin Guthrie, letter to and agreement with Richard Coleman, September 17, 1997.
[25]Eileen G. Fenton, "Re: retro qc," email to the author, August 3, 2001.
[26]Packet for the JSTOR board of trustees meeting of July 30, 1998.
[27]Visiting Michigan in early 1998, Kevin Guthrie reported that "it is clear that everyone [the JSTOR—Michigan staff] has tremendous respect for Eileen's many talents, organizational tendencies, and management ability." Kevin Guthrie, "Meetings in Ann Arbor," email to Ira Fuchs, January 19, 1998.

the basic structure remained that which Bowen, Frank, and Fuchs had negotiated for the grant. By his very presence Landis had brought some measure of order to the previously uncoordinated production operation. This change and others reflected JSTOR's transformation from a foundation grant project to a business with goals and deadlines. But problems persisted in other areas. There were ongoing problems in coordinating the software development work, and the overall organizational arrangements in place since 1994 in the Michigan operations had not always kept pace with the rapid changes that had occurred "on the ground."

The lack of blatant problems in software development allowed Guthrie to focus his efforts elsewhere. Since the pilot phase, Spencer Thomas had coordinated the work of the technical group at Michigan. Thomas was still the only member of this group working on JSTOR fulltime, and his focus had fallen principally on improving the still-buggy printing tool and making other bug fixes. Once the Princeton office was created in mid-1996, Kirchhoff and Ratliff participated in weekly conference calls with the Michigan technologists, joined often by Goldstein and Fuchs. As had been the practice prior to the creation of the Princeton office, the group continued to set out tasks for the coming week and evaluate the accomplishments of the previous week. The system was one of consensual decision making coordinated by Fuchs and Thomas to some degree, rather than one responding to active management.[28]

In part because of the loose organization of the software developers, bringing them together with the other camp of Michigan staffers—the librarians who were split between user services and production—proved to be difficult. The technologists had offices at the engineering school, while the librarians had two offices, at some distance from one another, in Harlan Hatcher, the massive main campus library. The School of Engineering and the library are on two different campuses in Ann Arbor! Due to the origins of the grant relationship between Mellon and Michigan, there was no central organizing force between the librarian and programmer groups. Lougee has noted that this "strange organizational structure" complicated efforts to bring together the various JSTOR operational groups: "We had the librarians and the production people reporting to me, vying for programmer time."[29] This flaw in the reporting structure proved to be problematic, for example, when the new production process required software tools that had to be developed in partnership with the programmers, who naturally prioritized

---

[28]Kevin Guthrie, interview with the author, December 6, 2001.
[29]Wendy Lougee, interview with the author, May 30, 2001.

changes that would more directly affect users, such as those to the printing tool.

These organizational arrangements only served to magnify a more general problem. Programmers were in great demand and generally well paid, and they were used to being integral to the projects on which they worked. At the time, they tended to be guided by technical elegance and efficiency rather than user-experience. In contrast, all of the librarians working on JSTOR were recent library school graduates. Their training led them to a focus on user needs and style, and a preference for accommodating them. These differences in professional outlook led to differing priorities, and the programmers' usually won out. Some reports indicate that the programmers met the librarians' suggestions for functionality improvements with skepticism, questioning whether librarians could contribute usefully to a discussion about technology needs.[30] The result was often inaction.[31] The differences in perspective between the user-services librarians and technologists were understandable, and under other circumstances the tension might have been creative. At JSTOR in the year following independence, however, these tensions were interfering with the progress of work.[32] The gap between librarians and technologists at JSTOR was symptomatic of a larger set of questions in American higher education. For more than a decade, libraries and computer centers had been vying with one another for information primacy on campuses.[33]

Moreover, in differing degrees Frank and Lougee had stepped back further from direct oversight. Nominally, at any rate, Frank and Lougee remained Guthrie's principal contacts in dealing with the staff. When to-do lists grew too large, he turned to them. Yet it was unrealistic to

---

[30] Ibid.

[31] A later anecdote is illustrative. In considering what features to add to the interface, many perspectives must be reconciled. A simpler way to search all of JSTOR's journals concurrently would yield more readily comprehensive searches and was therefore favored by the user-service librarians. It was opposed by at least one JSTOR technologist as "enabling people's laziness," given that there were (longer) routes by which a user could reach the same outcome. Other concerns prevented the implementation of this "Search All" feature for some time. Kristen Garlock, interview with the author, May 25, 2001; Sherry Aschenbrenner, interview with the author, May 30, 2001; Spencer Thomas, interview with the author, May 29, 2001.

[32] There is a fair amount of clear documentary evidence on this topic, and it was also confirmed by many JSTOR staff at the time. Gilbert Whitaker, interview with the author, December 4, 2000; Kevin Guthrie, interview with the author, December 13, 2000; Kristen Garlock, interview with the author, May 25, 2001; Sherry Aschenbrenner, interview with the author, May 30, 2001; Wendy Lougee, interview with the author, May 30, 2001.

[33] See, for example, Larry Hardesty, ed., *Books Bytes and Bridges: Libraries and Computer Centers in Academic Institutions* (Chicago: American Library Association, 2000).

expect Frank and Lougee to be intimately involved in operations, and indeed we saw in chapter 7 that JSTOR itself had tried to move away from such an arrangement. JSTOR was not Frank's primary responsibility. Rather, his primary responsibility at the School of Engineering was the development of the Media Union, a large, striking building that housed all manner of digital resources for faculty and students, plus a library that brought together engineering, art, architecture, and urban planning. Meanwhile, the librarians working on JSTOR—the user-services and production staff—were coordinated by Lougee, who was busy planning for PEAK, supervising Making of America, and developing the University of Michigan's Digital Library Production Services.[34] "Randy and Wendy are often very busy," wrote Guthrie at the time, and so "tasks fall through the cracks."[35] Atkins's involvement was never direct, and in this period it grew still more limited to rare moments as a "firefighter."[36]

As the staffs grew larger and their work more interdependent, the disparate locations and Byzantine organizational structure were hindering progress. Without a clear leader on the ground, or an ability to step in and address problems, Guthrie recalls, "work was being done by committee."[37] No doubt JSTOR shared responsibility for this arrangement being put into place, but, regardless, no one actively involved at Michigan had responsibility for outcomes.

Instead of active campus management, the Michigan bureaucracy took over. The rules and regulations differed from division to division, and so JSTOR had to jump through different hoops depending on whether it was hiring an employee, for example, into the library, the School of Engineering, or the School of Information. When Frank and Lougee were more involved, this had not been problematic, but once they deferred to Guthrie, JSTOR no longer had the institutional expertise.[38] The formal organizational arrangements were no longer matched with the needs or expectations of either JSTOR or Michigan.

Finally, many of the staff at Michigan—the programmers, the librarians, the QC and preparation staff—were beginning to identify more and more with JSTOR. This shift seems to have begun soon after JSTOR

[34] See *www.umdl.umich.edu* and *www.lib.umich.edu/retired/peak*.

[35] Kevin Guthrie, "Michigan Report (Part One)," email to Sarah Sully, William G. Bowen, Ira Fuchs, and Gilbert Whitaker, October 14, 1996.

[36] Dan Atkins, interview with the author, May 31, 2001.

[37] Kevin Guthrie, interview with the author, December 13, 2000.

[38] For example, Guthrie agreed in August 1996 that Bill Landis should hire a deputy, a full-time person to manage the growing production staff. Yet it took nearly two months for the university's human resources procedures to allow Landis to hold interviews. Kevin Guthrie, "Michigan Report (continued)," email to William G. Bowen, October 14, 1996.

became independent from Mellon, and Bowen and Guthrie sought to accelerate it after the Princeton office was opened in mid-1996. The second university office reduced any tendency to consider JSTOR a Michigan project, although there was a concerted effort even after that point to develop staff identification with JSTOR.[39] In the months after the release of the Arts & Sciences I Collection, the staff's JSTOR identity solidified. Yet they had to attend university library or technology committee meetings and staff development sessions, and they retained formal reporting relationships to Frank and Lougee.[40] With identity shifts underway, there was pressure for the enterprise's organization, including the staff's reporting relationships, to keep pace.

All of these various pressures had emerged gradually. In part, they should be understood as resulting from JSTOR's failure to reorganize its Michigan operations after independence. For example, Bowen had suggested that JSTOR take responsibility for Mellon's 1994 grant to Michigan (see chapter 5), and had this been done there would have been an early opportunity for a changed relationship. Although little had changed organizationally at Michigan since 1994, JSTOR's needs had changed substantially. Guthrie was solely responsible for JSTOR and was obliged by his trustees to demand fast progress. He felt responsible for production and software progress in a way that Frank and Lougee, because of their positions, did not. It is not difficult to see how problems could develop.

JSTOR needed to have more direct oversight of its Michigan staff. It wanted to transform its ad hoc agglomeration of staff into a well-organized, deadline-driven enterprise that would be suited for the oncoming marketplace debut. Guthrie concluded in October 1996: "Michigan is still not organized to oversee our operations at the quality level and scale that we envision for JSTOR."[41]

For its part, Michigan was working to address some of the challenges before JSTOR, but to do so completely would severely strain the university's preexisting systems. Atkins recalls that "Bowen wanted JSTOR to have the autonomy of an independent non-profit, but he wanted it to also have the advantage of the business machinery of the university, for it to be accommodated in the university. He wanted the best of both of those worlds."[42] Some at the university envisioned JSTOR as a grant-based academic project, for which its primary interest was

---

[39] William G. Bowen, "U of Michigan," email to Kevin Guthrie, November 6, 1996.
[40] Kristen Garlock, interview with the author, May 25, 2001.
[41] Packet for the board of trustees meeting of October 29, 1996.
[42] Dan Atkins, interview with the author, May 31, 2001.

research and development, not a production-level, marketplace-driven operation.[43] While Frank believes that the two are compatible, the evidence, to JSTOR, suggested otherwise.[44] As one of a number of what Lougee refers to as a "market basket full of little projects I was working on with different partners on campus," JSTOR was frustrated by perceived inattention.[45] On the other hand, many of the projects in the basket would eventually congeal together as the university's Digital Library Production Service. This vision of a complete solution may have impeded the step-by-step resolution of some of JSTOR's pressing problems. Even though, as Atkins points out, JSTOR sought to benefit the system of scholarly communications, the university continued to envision it less as an independent organization operating at the university, like the university press or the alumni society, and more as a research and development grant, perhaps to be linked to the library's production service vision.[46] For this reason, it had been difficult for JSTOR to capture enough attention to generate the changes it sought.

Just as Guthrie was growing increasingly frustrated with Michigan's bureaucracy and inability of JSTOR staff there to work as a coherent team, he became concerned about the ownership of JSTOR's basic intellectual property. As we saw in chapter 3, Mellon had paid for critical improvements in the preexisting DIRECT/TULIP software to create JSTOR, and, because this work was paid for from a Mellon Foundation grant, Michigan retained the intellectual property. This arrangement had caused no problems so far. But in October 1996, Frank emailed Fuchs and Guthrie with a suggestion about the intellectual property (IP) in the software. Programmers at Princeton had for several months been writing code for JSTOR. Spencer Thomas had pointed out that this complicated the IP to JSTOR's software, which was no longer exclusively Michigan's. Frank wondered if Michigan and Princeton should "exchange some paperwork," each allowing the other rights to the IP.[47]

When Guthrie traveled to Ann Arbor later in October, he focused on the possible implications of the current intellectual property ownership

[43] The conflict of research and operations is discussed in Christine L. Borgman, "What are digital libraries? Competing visions," *Information Processing and Management* 35 (May 1999): 227–43.

[44] Randall Frank, interview with the author, July 10, 2001.

[45] Wendy Lougee, interview with the author, December 13, 2001.

[46] Atkins believed that "the university did need to figure out how to do things like JSTOR, where we were, in a financial sense, giving more than we were getting, but that it was for the collective good of the academic enterprise." Dan Atkins, interview with the author, May 31, 2001.

[47] Randall Frank, "Intellectual property rights to code," email to Ira Fuchs (copied to Kevin Guthrie), October 8, 1996.

arrangement more closely than he had before. He asked various Michigan staff how JSTOR software was being used, and he was surprised by the answers. Michigan was proposing to use the software that had been refined by JSTOR-Michigan staff and at Mellon's expense to mount Elsevier journals on a server for other libraries to access, as part of the PEAK experiment. Each party had its own perspective on this situation.

Guthrie was displeased. To many in the library community, Elsevier—despite a number of key contributions—had an extremely negative reputation.[48] JSTOR was taking great pains to build a reputation for balancing the needs of publishers and libraries and was going "live" in only a matter of weeks. Its reputation was one of its key assets, which had to be carefully guarded. Guthrie was concerned that JSTOR would be seen as subsidizing or assisting Elsevier's for-profit activities. He was also concerned that, since many did not yet appreciate the distinction between Michigan and JSTOR, they might assume that this was a backdoor move into the current issues market, which JSTOR had only recently renounced. Thinking as a software entrepreneur, Guthrie felt that software developed for JSTOR (with Mellon funds) should not be freely deployed just anywhere, especially if it could endanger Mellon's interests in JSTOR's success![49]

For its part, the university saw itself attempting to follow the letter and spirit of its agreements with Mellon. The software deployed for JSTOR was not developed uniquely for the Mellon project (see chapter 3). Michigan had created the DIRECT software, using grants from other funders and resources of its own, and then improved it for TULIP. The grantor-grantee relationship between Michigan and Mellon to fund the software for JSTOR called for the university to retain ownership of any resulting intellectual property. As a matter of general principle, Mellon would have permitted—indeed encouraged—Michigan to take on further projects with the products of its grants. Michigan's work on the JSTOR software continued to be both funded and governed by the original agreement with Mellon, and neither the letter nor the spirit of that original agreement was violated by redeploying the JSTOR software for the PEAK experiment. Indeed, Michigan's strategic interest in JSTOR lay in its ability to leverage the Mellon-JSTOR investments with other projects for the greater good of scholarly communications.

---

[48] It should be noted, in fairness, that Elsevier had engaged in experiments like TULIP and later PEAK and shared resources with the JSTOR pilot project. While Elsevier declined to allow its journals to participate in JSTOR, it had contributed significantly to progress in scholarly communications, and to JSTOR in particular, which contributions have gone largely unrecognized in the debate on Elsevier's place in the scholarly community.

[49] Kevin Guthrie, personal communication, August 28, 2001.

Clearly, the ingredients were in place for a major clash. By neglecting detailed conversations with Michigan about the shift of control of the project from Mellon to JSTOR, the seeds had been sown for confrontation. In retrospect, Bowen and Guthrie probably should have been even more explicit with Michigan in 1995 about changes in ownership and control of the project that would result in Mellon's spinoff of JSTOR. But for at least two reasons, this may have been impossible at the time. First, there is evidence to suggest that, at the time, Mellon-JSTOR did not have a clear vision of what its mission and activities would later become. Second, if Bowen and Guthrie had a clear vision of JSTOR's future in 1995, which for these purposes they did not, it is unclear that sharing it with Michigan would have been desirable. As discussed below, the revised arrangements that were put into place between JSTOR and the university in 1997 were less desirable, from the university's perspective, than the original arrangements. Had JSTOR insisted on the revised arrangements from the beginning, it is unclear that the university would have willingly partnered with it.

By coincidence, during the course of Guthrie's October visit to Ann Arbor, Frank shared new calculations indicating that the original Mellon grants would be spent down by approximately June 1997. Regardless of anyone's contentedness or displeasure, JSTOR and the university would have to establish a relationship of their own in the eight remaining months. It was obvious to JSTOR that this was a key opportunity to negotiate a revision to its organizational place at, and its intellectual property arrangements with, the university.[50]

Reorganization

To establish a basis for negotiations, Guthrie worked with JSTOR General Counsel Sarah Sully to draft an agreement with Michigan. To be certain that the proposal would accurately reflect JSTOR's development, Guthrie asked Ken Alexander to document the evolution of JSTOR's software. Alexander's report demonstrated how much the software had been improved since JSTOR came on scene.[51] And of the improvements, not all had been written by Michigan staff. A relatively small, but not insignificant, percentage had been written at Princeton, which Amy

---

[50] Kevin Guthrie, "Michigan Report (Part One)," email to Sarah Sully, William G. Bowen, Ira Fuchs, and Gilbert Whitaker, October 14, 1996.

[51] Ken Alexander, "JSTOR software history," email to Sarah Sully and Kevin Guthrie, February 11, 1997.

Kirchhoff of the Princeton technical staff confirmed a month later.[52] As Frank recognized, it was already impossible to consider the JSTOR working system to be exclusively Michigan's property.

One of JSTOR's principal goals at this point was "to prevent Michigan (or Princeton for that matter) from providing this software to others that might compete with JSTOR."[53] With Alexander's software history in hand, Sully continued to update her draft of an agreement.[54] Under the proposed terms, Michigan retained ownership of all software developed prior to the Mellon grants to Michigan (that is, to improve the DIRECT/TULIP software). But JSTOR was to "own all aspects of the software that [was] developed by Michigan for JSTOR prior to this Agreement [that is, under the Mellon grant], and that will be developed by Michigan for JSTOR [in the future] under this Agreement." In other words, JSTOR would retrospectively take ownership of the software that Michigan had improved, with Mellon funds, for JSTOR—software that, by the terms of the Mellon grant, was to be retained by the university.

Michigan administrators were plainly unhappy with the proposal. The retrospective terms for intellectual property were, from the university's perspective, clearly a nonstarter. The university expected to retain the intellectual property of research projects developed with outside funding, as it had with the DEC funding of DIRECT. The terms of the Mellon grant explicitly called for the university to retain ownership of the intellectual property it would create, with Mellon-JSTOR to receive a nonexclusive license for its use. Upon looking at the proposal, Michigan's lawyer told Lougee that "this feels like a divorce settlement, where it's not only who gets what property, but do you ever get to see your kids again?"[55]

Beyond differing from the letter and spirit of the original agreement, JSTOR's request would affect ongoing operations in a number of ways. Because the university had not worried about apportioning IP, the programmers had been able to work on JSTOR "in the morning" and another digital library project "in the afternoon," with intended cross-fertilization. This was the very essence of sponsored research.[56] Michigan's

---

[52] Amy J. Kirchhoff, "JSTOR software dependencies," email to Ira Fuchs, and Serge Goldstein, March 28, 1997.

[53] Kevin Guthrie and Sarah Sully, "First Draft of JSTOR/Michigan Agreement," confidential memorandum to William G. Bowen and Gilbert Whitaker, February 12, 1997.

[54] [Sarah Sully], "Cooperative Service and License Agreement," JSTOR draft of February 18, 1997.

[55] Wendy Lougee, interview with the author, December 13, 2001.

[56] Of course, research in U.S. academia has grown much more commercialized since the early 1980s, in the wake of the Bayh-Dole Act. Intellectual property agreements with outside funders, not to mention restrictions on publication, have become the norm.

strategic interest in digital library software development lay precisely in its ability to leverage software across multiple projects. Otherwise, it would be a service provider for JSTOR, rather than benefiting from it.

Michigan's objections were legitimate and sensible. But what the university perceived as a retrospective "grab" for intellectual property rights was to Guthrie integral for JSTOR's success. JSTOR did not want to sponsor research; it was looking to build a marketplace operation. And besides, it was becoming increasingly clear to Guthrie that Michigan was not exclusively interested in research, either:

> The problem is that there are some at Michigan who argue that Michigan is going to be a major player in the business of content provision to the research community at large. One example of this would be the possibility that Michigan would house and provide access for a fee to current issues of scholarly journal publications, including commercial publishers. . . . [W]e cannot accept the possibility that technology we pay for would be used for that purpose. JSTOR specifically chose to work exclusively on building a trusted archive so that we would provide a service that would be complementary to that provided by our publishers, not competitive with them.[57]

JSTOR had made the difficult decision to avoid the current issues business, worried that its publisher relations would become too complicated (see chapter 6). Now, it seemed to Guthrie that Michigan might take on this work. Of course, Lougee points out, "We're a library, and it's kind of hard not to do journal projects."[58] Yet Michigan's infrastructure for the journals project was JSTOR's software and it could in the process be risking JSTOR's good name. Indeed, Michigan had been showing JSTOR to others as the platform on which this service would be built, without consulting JSTOR itself.

One early compromise, suggested by Guthrie, was to prove key in the end. Rather than think of JSTOR software as having developed in two stages—that is, before and after the Mellon grant—he suggested that it be thought of in three stages, each treated individually. One stage would cover the period prior to Mellon funds being granted to Michigan in 1994; a second stage during the period of Mellon funding of Michigan's work; and a third stage, to begin forthwith, when JSTOR itself would begin paying for further software development work at Michigan. This tripartite division of the software development allowed each section, paid

---

[57] Packet for the JSTOR board of trustees meeting on April 3, 1997. Note that Guthrie probably wrote and distributed these words approximately two weeks earlier than the date of the board meeting.

[58] Wendy Lougee, interview with the author, December 13, 2001.

for by different funders under different initial agreements, to be treated individually.

In late March, using this tripartite basis, Michigan lawyers and Sully negotiated at some length about proposed solutions. Michigan proposed that the university grant JSTOR joint ownership of all of the relevant software—whether developed previously or into the future. In addition, the university would agree not to compete "directly" with "the service envisioned by the pilot project in a non-profit environment." But Sully expressed several concerns. First, joint ownership would allow Michigan to use the JSTOR software as it liked into the future, but JSTOR required "full ownership of all intellectual property developed . . . from the effective date forward." In addition, JSTOR wanted some sort of non-competition agreement that would cover indirect competition, which Michigan noted "seems to press most heavily against School of Information, Library, and Media Union concerns of freedom of operation."[59]

By this point, positions had hardened enough that it seemed JSTOR and Michigan might be forced to part company, even though such an action would have had disastrous consequences for JSTOR's production goals. The negotiations seemed ready to break down, and it is not surprising that, at approximately this point, JSTOR began to conclude that it had become overdependent on Michigan. Luckily, the Princeton software group, recently brought on board, was developing expertise and a mirror site in another location.[60] Consequently JSTOR began to seek an additional production facility (see chapter 11). "That was," Bowen has said, "no criticism of Michigan, it was just a sense that . . . it was not wise to be utterly dependent on one place because anything could have happened. . . . any number of disasters could have occurred."[61] But this decision to seek redundancy would contribute to the altered relationship between JSTOR and Michigan.

The ominous tone of developments kept Whitaker awake that night, and his sleeplessness led to a 4 A.M. email that suggested the issues were less complicated than was believed. With respect to intellectual property, he believed there were really only two issues at stake. First, the software that had been developed with Mellon funding for JSTOR should never be used in any ways "that harm JSTOR," but ownership

---

[59] Michael A. Kope, "JSTOR Contract," email to Sarah Sully, Kevin Guthrie, Dan Atkins, Randy Frank, Wendy Lougee, and Gilbert Whitaker, March 28, 1997.

[60] Indeed, at the time Fuchs asked Kirchhoff what would be necessary for JSTOR to begin running exclusively from Princeton. Kirchhoff estimated it would take months to rewrite the software so that it was independent of the Michigan-owned code. Amy J. Kirchhoff, "JSTOR software dependencies," email to Ira Fuchs and Serge Goldstein, March 28, 1997.

[61] William G. Bowen, interview with the author, November 20, 2000.

should remain with Michigan. Second, any further software developed would be owned by JSTOR "with a willingness to [allow] non-harmful use [by] Michigan."[62] Although positions continued to be refined further, it would be only several days later that Dean Atkins of the School of Information would report that "Kevin and I had a long telephone conversation . . . and I think [we] have come to agreement on the intellectual property issues."[63]

In the final agreement, Michigan's big concession in terms of the intellectual property was giving JSTOR joint ownership of the search engine, FTL, so that both JSTOR and Michigan had the absolute individual right to utilize, distribute, and even sublicense it. This was a significant concession because it gave JSTOR rights not only to the work for which Mellon had paid, but also for all of the development work that Michigan had undertaken for the DIRECT project. The search engine was clearly the most important part of JSTOR's software package, but also the piece that Michigan most wanted to keep. This arrangement allowed Michigan to continue owning future versions of the software while also allowing JSTOR to use them.

Other software was less critical and could therefore be divided more cleanly. Michigan retained full ownership of everything created before the effective date of the interim agreement (June 20, 1997), while JSTOR would own everything that was created after that date by full-time JSTOR staff. In addition, the university gave JSTOR an irrevocable license to all previously created software that had been used by JSTOR. These terms combined to protect JSTOR from any potential future problems. Finally, JSTOR agreed that the university could, with its permission, use its software for certain projects. In exchange, the university promised not to compete with JSTOR on projects that involved journal backfiles.[64]

Before these intellectual property agreements could be finalized, there were difficult negotiations about organizational change. Providing JSTOR with a satisfactory organizational home in the Michigan bureaucracy proved to be nearly impossible. Eventually, Michigan President Lee Bollinger (now president of Columbia University) instructed staff to accommodate JSTOR, asking the university's co-interim general counsel, Elizabeth Barry, to work out an agreement. Barry recalls unmistakably

[62] Gilbert Whitaker, "<no subject>," email to Dan Atkins, Randall Frank, Wendy Lougee, William G. Bowen, Kevin Guthrie, and Sarah Sully, March 29, 1997.

[63] Dan Atkins, "Telephone meeting," email to Kevin Guthrie, Gilbert Whitaker, Michael A. Kope, Randy Frank, Wendy Lougee, and Nathan Eriksen, April 1, 1997.

[64] "Research Agreement," signed by Kevin M. Guthrie and Lee C. Bollinger, dated October 3, 1997.

the reason for this high-level intervention. The University of Michigan had "a relationship with the Mellon Foundation, that was of significant enough interest to the university, of significant importance to the university, that we stretched very far to come up with an arrangement for JSTOR that, without that kind of interest coming from the president of the university, wouldn't have gotten done."[65]

Even though Mellon and JSTOR were formally separated, Bowen's position as president of Mellon clearly had an impact upon JSTOR's negotiating position with regard to the university.[66] Besides which, Bowen and Bollinger were good friends and could speak honestly and directly.

Once Bollinger decided that Michigan would accommodate JSTOR organizationally, it took very little time for Barry and JSTOR to complete negotiations. An interim agreement was signed in the early summer of 1997, followed by a final agreement in the fall. The most noteworthy provision was that JSTOR staff be formally supervised by a committee made up of Atkins, Frank, Lougee, and a provost's designee—a committee that, through mid-2001, never met. In practice, JSTOR had direct authority over the performance of its Michigan staff, all of whom would be devoted full-time to JSTOR. Guthrie, Sully, and, later, others could work directly with colleagues in Ann Arbor, bringing JSTOR together as a single organization with an undisputed mission. JSTOR's Michigan operations were organizationally freed from any semblance of ties to a research grant.[67]

The arrangements on intellectual property and organization did not cost the university anything in terms of money or prestige. Yet the cost in principle was high. A fair amount of the initial agreement between Mellon and Michigan on intellectual property had been altered retrospectively, especially for the search engine. Organizationally, Frank and Lougee lost control of an important digital library project they had worked to build as a Mellon grant project. The university, and the School of Information under Atkins, no longer had any role, even nominally, in setting directions for JSTOR; now a separate unit worked directly with an external organization.

[65] Elizabeth Barry, interview with the author, May 30, 2001.

[66] It is important to note that Mellon continued to award grants to the university, including the School of Information, for other purposes in this period.

[67] Guthrie recalls that, in the course of the reorganization, "I think the biggest thing that happened was that . . . we ended up reporting in [to the university] at one place, the School of Information. . . . it sent a message that JSTOR was an important project at the university, all the way up to the top." Kevin Guthrie, interview with the author, October 30, 2001.

Michigan administrators' recollections have probably faded in their passion over time. Even so, Atkins recalls that "people didn't use the term 'exploited,' but there was that implication. . . . the normal [feeling of] human ownership and a degree of ego involved."[68] Lougee characterizes JSTOR's concerns about IP as "legitimate" and believes that "Kevin needed to be in more direct control and that all of the parts needed to work together," but she remembers a bit of "separation anxiety."[69] Frank regrets that relations between JSTOR and the university became "unnecessarily polarized," concluding that lawyers were consulted before general principles were agreed upon.[70] Barry is unabashed in concluding that "everyone at the university perceived [the IP arrangements] as a free giveaway."[71]

JSTOR had become a more mature and professionalized organization, and now its paper agreements with Michigan reflected this new reality. And the list of benefits was significant. In the wake of the renegotiations, JSTOR's Michigan operations were consolidated in one off-campus building with larger spaces and dedicated facilities, helping to solidify their arrangement as a group apart from the normal university operations. JSTOR-Michigan was now something of a business unit, rather than a component of an academic library or a research group. At the same time, and also as a result of the reorganization, the remaining part-time employees shifted to full-time, and Michigan managers withdrew. For the first time, all of JSTOR's Michigan staff were housed together and working exclusively on JSTOR. As a result, JSTOR's software group was now much better positioned to work as a team on priorities set by and for JSTOR. Staff further solidified their identification with JSTOR, further attenuating the connection with Michigan.

Soon after this new agreement was signed, JSTOR's board held a meeting in Ann Arbor. Bollinger hosted a dinner for the board, which Guthrie describes as "a celebration of a broad relationship and a broad mutual understanding."[72] Although tensions had run high for a time, in its new form the JSTOR-Michigan relationship persevered. In the years that have followed, the agreement has worked well for JSTOR and it has been renewed annually.[73]

---

[68] Dan Atkins, interview with the author, May 31, 2001.

[69] Wendy Lougee, interview with the author, May 30, 2001.

[70] Randall Frank, interview with the author, July 10, 2001.

[71] Elizabeth Barry, interview with the author, May 30, 2001.

[72] Kevin Guthrie, interview with the author, December 6, 2001.

[73] For JSTOR's perspective, see Kevin M. Guthrie, "JSTOR and the University of Michigan: An Evolving Collaboration," *Library Hi Tech* 16, no. 1 (1998): 9–14, 36.

SUMMATION

JSTOR's efforts to create a viable production-scale digitization and soft-ware-development operation were lengthy and challenging. Regarding production, the arrangements that Guthrie and Lougee developed (see chapter 7), and Andrews and Landis then revamped, laid the groundwork for an efficient operation. By mid-1997, once the Michigan organization and management was sufficient for JSTOR's purposes, digitization be-gan to proceed smoothly. In addition, the critical addition of Eileen Fenton provided an effective manager with sufficient authority on the ground and support in New York to succeed. Software development had more initial capability, since it transitioned from a preexisting group at the university, but as a result it was more challenging to free it from preexisting Michigan structures.

The lesson of this chapter has been that, in order for all of this to oc-cur, JSTOR's relations with Michigan necessarily changed—explicitly, and several times implicitly—until the university viewed its relationship with JSTOR as retaining little synergy. Until 1997, Michigan was clearly not able to offer JSTOR the digital library production services it required. Only in exceptional enterprise arrangements are research universities set up for production and deployment. JSTOR required a sense of inde-pendence like that of a university press, in which staff view their pri-mary responsibility as meeting the needs of a business unit. Michigan struggled to operate JSTOR as a grant-funded development project. When its operations were given the independence and organization to work as a production office—somewhat akin to the arrangements of a university press—JSTOR was far more satisfied. The effect was to take the JSTOR-Michigan groups out of the university organization and place them, in effect, "inside" the JSTOR organization. JSTOR needed "inter-nal" capacity, rather than the sort of outside partnership or contract that had earlier developed at Michigan.

It was only when JSTOR actively stepped in that the Michigan pro-duction operation became viable. This is not to denigrate the contribu-tions made by Michigan administrators like Lougee; it is inconceivable that JSTOR's production operation could have been developed without her important contributions. But in the end, the sustained attention that full-time JSTOR staff brought to bear was integral to the necessary on-going production work. Guthrie and Bowen were able to give attention to good ideas, like a sampling process, as soon as they were suggested. Working with Guthrie and Sully, Fenton had both the responsibility and the authority to bring managerial order to the production group.

Preexisting university organizational structures would have been less likely to have reached the same ends.

In the realm of software development, it had to be clearly established that the mission was related to JSTOR, rather than to DIRECT, or FTL, or the university. Again, this is not to denigrate anyone's contributions at the time. But it was difficult for a team of technologists that continued to work on a number of digital library projects—of which JSTOR was only one—to view JSTOR's needs as primary. In this regard, the Princeton mirror site not only gave Michigan some competition, but also helped to clarify the primacy of the JSTOR organization.

It was perhaps unfortunate, but altogether necessary, that JSTOR evolve away from a close relationship with Michigan and its other digital library projects. There was (and still is) much innovative work taking place there, and the synergies that did not occur were certainly a loss. In particular, the Digital Library Production Service that was subsequently developed under Lougee's leadership might have been an important partner. But the DLPS's production capacity was not available in time for JSTOR's needs. JSTOR had to build an independent production operation of its own.

To underscore, the synergy that has resulted has, for Michigan, been less than optimal. While JSTOR focused on completing Arts & Sciences I in the time remaining, Michigan had digital library goals of its own. For example, Michigan had secured funds for a digital library project on space science, and Dan Atkins tried to convince JSTOR to digitize geology journals as a complement. Atkins believes that, given the university's special arrangements to accommodate JSTOR, "it would not be unreasonable to assume that they might do something a little bit out of order or a little bit different, in the same spirit of specialness," to accommodate the university.[74] JSTOR would later include some geology journals in its Arts & Sciences II Collection, but at the time the principal scholarly society was not an enthusiast.[75] JSTOR was not able to devote enormous time and resources to securing the participation of a discipline that did not fit squarely into the first collection it was building. Had JSTOR been constituted under a different organizational structure—perhaps as a unit of Michigan's library or university press—a different outcome would have been likely. This is an indication of the sorts of pressures for new priorities that would likely have faced it had JSTOR been in some sense a satellite of the university—a scenario that Bowen considered and rejected.

---

[74] Dan Atkins, interview with the author, May 31, 2001.

[75] Kevin Guthrie, "1st day of meetings at the University of Michigan," email to William G. Bowen, January 19, 1997.

JSTOR's arrangement of keeping a skeletal central office with a production operation at Michigan had several advantages. First, while Guthrie traveled to Michigan frequently to keep apace of events there, his distance allowed or forced him to concentrate on publisher and library relations. Focusing on production and software could easily have used up all of Guthrie's time. By locating JSTOR's administration away from the Michigan staff, he was able to stay more strategically and externally focused rather than becoming consumed by operations. Second, JSTOR did not rapidly build up production staff until it had developed a satisfactory operation. This decision allowed JSTOR to "burn" through very little money during its first two years after independence, thereby stretching its grant funds to their maximum. Although the staff grew, it grew only gradually. In general, JSTOR acted conservatively in its growth, determined to get its initial procedures in place before expanding.

In no domain other than intellectual property did JSTOR's needs change so radically from its days as a Mellon project. Rather than assuming that "friendly organizations" like JSTOR, Mellon, and Michigan would work things out, JSTOR began to behave like a business, with proprietary rights that required protection. Ideally, Mellon would have established a different intellectual property understanding in its 1994 grants to Michigan, and Bowen's early comments about JSTOR's need to seek independence suggest that this was something more than a remote possibility (see chapter 3). But the case of JSTOR does not show any clear error. Mellon reserved the rights that it believed to be necessary in order to create the database; it was not thinking two or three years ahead about the marketplace needs of a business. A renegotiation at the time of JSTOR's independence might have been desirable, but it might also have been awkward. In the years that followed, Mellon would develop a more systematic approach to intellectual property issues, and it has undertaken other major digitization projects with complicated software arrangements (the foremost of which being ArtSTOR), the outcome of which are yet to be determined.

As an increasingly professionalized organization, independent of both Michigan and Mellon, JSTOR was ready to take on further challenges. A large motivating influence for all of these changes had been the knowledge that, per the terms of the plan, JSTOR would be launched publicly at the beginning of 1997. Indeed, while its organization and operation were being brought to a higher standard, JSTOR was already working to present itself to the library community as an appealing service on which to expend scarce resources.

CHAPTER 10

Public Availability and Library Participation

SEPTEMBER 1996–DECEMBER 1997

By late 1996, JSTOR had completed all of the work necessary for public release. Even though only seventeen journals had been digitized by January 1997, JSTOR was not willing to delay its entry into the marketplace any further. The extent, speed, and distribution of library participants would determine whether JSTOR could reach the scale necessary for success. This chapter explores how JSTOR marketed and licensed its first collection, Arts & Sciences I, through the close of 1997. First, going back to 1996, it will document the actions that followed the adoption of the business plan. Some of JSTOR's most important policies on library relations—including its stance on consortia—were formulated at this time. Then, it will describe how and why some libraries opted to license this collection (mostly under the charter provision) while others did not. The libraries that signed on during the first year or so tended to think of themselves as being in the vanguard of an experiment rather than as customers of a business. In this year, JSTOR signed on mainly the risk-takers. Only later would a broader group of libraries clamor to participate.

LIBRARY LICENSE

In implementing the business plan, one of the first steps was for Sarah Sully to craft the license terms by which academic libraries could participate in JSTOR. In a sense, these agreements would be the parallel to the publisher licenses that JSTOR had been signing for the past year. Much as standard agreements were an integral part of JSTOR's ability to encourage journal participation, so a standard license was seen as critical to JSTOR's ability to take on numerous library participants. But just as many publishers were unfamiliar with licensing their journals to an electronic database, so many libraries were only just beginning to license online resources like JSTOR.[1]

---

[1]For an overview of the licensing environment in this period, see Ann S. Okerson, "The Transition to Electronic Content Licensing: The Institutional Context in 1997," in Richard Ekman and Richard E. Quandt, eds., *Technology and Scholarly Communications* (Berkeley: University of California Press, 1999), 53–70.

Libraries were accustomed to collections development by outright purchase of materials in traditional formats such as books, serials, and microfilm. Licensing digital resources, rather than purchasing printed materials outright, presented a challenge for both librarians and publishers. At first, publishers traditionally sought the most restrictive and comprehensive terms, and the librarians that were in the vanguard of interest in e-resources were willing to accept them. But when librarians began reading licenses more carefully—as Ann Okerson did when she took on responsibility for all collections development at Yale University—they grew concerned lest they abandon their traditional commitment to broad and free availability of information. Licensing digital resources should not, they believed, result in an abandonment of librarians' long-held values, such as the ability of readers to make "fair use" of copyrighted publications for research and education. In 1995, when negotiating a license for the Biosis database, Okerson noticed the phrase, "no reproduction by any means, mechanical or electronic," which could be interpreted to bar fair use of the resource. She "contacted Biosis and said we could not renew the sub[scription] under those terms."[2]

In 1996, Okerson identified several of the most commonplace shortcomings in digital library resource licenses.[3] Okerson's thoughts are important for several reasons, most importantly because they offer a useful summary of the most common licensing flaws, from a librarian's perspective, at approximately the time that JSTOR was creating its own library license. First, according to Okerson, licenses often defined "users," seeking to limit use of the resource only to the library building and only to students, faculty, and staff. Academic libraries often admitted unaffiliated walk-in users in addition to the campus community, and they wanted to be able to give such users access to their digital resources. They also wanted the resource available anywhere on the campus network. The licenses sometimes also defined acceptable use, which librarians interpreted as prohibiting fair use of the resource. Librarians wanted readers to retain the right to copy "reasonable" amounts of content and to incorporate these copies into scholarly works and teaching materials.[4] Second, licenses often attempted to impose legal responsibility

[2] Joyce Ogburn, "A Look Back at Licensing," *Against the Grain* 13, no. 4 (September 2001).

[3] Ann Okerson, "What Academic Libraries Need in Electronic Content Licenses," presentation to the STM Library Relations Committee, October 1, 1996; available online at *http://www.library.yale.edu/~okerson/stm.html*.

For a somewhat earlier, but largely consonant, view, see Edward A. Warro, "What Have We Been Signing? A Look at Database Licensing Agreements," *Library Administration & Management* 8, no. 3 (Summer 1994): 173–77.

[4] In other words, they did not want "fair use" provisions of the copyright code to be impaired by licensing restrictions.

on libraries for any impermissible user behavior, even though libraries had no established way of monitoring (and no desire to monitor) their users. Third, licenses often included vague or impossible-to-satisfy technology expectations, such as the need to include resource-specific copyright statements on all printouts. Fourth, licenses occasionally obscured, whether intentionally or accidentally, the pricing plan over the life of the agreement. Finally, licenses often included no guarantee of archiving or perpetual access, and when they did, the terms were often vague.

The situation looked extremely different to publishers. Perhaps in part because they had experienced cancellations in the face of the serials crisis, their executives saw the opportunity to correct perceived imbalances in the system. Although it has not been possible to identify contemporaneous commentary, by the spring of 1999, one commentator reflected that, after much progress, several divisive issues still remained: whether and how fair use would apply, and the place of ILL.[5] Reflecting on her experience with licensing, Eileen Lawrence of Chadwyck-Healy made clear that "publishers are afraid that their painstakingly created data will be misused, resold, or copied—that what they've created to sell may not remain salable." But recalling her own education in licensing techniques, Lawrence explained the virtues of the vague but legally enforceable term "reasonable" to limit the actions of researchers and libraries—and who would oppose the reasonable! In looking back, she explained that "the task has become at least neutral, if not enjoyable."[6]

Of course, librarians and publishers differed—and JSTOR sought to position itself in the precarious middle ground. Okerson was one of several early advocates of library action to negotiate, rather than simply accept, the terms of licenses, and her article drew some lines in the sand that she believed librarians should not cross. Librarians began attending licensing seminars and discussing collective actions to force publishers to compromise. Libraries signing a license with JSTOR were likely to demand especially advantageous terms because of its nonprofit, library-friendly mission. And JSTOR wanted its license to be, from the beginning, appealing to librarians and responsive to their needs. Yet it also had to meet the legitimate needs of publishers and be acceptable to them.

Consequently, JSTOR's library license was crafted with the input and active collaboration of several librarians and publishers. On the librarian side, Wendy Lougee of Michigan (now at the University of Minne-

[5]John E. Cox, "Publisher/Library Relationships in the Digital Environment," report commissioned by the STM Library Relations Committee, April 1999.

[6]Eileen Lawrence, "Licensing: A Publisher's Perspective," *Serials Librarian* 38, nos. 1 and 2 (2000): 147–153. For a more contemporaneous publication, see Joseph P. Bremmer, *Guide to Database Distribution: Second Edition* (Philadelphia: NFAIS, 1994).

sota), David Pilachowski of Denison (now at Williams College), Nancy Cline of Harvard, and Okerson herself all reviewed the license, offering feedback that led to a number of changes.[7] On the publisher side, JSTOR went to a commercial publisher, John Wiley, for what it presumed to be a self-protective perspective.[8] Only with these inputs did the license become a document that worked for all parties.

A brief summary of some of the most important terms illustrates how JSTOR addressed key issues.[9] The archive was available not only to anyone present in the library, whether an affiliate or a visitor, but also to all campus-based affiliates, no matter where they were located. These users were allowed to make any use of the database that was permitted by copyright law, so long as no fees were charged for use. (As we saw in chapter 8, JSTOR's leaders believed that the best outcome would be maximum possible use of the database and that by-the-drink pricing would inhibit usage.) If a user were to abuse the database, JSTOR required libraries to cooperate, but it did not impose unrealistic requirements of users or libraries about prohibited uses or controlling usage. The pricing plan, as we saw in chapter 8, was very explicit. Finally, JSTOR's archival responsibilities were clear: If its business declined and it could no longer remain accessible, JSTOR would provide a copy of the digitized page images to the participating libraries.

One subject that Okerson had not mentioned proved to be important for JSTOR's initial library license. Licenses for digital resources in 1996 and 1997 generally barred the use of the resources for ILL, because publishers feared that it would substantially reduce the numer of library subscribers.[10] While JSTOR also had such concerns, ILL had become symbolic of a core value of librarians, that information should be available, when needed, even to those who could not pay. As a result, anti-ILL provisions provoked great objections by librarians.[11]

[7]Ann Okerson, "JSTOR License," email to Kevin Guthrie and Sarah Sully, October 23, 1996.

[8]Kevin Guthrie, interview with the author, October 30, 2001.

[9]A copy of the license at the time may be found in the packet for the JSTOR board of trustees meeting of October 29, 1996.

[10]For an excellent and succinct summary of the publisher perspective at this time, see item 6 of Karen Hunter, "Things that Keep Me Awake at Night," *Against the Grain* February 1997: 42.

[11]Publications by a number of librarians had made clear that at least some of them viewed ILL as a substitute for purchases, so it is not difficult to appreciate publishers' concerns. While ILL had been created to allow patrons access to materials that their libraries could not justify purchasing, now it was being used to justify cutbacks. See, for example, Terry Mackey, "Interlibrary Loan: An acceptable alternative to purchase," *Wilson Library Bulletin* 63 (January 1989): 54–56; and Valerie J. Payne and Mary Burke, "A cost-effectiveness study of ownership versus access," *Serials Librarian* 32, no. 3–4 (1997): 139–52.

At a meeting of the Association of Research Libraries just before JSTOR became publicly available, Harvard College librarian Nancy Cline suggested a compromise.[12] There would be a trial period during which libraries would be able to make use of JSTOR for ILL, by printing out articles and sending them by traditional means but not by forwarding them electronically.[13] The ILL departments would keep records of the amount of JSTOR use for ILL purposes. As Guthrie explained to the board, "Publishers claim that ILL is rampant; librarians claim that it is minimal. We will offer a service by ascertaining where the truth lies."[14] At the end of the two-year experimental period, JSTOR would determine whether the amount of ILL was significant enough that it was proving to be a threat. The trustees adopted this plan as "a workable compromise."[15] It would turn out that JSTOR use for ILL was not only not a threat, but essentially nonexistent.[16]

PUBLICITY AND SELF-PRESENTATION

Well before JSTOR's public release, Guthrie gave serious thought to crafting an image for the organization. He wanted it to be perceived in the marketplace as uniquely library-friendly, and to take advantage of JSTOR's central mission, historical roots, and nonprofit status. One result of this determination was in nomenclature. Whereas other resource-providers were "vendors," JSTOR was a "collaborator"; vendors targeted a "market," but JSTOR embraced a "community"; successful marketing would yield "subscribers," but JSTOR sought "participants"; and whereas subscribers paid a "price," JSTOR charged "fees." Guthrie believed that JSTOR's mission entitled it to be perceived by libraries differently than the typical vendor.

---

[12]Kevin Guthrie, "ARL meeting/presentation," email to William G. Bowen, October 18, 1996.

[13]In discussing ILL, it is important to recognize that all that is at stake is the journal articles themselves. There has never been any consideration of an ILL of the *database*—the searching functions that add so much value to JSTOR. Thus, even if a small public library can obtain a given article for a patron via ILL, the searching functions are altogether inaccessible. From JSTOR's perspective, ILL would have been of only moderate concern.

[14]Packet for the JSTOR board of trustees meeting of October 29, 1996.

[15]Minutes of the JSTOR board of trustees meeting of October 29, 1996.

[16]It is conceivable that some librarians, recognizing that a test was at hand, resisted using JSTOR for ILL during the test period. Guthrie believes that many ILL departments may have found it easier to continue using print sources at the time, rather than tracking those sources available online. It is quite possible that since then use of JSTOR for ILL has increased. Kevin Guthrie, interview with the author, October 30, 2001.

JSTOR's desire to be perceived differently was legitimate only insofar as it behaved differently. In part to save money and in part because they were not believed to be necessary, JSTOR placed no advertisements in trade publications and did not set up marketing booths—which were often flashy and always pricey—at conferences.[17] Perhaps even more importantly, there was no sales staff. Unlike many vendors and subscription agents, JSTOR did not hire salespeople to travel the nation. JSTOR believed that only those libraries that chose to participate should do so; while it believed many would want to participate, it was not seeking profits.[18]

Instead, JSTOR created an "about" section on its website to distribute information it believed librarians would value. Rather than providing a phone number to contact a salesperson for pricing information, as was and continues to be standard practice, JSTOR shared all pricing and access information publicly, thereby underscoring its standard, transparent terms. Eventually, the website would even include printable versions of the library license that could be sent to JSTOR with a check or purchase order enclosed; because the terms were publicly available, there was no need for the truly convinced even to speak with a representative. In addition, there was a demonstration database with one journal's early issues, those whose copyright had expired. This allowed anyone to test out JSTOR, obviating the need for a traveling salesperson to "demo" its features locally. In these ways, JSTOR took advantage of the web for its library relations.

While some aspects of its approach were unusual, JSTOR made use of standard techniques when they seemed appropriate and efficacious. It engaged in marketing and sales techniques such as sending letters and promotional materials to librarians. It created a newsletter, to provide updates about its progress. There were also less formal means to build awareness, such as dispatching representatives to speak at conferences. At the meeting of the Association of Research Libraries, when Guthrie and Cline developed the ILL policy, about twenty-five major libraries expressed interest in signing up.[19] While these standard methods were without question useful, JSTOR did not allow its approach to be defined by the industry standard.

It is important to note that JSTOR had a number of choices in how to present itself publicly. Space-saving and resource-saving remained

[17] As Bruce Heterick, later JSTOR's director of Library Relations, explains, advertising and booths are a given in the industry, "but then you are just one of the [hundreds of] exhibitors." Bruce Heterick, interview with the author, February 4, 2002.

[18] Kevin Guthrie, interview with the author, October 30, 2001.

[19] Kevin Guthrie, "ARL meeting/presentation," email to William G. Bowen, October 18, 1996.

critical features, but for some time Bowen had also been presenting JSTOR as an access mechanism. In early 1995 he reflected on the shift: "We are now giving more attention to [JSTOR's] immediate utility to users [as a result of] what we have learned about the abundant technical possibilities for creating a highly accessible database."[20] In a mid-1995 speech, he presented JSTOR as of greatest interest to research-intensive schools, closed-stack libraries, and institutions that lacked paper copies. His emphasis was no longer on the ability to move paper backfiles off-campus or discard them.[21] Bowen, Guthrie, and others speaking on JSTOR's behalf remained convinced of its cost-saving potential, and spoke of it frequently. Even so, it had become clear that access was, for librarians, a most resonant feature. Remarkably, a scholarly resource that had been conceived amid constrained resources and tightening belts was of great interest for its searchability and desktop access, features that did not really save money. Although JSTOR remained both better and cheaper, its emphasis changed to focus on the former in addition to the latter.

How and why did JSTOR become more than just a cost-saving resource? For one thing, many of the most important access features were not fully conceived of when JSTOR was first created in 1994. Fulltext searching and 24-hour desktop availability were not envisioned in the earliest plans for a CD-ROM nonsearchable resource, and these features were added only at the urging of a number of advisors, including Fuchs, the test-site librarians, and the rest of the advisory committee. Once the features were available to the test sites (and to Guthrie and others), their utility became increasingly clear. The library take on JSTOR's value, and its implications, are discussed further in this and future chapters.

CHARTER SUBSCRIBERS:
DEGENNARO AND THE FIRST 190 LIBRARIES

During the four months at the beginning of 1997 when charter membership was available, 190 libraries joined JSTOR. This number was significantly greater than the most optimistic predictions. The Strategic and Operating Plan, which was completed before the charter period began, called for only about 120. Retrospectively, Bowen would write that

---

[20] William G. Bowen, "The Foundation's Journal Storage Project (JSTOR)," in *Report of the Andrew W. Mellon Foundation 1994* (New York: Andrew W. Mellon Foundation, 1995).

[21] William G. Bowen, "JSTOR and the Economics of Scholarly Communications," speech to the Council on Library and Information Resources, Washington, DC, September 18, 1995; revised version online at *www.mellon.org/jsesc.html*.

Guthrie "hoped to sign up 50 to 75" charter participants.[22] In either case, expectations were exceeded. How was this success achieved?

JSTOR faced the immediate challenge of legitimacy in the library community. Guthrie was unknown to most librarians, and the JSTOR "brand name" was equally unknown. With less than one-fifth of the planned journals available, JSTOR was selling only a promise, yet its pricing policy required a large up-front payment. JSTOR clearly faced a challenge, and its leaders recognized the need to establish legitimacy. They did not simply assume that a good service would achieve success—they were attuned to the need for the right people to support it. To help, they needed someone who could talk with senior librarians as a peer.

Board member Richard DeGennaro offered to introduce JSTOR to his extensive network of contacts among library directors, and his help was gladly accepted. He telephoned many dozens of head librarians, particularly at the largest and more research-oriented academic libraries. These directors gladly accepted the call of the emeritus director of the Harvard College Library when they might have passed Guthrie along to a deputy.[23] With the ear of the director or dean, DeGennaro explained JSTOR's mission, the journals collection it was building, and the qualifications of its leadership. Beyond simple salesmanship, DeGennaro remembers his role as "putting my own reputation on the line . . . to stand behind" JSTOR's leadership, Guthrie in particular.[24]

Notably, DeGennaro relieved Guthrie of some of the onerous work of reaching out to libraries. Guthrie nevertheless made numerous contacts of his own, and he always had to follow up after DeGennaro's initial contact.[25] This work alone occupied perhaps 60–70 percent of his time for nearly a year.[26] As a result of this approach, it was possible for every

[22] William G. Bowen, "University of Chicago Press Journals—JSTOR," memorandum to Arthur Sussman, May 26, 1997.

[23] DeGennaro was well known not only because he had also served as library director of Harvard, and previously of Penn and the New York Public Library. He had served on the board of RLG (for a time as chairman) and had been an important voice urging library automation. His name was a familiar one to a generation of academic librarians.

[24] Richard DeGennaro, interview with the author, March 30, 2001.

[25] In retrospect, Guthrie is glad that he and DeGennaro did this early library outreach work themselves, rather than hiring a professional salesperson. "I learned a lot about what librarians were worried about. . . . I think I understood what the issues were. Those lessons are important all the time. . . . Looking at our website, seeing how it emphasized things, I think a lot of those lessons were learned in that intense six-month period—hearing what kinds of questions people were asking, and why they had problems, and what they needed solved." Kevin Guthrie, interview with the author, March 25, 2002.

[26] Kevin Guthrie, "RE: time costs for licensing agreements," email to Gerard J. Aurigemma, November 12, 1998.

library that was solicited in this period to speak with the chief executive of JSTOR, in addition to the many who also spoke with the emeritus director of the Harvard College Library—rather than speaking with a regional sales representative of a new and unknown firm.

DeGennaro's extensive phone conversations, some with old friends and others with previously unintroduced colleagues, led dozens of libraries to participate. Many librarians saw JSTOR's promise immediately. DeGennaro recalls most of this enthusiasm deriving from the access improvements that JSTOR would bring—both the desktop availability of core journals and the new fulltext search capability—rather than any potential cost savings. Some library directors were so enthusiastic about the new project that they even offered to speak with other colleagues to encourage their participation. DeGennaro explained the charter period, whose deadline gave some library directors the excuse to cut through local bureaucracy to sign up quickly.[27] Working as a tag team, DeGennaro and Guthrie signed on dozens of libraries per month in this period.

Some library directors, albeit the minority of those initially contacted, were less enthusiastic: DeGennaro recalls their hesitancy having three distinct sources.[28] First, some libraries wanted to participate via consortia (discussed below). Second, some felt that they had already purchased the journals in original paper format and again in microfilm. Every time some new technology arose, were they to be expected to buy the same scholarly journals again and again? These directors simply did not, on first blush, value JSTOR's access features, let alone its space-saving promise. With the novelty of the resource and especially its untested claim of savings, and with budget constraints to be considered, their skepticism was understandable.

Finally, some library directors were simply not convinced of the promise—or the stability—of the yearling organization. Such questions would prove to be the most difficult to handle, and only time would have any hope of answering them. JSTOR would do fine while using the Mellon Foundation's grants and its initial capital accumulation from DDFs. But it was dependent on ongoing annual fees. If at some point library budgets tightened further and libraries cancelled their participation, JSTOR's viability could be endangered. Such long-term worries about JSTOR's viability were based in legitimate uncertainty. On the other hand, librarian skepticism could have become a self-fulfilling prophecy if no libraries had been willing to take a considered risk and participate. The concerns of the risk-averse would only be adequately

---

[27]Richard DeGennaro, interview with the author, March 30, 2001.
[28]Ibid.

answered as JSTOR built up sufficient standing in the library community, and commensurate financial reserves, to assuage the fears of the doubters.

JSTOR had long recognized that finding additional money in library budgets would be difficult and presidents and provosts would have to be made to see the value of participating. In dozens of routine meetings with higher education administrators visiting the Mellon Foundation, Bowen demonstrated the JSTOR database. He would often perform a search for articles written by his guests, or someone they selected, to show how comprehensive the database was becoming. Bowen underscored JSTOR's commitment to save costs for institutions, an argument that may have had greater appeal with administrators, who had an institution-wide perspective, than with librarians, who had a more focused responsibility. And as the list of likely (and some unlikely) charter participants was developed, other avenues were pursued. Bowen called a number of the presidents and other administrators of the "unlikelies" to alert them to the rapidly closing charter opportunity. As President of Bryn Mawr, JSTOR Trustee Pat McPherson called several of her fellow college presidents to alert them to JSTOR's usefulness. These calls undoubtedly added participants at the close of the charter period.

Sometimes, other enthusiasts pushed JSTOR, as well. As a member of the second set of test sites, Yale's JSTOR access was enabled prior to the charter period, and the Yale president had become an even bigger believer than many in the university library. Bowen wrote to Guthrie,

> I had a long meeting with Rick Levin yesterday afternoon. In the course of it, he mentioned that he had had great fun not long ago providing a JSTOR demo in his office. . . . He is a true believer and will help us in every possible way. I mumbled something about our hope that Yale would be an early participant, and he assured me that that would definitely be the case.[29]

At Yale, the decision to participate may have been made, or in any case strongly endorsed, in the president's office. Later, President Levin would join the JSTOR Board of Trustees.

Several librarians have subsequently described their early decision to participate as responding in part to the endorsement of the Mellon Foundation, which after all made more grants to academic and research libraries than any other foundation.[30] DeGennaro himself was not bashful in "calling in chits" from friends and colleagues.[31] Some sought to support a particularly appealing experiment, while others wanted

---

[29] William G. Bowen, "Rick Levin and Yale," email to Kevin Guthrie, December 4, 1996.
[30] Foundation Center, *Foundation Grants Index* [database].
[31] Richard DeGennaro, interview with the author, March 30, 2001.

TABLE 10.1
Charter Participants by Carnegie *Classification* Groupings

Carnegie *Classification* Grouping	Charter Participants
Research I	56
Research II	14
Doctoral I	10
Doctoral II	7
Master's I	22
Master's II	0
Baccalaureate I	48
Baccalaureate II	8
Other[i]	25
Total	180

[i]Including Canadian and nonacademic libraries.

simply to encourage any sort of experimentation to save library costs; they may have been thinking more of the "greater good" than of their own campus-specific needs. It is impossible to quantify the extent to which the foundation's, and Bowen's, association with JSTOR contributed to its high library participation rates.

It is possible, however, to quantify the outcome at the close of the charter period. During those four months, JSTOR signed a total of 190 libraries. Among these were a significant percentage of the most well-respected American academic libraries. JSTOR leaders at the time, including Bowen, DeGennaro, and Guthrie, are convinced that this list of early signers contributed mightily to the perceived legitimacy of the nascent enterprise. Without the impending closure of the charter period, many of the prestigious research libraries might well have delayed participation, perhaps for years, until more of the database had been made available or committees had deliberated at greater length. Without this banner list of prestigious libraries signed on virtually from day one, they have suggested, JSTOR might have foundered. With these libraries participating, JSTOR could demonstrate that it had earned substantial backing when talking with other potential participants. And although many of these participants were the largest and richest libraries that certainly would have signed on eventually, some seventy-eight Master's and Baccalaureate libraries joined, as well.

Although JSTOR was extremely pleased with the outcome of the charter period, its success is difficult to evaluate. Certainly, a number of the 190 charter libraries participated sooner than they might have without the charter provision in place. Yet a look at the Carnegie *Classification* groupings of the charter participants indicates that the majority are either large and wealthy research universities (Research I or II) or small, selective, wealthy liberal arts colleges (Baccalaureate I). All of the charter participants were risk-takers, and all 190 would have participated eventually. It was critical to JSTOR, for both public-relations purposes and for budgetary reasons, that many libraries participate rapidly. As it turned out, however, it was precisely those libraries least needing a discount that received one. Libraries at less selective colleges and universities, which in turn had tighter budgets and less ability to take risk, paid a higher price, and not just for Arts & Sciences I but for subsequent collections, as well, which is not to suggest that discounts should have instead been offered to the laggards![32] This phenomenon is notably similar to the endowment-investing patterns of colleges and universities in the 1990s, when existing wealth permitted risk-taking that resulted in remarkable rates of return and greater disparities between the wealthy and the others.[33]

JSTOR's own needs mandated the charter arrangement, and within that context it was clearly a success. Although dozens more libraries than expected received the generous discounts, each library was an early and long-term participant. It is when viewed in contrast with those libraries that would have liked to participate, but in the early stages felt they could not, that the generous charter discounts to numerous wealthy libraries become problematic, as we shall now see.

CONSORTIA

JSTOR's enthusiasm for the charter provision contrasted with its forbearance with library consortia, which sought a different kind of discount. Numerous academic libraries wanted to participate via consortia, and sometimes their participation depended on working through their consortium. Beginning even before the charter period and continuing at

[32]Both DeGennaro and Bowen in retrospect believe that the charter discounts may have been too generous. The discounts for the Arts & Sciences I collection may have been appropriate, but the discounts for subsequent collections may have been excessive and too speculative to be effective inducements. Richard DeGennaro, interview with the author, March 30, 2001; William G. Bowen, personal communication, May 3, 2001.

[33]Cara C. Nakamura, *Wealth Disparities*, unpublished manuscript on deposit at the Nathan Marsh Pusey Library, the Andrew W. Mellon Foundation.

least through 2001, JSTOR took the stance that consortia should receive discounts only based on the amount of system-wide savings that they brought with them (see chapter 8).

One of JSTOR's earliest encounters with consortia was at the first meeting of the monolithic-sounding Consortium of Consortia, which provided an opportunity for vendors to meet at one time with the directors of dozens of consortia representing hundreds of libraries. In February 1997, Guthrie presented JSTOR to this group, and he explained that discounts to consortia would be extremely modest, since it was unlikely that they would save costs for JSTOR. Their response "was that consortia provide additional [participants and thereby] revenue, not savings in cost."[34] He suggested that they encourage their members to participate during the charter period, to receive the 25 percent discount. At the meeting itself, recalls one of the consortia directors of Guthrie, "here we had someone who was supposed to be one of us [librarians] . . . here we had a guy who supposedly was creating a project from the inside and here we saw all these flaws in it and we probably—at some level—treated him like family. Then you're really nasty."[35] While some attendees were strongly supportive of the JSTOR approach, the overall tone that was set at this meeting cannot have been helpful for future compromises.

Before examining the case of the consortia, it will be important to keep in mind that they came in many different varieties. From a vendor's perspective, there are essentially two types. The first type of consortium, the decentralized buying cooperatives, aggregated purchaing power to save money for libraries without cutting any costs. With this type, the money that was saved would have to be made up via increased prices to others or lower returns for the vendors. The second type, the centralized service providers, fostered interlibrary lending, provided union catalogs, built remote storage facilities, or negotiated standard deals with resource vendors for all of their members. It is this group that had the potential to offer system-wide savings, by centralizing services such as licensing and thereby cutting costs for libraries without raising them for vendors. There is also another axis, not of savings but of revenues. If a consortium is composed of libraries with a diversity of wealth, it might be able to bring a vendor otherwise-unlikely participants. This sort of consortium might be able to save costs, too, but its asset was to provide a vendor with increased revenues.

[34]Kevin Guthrie, "A long day," email to JSTOR staff, February 4, 1997.

[35]Tom Sanville, interview with the author, October 29, 2001. Bill Potter, who attended the meeting on behalf of the GALILEO consortium, recalls that "we really raked him over the coals." Interview with the author, April 26, 2002.

The first group of consortia is perhaps best typified by NERL, the NorthEast Research Libraries. NERL brought together eighteen major research libraries, all of which could be expected to want access to virtually every resource imaginable.[36] Because they are prestigious research libraries, acting as a group they can exercise a great deal of market power in negotiating with a vendor. In this way, NERL saved a great deal of money for its members in several deals, and obtained improved terms on many standard provisions. (It should be noted that NERL never approached JSTOR for a deal.) Such a consortium did not, however, bring any meaningful efficiencies to the market. Money was "saved" by NERL but no substantial costs were reduced, and so the savings presumably had to be recouped elsewhere by a vendor.

OhioLINK was just the opposite. In late 1996, OhioLINK counted as members about seventy academic libraries in the state, from Ohio State University to the smallest community colleges. Although many of Ohio-LINK's members would prove to be willing to participate independently, a single deal with the consortium could mean that institutions like the Mount Carmel College of Nursing and Muskingum Area Technical College could participate in JSTOR. Hypothetically, such an agreement could save seventy institutions the costs of negotiating a deal with JSTOR, and JSTOR the costs of negotiating seventy deals. To JSTOR, such an arrangement might be worth two months or more of the salary of a library-relations professional—savings that could in turn be passed along to the consortium. But in addition to this cost savings, it is clear that OhioLINK could have had real value to JSTOR by bringing it dozens of otherwise-unlikely participants.

JSTOR was happy to pass along savings, which were far more likely from the centralized service providers than from the decentralized buying cooperatives. But to agree to pass along savings did not mean it was at all prepared to price its database at or approaching marginal cost.[37] It was in this setting that JSTOR and OhioLINK began discussing the outlines of an agreement in late 1996.

OhioLINK approached such negotiations by considering the number of its members likely to have participated without a consortium-related agreement, and it then would offer to pay the standard costs of participation for these institutions, plus a small increment, in exchange for all

---

[36] NERL's membership counts Boston College, Boston, Brown, Columbia, Cornell, Dartmouth, Harvard, MIT, NYU, Princeton, Rutgers, Stanford, Syracuse, Temple, the University of Connecticut, the University of Massachusetts, the University of Notre Dame, the University of Pennsylvania, the University of Pittsburgh, the University of Rochester, and Yale.

[37] Kevin Guthrie, "Big Consortia," email to William G. Bowen, November 5, 1996; William G. Bowen, "Re[3]: St. Louis," email to Kevin Guthrie, February 4, 1997.

of its membership receiving access. Tom Sanville, the director, gives an example of one "big database" that OhioLINK believed would have a maximum of six likely subscribers in its consortium. "Six big libraries could get this, or we can guarantee that we'll pay the price tag for six large libraries but in return we get full access across the state. Because [at the time] they weren't getting six schools."[38] In the case of JSTOR, OhioLINK proposed paying only for the Doctoral and Research libraries.

Therein lay the problem for JSTOR, for in late 1996 no one could reasonably foresee how many academic libraries would likely participate, and the trustees had set an ambitious goal. Guthrie offered, instead, a deal in which all Baccalaureate II and community colleges could participate without the one-time DDF and with a reduced AAF of $1000 per year, so long as all other schools paid the full (charter) price.[39] This would recognize the savings brought by a single deal for dozens of libraries. But with OhioLINK believing that most of these twenty-eight Baccalaureate II and community colleges would be unlikely to participate to begin with and that $1000 per year remained far too high, it did not view the proposal as at all reasonable.[40] JSTOR in turn was hesitant to reduce AAF revenues for its Small and Medium classes beyond the 25 percent charter discounts. As of 2002, JSTOR and OhioLINK still had not reached an agreement.

Even without a consortium-related agreement, however, a large number of the four-year OhioLINK members chose to participate on their own, as illustrated in table 10.2. Indeed, the participation rate for four-year institutions rose to 42 percent; for four-year institutions other than Baccalaureate II, the rate is 68 percent. By 2001, even one Baccalaureate II college, which Sanville would never have expected to participate on its own, had done so. Perhaps more would do so in the future. Only the community colleges would not show interest in participating.

The plan proposed by OhioLINK would have left JSTOR with Arts & Sciences I AAFs of perhaps $41,000, with the responsibility to provide access for seventy-nine libraries, rather than the twenty libraries (with AAFs of $73,000) participating at the close of 2001. In other words, revenues were 75 percent higher than they would have been, while costs were lower.

Dealing with consortia on a national basis, JSTOR would not have been able to break even, let alone reach self-sustainability. Those consortia that advocated that JSTOR steeply reduce its prices obviously did not understand fully the economics of an archive striving for perpetual

---

[38] Tom Sanville, interview with the author, October 29, 2001.
[39] Kevin Guthrie, letter to David Barber, December 12, 1996.
[40] Tom Sanville, letter to Kevin Guthrie, January 6, 1997.

TABLE 10.2
JSTOR Participation among OhioLINK Members

Carnegie Classification Grouping	OhioLINK Libraries	Number in JSTOR		Participation Rate, Close of 2001
		Close of 1997	Close of 2001	
Research I	3	3	3	100%
Research II	2	1	1	50%
Doctoral I	4	1	4	100%
Doctoral II	2	0	2	100%
Master's I	8	0	2	25%
Master's II	1	0	1	100%
Baccalaureate I	8	3	6	75%
Baccalaureate II	20	0	1	5%
Associate of Arts or other	31	0	0	0%
Total	79	8	20	25%

self-sustainability. Unlike some other resource providers, which no doubt calculated their prices and then raised them a percentage that consortia could then "save" libraries, JSTOR's prices were developed to reflect its anticipated costs. Some other nonprofit projects, which like JSTOR priced themselves at cost, then succumbed to pressure by the consortia to reduce them—an arrangement that was obviously not sustainable.[41] JSTOR instead would suffer through a few years of lower participation rates, waiting patiently to achieve its goals.

In one documented exchange on the topic, David Carlson of Bridgewater University—a JSTOR participant—wrote to a listserv on licensing (operated by Ann Okerson) to report that some librarians were "offended" by JSTOR's "stance not to deal with library consortia." He argued that more libraries would participate if arrangements for consortia were available.[42] He probably spoke for many in wondering why

[41]Richard E. Quandt, "Mellon Initiatives in Digital Libraries: 1994–1999" unpublished manuscript on deposit with the Nathan Marsh Pusey Library, the Andrew W. Mellon Foundation, 2002, 2–17.

[42]David Carlson, "Re: Consortia pricing," email to Liblicense, January 30, 1998; available online at http://www.library.yale.edu/~llicense/ListArchives/9801/msg00033.html.

JSTOR, representing itself as a member of the library community, would not want to increase its number of participants via consortia.

Vacationing in Hawaii with his family, Guthrie did not respond until the following day. He focused on JSTOR's economics and how they differed from those of a traditional publisher.[43] He also noted his belief that there was a fairness issue implicit in the debate about consortia—why should two otherwise similar libraries pay different fees because one was part of a consortium and the other was not? JSTOR had already sought to price its database fairly, in a way that ensured its success but would yield no profits. It had taken account of the research intensity and size of colleges and universities in its plan. Discounts for consortia would only detract from fairness and transparency, while threatening JSTOR's careful financial planning. There were no further responses to this thread, suggesting that Guthrie's arguments were largely persuasive.[44]

In his email, Guthrie explained that if any consortium were able to achieve significant system-wide savings, JSTOR would eagerly work with it. But few traditional American library consortia were able to do so to JSTOR's satisfaction, even though the dominance of these players increased notably during the course of 1997.[45] Eventually, as discussed in chapter 12, JSTOR would work with a number of consortia. Among American libraries, it would work mainly with state university consortia. Among international libraries, it would work mainly with nationwide consortia. The first two consortia to participate in JSTOR, however, had special characteristics and presented special opportunities of a different kind.

[43]Kevin Guthrie, "Re: Consortia pricing—JSTOR Response," email to Liblicense, January 31, 1998; available online at *http://www.library.yale.edu/~llicense/ListArchives/9801/msg00035.html*.

[44]The only response other than that of Guthrie had been by Paul Gherman of Vanderbilt, who argued that, as a nonprofit, JSTOR should receive a greater deal of trust than most other vendors. Paul M. Gherman, "Re: Consortia pricing," email to Liblicense, January 30, 1998; available online at *http://www.library.yale.edu/~llicense/ListArchives/9801/msg00034.html*.

[45]Karen Hunter of Elsevier Science wondered in early 1997 if consortia might be "just the flavor of the month," but by 1998 she was convinced that they were an important presence. She noted, however, that the emerging economics of such organizations were not "win-win," but rather little more than "collective price bargaining." Ann Okerson also reflected on 1997 as being a formative year for consortia, which she considered to be "an extremely promising development in the marketplace of scholarly and scientific communication." Karen Hunter, "Things That Keep Me Awake At Night," *Against the Grain* February 1997: 41; Karen Hunter, "Sleepless Nights Redux," *Against The Grain* February 1998: 29; Ann Okerson, "Are We There Yet? Online E-Resources Ten Years After," *Library Trends* 48, no. 4 (March 22, 2000): 671.

HISTORICALLY BLACK AND APPALACHIAN SCHOOLS:
AN EARLY EFFORT TO ADDRESS THE DIGITAL DIVIDE

Arrangements with consortia representing the Historically Black Colleges and Universities (HBCUs) and the Appalachian colleges allowed two groups of disadvantaged institutions to participate in JSTOR while saving costs for the system. Since the Mellon Foundation had a long-standing commitment to support both private HBCUs and Appalachian colleges, bringing JSTOR to them can be understood as a means of leveraging the foundation's JSTOR investment for the benefit of other areas of interest. Mellon's program for HBCUs stretched back to 1971, helping to support schools that, ironically, did not benefit from the desegregation of education that began in 1954 with *Brown* v. *Board of Education*.[46] Mellon had also developed an interest in small Appalachian colleges, which dated back to some investments Andrew Mellon himself had made in the region.[47] In both cases, investments in library resources had been an important part of Mellon's grants.[48]

As a group, both sets of colleges lacked extensive library resources, and JSTOR could bring them access to numerous new journals. But because they were generally very small and poor, they could not afford the paper backfiles and there was no reason to suspect they could now afford JSTOR participation. (Some schools had annual collections budgets of $20,000 or less.)[49] Virtually every one of these schools fell into JSTOR's Very Small pricing class, yet even finding the $10,000 DDF would have been challenging or, more often, impossible.

Foundation Senior Advisor Henry Drewry was one of several who had become convinced of JSTOR's potential for colleges that lacked extensive backfiles. As director of Mellon's HBCU program, Drewry had worked through the Southern Educational Foundation (SEF), a consortium comprised of twenty-four private HBCUs, to stabilize and improve these colleges' libraries. Now, in late 1996, the SEF was proposing to upgrade the HBCUs' computing and network infrastructure and Fuchs had been consulting with Drewry on how best to tackle these problems.

---

[46] A fascinating study of these schools can be found in Henry N. Drewry and Humphrey Doermann, *Stand and Prosper: Private Black Colleges and Their Students* (Princeton: Princeton University Press, 2001). Mellon in this period dealt with only a subset of the institutions that Drewry and Doermann examined.

[47] Alice F. Emerson, interview with the author, June 15, 2001.

[48] The grant totals prior to this point, much but not all of which had gone toward libraries, included more than $12 million to the Appalachian colleges and nearly $35 million to the HBCUs.

[49] Tony Krug, interview with the author, March 26, 2002.

In December 1996, just as JSTOR was beginning its charter push, Drewry and Bowen spoke about the plans Drewry was developing for the HBCUs.[50] Bowen was enthusiastic about a proposal to make electronic resources more broadly available on campus. It became immediately clear that such a grant could help to enable JSTOR participation. Bowen suggested that the Appalachian colleges would benefit from similar assistance. For these colleges, Mellon traditionally worked through the Appalachian Colleges Association (ACA), which consists of thirty-three colleges in central Appalachia. (Further investigation would reveal that, in mid-1997, one school had an entire campus without an Internet connection.) The ACA's director, Alice Brown, had already become interested in JSTOR's potential.

Plans were refined for the grants, to be funneled through the SEF and ACA. Toward supporting JSTOR participation, they would pay for the DDF, in addition to three years of funding for the AAF. Then, if the colleges wanted to continue to participate, they would have to find resources of their own. In addition to the JSTOR component, the grants included provisions to update networking infrastructure, provide email accounts for the campus, offer training for librarians, faculty, and students, and bring more modern computers onto campuses. On some campuses, these grants added 10 percent more computers.

To the officers and trustees of the foundation, the arrangement allowed it to meet two of its goals at once. First, the library (and computing) resources of the HBCUs and the Appalachian colleges were improved with a nonrecurring grant. Second, JSTOR gained participants that otherwise could not have joined, helping its participant base reach adequate scale. The foundation's board approved the grants of around $2 million each to the two sets of schools in mid–1997.[51] The SEF and ACA held competitions among their members for the funding, which eventually benefitted about twenty HBCUs and twenty-five Appalachian schools.

In early 2001, JSTOR's head of American library relations, Carol Mac-Adam, contacted all of the HBCUs that participated via the SEF grant, to gauge their interest in continuing to participate given that the subsidy had expired at the end of 2000. According to her detailed notes, there was a range of savvy with regard to digital resources. Although several schools had been wracked by troubling leadership transitions in the past three years, there was near-unanimous enthusiasm. MacAdams's

[50] William G. Bowen, "JSTOR, HBCUs and Appalachia," email to Henry Drewry, December 13, 1996.

[51] The grant applications and docket items are for Mellon Grants #19700671 (SEF) and #29700685 (ACA).

notes suggest that all twenty SEF participants were willing to begin paying the Annual Access Fees necessary to continue participation, and all did so for the year 2001.[52]

Tony Krug, who was then the library dean at ACA member Carson-Newman College, recalled that JSTOR was the first networked library resource to get his attention and that of his colleagues. Its full backruns and page images were, from his perspective, ideal. And JSTOR provided a clear example of the value of networked information, helping to convince faculty and administrators of the educational necessity of making investments in information technology. He also points out that JSTOR's curated bundles of titles have an especially high value when a library has few other peer-reviewed resources. In part as a result of substantially increasing the amount of peer-reviewed literature available to researchers there, Krug believes that JSTOR "became a significant cornerstone to the academic libraries of these small colleges."[53]

Is is remarkable that all of the SEF and ACA beneficiaries continued to participate in JSTOR on their own. Although there is little doubt that some believed this helped foster their relationship with Mellon, the unanimity seems to indicate broad satisfaction. Mellon grants to the Appalachian colleges and HBCUs, like later grants for international participants (see chapter 12), helped to broaden JSTOR's participant base while also assisting these important institutions. But while the schools receiving the grants benefited by obtaining JSTOR access, the grants suggest a deeper problem: just because a school values a resource does not mean it can afford to pay for it.

INTERNATIONAL EXPANSION: WORLDWIDE MIRROR SITES

Even as JSTOR's staff was laboring mightily to fulfill its goals as stated in the business plan, it was receiving enquiries from libraries across the globe that wished to participate. Several concerns, including connectivity and pricing, had compounded to give pause to JSTOR's staff and trustees. But there was no question that, in the end, the archive would be made available to students and scholars throughout the world.

Of the various causes for delay in 1996–1997, perhaps the most important was JSTOR's intensive use of bandwidth, which meant that Internet connectivity became a limiting factor. JSTOR was far more dependent on bandwidth than text-based databases. As an example, Lexis-

---

[52] Carol MacAdam, "Conversations with SEF librarians," email to Danielle D. Carr, March 30, 2001.

[53] Tony Krug, interview with the author, March 26, 2002.

Nexis had long been available worldwide, but it transmitted only text, at perhaps 1-2 KB per page. JSTOR's image-based display was far more bulky—approximately 50 KB per page—and so was dependent on the availability of far more bandwidth. If bandwidth was not adequate, JSTOR was very slow. Relative to the United States and Canada, Internet connectivity was very poor almost everywhere else. For a 2002 publication, Richard Quandt has made efforts to document bandwidth growth in Eastern Europe, where he found several countries in the early to mid-1990s with total connectivity of 9.6 Kbits/second.[54] Closely correlated with bandwidth is Internet usage; in 1996, 83 percent of Internet users were based in the United States.[55] There were two principal aspects to the poor connectivity that are reflected in the low rate of use in the rest of the world, and each would have a different solution.

"Big pipes" to the United States, and JSTOR's servers there, were in place from some, but really very few, countries. If these were missing, but local infrastructure was adequate, the solution might be a local server to "mirror" JSTOR's database for nearby distribution. Unfortunately, this could have prevented the archive from becoming available in many regions, especially those with few arts and sciences institutions. There, the participation fees would not justify the expense of a mirror. Establishing mirror sites would also force JSTOR to station technical staff around the world to maintain the servers, or else it would have to find trustworthy organizations to take on the work as its partners.

An equally problematic circumstance was when the so-called "last mile" connecting the local college or university to an Internet backbone was insufficient or nonexistent. For this there was no solution. JSTOR could never be available on a campus whose local network was slow. The network would have to be improved before the database could be available. (We will return to the last mile in chapter 14, in the section on South Africa.) Thus, the story of the internationalization of JSTOR's participant base is closely intertwined with the growth of worldwide Internet connectivity and the concomitant reduction in connection fees.

[54] Richard E. Quandt, *The Changing Landscape in Eastern Europe: A Personal Perspective on Philanthropy and Technology Transfer* (New York: Oxford University Press, 2002): 89–90.

[55] In 1995 an astounding 75 percent of Internet users were based in the United States; in 1996 the percentage rose to 83 percent. By 1997, North Amercan accesses were 63 percent of the worldwide total, and by 1998 57 percent. Nua Internet Surveys, available at *http://www.nua.ie/surveys/analysis/index.html*. Similarly, China had less than one million Internet users before 1998, but by 2000 users had grown to approximately twenty-two million. Nina Hachigian, "China's Cyber Strategy," *Foreign Affairs* March/April 2001: 121. The early prevalence of U.S. users may have been due in part to earlier deregulation of Internet access in the United States. Sari Kalin, "Deregulation; Foreign Internet access costs soar above United States," *InfoWorld* October 28, 1996: TW 2.

In addition to connectivity, the other major impediment to international distribution was uncertainty about the database's value from country to country. Abroad, there were several additional factors in the value-equation for pricing. First, in some countries English was not the language of instruction, which JSTOR staff believed would lessen the value of English-language journals to students and scholars.[56] Second, different countries have different priorities for scholarship. In Latin America, for example, the more practical scientific disciplines, such as biology, medicine, and agriculture, took hold well before mathematics and physics.[57] One might assume that other less "useful" disciplines would be slow to develop, as well.

Beyond uncertainties about the value of the JSTOR database abroad, there were also real concerns about how to set the pricing. There would clearly need to be a great deal of pricing variance by country, but JSTOR's small staff did not have the competence to determine, country by country, the value and price. And in terms of pricing variants within countries, the Carnegie *Classification* covered only U.S. colleges and universities; elsewhere, JSTOR would have to adopt its own pricing classifications.

The connectivity issues meant that, when considering its business plan in mid-1996, JSTOR would have been unappealing in many regions of the world, especially in developing nations whose Internet

---

[56] India has a number of well-established journals in subcontinental languages. Malaysian national policy calls for the use of the national language for the purposes of scholarship, but scholars nevertheless retain "an overwhelming dependence on scholarship produced in the industrialized nations, and Malaysian scholars are still keen to have their work published in English abroad." "African scholars," one author mused, "are not at as much of a disadvantage as colleagues in some other developing countries since African universities generally use English or French as the medium of instruction." Philip G. Altbach, "The Role and Nurturing of Journals in the Third World," in Philip G. Altbach and Damtew Teferra, eds., *Knowledge Dissemination in Africa: The Role of Scholarly Journals* (Chesnutt Hill, MA: Bellagio Publishing Network, 1998), 5, 6, 11.

Despite the exceptions, the English language has been growing more universal in scholarly communications. In Latin America, Spanish and Portuguese have a great deal of critical mass, although this region has been turning increasingly to English recently. Ana María Cetto and Octavio Alonso-Gambosa, "Scientific and Scholarly Journals in Latin America and the Caribbean," in ibid., 117–18. There are very few languages other than English sufficiently widespread to permit extensive scholarly communications, though there is no reason to assume that the number is shrinking. Ian Buruma wrote that, in addition to its role in entertainment, "English is becoming the language of science and higher education too, replacing Latin as the lingua franca of learning." Ian Buruma, "The Road to Babel," *New York Review of Books*, May 31, 2001, 23.

[57] Ana María Cetto and Octavio Alonso-Gambosa, "Scientific and Scholarly Journals in Latin America and the Caribbean," in Altbach and Teferra, eds., *Knowledge Dissemination in Africa*, 102.

infrastructure was particularly poor. On top of this, the pricing impediments suggested that even where connectivity was robust, such as
Australia and a good deal of Western Europe, delay might be wise.
Some initial experience with American institutions would give JSTOR a
much more accurate sense of its baseline value from which to make
more speculative decisions abroad. So in 1996 and 1997, the focus was
almost exclusively on North American academia.

JISC and the United Kingdom

But the focus on America notwithstanding, British higher educational
institutions expressed particular interest in participating. Of all possible
places to expand JSTOR, the United Kingdom was one of the most logical for a number of reasons. The language of instruction is English.
There is a long tradition of transatlantic movement of scholars and
ideas. Universities in the United Kingdom are, arguably, more similar
to American institutions than are those in other countries. Most British
universities were established in the later twentieth century. For this
reason, or because of budget constraints, many British universities did
not hold backfiles of many of JSTOR's journals. And networking was
generally robust. Given all of these factors, British universities perceived
the value of participation to be high. JSTOR therefore began searching
for an organization that could host a mirror site to provide the United
Kingdom access to the archive.

Richard DeGennaro attended a CNI-CAUSE meeting in San Francisco,
which brought together many of the librarians, computer scientists, IT
staff, and others most interested in networked information resources.
DeGennaro attended as a representative of JSTOR, and while there he
was approached by Lynne Brindley and David Cook of the Joint Information Systems Committee (the JISC), the suprainstitutional U.K.
governmental organization with responsibility for networking and computing resources at universities and colleges.[58] In part through Brindley's
good offices, the JISC had recently received a substantially increased
government appropriation, to be applied largely to electronic information resources.[59]

---

[58]Brindley was at the time the librarian of Leeds University in the United Kingdom and
has since become the director of the British Library. She was the chair of an important
working group of the Joint Information Systems Committee (JISC). Cook was staff director of that working group.

[59]In the past decade, increased enrollments in United Kingdom higher education had
been coupled with stagnating budgets. The Follett Report sought solutions to the short-
ages and other problems that resulted. It recommended, among other things, substantially

In 1993, in one of its earliest grants with these new monies, the JISC funded a project rather similar to JSTOR, with the goal of digitizing the backfiles of academic journals. This project focused, naturally, on British titles, but its success was limited by the lack of a suitable organization to take responsibility for the long-term operation of its database. Having heard of JSTOR's similarity to the project they had funded, representatives of the JISC wanted to avoid duplication of effort. If JSTOR's infrastructure and potential for success were high, then the JISC could devote its efforts to other important projects and encourage JSTOR to make its database available in the United Kingdom. Viewing JSTOR as a possible way of increasing the JISC's efforts with journal backfiles, Brindley, Cook, and DeGennaro spoke about JSTOR's achievements and plans. Brindley and Cook were sufficiently pleased with what they heard that they inquired whether JSTOR might consider working with the JISC as a partner to distribute its archive in the United Kingdom.[60]

The JISC was convinced that, as part of such an agreement, a mirror site had to be established in the United Kingdom. As the provider of network access to U.K. higher education, the JISC managed, among other network infrastructure, transatlantic connectivity. The JISC needed to recover approximately 10 percent of its networking costs from higher-educational institutions, which it did via a formula based on an institution's usage of international bandwidth. Although JSTOR was bandwidth-intensive, the JISC could provide British access to JSTOR's U.S. servers, but this would force it to increase its transatlantic connectivity and therefore to charge participants twice: once for access to JSTOR, and again for the necessary international bandwidth. Such an arrangement seemed prone to criticism. A mirror site, on the other hand, would guarantee that institutions would only be charged once.[61]

From JSTOR's perspective, such a relationship brought a number of advantages. With a JISC-funded mirror site, JSTOR could lower its fees somewhat, to take account of not having to increase its own server infrastructure to provide access to British participants. Critically, the JISC was part of the academic community, just as were Michigan and Princeton. The JISC would, if anything, ease JSTOR's entry into this new

---

increased funding for electronic resources as a solution to increasingly inadequate library facilities and collections. See Joint Funding Councils' Libraries Review Group, *Report* (Bristol, England: HEFCE, 1993). Brindley had chaired the Follett subcommittee on libraries that made this recommendation, and when the funds were provided as suggested, she was selected to manage their appropriation.

[60]David Cook, interview with the author, April 13, 2001.

[61]Ibid. The JISC's policy was eventually applied to all manner of resources based outside of the United Kingdom, and its datacentres eventually hosted dozens of mirror sites for higher educational institutions in the United Kingdom.

market, somewhat as DeGennaro did for many elements of the domestic market.

Once they agreed to work together, representatives of JSTOR and the JISC negotiated easily. Guthrie would report to the board that "relationships between the JISC and JSTOR have been extremely positive and candid."[62] The JISC would essentially purchase access to the JSTOR archive for British higher education, for three years. Then, it would attempt to recover its costs by charging institutions an annual fee for access. This made good sense for JSTOR, by guaranteeing a minimum payment without regard to the number of eventual British participants; the JISC assumed the risk if few institutions signed on. For the JISC, it would speed British access to JSTOR and give the JISC some influence in JSTOR's future development. The JISC would also provide library relations and user services to U.K. participants.

In exchange for the JISC providing hardware and staff, a new pricing structure was negotiated. Although it would pay JSTOR both a DDF and an AAF, the JISC planned to charge participants no up-front fee but a higher annual fee, recouping at least some of its costs. For JSTOR, the arrangement allowed it to earn substantial revenues with no additional costs or risks, helping it to spread further its fixed costs of creating the database and its annual costs of maintaining it. It would locate a copy of its database outside the United States with a trusted partner. This relatively straightforward partnership would be an ideal experiment to see if establishing further international mirrors made sense.[63]

To the JISC, the arrangement made good sense, as well. JSTOR was just the type of resource that the JISC hoped to deliver to British academia. With the mirror site, the JISC was able to leverage its preexisting commitment to operating a host of data services locally rather than purchase additional transatlantic connectivity. It was able to obtain significant cost savings for both the U.K. higher-education community and for JSTOR, exactly the sort of consortium-type effort that in Guthrie's mind justified offering a reduced price.

In other words, the JISC was able to offer JSTOR just the sort of money-saving consortium with which it would most want to work, but which had been unavailable in America. Since Amy Kirchhoff and Mark Ratliff (both at Princeton) had already developed the technology for mirror sites, relatively little work was necessary to build one in the United Kingdom. The JISC would cover almost all of JSTOR's incremental expenses, taking care of on-the-ground arrangements relating to the mirror and even providing the bulk of user-services needs. The rev-

[62]Minutes of the JSTOR board of trustees meeting of July 31, 1997.
[63]Kevin Guthrie, interview with the author, April 11, 2001.

enues that the JISC generated could therefore be directed toward recovering the investment that JSTOR had made in its one-time costs.

For both parties, the agreement offered potentially fruitful areas for collaboration. As examples, both the JISC and JSTOR had struggled with authentication, authorization, and linking concerns, projects on which they could now pool ideas and resources.[64] Representatives of JSTOR and the JISC quickly negotiated this agreement. It was formally signed in a ceremony at the U.S. Embassy in London, an event that Bowen, Cook, and Guthrie all agree indicated the collaborative nature of the JISC-JSTOR relationship. In 1998, access to the U.K. mirror site was launched.[65]

Central and Eastern Europe

At the same time that JSTOR was reaching the final agreement with the JISC in the spring of 1997, it was also beginning to speak with the Soros Foundation about Central and Eastern Europe. The Board had focused on the "social utility of JSTOR in countries like South Africa,"[66] and JSTOR's economics journals alone would have clear benefit in the former Soviet bloc. Guthrie envisioned a "parallel path between the developed world and the developing world, a mirror site in the UK and then a mirror site in Eastern Europe."[67] Yet while the board was generally enthusiastic about the JISC and the United Kingdom, it recommended caution in dealing with Eastern Europe. "The Board suggested that [JSTOR] make certain Soros has the staff and technical capacity" to undertake a mirror site relationship with JSTOR. Bowen "concluded the discussion on international questions by stating that JSTOR should move forward carefully on international fronts, making sure that access is made available through stable partners with whom we have strong relationships of mutual trust."[68] JSTOR leaders adopted this informal policy to govern further worldwide expansion.

Guthrie and the trustees agreed to "pursue an agreement with [Soros] along the lines of the JISC model."[69] JSTOR agreed to provide the Arts

[64]David Cook, interview with the author, April 13, 2001.

[65]To celebrate their relationship publicly, Lynne Brindley and Kevin Guthrie published a summary of it. See "JSTOR and The Joint Information Systems Committee: An International Collaboration," *Serials* 11, no. 1 (March 1998): 41–45.

[66]Minutes of the JSTOR board of trustees meeting of June 20, 1996.

[67]Kevin Guthrie, interview with the author, April 11, 2001. Other future plans at the time included a mirror site in Africa.

[68]Minutes of the JSTOR board of trustees meeting of April 3, 1997.

[69] Minutes of the JSTOR board of trustees meeting of July 31, 1997.

& Sciences I Collection for distribution by a Soros-funded mirror site in Budapest at a 50 percent discount from the U.S. rate, since it seemed unfair to charge the U.S. rate to relatively impoverished institutions that did not use English as the sole language of instruction. Yet eventually, the negotiations fell through, in part because the Soros organization preferred to spend its resources to provide a current issues aggregation,[70] rather than JSTOR's backfiles.[71]

USER SERVICES AND SOFTWARE DEVELOPMENT

As JSTOR grew in scale to a production-level operation, the software and interface had to keep pace. Thus, while the production team was vastly expanding JSTOR's online collection, the user-services and software-development groups worked to make this content more accessible. Following JSTOR's public release, far more researchers than ever before were using the system. Much praise was received. User feedback suggested a number of ways in which the software and interface should be modified to make it more user-friendly. Inevitably, users found bugs, and JSTOR was determined to fix them. In addition, a great deal of behind-the-scenes work went into making the software run more efficiently.[72]

The JSTOR user-services group in Ann Arbor had set up both a toll-free number and an email address to receive user feedback, including questions about how to use the database. JSTOR opted to set up an email address at the University of Michigan domain, to underscore its academic association. Whether user comments arrived via this email address or telephonically, their problems (or praise) generated a system-wide email, sent to Guthrie, the user-services librarians, the technical group, and the production manager. Initially, it was useful for such a large group to see how the system was being used, and what problems existed.

Aschenbrenner and Garlock, the user-services librarians, worked in conjunction with Guthrie to develop standard ways to respond to users. The goal was to incorporate a systemic "JSTOR tone," to enunciate its nonprofit, academic-oriented mission, providing as much information

[70]"Scholars in 39 Developing Countries Benefit from Database Project," *Chronicle of Higher Education*, December 15, 2000, A47.

[71]Kevin Guthrie, "Conversation with Michael Kay, OSI," email to William G. Bowen, Richard E. Quandt, Glenda Burkhardt, Sarah Sully, and Gerard J. Aurigemma, February 18, 1999.

[72]This section is based on a number of interviews, including with Amy Kirchhoff, December 21, 2001; Spencer Thomas, May 29, 2001; Kristen Garlock, May 25, 2001; and Sherry Aschenbrenner, May 30, 2001.

as was useful. By standardizing responses, Aschenbrenner and Garlock did not have to write new responses to the same questions time and again, but instead could focus on other needs.

Even with standardized messages, responding to this feedback soon became difficult. It was rare that users experiencing difficulties would email all of the information necessary for JSTOR staff to resolve the problem, and a lengthy back-and-forth often ensued. To help user-services librarians with their responses, Kirchhoff developed a set of feedback forms. These forms used Java to gather automatically as much information as possible while giving structured space for the data that the user needed to input—about, for example, the operating system, the web browser and version, and the printer—with the user-services staff receiving the information needed to respond. This seemingly small change made it far easier for users to receive the timely assistance they required.

Another software change that brought greater efficiency allowed some ongoing work to be shifted away from software developers. As the number of library participants skyrocketed during the charter period, JSTOR required a more robust means of authorizing users. Previously, the web-server had contained a list of the Internet addresses at which JSTOR could be accessed, but it became apparent that, as the number of participants grew, this system would not be sufficient. Most importantly, it meant that every time a new participant signed on (and every time existing participants increased or altered their Internet domains), a software developer had to "open up" the webserver. Ratliff created an authorization database, allowing user-services staff to input new library participants and their Internet addresses. This database would prove to be important in the future, as many participants would subscribe to more than one collection.

One of JSTOR's key shortcomings, it was always understood, was the large size of the page images that downloaded to a user's computer for viewing and printing. Scarce bandwidth, even at the largest American research universities, meant that printing an entire article could take fifteen minutes or more. One appealing option, initially identified by Fuchs, was to send the images in an extremely compressed form. After the user downloaded a "plug-in" to the local machine, the images could be sent in far less than half the time, and expanded almost immediately to be printed or viewed.[73] In one of her earliest projects for JSTOR,

[73]For a general discussion of delivery speed and compression, see Anne R. Kenney, "Digital Benchmarking for Conversion and Access," in Anne R. Kenney and Oya Y. Rieger, eds., *Moving Theory into Practice: Digital Imaging for Libraries and Archives* (Mountain View, CA: Research Libraries Group, 2000), especially at 51–57. For more on CPC, see

Kirchhoff designed an experimental interface incorporating the compression technology, and Guthrie found the technology promising, downloading a seven-page article in six seconds.[74] The technology had only one shortcoming: the requirement for local customization; that is, that users download the plug-in. But this shortcoming cut against JSTOR's emphasis on ease of use. Although it would have solved one ease-of-use problem—making the system faster for most users—it would make it more complex for all. As a result, JSTOR decided against making use of this form of compression for delivery, although it was used for internal-storage purposes.

As user feedback continued to amass, many comments suggested a real problem in the interface design. Initially, there was a vertical interface bar running along the left side of many JSTOR web pages. But users rarely realized that this was where they had to click in order to go to the next page of an article. A substantial number of user queries were simply to find out how to reach page two of an article! Eventually, JSTOR added links to the next and previous pages above and below the image of the journal page. With this simple innovation, users were able to navigate JSTOR much more easily, and the corresponding feedback messages virtually ended.

Similarly, links were included that obviated the need to view an article before printing it. This certainly raised the ratio of printing to page-views, but also probably resulted in some measure of unnecessary printing, in the sense that reading the first paragraph on screen would have indicated that the article was not desired.

In addition to all of this tangible progress, Guthrie had in mind that the Princeton technologists would undertake some effort to serve as "outside consultants," examining the bulk of the software that JSTOR had inherited from Michigan. He wanted a "soup-to-nuts evaluation of the architecture, software, database structure, etc."[75] In this role, Kirchhoff and Ratliff researched other search engines, including free-WaisSF.[76] Eventually, they concluded that no search engine was more efficient for JSTOR purposes than FTL. Similarly, they found the helper application

http://www.cartesianinc.com/. Some of JSTOR's options for CPC are discussed in Serge Goldstein, "Re: Rough Draft of tech retreat report: Try 2," email to Kevin Guthrie, Ira Fuchs, and JSTOR technical staff, October 9, 1996.

[74]Kevin Guthrie, "Conference Calls/Technology Issues," email to JSTOR staff, August 15, 1996.

[75]Kevin Guthrie, "Conference Calls/Technology Issues," email to William G. Bowen, Bill Landis, Sherry Aschenbrenner, Randy Frank, Ira Fuchs, Kristen Garlock, Serge Goldstein, and Spencer Thomas, August 15, 1996.

[76]Serge Goldstein, "Re: Rough Draft of tech retreat report: Try 2," email to Kevin Guthrie, Ira Fuchs, and JSTOR technical staff, October 9, 1996.

for local printing to be acceptable, although their enquiries eventually led to the creation of an Adobe Acrobat mechanism, which soon became the standard print option.[77]

Beyond their role in helping to improve software and the interface, the user-services librarians also kept users informed about the archive and encouraged its use. They developed discipline-specific materials that encouraged faculty to consider the advantages of using the archive. On the recommendation of a participating librarian, they created shelf labels, designed to be placed on shelves that held the journal backfiles (or used to), to alert researchers to the JSTOR option. In this same vein, they cataloged each journal in the OCLC catalog, so that libraries could directly import their JSTOR holdings information into their online library catalogs, often allowing a direct link from holdings information to archive. Finally, they held a meeting of library participants twice a year, at the American Library Association meetings. Because those meetings attracted numerous staff from every academic library in the country, it afforded an opportunity for JSTOR to interact in person with its participants. This would often be the first time the participants and JSTOR staff had met, and it allowed JSTOR to gather feedback while offering updates about its own plans.

While so much was accomplished, not everything ran smoothly. The user-services group remained small—three librarians, all in Ann Arbor—but the software group had grown with the opening of the new office, with two staff in Princeton and two in Ann Arbor, making management more difficult. Although by late 1997, all JSTOR technical staff were employed full-time, other problems remained. Guthrie recalls being frustrated "that nobody could give me any sense as to how long things were going to take," a problem typical of software development, but one that made it difficult at times to know the cost of certain projects, and therefore whether they were justified.[78] In early 1998, Fuchs was to take responsibility for software development, but it is inconceivable that he would have been able to devote very much time to this task.[79] Eventually, Amy Kirchhoff took the lead role in coordinating the work of the growing technology staff.

USAGE STATISTICS

Well before the public release of the database, software developers in Michigan began to create a system allowing JSTOR and its library

[77] Amy Kirchhoff, interview with the author, December 21, 2001.
[78] Kevin Guthrie, interview with the author, December 6, 2001.
[79] Kevin Guthrie, "Meetings in Ann Arbor," email to Ira Fuchs, January 19, 1998.

participants to study usage of the database. Spencer Thomas designed the initial system, and implementing it was the initial task of Karthik Ramamoorthy, who was hired in May 1996.[80]

Developing this statistics interface was extremely challenging. Because of the massive and ever increasing amount of information that had to be captured, it would be difficult to calculate results on the fly. Instead, to ensure adequate speed, much of the data was precalculated. This, however, imposed a key challenge. The system had to be designed in advance, rather than designing a piece of it, then developing that, then redesigning and so forth. Progress was slow in 1996.[81]

At the January 1997 participants meeting at ALA—the first one immediately after the public release—a number of librarians mentioned the need for JSTOR to make usage statistics available. This task already was on the backburner, but in response to these requests, JSTOR committed to making this feature available. Usage statistics seemed to involve a big risk to many resource providers—would librarians use low usage numbers to justify canceling a database? Nevertheless, librarians wanted the information and JSTOR agreed to make it available.

Garlock began working with a small committee of interested participants to develop the list of needed functionalities. While that group identified the list of functionalities, Alexander took over responsibility for implementing them. The guidelines composed by Garlock's committee were eventually formalized and handed off to an international organization that lobbied other resource-providers to implement them.[82] By taking on early leadership in the matter, JSTOR impressed many of its participants, some of whom continued into 2001 to believe that JSTOR's usage data were the only that were presented objectively and accurately.

JSTOR's system brought a number of important innovations. First, it attempted to define what was being counted (and it counted conservatively), rather than using the meaningless notion of "hits." It also allowed librarians to track usage compared with the average usage of their library class: for example, a librarian at Oberlin College could see how usage at Oberlin compared with usage at other colleges in the Small classification. This allowed for comparison without sharing information confidential to one library with others. The system would continue to be refined into the future; one development allowed publishers to track usage of their titles.

[80] Spencer Thomas, "Programming Report," email to Kevin Guthrie, May 13, 1996.

[81] Amy Kirchhoff, interview with the author, May 3, 2002.

[82] See International Coalition of Library Consortia, "Guidelines For Statistical Measures Of Usage Of Web-Based Indexed, Abstracted, and Full Text Resources"; available online at *http://www.library.yale.edu/consortia/webstats.html*.

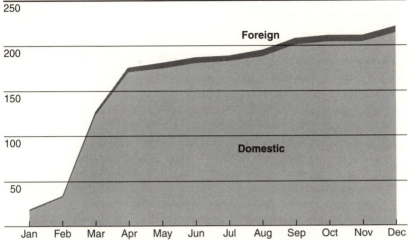

Figure 10.1. Libraries Participating, 1997

The statistics interface was far more than just a tool to impress libraries with JSTOR's goodwill. It allowed JSTOR itself to understand how the archive was being used. User-services staff could examine which disciplines were being underused. Technology staff could examine what factors were causing usage to skyrocket, in a bid to predict future hardware needs. And in 1998, usage statistics made the essential contribution of allowing a data-driven reexamination of certain assumptions in the business plan. This reexamination allowed JSTOR to adjust its pricing model for libraries and led to an increase in library participation (see chapter 12). Usage statistics were a major development.

SUMMATION

In the year following its public release, JSTOR's list of library participants grew dramatically. The spurt during the charter period, however, quickly slowed to barely a trickle, as Guthrie had predicted to the board. By year's end, of 275 anticipated participants, only 233 had materialized. In other words, in the eight months following the expiration of the charter period discounts, only forty libraries, or five per month, had signed on to participate (see figure 10.1). And many of these noncharter

TABLE 10.3
JSTOR Participation at the Close of 1997, by Pricing Class

Pricing Class	Anticipated Participants	Anticipated Annual Revenues	Actual Participants	Actual Annual Revenues	Revenue Variance
Large	100	$427,556	96	$353,750	−17%
Medium	100	$342,044	36	$118,000	−65%
Small	75	$129,400	57	$123,750	−4%
Very Small	N/A	N/A	33	$52,500	N/A
Total	275	$962,000[i]	233	$648,000[ii]	−33%

[i] The figures for "Anticipated Annual Revenues" are estimates that have been made to conform with Guthrie's projections that approximately 43 percent of the libraries participating in 1997 would do so under the Charter discount. The "Total" figure is Guthrie's, from the Strategic and Operating Plan, as revised July 22, 1996.

[ii] JSTOR reported AAFs of $663,000. The larger figure is accounted for by the 11 "special" library participants—generally, foundations and other nonacademic nonprofits.

libraries participated with the assistance of the Mellon grants to the ACA and the SEF. Clearly, growth in participation had slowed.

The lower-than-anticipated level of participation illustrated in table 10.3 was not surprising. Any library that had been likely to participate in the first year knew about the advantage of the charter period and sought the discount that it brought. And since only one-third of the promised journals were as yet available online, libraries had little incentive to rush to participate in the absence of the discount or some form of grant funding. JSTOR had enough reserves at this point to wait patiently, as it did through the latter half of 1997.

But a careful analysis left no doubt that there were disturbing findings in the participation data. Rates of participation varied greatly among the pricing classes, with major long-term implications for participation and revenue. JSTOR had done well for Large participants, and if Very Small and Small are combined, it had exceeded expectations with this group. For Mediums, on the other hand, participation was much lower than planned. Some anecdotal evidence suggested that the pricing policy was to blame, but it could just as well have been that Mellon and De-Gennaro had earlier focused on the most prestigious institutions, leading to the unintentional exclusion of the Mediums.

Guthrie presented this situation, and the operating statement for the past year, to the trustees in early 1998.[83] Revenues had been $5.1 million, almost 40 percent off of the $8.2 million predicted in the Strategic and Operating Plan. Expenses were $3.1 million, just 13 percent higher than anticipated, almost exclusively due to the increased cost of production and digitization. The bottom line was that lower-than-expected revenues lessened JSTOR's operating surplus, which was earmarked for the endowment fund designed to assure the JSTOR archive's permanence.

At the same time, JSTOR had taken on numerous responsibilities unanticipated a year before. Guthrie explained to the trustees that "we are now establishing international mirror sites, identifying, signing and beginning production on Phase II content [see chapter 11], and participating in the national discussion on archiving of electronic resources [see chapter 15]. These efforts are essential if JSTOR is to reach its potential." Had JSTOR followed the Strategic and Operating Plan to the letter, it never would have undertaken these absolutely critical challenges, underscoring the importance of the nimbleness of the JSTOR organization. With more new goals, but less progress than anticipated on its preexisting goals, JSTOR finished its first year in the marketplace.

[83]Packet for the JSTOR board of trustees meeting of March 5, 1998.

CHAPTER 11

Developing Two New Collections

MAY 1997–DECEMBER 1999

WITH THE ADVENT of hundreds of paying charter participants, JSTOR's goal of completing Arts & Sciences I by the end of 1999 had become not just a promise, but rather something of a contractual obligation. At the same time, pressure for further collections growth was mounting from multiple quarters, even though library participation was coming in fits and spurts. It was necessary to manage expectations, as well as accommodate some of the pressure for expansion. This chapter focuses on how JSTOR managed the ongoing operations necessary to meet its initial obligation, while also confronting the future.

MUCH IN FLUX

The context for strategic planning in mid-1997 was the progress that JSTOR was making, albeit tentatively, in signing libraries to participate. By May, under the influence of the charter period discounts and the broad outreach of DeGennaro and others, some 190 libraries had elected to participate. JSTOR was no longer a pilot project, an experiment, or a theory. It had long-term contractual responsibilities to libraries and publishers and a renewed sense of obligation to be responsive to their needs.

Again as of May, JSTOR's cumulative publisher agreements allowed it to digitize 1.6 million pages beyond the 1 million pages that were already available online. In the Strategic and Operating Plan, Guthrie assumed that production could be maintained at 100,000 pages per month and that future journals signed would average 30,000 pages each. Based on these assumptions, a back-of-the-envelope calculation in May would have suggested that completing Arts & Sciences I would take thirty months, or until November 1999.[1] There was precious little margin for error. Given that these rates had as of then been successfully achieved

---

[1] The 2.6 million pages of signed journals represented fifty-four titles, leaving forty-six of uncertain lengths to be signed. Assuming the forty-six titles would average 30,000 pages each, as Guthrie estimated in the Strategic and Operating Plan, JSTOR had 1.38 million pages from unsigned titles, plus 1.6 million pages from signed titles, to digitize before the deadline. Thus, at 100,000 pages per month, this project would take another thirty months.

only for one month, such a calculation, had it been performed, would have given cause for concern.

Although these figures were simple to calculate, it has not been possible to locate any documentation to suggest that Guthrie made projections this early about the likelihood of completing Arts & Sciences I on time. There were many variables in mid-1997, and the long time-horizon would have involved much uncertainty. It may simply have seemed too early for the organization to make comparisons between plausible rates of production and likely page counts of signed journals. Much was still in flux at Michigan: it was in the month of May 1997 that JSTOR most directly contemplated removing its operations from Ann Arbor. Guthrie's analysis of the production operation was not so much focused on month-to-month capacity at Michigan as it was on whether the partnership could be made to work at all. It seemed likely that future management and process improvements at Michigan, or at a new location, would result in an increased digitization rate.

In retrospect, Guthrie has explained that he was not concerned about rates of production for several reasons. First, he had "begun to sense that the per-title average was going to be less than 30,000 [pages], since] the later journals were getting much smaller."[2] And he was not worried about expanding capacity if it proved to be necessary.[3] As a result, the pressure was subtly shifting from the need to complete Arts & Sciences I to the need for further growth.

FURTHER COLLECTIONS?

The loudest and most important criticism of JSTOR was heard before public release and had continued to grow louder ever since: librarians, scholars, and students wanted the database to grow more rapidly than JSTOR had ever envisioned. By the fall of 1996, numerous publishers were contacting JSTOR to see if their titles could be included.[4] In November 1997, Guthrie would report to the board that "the biggest complaint of JSTOR users and librarians is that they want more journals and they want them available as soon as possible."[5] It is difficult to be certain that, at the time, Guthrie was using the word "complaint" in order to underscore the weight of demands that were in fact little more than compliments of JSTOR's success. It is also possible that some of these

---

[2] Kevin Guthrie, personal communication, January 10, 2002.
[3] Kevin Guthrie, interview with the author, July 23, 2001.
[4] Packet for the JSTOR board of trustees meeting of October 29, 1996.
[5] Minutes of the JSTOR board of trustees meeting of November 6, 1997, 2.

"complaints" represented a sense that JSTOR would not reach critical mass at its planned rate of growth, as well as frustration by scholars and librarians interested in fields that had been omitted thus far. Some publishers were also requesting the inclusion of titles or further titles. Guthrie has reflected that "it had started to become evident that people were not going to be satisfied if JSTOR did only 100 titles."[6] It seemed likely that JSTOR would want to accelerate its plans to expand beyond its initial hundred-journal target.

Thus, even as JSTOR continued its initial marketing efforts, recruited additional journal participants, and digitized additional titles as rapidly as possible, Guthrie and Bowen began strategizing for future growth beyond the first collection. With about a quarter of Arts & Sciences I released, and with a satisfactory rate of library participation, JSTOR believed it was ready for expansion.

To begin with, they recalled the previous year's conversations with the AAAS, the publisher of *Science,* and the board's conclusion that this journal title could be absolutely key, particularly if bundled with *Nature* (see chapter 6). Bowen began to make arrangements to contact the Howard Hughes Medical Institute, a funder in the sciences, but Guthrie urged caution. "Because of the size and complexity of this title," he wrote in an email to Bowen, "doing a real assessment of what will be involved in its conversion, assessing the cost, and making a proposal [to a foundation like Hughes] will be a *major* undertaking. We must get some other things stabilized first," including, he added, "trying to meet the 100,000 page [per month] goal" for Arts & Sciences I production.[7] Bowen concurred, but added that "it probably does make sense to get a sense of interest and, more specifically, to discourage folks like those at SCIENCE from going off in another direction. That remains a concern."[8] The combination of Bowen's ever forward thrust and Guthrie's caution would define their relationship as the leadership of JSTOR, even though it is rarely so clearly documentable as in this case.

Here, Bowen voiced his concern that if JSTOR did not offer itself to publishers, other JSTOR-like entities would crop up and fragment journal backfiles in a way that would be detrimental for scholarly users. As a result of this email exchange, Bowen and Guthrie began to plan for expansion, given the long time-horizons involved, even while they agreed that Arts & Sciences I production was the most important immediate concern. Either way, production capacity had to be increased.

[6] Kevin Guthrie, interview with the author, July 23, 2001.

[7] Kevin Guthrie, "Re: SCIENCE-JSTOR," email to William G. Bowen, May 8, 1997.

[8] William G. Bowen, "Re[2]: SCIENCE-JSTOR," email to Kevin Guthrie, May 8, 1997.

PRODUCTION CAPACITY AND TENTATIVE PLANNING

Fortuitously, just as Bowen and Guthrie were considering the addition of new collections, JSTOR's production operation began functioning more efficiently, though perhaps at a rate that was still inadequate. It was clear that there was no excess production capacity; to begin building any new collections before completing Arts & Sciences I, JSTOR would have to expand its physical facilities and the ranks of skilled personnel. Such an enlargement of capacity would happily provide a margin of error for Arts & Sciences I that did not then exist.[9]

At the same time that JSTOR decided to create additional production capacity in the summer of 1997, it was feeling the after-effects of the renegotiations with Michigan. Even though JSTOR and Michigan were able to come to a satisfactory agreement, JSTOR leaders never again wanted to be overly dependent on another entity. If somehow the relationship had been severed, JSTOR's promise to libraries might well have gone unmet. Prudence suggested JSTOR should become less dependent on its one partner by establishing a second site for production.

Thus JSTOR's strategic need to establish a redundant production capacity was consonant with its immediate need for additional production capacity to build new collections. Even if a new production facility would not literally provide a fail-safe redundancy, it would ensure that skills and processes were secure, independent of shifting political winds. It should be underscored that Guthrie was not unhappy with the recent progress of Michigan production. In point of fact, Bill Landis was able to hire Eileen Fenton as his principal deputy in the summer of 1997, and they kept the production process flowing smoothly, even as Landis made plans to leave JSTOR. Rather, the decision to seek an alternative production site was an organizational choice, mostly unrelated to the quality and progress of Michigan's production operation.

Princeton was chosen as the second production site. It was ideal because it already had a relationship with JSTOR through hosting a number of programming staff as well as the mirror site (see chapter 9). The production facility would also provide improved offices for the programmers. Moreover, it was hoped that Fuchs's presence as a vice-president on campus (and Bowen's affiliation as president emeritus)

---

[9] While there would have been some risk in assuming that Arts & Sciences I would only require three million additional pages to be digitized and in assuming that the rate of production could be maintained, these estimates would not have been unreasonable. In other words, in 1997 there was no need to expand production capacity except to build additional collections.

would continue to ensure that relations with Princeton never became as complicated as they had with Michigan.

The production facility would be designed to accommodate a production team the same size as the one at Michigan—a coordinator and four technicians. The Princeton site would presumably have the same capacity as Michigan, thereby doubling JSTOR's total monthly rate of production to about 200,000 pages. It would take another year for the space to be fully renovated and staffed. But the arrangements fulfilled the two desired effects: future collections (including the journal *Science*) had a place to be digitized and JSTOR had its redundant production facility.[10]

Spurred along by the new Princeton space, Guthrie brought several further suggestions for expansion to the board for discussion and consideration.[11] First, JSTOR could take its large database and bundle it into smaller clusters that would have greater appeal to institutions that had not yet chosen to participate. Elton White suggested that JSTOR focus on "making the most of what we have already created." By offering "sub-bundles" in addition to the larger Arts & Sciences I, JSTOR would offer greater choice to future participants, a range of choices that had not previously been available and that had cost it a number of participants.[12] Bowen suggested that an obvious example of such a cluster would be one that encompassed the titles in economics, finance, and statistics. Such a cluster would target those universities less focused on the liberal arts and more on business (as well as central banks and nonprofit research groups). Although JSTOR by this point was aware that more professionally oriented comprehensive universities were not signing on at the same rate as other schools (see chapters 10, 12, and 13), it had not yet acted. So it may have been that Bowen's suggestion was offered in response to JSTOR's desire to interest more of these universities, which he believed to be more focused on teaching business courses and less on the liberal arts. It is clear that Guthrie's proposed sub-bundles, and White's and Bowen's endorsement of them, reflected JSTOR's desire to be responsive to the libraries that had expressed a preference for only a subset of journals.

The second option was to expand, scanning additional titles that would take JSTOR well beyond its initial hundred-journal goal for Arts

---

[10] Packet for the JSTOR board of trustees meeting of July 31, 1997.

[11] Minutes of the JSTOR board of trustees meeting of July 31, 1997.

[12] A relatively small number of colleges and universities had been unwilling to license the entire Arts & Sciences I Collection but were interested, conceptually, in electronic access to more focused groups of backfiles. This may have been about ten such libraries at this point. Kevin Guthrie, interview with the author, December 6, 2001.

& Sciences I. The board considered criteria for such further growth, which would focus on fields that were intellectually important, could benefit from backfile access, and would attract external funding. In this regard, the board discussed the specific title *Science*, which had earlier expressed interest in participating, as well as a variety of disciplines, including art history, ancient studies, agriculture, and ecology. It also recognized that there was further work to be done in other areas of the arts and sciences, including some disciplines already included in Arts & Sciences I. The options were so plentiful that it was difficult to know where to begin.

The board concluded that both approaches—redeployment of existing content and digitization of further titles and fields—would be desirable.[13] But the redeployment, especially, would cause concern. Would JSTOR's existing library participants continue to take the large bundle of titles, or would many choose to replace it with only the most desirable of the minibundles to save money? If the latter, redeploying existing content, to create previously unavailable options, might radically transform the economics of the Arts & Sciences I Collection. JSTOR's carefully constructed business plan might no longer be viable. One way around this dilemma would be to create disciplinary clusters that combined a number of existing titles from Arts & Sciences I with new ones. Thus an economics cluster could combine the dozen relevant titles from Arts & Sciences I with perhaps two dozen new titles that had not fit into the original collection. Arts & Sciences I participants would pay only for the new titles they received; a library choosing solely the disciplinary collection would pay a higher price. Existing participants, it was thought, would not abandon Arts & Sciences I because so many of its titles would not be available in any of the new disciplinary bundles. Moreover, the lower price they paid for the new journals would represent a discount. Under this plan JSTOR could reach new markets by combining existing and new content, without unbundling Arts & Sciences I. Although this model was a bit more complicated, it had the clear advantage of allowing both new and existing participants to receive additional titles without threatening the original business plan.[14]

At this point, Guthrie also determined that it was time to begin assessing *Science*, to see exactly what a digitization project would involve

---

[13] Minutes of the JSTOR board of trustees meeting of July 31, 1997.

[14] Where scholars have worked on bundling strategies for information goods, they have stressed the advantages of creating bundled subsets of larger bundles. Yannis Bakos and Erik Brynjolfsson, "Bundling Information Goods: Pricing, Profits, and Efficiency," *Management Science* 45, no. 12 (December 1999): 1613. It has not been possible to locate any analysis of mixed bundling as practiced by JSTOR, in which the "sub-bundle" includes items that are not included in the larger bundle.

in terms of staff, technology, and funding. This was necessary for planning purposes in general, and it would allow him to write a grant proposal to HHMI or other potential funders. This planning was seen as important enough to divert some production staff time at Michigan from their Arts & Sciences I responsibilities.[15]

For a number of reasons, the board concluded that accelerating the pace of collections growth was highly desirable. Most important, librarians and scholars were demanding more journals more quickly. Also, Bowen had become increasingly concerned that if JSTOR did not increase its journal titles rapidly, individual publishers would more and more begin to take on retrospective digitization themselves. Guthrie and the rest of the board agreed that such a fragmenting of JSTOR's potential for critical mass was undesirable and worth taking risks to avoid.

SCIENCE MAGAZINE

Once JSTOR arranged to acquire the Princeton space, it had to secure journals to be scanned there. Although the space would not be available, and production work could therefore not begin, for some time, this time would most properly be used to secure a significant number of journals for that office to digitize. While there was strong reason to believe that *Science* would participate, a formal agreement was obviously necessary. Discussions between Guthrie and the AAAS in the fall of 1997 revealed both exciting opportunities and new challenges.[16]

In a memorandum to JSTOR trustees, Guthrie discussed some of the pricing and access options. He noted that *Science*'s backfile was sufficiently large that it would not fit into Arts & Sciences I; it was so large it could almost have been a collection of its own. The idea had appeal: Guthrie wondered if the AAAS might not be a better distributor of its own backfiles than JSTOR, given *Science*'s huge and broad subscription base. Just as JSTOR was using the JISC as seemingly the most efficient distribution mechanism in the United Kingdom, so it might use the AAAS as the most efficient distributor for *Science*. This was one interim conclusion in conversations between JSTOR and the AAAS, but it would rapidly be changed.[17]

While this option had been discussed, neither the AAAS nor JSTOR was committed to it. In a single-title collection, the price of the *Science*

---

[15] Kevin Guthrie, "*SCIENCE* and Princeton Production," email to Eileen G. Fenton, August 4, 1997.

[16] Kevin Guthrie, "Meeting with AAAS re: Science," email to William G. Bowen, Ira Fuchs, Richard DeGennaro, Mary Patterson McPherson, and Sarah Sully, October 21, 1997.

[17] Packet of the JSTOR board of trustees meeting of November 6, 1997.

backfile would be totally transparent, rather than being priced in conjunction with other titles. The value of the "collection" would be indistinguishable from the value of the individual title. As a result JSTOR's pricing might have put direct pressure on the AAAS's pricing for *Science*'s current issues, pressure that both the AAAS and JSTOR sought to avoid.

At the board meeting, the matter was discussed and it was decided that the existing business model was adequate for *Science*, as well, a key example of how the board was actively involved in JSTOR's ongoing development. As a result, subsequent conversations with the AAAS were based on JSTOR's existing business model of building multiple-title collections, then licensing access to academic libraries.

ECOLOGY & BOTANY

Even while JSTOR was working out early arrangements for the digitization and distribution of *Science*, an unusually broad scholarly title of appeal to numerous students and scholars, it was being encouraged to create collections of substantial depth—collections that, for a smaller discipline, would contain nearly all of the core journal backfiles. This was one version of the quest for critical mass. For nearly two years, Mellon Program Officer William Robertson had been lobbying for additional ecology titles. An enthusiastic proponent of digitized collections in his program domain of Conservation and the Environment (see chapter 6), Robertson saw JSTOR as a resource of particular value to ecologists and allied scholars.

Although ecology and related disciplines would benefit from having their journals included in JSTOR and Robertson was willing to recommend funding for this purpose, there was also the question of whether these were the journals that would be best for JSTOR. Given the ability to produce only one or two new collections per year, where on the ranked list of librarian priorities did Ecology & Botany fall? A survey found high interest there, and the interest of a potential funder was reassuring. Although consultation with librarians did not fully assuage Guthrie's concerns, he and the board elected to begin moving forward with an Ecology & Botany collection.

Grant support was particularly important for a collection like Ecology & Botany, because the journal content was substantially more specialized and the audience more limited than some of the individual disciplines of Arts & Sciences I. As JSTOR expanded, of course, new journals included would inevitably become less broad in their coverage but more important to their specific disciplines. Whereas Arts & Sciences I included the core title *Ecology*, Ecology & Botany included the somewhat more specific title, the *New Phytologist*. A collection of these journals would, breadth of Arts & Sciences I. In addition, a subject-centered collection would appeal to fewer disciplines at a given college or university than Arts & Sciences I's massive multi-interdisciplinary bundle. As a result, fewer colleges and universities were likely to license it. The collection would generate lower revenues, and recover a smaller percentage of its costs, than Arts & Sciences I. Some sort of subsidy would consequently be necessary, and Robertson was willing to recommend that the Mellon Foundation grant funds toward the creation of such a collection.

But JSTOR was not initially in a position to take on further responsibilities; it lacked the production capacity to add to its digitization commitments. And even the new Princeton office being established was committed to digitizing *Science* and so could not be charged with digitizing ecology journals. For these reasons, Guthrie was justifiably conservative about JSTOR diverging from its focus and spreading itself too thin.

But soon after Guthrie and the board concluded that expansion of some sort was desirable, and just after they secured the Princeton space, additional space became available in Ann Arbor contiguous with JSTOR's existing offices. Fortuitously, JSTOR had obtained the right of first refusal on the space. Now, it had to take the space or lose the option. In a fairly bold stroke, Guthrie and the trustees opted to rent this additional office space, which could be used to accommodate an expanded production staff.[18] (It was foresight that JSTOR had secured the right of first refusal.) So while in May of 1997 JSTOR appeared to have a capacity of 100,000 pages per month, by October it seemed to be on the verge of increasing this capacity to nearly 300,000 pages per month. Without this fortuitous development, JSTOR would not have moved so rapidly toward its third collection.

Independently, Robertson and Katherine McCarter, the new executive director of the Ecological Society of America (ESA), had been discussing the possibility of a grant to cover access to its three JSTOR titles for ESA members that were not affiliated with JSTOR-participating colleges and universities. In essence, the proposal would fund a revamped membership database that could, in an experiment to see if this was feasible for other society publishers, link with JSTOR.[19] The effort to make access available to individuals is covered in chapter 12.

[18]It is not possible to document any internal discussion about whether the production operation could be scaled so radically; it seems that the only constraint was believed to be the physical space to accommodate staff.

[19]Katherine McCarter, letter to William Robertson IV, October 7, 1997, in Grant file #49700620 of the Andrew W. Mellon Foundation.

While Robertson was considering this request, even before JSTOR's new space was absolutely committed, he and Guthrie discussed further arrangements for an Ecology & Botany Collection. With such a collection seeming increasingly likely, Roberston recalled McCarter's interest in working to expand the ESA's access to, and participation in, JSTOR. It seemed there was an opportunity for the ESA to aid in the development of the Ecology & Botany Collection, and so he contacted McCarter to see if the ESA would be interested. McCarter recalls that Robertson "called up and said, 'Katherine, I've got your letter here [requesting funds for individual access], what would you thing about $1.5 million?' And I said, 'Okay, Bill, that sounds good—what do you want?'"[20] The stand-alone Ecology & Botany Collection, noted ESA Program Officer Mary Barber, would allow them to serve the membership in a new way. "These are the journals that our members . . . use, and now they are going to be part of JSTOR, which is going into [virtually] all institutions, and therefore [the journals] will be [broadly] available."[21] So just two weeks after McCarter's first letter, requesting $129,000, she sent a revised request for $1.5 million. Such a grant would fund work by the ESA to organize societies and other ecological publishers to participate, as well as cover JSTOR's one-time expenses to digitize the materials (in addition to the original plans for the individual access experiment).[22] For Mellon, these arrangements would offer an exciting opportunity, since the relatively small size of the discipline allowed an incredibly deep collection.[23]

Another special characteristic of the grant was the ESA's role as a bridge between Mellon and JSTOR and between JSTOR and potential publishers. The ESA had as members virtually all of the editors of the possible titles, and as a result it was well-placed to encourage their participation. Also, it would assemble a committee of scholars to help identify the desired titles, getting JSTOR invaluable input. The involvement of the ESA and this group of scholars would give the collection an important stamp of approval, thus conferring more scholarly credibility on the collection than it might otherwise have had.

Within a matter of weeks, JSTOR outlined a digitization project for Ecology & Botany, totaling approximately 700,000 pages, to be funded by the ESA via a grant from the Mellon Foundation.[24] By securing the grant concurrent with the space, JSTOR was able to use grant funds to

[20] Katherine McCarter, interview with the author, September 20, 2001.

[21] Mary Barber, interview with the author, September 20, 2001.

[22] Katherine McCarter, letter to William Robertson III, October 23, 1997, in Grant file #49700620 of the Andrew W. Mellon Foundation.

[23] The docket item, in Grant file #49700620 of the Andrew W. Mellon Foundation.

[24] Packet for the JSTOR board of trustees meeting, of November 6, 1997.

pay the capital costs of outfitting its new offices. The capacity that these funds would create would prove useful to additional digitization projects beyond Ecology & Botany.

In December 1997, Mellon awarded $1,476,000 to the ESA, allowing work to proceed. Guthrie would write later of his ongoing concern about the possibility "that the ecology/botany cluster wouldn't be the first [cluster that librarians] would choose and that we might be subject to criticism for the choice."[25] It seems that the enthusiasm of Bowen and Robertson pushed JSTOR to move ahead with this collection when Guthrie was not fully convinced that the move was right. In any case, the ESA immediately organized the committee of scholars to plan the collection. Only after they had developed plans and spoken with publishers themselves would JSTOR's publisher-relations staff—principally Sarah Sully—contact publishers. This arrangement allowed JSTOR's overtaxed publisher-relations operation to focus its energies where they were most urgently needed—Arts & Sciences I.

GENERAL SCIENCE

Prompted by the board's conclusion that the ways in which *Science* was different did not merit a departure from the traditional business model, Guthrie began to consider how *Science* could fit into a cluster. At one point, Guthrie thought there might be a way for JSTOR to expand the Ecology & Botany Collection to encompass *Science*, but he quickly realized that this would not work.[26] Instead, Guthrie and Bowen consulted with others on the other components of a collection expressly built around *Science*. Such a collection would adequately meet the AAAS's need that pricing be based on more than one title, while preserving JSTOR's curatorial role. It was in this way that the collection, titled "General Science" by Bowen, was born.[27]

In addition to Morawetz's recommendation that JSTOR pursue *Nature*, Guthrie began to research other broad scientific titles. With the assistance of Mellon Foundation Librarian Kamla Motihar, he determined that, of the multidisciplinary science titles, three—*Science, Nature,* and *Proceedings of the National Academy of Sciences (PNAS)*—had a massive number of total citations in the scientific literature, an order of magnitude

---

[25]Kevin Guthrie, "Ecology cluster and SCIENCE," email to Sarah Sully, January 17, 1998.

[26]Ibid.

[27]William G. Bowen, "Re[3]: Science Online," email to Kevin Guthrie, January 17, 1998.

greater than the fourth most-cited title.[28] The four Royal Society publications did not seem to be so high on the list because they were treated as discrete publications; when combined as one, they were solidly fourth on the list. The Royal Society titles were of extraordinary historical importance. Dating back to 1665, they included articles by Isaac Newton on optics, Benjamin Franklin on electricity, and many other distinguished contributions. On the recommendation of a number of prominent scholars including Harriet Zuckerman, senior vice president of the Mellon Foundation and an expert in the sociology of science, the Royal Society titles were added to the target list.[29] In addition to these seven titles, JSTOR sought several other possibilities, including *Scientific American*. A collection consisting of this group of titles would be of great importance to historians, sociologists, and other scholars of science and industrialization, not to mention scientists themselves.

JSTOR's production staff determined that the costs of creating a General Science Collection would be extremely high. The newer issues, especially in *Science*, had more complicated layouts, using color, insets, and numerous illustrations, all of which required special attention. All in all, initial estimates called for the General Science Collection to cost between two and three times more, per page, than Arts & Sciences I.[30]

Despite the high costs involved, JSTOR staff was convinced from conversations with librarians and scholars that the collection would be in great demand, if prices could be held low. Indeed, it seemed that demand for the General Science Collection might exceed that for Arts & Sciences I. And General Science might well expose JSTOR to a broader user-pool, possibly including high schools, public libraries, and a large number of community colleges. Guthrie was determined to keep prices as low as possible, so that high demand could substantially enlarge JSTOR's user-base.

Guthrie created a detailed budget focused on the costs of creating the collection, based on estimates from JSTOR production staff. JSTOR would put the scanning and indexing out for bid in the hopes of retaining a second able scanning bureau in addition to DIT, to give flexibility and redundancy in digitization, just as the new Princeton production site would give for preparation and quality control. Taking into account the need for some sort of manual OCR and many, many images, Guthrie's

[28]Kevin Guthrie, "Science interdisciplinary cluster," email to William G. Bowen, Sarah Sully, and Harriet Zuckerman, February 7, 1998.
[29]Harriet Zuckerman, "Re[2]: Science interdisciplinary cluster," email to William G. Bowen, Kevin Guthrie, and Sarah Sully, February 8, 1998.
[30]See, for example, the JSTOR grant request of May 14, 1998, in Grant file #29800655 of the Andrew W. Mellon Foundation.

budget totaled $2.5 million. With this budget in hand, JSTOR sought foundation subventions for the up-front costs of the collection.

While beginning to speak with representatives of several foundations, Guthrie worked to finalize publisher agreements. Without signed publisher agreements, any proposal to a foundation would be little more than a creative, unproven idea. (Of course, the Catch-22 was that, without funding, it was more difficult to secure publishers.) With signed agreements in hand, potential funders could see that JSTOR had both the resources and the ability to undertake the new collection.

Agreements in principle were reached with every publisher well before final terms were determined and licenses signed. The license for *Science* and its related publication, *Scientific Monthly*, was the first to be signed for General Science, at the end of May 1998. The announcement that the entire *Science* backfile would be put online was considered to be so important on its own, without the other potential titles, that the *Chronicle of Higher Education* published an article reporting the news.[31]

Meanwhile, Bowen had contacted Bruce Alberts, the president of the National Academy of Sciences, whom he had known at Princeton. Following an enthusiastic conversation between Bowen and Alberts, Guthrie arranged to meet with staff of the *PNAS*. In March 1998, he spoke at length with Nick Cozzarelli, the editor-in-chief, who "is not as concerned by the economic ramifications of electronic publishing as are most publishers. He is the first to admit that he is an academic and his heart lies with getting things up and available [online] without restriction." More to the point, Guthrie reported that Cozzarelli "seemed both interested [in JSTOR in principle] and positively disposed to participating."[32] In July, the formal publisher license was signed, making possible the digitization of the *PNAS*.

Nature seemed less likely, and it initially declined to participate. When the collection began to take form, with both *Science* and the *PNAS* signed on, *Nature* publisher MacMillan met with JSTOR Board member Charles Ellis to reconsider. Nothing, however, developed, and the collection was built without *Nature*.[33]

With a number of publisher agreements secured, grant requests were finalized. In his May request to Mellon, Guthrie noted that the collection "would be of inestimable value" as a research resource.[34] Mellon's

---

[31]"'Science' to Appear in Journal Archive on the Web," *Chronicle of Higher Education*, July 24, 1998, A17.

[32]Kevin Guthrie, "Conversation with Nick Cozzarelli, PNAS Editor-in-Chief," March 11, 1998.

[33]Packet for the JSTOR board of trustees meeting of October 6, 1999.

[34]Guthrie grant request of May 14, 1998, at 5, in Grant file #29800655 of the Andrew W. Mellon Foundation.

award of $1.3 million was contingent on other grants being awarded, but such grants were all but assured and so its trustees acted at their July meeting. An award letter was sent with the first payment later in July.[35] It should be noted that accepting the Mellon grant was a calculated risk, since it further increased JSTOR's challenge in diversifying its revenue-base for tax purposes. In August, the trustees of the Howard Hughes Medical Institute awarded $800,000 to JSTOR for the collection. As a funder of biomedical research, Hughes's vice-president explained in his award letter, the institute recognized that "data only becomes useful information when organized for rapid retrieval and accessibility."[36] The support of Mellon and Hughes and the signing of the *PNAS* led to a second laudatory *Chronicle* item.[37] Another medical funder, the Josiah S. Macy Foundation, also provided $500,000 toward the General Science Collection.

SIGNING ECOLOGY & BOTANY

Whereas JSTOR worked hard to secure funding and publisher participation in General Science, its approach with Ecology & Botany was significantly different. The ESA itself took on responsibility for identifying titles of interest (in consultation with JSTOR) and initial publisher outreach. After the ESA completed this work, JSTOR negotiated final agreements. Then, the collection entered JSTOR's production process like any other. The differences between General Science and Ecology & Botany (and between both of them and Arts & Sciences I) offers an important opportunity to consider the work for which JSTOR possessed a comparative advantage and the work for which it could partner with other organizations.[38]

The ESA committee consisted of nine scholars and other leaders in the field, who considered the contours of such a collection and began working from a list of eighty-five titles. Eventually the committee recommended about forty titles, and ESA staff began to contact the editorial and publishing arms of the publishers, especially the scholarly societies, with which the ESA was especially well positioned to work. In the case of the university and commercial presses, whose interests were more

---

[35] William G. Bowen, letter to Kevin M. Guthrie, June 15, 1998.

[36] Purnell W. Choppin, letter to Kevin Guthrie, August 24, 1998.

[37] "Project to Digitize Back Issues of Scientific Journals Gains Support," *Chronicle of Higher Education*, October 23, 1998, A23.

[38] This section is based on Mary Barber and Katherine McCarter, interviews with the author, September 20, 2001; and Heidi McGregor, interviews with the author, May 18, 2001, and June 5, 2001.

complex, JSTOR staff, who may have had previous contact with those presses on other titles, often made the contact.

Several factors complicated the work. JSTOR did not provide as much up-front advice about publisher outreach as it might have to the ESA, which, after all, was new to this game. In turn, the ESA may have consulted JSTOR less then it might have, as a result of which some negotiations became unnecessarily complicated. Neither the ESA nor JSTOR fully appreciated, at the onset of this novel partnership, how closely they would have to work together in order to succeed, which in turn lessened the value to the overtaxed JSTOR of having the ESA involved. Challenges aside, the collection was built successfully.

Because there was a clearly developed list of titles desired for Ecology & Botany, it is possible to judge the success of JSTOR and the ESA in soliciting their participation. (This was not effectively possible for Arts & Sciences I because the list of desired titles and disciplines was constantly evolving in response to developments.) Table 11.1 shows all of the titles eventually approached. Whereas it was possible to secure the participation of 83 percent of the noncommercial titles, JSTOR only secured two of the nine commercially published titles—both of which were published by Blackwell's, which had contributed titles to Arts & Sciences I. No new commercial publishers agreed to participate in JSTOR at this stage—a stark demonstration that JSTOR's terms were more appealing to the scholarly societies and university presses than to the commercial players. Happily, most of the highest-ranked titles were published by the nonprofits and would eventually participate. Of the four noncommercially-published titles that did not participate, it cannot have been a coincidence that three were based outside of the United States.

Although the ESA-JSTOR team approach did not work perfectly, it accomplished its goals. The Ecology & Botany Collection that was ultimately created is an extraordinarily rich and deep resource for scholars working in the fields, and it has generated significant interest in further expansion in these areas.

SUMMATION

In this period, JSTOR was able not only to develop plans for two important new science collections, but also to expand its production capacity by a factor of three. Expanding production capacity was a critical move. Not only did it ensure that Arts & Sciences I was completed on schedule, but it also gave JSTOR substantial capacity for further projects (as

TABLE 11.1
Journals Invited to Participate in Ecology & Botany
(Excludes Six Arts & Sciences I Participants)

Title	Publisher	Type[i]	Participant?
American Journal of Botany	Botanical Society of America	SS	Yes
American Midland Naturalist	University of Notre Dame	UP	Yes
American Naturalist	University of Chicago	UP	Yes
Annals of Botany	Academic Press / Elsevier Science	Commercial	No
Annals of the Missouri Botanical Garden	Missouri Botanical Garden Press	UP	Yes
Aquatic Botany	Elsevier Science	Commercial	No
Biodiversity Letters	Blackwell Science	Commercial	No
Biotropica	Association for Tropical Biology	SS	Yes
Brittonia	New York Botanical Garden Press	UP	Yes
Canadian Journal of Botany	NCR Research Press	UP	No
Canadian Journal of Forestry	NCR Research Press	UP	No
Conservation Biology	Society for Conservation Biology	SS	Yes
Evolution	Society for the Study of Evolution	SS	Yes
Evolutionary Ecology	Kluwer Academic Publishers	Commercial	No
Functional Biology	British Ecological Society	SS	Yes
Global Ecology & Biogeography Letters	Blackwell Science	Commercial	Yes
International Journal of Plant Sciences	University of Chicago Press	UP	Yes
Journal of Applied Ecology	British Ecological Society	SS	Yes
Journal of Biogeography	Blackwell Science	Commercial	Yes
Journal of the Torrey Botanical Society	Torrey Botanical Society	SS	Yes

[i]University press, scholarly society, or commercial publisher.

continued

TABLE 11.1 *(Continued)*

Title	Publisher	Type[i]	Participant?
Journal of Tropical Ecology	Cambridge University Press	UP	Yes
Journal of Vegetation Science	Opulus Press	Commercial	No
Limnology and Oceanography	American Society of Limnology and Oceanography	SS	Yes
Missouri Botanical Garden Annual Report	Missouri Botanical Garden Press	UP	Yes
New Phytologist	New Phytologist Trust	SS	Yes
Oecologia	Springer-Verlag	Commercial	No
Oikos	Nordic Ecological Society	SS	No
Paleobiology	Paleontological Society	SS	Yes
Quarterly Review of Biology	University of Chicago Press	UP	Yes
Systematic Biology	Society of Systematic Biologists	SS	Yes
Systematic Botany	American Society of Plant Taxonomists	SS	Yes
Taxon	International Association for Plant Taxonomy	SS	No
Theoretical Population Biology	Academic Press / Elsevier Science	Commercial	No
Trends in Ecology and Evolution	Elsevier Science	Commercial	No
Vegetation / Plant Ecology	Kluwer Academic Publishers	Commercial	No

[i]University press, scholarly society, or commercial publisher.

we shall see in chapter 13). The collections that were planned in this period did not become available until 2000, and library response to them is discussed in chapter 14. The leadership balanced the prioritization of Arts & Sciences I against the need to look forward, even in the face of slow increases in library participation. In so doing, it operated opportunistically in planning collections in response to publisher and funder interest.

CHAPTER 12

Increasing Availability and Participation

JANUARY 1998–DECEMBER 1999

ALTHOUGH the two new collections represented something of a risk, since JSTOR committed to them in a period of little new library participation, they also held forth a great deal of opportunity. It was believed that the General Science Collection would bring greater exposure for JSTOR, and the up-front costs of both collections would be paid for by outside funders. For the year following the close of the charter period, with the Michigan renegotiations and planning for the new collections taking center stage, library participation was not as much of an institutional priority. By the summer of 1998, however, a number of factors would refocus Guthrie's attention on library participation.

LAYING THE GROUNDWORK

In preparing for the first trustee meeting of 1998, Guthrie reflected on the mixed success of 1997 and sounded an upbeat note for the future.[1] Some of the upcoming priorities included bringing international mirror sites online (see chapter 10), getting post-Arts & Sciences I production underway (see chapter 11), linking JSTOR's archive with current issues (see chapter 14), permitting outside databases to link to JSTOR (chapter 14), and developing new pricing approaches for new types of libraries (see below). Not least, Guthrie anticipated adding 175 new library participants (25 fewer than called for by the Strategic and Operating Plan) to the existing 233. All of this would take new staff.

For one, managing the expenses of three offices and the billing of hundreds of participants would require a controller. In the spring of 1998, JSTOR hired Gerard Aurigemma, who had experience working in higher education at New York University. Aurigemma would introduce more refined financial reporting and a formal invoicing system. More generally, he would provide back-office capacity for growth in collections, participants, and the staff necessary for both.

In addition to Aurigemma, JSTOR needed to staff the new production operation at Princeton and the larger one at Michigan. Production

---

[1]Packet for the JSTOR board of trustees meeting of March 2, 1998.

technicians, as well as a coordinator for Princeton, would add nine staff members. A new associate director for Publisher Relations would add capacity now that there were three collections on which to focus.[2] Heidi McGregor, who had worked for Simon and Schuster and had experience in licensing the electronic rights to retrospective materials, accepted the position. Finally, the growing Michigan office was ready for a local office administrator and Princeton needed to hire a systems administrator to coordinate all of the mirror sites that were expected abroad.

But in many areas there was to be no growth. Software development, with four programmers, was forecast for no growth, as were user services (three librarians) and library relations (two staffers). The priority was collections growth; it was believed that libraries would participate if the content was there, and that new software features could be added later.

MIDWAY ADJUSTMENT

In the first half of 1998, even with the support of a full-time library-relations staffer recruited late the previous year, JSTOR was having difficulty adding library participants. The enthusiasm accompanying the charter period was impossible to sustain. After the initial spurt of 190 participants in the four-month charter period, it took about a year to add another hundred. At this rate, the target of 750 libraries foreseen by the business plan as participating by the end of 1999 would not have been reached until mid-2002. Guthrie had firmly resisted making exceptions to the pricing structure, preferring to wait for participants to appreciate what he believed to be JSTOR's principled stand for fairness.[3] Yet many of the most important state library systems, in particular, were not budging from their demands for agreements for consortia or reduced prices.

And for good reason. The U.S. Department of Education's 1998 Academic Library Survey, not released until 2001, allows the calculation of

---

[2] In general, we have presented JSTOR's publisher-relations operation as focused on the necessity to recruit new publishers. In addition, Sully was acting as general counsel on all manner of legal and licensing issues, in addition to functioning as liaison with existing publishers. "Keeping one-hundred publishers well-informed, managing links with their sites, and coordinating the projects we are undertaking [such as individual access] . . . is getting to be a significant responsibility" in itself, Guthrie wrote to the board. For this reason, in the summer, JSTOR began to search for an associate director of Publisher Relations, someone who could handle existing relationships in addition to assisting with new developments. Packet for the JSTOR board of trustees meeting of March 5, 1998.

[3] Kevin Guthrie, interview with the author, October 30, 2001.

TABLE 12.1

Average Spending on Electronic Information Resources per School,
by Carnegie *Classification* Groupings

Carnegie *Classification* Grouping	Avg. Spending on Resources	JSTOR DDF
Research	$446,000	$40,000
Doctoral	$170,000	$30,000–$40,000
Master's	$64,000	$30,000
Baccalaureate	$25,000	$20,000

average annual expenditures on electronic resources. As table 12.1 suggests, JSTOR's one-time fee was 9 percent of the Research universities' average electronic spending, but for the Baccalaureate schools, it was 80 percent! Although JSTOR's DDF was sometimes funded by the central administration or spread across two years, participation was clearly more difficult for the smaller libraries than the larger.

By mid-1998, JSTOR staff were in a better position to evaluate the pricing structure, since usage statistics were now available (see chapter 9) and more than a year of participant and usage data had accumulated. At the same time, JSTOR's leadership was involved in a sustained negotiation with the California State University system, whose participation would have added 22 Medium institutions, for an overall 10 percent increase in JSTOR's participant-base. Guthrie described his dilemma in materials he prepared for the board's July 30 meeting. "Although the idea of offering Cal State a special group deal is not appealing" because of the decision to avoid discounts for consortia, he wrote,

> I am sympathetic to the fact that the price they would have to pay—especially the $30,000 [DDF] for each school—seems high. Put another way, it doesn't seem appropriate that an institution like Cal State-Chico should have to pay [a DDF] of $30,000, while an institution like UC-Berkeley pays [a DDF] of $40,000. Shouldn't there be a greater gap? The difference between the value of JSTOR to large research institutions and master's granting institutions is disproportionately larger than the difference in our prices offered to these institutions. It seem[s] that a reassessment of our prices might be in order.[4]

[4]Packet for the JSTOR board of trustees meeting of July 30, 1998.

**Number of Articles
Viewed, Articles Printed,
and Searches Conducted**

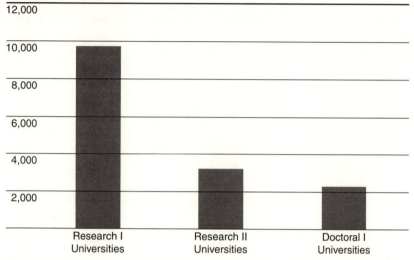

Figure 12.1. Median per-Institution Arts & Sciences I Usage in the First Half of 1998, by Carnegie *Classification* Groupings, U.S. Participants Only

As a result, Guthrie and his staff had undertaken a summer-long examination of library sizes and usage rates, to understand in greater detail the value bases for the pricing categories.

Most significantly, the study found a huge disparity in usage among the Research I, Research II, and Doctoral I universities, the Carnegie categories that JSTOR had combined to form its Large pricing class. Usage at the Research Is, which were the largest, wealthiest, and most research-oriented universities, was astronomical by comparison with the others, as figure 12.1 illustrates.[5] Although usage was only one of the many potential value indicators, the gap between the Research I universities and the rest of the Large class was evident. Indeed, it was not even clear that this was the full extent of the gap; as more journals in more disciplines went online, the gap might have become even more pronounced.

---

[5] In mid-1998, sufficient data were first available to allow such an analysis. The average, or median, per-school use over a period of time should include only those institutions participating throughout the entire period. Consequently, there was a necessary delay between JSTOR's signing on new schools in 1997, those schools effectively publicizing the resource so that statistics would have meaning, and finally having a period that could be analyzed.

In response, JSTOR staff proposed splitting the Research I universities out of the Large class into a new group: the Very Large universities. JSTOR would not raise retrospectively the DDFs of the so-called Very Large institutions that had already signed on, but any new Very Large participants would be invoiced at a higher DDF immediately. The DDF for the remaining Large class would be reduced slightly, for existing and future participants, to $35,000.

The Research I universities had signed up in great numbers—three-quarters were already participants, compared with 40 percent of the rest of the Large class—and their usage was much higher than was anticipated, suggesting that they valued the database more than JSTOR's pricing plan had foreseen. Meanwhile, the Medium institutions—the Doctoral II and Master's I and II—constituted some 600 potential participants, of which only about 60 were actually participating in mid-1998. In particular, of the Master's II universities, only about 6 percent had elected to participate, the lowest percentage of any Carnegie class. These schools clearly did not value JSTOR as much as the pricing plan had imagined.

In examining the characteristics of libraries at these universities, JSTOR staff discovered the great disparity between the Doctoral II and Master's I, on the one hand, and the Master's II on the other. This latter group of academic libraries had far smaller collections, measured by titles and journal subscriptions, than the other Carnegie groups making up the Medium class. And because there were only seven Master's II participants, it was impossible to analyze their usage in a meaningful way.

Consequently, Guthrie brought to the board several proposals related to the Medium institutions. First, he hoped to move the Master's II universities from the Medium to the Small pricing class, based on the different characteristics of their library collections. Then, he proposed a reduction in the one-time fees, but not the AAFs, for both the Medium and the Small classes. This second change seemed like an obvious way to increase JSTOR's anemic participation rates in these categories.

Finally, Guthrie proposed moving all Baccalaureate II colleges into the Very Small class, eliminating the enrollment cap of one thousand above which they were considered Small. The Bachelor's IIs were defined as those colleges that award fewer than 40 percent of their degrees in the liberal arts, and they were generally less restrictive in admissions—and both of these factors diminished JSTOR's value to them. In fact, only one Baccalaureate II had licensed JSTOR since the charter period as a Small, and it seemed that if JSTOR were to make any substantial inroads at these schools, it should price them all as Very Small.

The effect of all of these changes, which are summarized in table 12.2, was to lower prices for a large number of JSTOR's potential participants.

TABLE 12.2
Pricing Categories before and after Readjustment,
by Carnegie *Classification* Groupings

Carnegie *Classification* Grouping	1997 Arrangement			Post–July 1998 Classes[i]		
	JSTOR Class[ii]	DDF	AAF	JSTOR Class[ii]	DDF	AAF
Research I	Large	$40,000	$5,000	Very Large	$45,000	$5,000
Research II	Large	$40,000	$5,000	Large	$35,000	$5,000
Doctoral I	Large	$40,000	$5,000	Large	$35,000	$5,000
Doctoral II	Medium	$30,000	$4,000	Medium	$25,000	$4,000
Master's I	Medium	$30,000	$4,000	Medium	$25,000	$4,000
Master's II	Medium	$30,000	$4,000	Small	$20,000	$3,000
Baccalaureate I	Small	$20,000	$3,000	Small	$20,000	$3,000
Baccalaureate II	Small	$20,000	$3,000	Very Small	$10,000	$2,000

[i]Note that some of these prices have since risen.
[ii]Institutions with relatively low enrollments are bumped down to next-lower class.

Master's II schools were moved to the Small class. The one-time DDF fees were reduced for the Large and Medium classes. And all Baccalaureate II colleges were assigned to the Very Small class. Had JSTOR simply been overpriced?

It is critical to note that the changes being made at this point sought to radically readjust the value basis of the pricing. Rather than value being calculated based on space-saving, as the Strategic and Operating Plan had anticipated, JSTOR finally had data indicating the ways in which value derived from access and usage, as well. It should be underscored that Guthrie continued to believe that JSTOR's primary value was its potential to achieve system-wide savings by freeing up shelf space—even if many colleges and universities were as yet unwilling to pay for this value.

In the context of access value, the principal flaw identified was that the pricing difference between the largest and smallest schools was too small. The 1998 pricing adjustments are best understood as an attempt to ameliorate the situation by recognizing that access value recommended a larger pricing difference.

These readjustments were only a partial correction. A number of critics have pointed out that a simple way to correct for the insufficient pricing differential would have been to make arrangements for consortia, which could themselves take responsibility for making the internal arrangements necessary, to lower fees for the smaller schools.[6] JSTOR continued to resist such an approach, preferring instead to adopt revised, but fully transparent, pricing that treated similarly situated libraries the same. Working with consortia would have meant that the consortia would have done the same thing, but with the danger that two identical libraries (one in and one out of the consortium) could have paid significantly different prices—an outcome that, in JSTOR's eyes, would be fundamentally unfair. Even though working with consortia would have delivered additional participants more quickly, JSTOR preferred to fix its own prices since, in Guthrie's words, JSTOR and its libraries are "in it for the long haul" and the principles of transparent pricing and fairness were fundamental.[7]

Under the 1998 pricing readjustment, JSTOR did not seek to raise the prices for the largest libraries so far as to recognize access as being its primary value. For one thing, the largest libraries had already joined at relatively modest prices (many during the charter period), which prices were grandfathered in by JSTOR. Raising prices for any subsequent Large or Very Large participants would have had relatively little impact.

Thus, rather than raising the prices for the largest libraries very much, JSTOR lowered the prices for virtually every other library, sacrificing per-library revenue in order to encourage more library participation. Because fewer libraries were participating, the pricing readjustment was designed to help meet the original target of 750 libraries. This important goal notwithstanding, the repricing decision could have had deleterious effects. While in the long term JSTOR as a whole would become self-sustaining (and its prices, when combining all available collections, would seem far more sensible), the Arts & Sciences I Collection would not. Nevertheless, there is some evidence that the repricing contributed to a dramatic increase in participation.

ADJUSTMENT AFTERMATH:
PARTICIPATION THROUGH THE CLOSE OF 1999

The repricing presented JSTOR with a choice. Many libraries in categories now assigned lower prices had signed on with the original pricing. To preserve fairness, JSTOR chose to give them refunds, at a cost of $195,000.[8] Carol MacAdam, who joined JSTOR as associate director for Library Relations in mid-1998, reported to the board:

[6] Tom Sanville, interview with the author, October 29, 2001.
[7] Kevin Guthrie, interview with the author, October 30, 2001.
[8] Packet for the JSTOR board of trustees meeting of July 30, 1998.

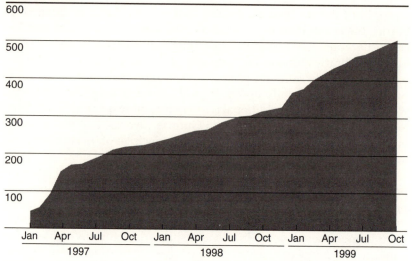

Figure 12.2. American Libraries Participating, Arts & Sciences I Only

The first task I undertook in August was to contact those JSTOR participants that were due rebates. . . . Not surprisingly, these institutions were
glad to hear from me, but I was struck by [the] enthusiasm evident in the
many positive comments about the JSTOR database, about JSTOR usage
on participating campuses, and about the "JSTOR way" of doing things.
One librarian said that . . . she didn't want a rebate, she just wanted us to
use it to get more journals in.[9]

JSTOR had come a long way in two years, building a reputation for fairness driven by data. That reputation began to pay off as more and more
libraries participated.

Beginning in early 1999, in the wake of the pricing adjustments, the
rate of new American library participation increased, which can be seen
in the changed slope on figure 12.2. In part, credit should be given to the
1998 pricing readjustments and the increased outreach that followed,
such as MacAdam's mailing to Medium nonparticipants. In addition,
several other factors combined to drive growth. Principal among these,
surely, was the growing heft of the database itself.

[9] Packet for the JSTOR board of trustees meeting of November 4, 1998.

Libraries with less "risk capital," in the words of JSTOR Board member Taylor Reveley, preferred to see JSTOR's title list in place, and its journals digitized, before committing to participation. Those libraries that were willing to buy "on faith" tended to be charter participants that paid a large sum up front when the database consisted of at most twenty-one titles, with fifty not even licensed from publishers. The risk taken by these early faithful libraries was rewarded with a discount. Many of the 1999 (and subsequent) participants had been waiting for the Arts & Sciences I database to reach (or at least near) completion. Seeing JSTOR's promises realized and the positive experience of existing participants, they elected to participate; a number expressed regret that they had not participated earlier, during the charter period.

To reach the libraries that would participate after the repricing, MacAdam recalls making a number of cold calls to librarians. A number of those with whom she spoke were not yet familiar with JSTOR. But this did not disappoint her. She was pleasantly surprised to find a high number of librarians who were themselves "cold calling" JSTOR with interest in participating. While in the future, libraries would participate in response to faculty interest, MacAdam recalls that in this period librarians more often participated based on their own judgment.[10]

Late in 1998, MacAdam reported to the board that the biggest impediment to further participation was money.[11] And while that impediment never disappeared, JSTOR was able to work with libraries to ease the problem. Although the DDF was intended to be an up-front charge, libraries that sought to do so were able to spread it out across two or even three years, substantially cushioning its impact. In addition, MacAdam would suggest that libraries seek on-campus grants, pools of money reserved by administrators for innovative proposals, to pay the one-time fee. In many cases, such nonlibrary sources paid the DDF (which, it should be noted, brought together in a nonlibrary office the payment for JSTOR with the savings it might bring—see conclusion). Finally some libraries utilized end-of-fiscal-year reserves to join.[12]

It is critical to appreciate why librarians participated—what it was that they valued so much about JSTOR to pay the participation fees. In 1997, many libraries were strongly influenced by the charter period, the Mellon connection, and grant funding (see chapter 10). By 1998 and 1999, these sources of influence had subsided and could no longer be said to be significant factors in library judgment. Instead, there were two principal drivers. MacAdam believes that for roughly two-thirds or

[10] Carol MacAdam, interview with the author, March 13, 2002.
[11] Minutes of the board of trustees meeting of November 4, 1998.
[12] Carol MacAdam, interview with the author, March 13, 2002.

TABLE 12.3
U.S. Participation as of December 31, 1999

Pricing Class	1999 Actuals	Strategic and Operating Plan	Variance
Very Large	83	175	−17%
Large	63		
Medium	133	300	−56%
Small	103	275	−26%
Very Small	101		
Other	37	N/A	N/A
Total	520	750	−31%
Total aafs (millions)	$1.220	$2.737	−55%

more of those libraries that elected to participate, the increased accessibility of having journals online and fully searchable was the key factor. For perhaps one-quarter, space-savings was primary. As MacAdam explains, the decision to use JSTOR to save space "down the line" could only sometimes be made concurrently with a decision on whether to participate. Other factors of less importance were collection-building, and, although rarely foremost, concerns about prestige or peer-pressure were often in the background.[13]

By the close of 1999, when Arts & Sciences I was completed on time, virtually all of the obvious U.S. candidates had opted to participate. The expectations of the Strategic and Operating Plan had not been met for the year, and overall participation continued to lag by about one-third. This shortfall was concentrated among the Medium schools (see table 12.3). The participation level of the Research I universities—that is, the Very Large class—was remarkable, as was that of the most selective liberal arts colleges. Revenue levels were lower than called for by the plan in part because of the creation of the Very Small pricing classification; the recent repricing also played a small role. But there was no negative feeling that numbers were not being met. JSTOR had built an extraordinarily strong and committed participant base, and the plan overall had so much built-in flexibility that there was little cause for concern.

[13]Ibid.

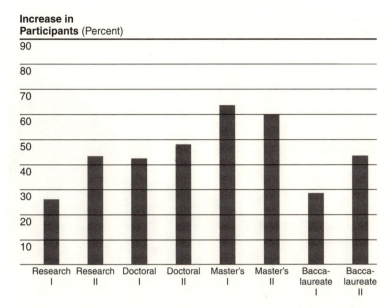

Figure 12.3. Increase in Participants, July 1998 to December 1999, by Carnegie *Classification* Groupings

And the positive effects of the repricing can be seen clearly. Figure 12.3 shows its effects on each of the Carnegie classes, with the effects clearly most pronounced among the Master's schools. Cal State's twenty-two Master's campuses joined soon after the pricing readjustments, causing an appreciable blip in the Master's I graph in early 1999 (see figure 12.4), with commensurate ongoing annual payments. This alone could be seen as a sufficient achievement to justify the pricing change for Master's institutions.

COMMUNITY COLLEGES

In 1999, the sustained interest of a number of community colleges led staff to focus more attention on them. Previously, JSTOR had never anticipated any significant number of community colleges being interested in its database. Community colleges participated either as part of a state university system or in the Very Small category. But most community colleges were not affiliated with state universities and would not participate even at the Very Small rate. JSTOR had not anticipated

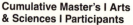

Cumulative Master's I Arts & Sciences I Participants

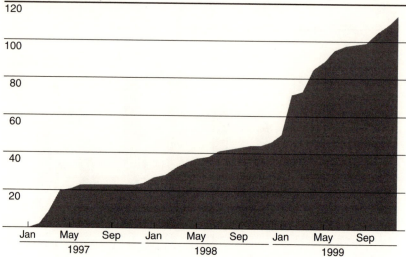

Figure 12.4. Cumulative Master's I Arts & Sciences I Participants, by Month

that these libraries would want to participate at any price, so it had not set up value-based pricing for them.

Increasingly, community colleges expressed interest in JSTOR as their curricular aims shifted. Although initially envisioned as an entry-point to four-year universities, many community colleges had offered vocational education and terminal two-year programs.[14] Yet for a number of reasons, in the late 1990s these colleges were moving back to their roots. Increasingly, they offered the first two years of a baccalaureate program, after which students transferred to a four-year campus for their junior and senior years and a degree.[15] As a result of this expansion in their work, community colleges were expanding their curricula. Their libraries had to support this expansion. For some, the JSTOR journals would be a desirable addition.

MacAdam, Aurigemma, and Guthrie together considered how to establish pricing for community colleges. They recognized that these

[14]Steven Brint and Jerome Karabel, *The Diverted Dream: Community Colleges and the Promise of Educational Opportunity in America, 1900–1985* (New York: Oxford University Press, 1989).

[15]See, for example, Karla Haworth, "Many 2-Year Colleges Impose Tougher Academic Standards," *Chronicle of Higher Education,* January 22, 1999.

**Community College Arts &
Sciences I Participants**

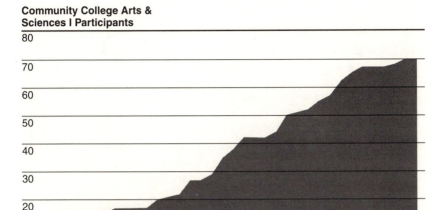

Figure 12.5. Community College Arts & Sciences I Participants

schools "don't really have a role as keepers of archives," so archiving was of trivial importance.[16] (This might well have also been the case for many other existing participants.) Rather, the value basis of the pricing would reflect collection-building. As a result, they developed a fee structure that had a one-time "installation fee" of $1,000, charged once per institution, not per collection like a DDF, and an annual fee for the collection. This fee arrangement recovered little if anything more than the marginal cost to JSTOR of a college's participation, and it was JSTOR's first departure from the DDF-AAF structure.

While there was no stampede of community college participants, the new pricing plan had a quantifiable effect. Figure 12.5 illustrates participation in Arts & Sciences I under this arrangement. It offers dramatic evidence that even the least research-oriented academic libraries have demand for scholarly resources like JSTOR, when the price is right.

Even among those who agree with this conclusion, JSTOR's approach was not universally admired. Tom Sanville, the director of the OhioLINK consortium that counts as members dozens of these two-year colleges, believes that it impedes access to information. He says that the majority of such schools will "never ever pay a nickel for [JSTOR] because they

---

[16]Carol MacAdam, interview with the author, March 13, 2002.

have many other things that have much, much more value, and they'll run out of money way before they ever assign JSTOR a high enough value rating to pay anything for it."[17] JSTOR had believed from the start that libraries had to demonstrate that they attached at least some value to participating—otherwise, Bowen and others wondered, why make the resource available to them? The question of whether JSTOR should respond to schools without any dollar-driven demand is an important one. But it is not clear that there is a way to do this other than arrangements that would have the effect of reducing the fees paid below the marginal cost to JSTOR of their participation, thus imposing a net cost to JSTOR. And it is notable that about 100 two-year colleges were willing to pay at least the marginal costs of participation.

NO MORE MIRRORS:
PLANS FOR INTERNATIONAL EXPANSION

In late 1997, given the level of international demand, the board reviewed the desirability of establishing mirror sites around the world. "It will not be possible to meet all international demand taking this approach," but given the "performance problems [and] pricing issues, . . . the Board decided it would be best at this early stage to continue with JSTOR's present approach" of mirror sites.[18]

While American library participation grew slowly in 1998, Guthrie and the board began strategizing about how to expand JSTOR's international presence. The stalled negotiation with Soros led JSTOR's leadership in mid-1998 to begin rethinking its intention to place mirror sites around the globe. Negotiating through local complexities had proven a great deal more difficult in Eastern Europe than it had in the United Kingdom, and there were reasons to think that other locales might prove even more intractable. Even in Western Europe, Guthrie had the sense that "because of the politics involved, . . . even though a single mirror site in Europe should be able to handle demand from European higher education institutions, . . . Southern Europeans, Northern Europeans, and Scandinavians would not stand for accessing JSTOR from a single site."[19] Who would decide where to locate it?

Were local mirrors truly necessary? Previously, the JSTOR Board of Trustees had been so pessimistic about the growth of international bandwidth as to consider distributing JSTOR on CD-ROM to some regions;

---

[17] Tom Sanville, interview with the author, October 29, 2001.

[18] Minutes of the JSTOR board of trustees meeting of November 6, 1997.

[19] Packet for the JSTOR board of trustees meeting of July 30, 1998.

mirrors seemed optimistic.[20] But if mirrors somehow proved unnecessary, it would be only the pricing (complicated enough in itself) that would stand in the way of worldwide distribution. While in Eastern Europe that summer, Guthrie had realized that connectivity was far better than generally assumed.[21] This realization would bring a major shift in JSTOR's policy. With so much worldwide interest, the mirror strategy was seen as not only increasingly challenging, but perhaps even altogether unnecessary.

In the summer of 1998, JSTOR staff began thinking about how to proceed in the absence of worldwide mirror sites. First, they used published information on libraries across the globe to examine the structure of the potential markets. They determined the number of libraries that would roughly fall into each of the American pricing classes, as measured by size of holdings and breadth of serials subscriptions. With these data, JSTOR was able to gain some sense of which countries had significant numbers of potential participants. In addition to the published data, staff also analyzed all emails from abroad requesting access that had been sent since JSTOR's inception. From these 243 emails, it was clear that interest in participation was worldwide. Generally speaking, the largest countries with presumably the most postsecondary education had expressed the greatest interest. More than ten emails had come from individuals in Australia, Brazil, Canada, Mexico, and South Korea; six or more had come from Argentina, China, Colombia, France, Germany, Israel, Italy, Russia, Spain, and Turkey. These countries were largely not a surprise. But individuals in Gambia, Ghana, the Dominican Republic, and other smaller, less affluent countries had also expressed interest.[22]

Had demand been more concentrated, JSTOR might have focused on a few regions. But with demand fairly widely distributed, a less prescriptive strategy was in order. In those regions where connectivity was adequate, JSTOR could offer access from the U.S. servers. "Rather than focusing on certain regions and expending resources attempting to market to those regions," wrote Guthrie, "better to be prepared to respond to demand for access from individual institutions" wherever it manifested itself.[23] JSTOR had to establish a pricing policy for interested institutions.

Guthrie worked with Bowen and Aurigemma to study various possible pricing models. Their challenge was to find a model that would reflect JSTOR's commitment to value-based pricing while remaining

---

[20] Minutes of the JSTOR board of trustees meeting of June 20, 1996.
[21] Kevin Guthrie, interview with the author, April 11, 2001.
[22] Packet for the JSTOR board of trustees meeting of July 30, 1998.
[23] Ibid.

true to the board's mandate "not to subsidize overseas access with fees from U.S. libraries."[24]

JSTOR staff were convinced that the pricing classes should be maintained for international libraries, both because they had proven effective in the United States and the United Kingdom and because worldwide uniformity seemed wise. Because the Carnegie classifications were not available for international institutions, JSTOR had to find another mechanism to determine the pricing classes. Guthrie was familiar with the published data (on the number of volumes in a library and its periodicals subscriptions) that he had examined over the summer to get a sense of worldwide demand. He had determined that, for American libraries, such data mapped well with the JSTOR pricing classes, yielding fairly clear natural breaks. He believed that the equivalent numbers could be used for international libraries to determine the JSTOR pricing class.

JSTOR then proceeded to set base fees, both one-time and annual, for each pricing class, which were essentially equivalent to, though in some cases slightly lower than, the American equivalent. "The baseline is intended to make an adjustment in the relative prices between the classes," yielding "a steeper decline in the prices for Large, Medium, and Small institutions relative to the Very Large price."[25] In other words, it was intended to remedy the value gap that had been identified among American participants. But the baseline international prices were not intended to be offered to specific institutions; they were only the first step.

Guthrie then intended to calculate a discount of between 10–50 percent off the baseline price. The discount would take into account several factors, including

> the extent of development in the country or region, the financial resources available, and the level of comfort and facility with English. We have decided not ever to discount fees for any institution more than 50 percent. We believe that a discount beyond that level constitutes philanthropy, and that if an institution requires that much of a discount, we should seek funding from other institutions or foundations to subsidize participation.[26]

While believing that discounts were fair, JSTOR's leadership did not want to cut prices so much as to endanger the broader enterprise. The ratio of marginal to fixed costs associated with an additional participant suggested to Guthrie that a discount in excess of 50 percent would result in the wealthier institutions subsidizing the cost of participation at poorer schools—through radically discounted prices.

[24] Minutes of the JSTOR board of trustees meeting of November 4, 1998.
[25] Packet for the JSTOR board of trustees meeting of November 4, 1998.
[26] Ibid.

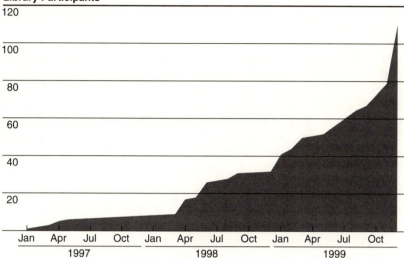

Figure 12.6. International Library Participants

Prior to 1999, virtually all international participation was due to the agreement with the JISC for U.K. libraries (whose participation slowed after the first twenty-five participants, perhaps because of the incomplete Arts & Sciences I Collection)[27] and the Canadian libraries that had sought to participate in a new American library resource. In the year that followed the introduction of this pricing plan, JSTOR did little outreach to international libraries. Its most direct efforts consisted of alerting libraries that had in the past requested participation information (and been told that JSTOR was not yet in a position to provide them) of the newly established terms. The separate pricing arrangements for non-American libraries gradually bore fruit in 1999, as illustrated in figure 12.6, and its success quickly overwhelmed library-relations capacity. Soon, JSTOR staff member Dawn Tomassi took responsibility for relations with foreign libraries, shepherding them to participation. With attractive terms and Tomassi focused full-time on foreign libraries, participation accelerated in the fall with steady growth. By the close of 1999, foreign participation added 111 libraries—and commensurate revenues.

[27]David Cook, interview with the author, April 13, 2001.

INDIVIDUAL ACCESS

As was made clear in chapter 8, JSTOR considered whether to focus its sales on libraries or individuals, and it opted for the former. Yet we have seen at length the pressure at some scholarly societies, which were worried that as journals went online their membership rolls would decline. Any new benefits that they could offer to their members would help to encourage their transition to online publishing, as well as their JSTOR participation. This dynamic is a significant part of the explanation for Guthrie's report to the board in October 1996 that "several publishers have inquired as to whether we intend to offer individual subscriptions to [the backfiles of] their journals." He was enthusiastic about this development:

> It appears that not only is there some demand for this in the community, it might also be a benefit to scholarly associations if they could offer subscriptions to their journal to their members at a discount. We have so far tabled any conclusions on this subject with publishers, agreeing to discuss it at a later time. As an alternative to JSTOR delivering the archives of journals to individuals, we might provide publishers with the ability to perform this function, with a payment to JSTOR.

In other words, individual publishers could maintain relationships with individual subscribers for their journal(s). Guthrie was less enthusiastic about JSTOR providing the entire archive to individuals, which would presumably have been even more popular for the sake of research but without bringing any benefits to the publishers.[28]

As part of its Mellon grant to develop the Ecology & Botany Collection (see chapter 11), the ESA also received funds to participate in a pilot toward these ends. At $50 each, fifty ESA members signed on to access the three ESA journals in JSTOR during 1998. Subsequently, an average of about 300 individuals participated in the ESA program annually, at $40 each.[29] For a scholarly society, an additional gross of $12,000, with very little added expense, was significant.[30] Other publishers were interested, leading JSTOR to expand the initiative for 1999.[31]

The program in 1999 attracted about half a dozen publishers, including a university press (MIT). Because some societies included the journal

---

[28] Packet for the JSTOR board of trustees meeting of October 29, 1996.

[29] Katherine McCarter, interview with the author, September 20, 2001.

[30] Administrative costs were minimal because the service was offered with the annual membership renewal.

[31] Packet for the JSTOR board of trustees meeting of November 4, 1998.

itself with membership, JSTOR access was sometimes enabled only for the higher contribution rates. Some societies made access available to nonmembers for a fee, or only to their members who contributed at higher fee levels, thereby raising funds. The *William & Mary Quarterly*, whose earliest issues were of deep interest to genealogists, attracted numerous nonmembers who could search the fulltext for their ancestors. JSTOR charged the publishers $10 per individual, or a smaller fee for larger numbers.[32]

The purpose of the fee was only to break even, and JSTOR remains clear about the program's purpose. "It's purely a benefit to publishers," says McGregor, and especially to "those publishers that have individual members."[33]

An obvious way to alter the individual access program would have been for JSTOR to make its entire collection available for a fee to individuals and pay some proportional amount to publishers. But in part because this would undermine both JSTOR's focus on nonprofit organizations and the uniqueness of the services it offered to libraries, it did not follow such an approach.[34] Instead, in 2001, publisher-relations staff began exploring how a number of publishers from a given discipline—in the case of the first pilot, political science—could offer a discipline-specific bundle of titles to individuals.[35] It was too early to know whether this type of "loose" bundle would prove to be manageable, or whether individuals would have demand for it.

SUMMATION

This chapter has witnessed several crucial developments in JSTOR's quest toward self-sustainability. It began to recognize the multiple sources of value to its archive, repricing Arts & Sciences I and setting fees for subsequent collections with this in mind. Second, it began to include significant numbers of non-U.S. library participants. Just at the end of this period, it released the final segment of the Arts & Sciences I Collection, thereby completing the collection on time and for the promised price, bolstering its reputation with libraries (and publishers). With these

---

[32]Packet for the JSTOR board of trustees meeting of October 6, 1999.

[33]Heidi McGregor, interview with the author, April 9, 2002.

[34]Bruce Heterick, interview with the author, April 30, 2002.

[35]Heidi McGregor, interview with the author, April 9, 2002.

achievements, and additional collections on the way, JSTOR was transformed from a well-connected promise-maker to a trustworthy partner.[36]

The pricing corrections were an important departure, but not enough to correct all of the problems. As further collections were released, Guthrie would make a savvy decision to set their fees to correct for the flaws in the pricing of Arts & Sciences I (see chapter 14). Thus, as JSTOR grew further, its fees were designed to become fairer for libraries. In 2000 and 2001, ever fairer pricing combined with other factors to yield striking results.

[36] For publishers, the individual access program seems to have helped to make the case for JSTOR.

CHAPTER 13

Completing Arts & Sciences I
and Strategizing for the Future

JULY 1998–DECEMBER 1999

WITH TWO science collections being developed, JSTOR began to respond to the knowledge that Arts & Sciences I would soon be completed. The interplay between this response and the rapid increases in library participation, covered in the previous chapter, were key. As more libraries participated, JSTOR's ambitions increased. This chapter charts the organization as it rapidly gained self-confidence.

TENTATIVE FURTHER PLANS

In mid-1998, even before any production work began on General Science or Ecology & Botany, Guthrie began to push the board to consider additional collections. He was well aware of the substantial lead-time between proposing a collection and beginning production work on it. Experience had shown that well over a year had to be allowed for securing funds, selecting titles, negotiating with publishers, and obtaining the physical backruns before the first steps of production could begin. There was only a little more than a year before the Arts & Sciences I Collection would be substantially completed, and the combined General Science and Ecology & Botany collections totaled less than two million pages. With an impending capacity of nearly 300,000 pages per month,[1] JSTOR's voracious production teams would claw through the planned collections in no time. To make efficient use of this newfound capacity, it was clear that planning for future titles and collections had to begin, and soon.

In mid-1998, the board considered two proposals for subsequent collections. First, the 1997 suggestion to digitize business and additional economics journals and combine them with the existing economics titles into a Business Collection was still very much on the table, with Gil

---

[1]In addition to this being the straightforward calculation, the figure was published in Lynne Brindley and Kevin M. Guthrie, "JSTOR and the Joint Information Systems Committee: An International Collaboration," *Serials* 11, no. 1 (March 1998): 41.

Whitaker a sustained enthusiast. Additionally, the JSTOR Board discussed a multidisciplinary "enhancement" to Arts & Sciences I. This enhancement would include fields and titles that had, for one reason or another, been omitted from the original collection. The plan would eventually grow to be more ambitious than just an enhancement; indeed it would garner the name Arts & Sciences II.[2]

In the cases of both proposed collections, conversations in the summer of 1998 should have led rapidly to concrete plans. Then, Sarah Sully and the new Assistant Director of Library Relations, Heidi McGregor, would have begun to secure publishers while Guthrie sought funding. Guthrie pointed out to the board in November 1998 that "we will need to have a list of [signed business] titles and backruns in house by one year from now in order to keep our Ann Arbor production staff busy after the completion" of Arts & Sciences I.[3] Arts & Sciences II would follow Business in the queue.

In the summer and fall of 1998, JSTOR's growth strategy sought to meet library demand by fully utilizing the then-tripling production capacity. But with library participation below expectations, this large production capacity presented something between a risk and a liability. Although existing participants called for growth, they would not constitute a base large enough to support it. As a result, new collections did not have to respond to the demand of existing participants but might be used to attract a broader group of libraries. Obviously, radical immediate growth posed considerable risk; cautious, steady, incremental expansion was the plan.

CONSULTING: THE LIMITS OF GROWTH

The calls for expansion were unquestionable. JSTOR's planned rate of growth, in terms of titles available online, was steady but intentionally not astronomical. The most optimistic projections called for the completion of the General Science and Ecology & Botany Collections by early 2000. Other collections would presumably follow later in 2000, in 2001, and after. Unable to risk rapid growth itself, should JSTOR address the pressure to grow by other means?

The first idea, discussed at some length in early and mid-1998, was that JSTOR in a sense franchise itself around the globe.[4] This was during the height of the discussion of mirror sites, and JSTOR was begin-

---

[2]Minutes of the JSTOR board of trustees meeting, July 30, 1998.
[3]Packet for the JSTOR board of trustees meeting of November 4, 1998.
[4]Ibid.

ning to cultivate partners worldwide that shared its values and interests. The JISC, for example, might be interested in developing its own JSTOR-compatible production facilities, perhaps for journals from the United Kingdom. That way, production rates could be increased without JSTOR having to add production capacity of its own. The risk of expansion would thereby be spread.

Such a franchising arrangement would have been exceedingly difficult to develop—even if partners were willing, it would have been enormously difficult to transfer JSTOR's production systems to new locations abroad. While it is not clear that this was the main reason that franchising was never pursued, the plan that replaced it addressed the problem.

Since the problem with franchising was that its advantage of being hands-off seemed to doom it to failure, JSTOR began considering ways to become more directly involved with knowledge-transfer to willing partners. These ideas began to congeal into what would be termed the "consulting" or "advisory" service. The basic idea remained the same: "JSTOR obviously cannot convert all the journals in existence all over the world. Nor can we expect that others will wait for us to do so if we could. . . . Providing advice [to other projects, as JSTOR had been doing] is consistent with our mission to be of service to the academic community, but it is a drain on staff time and resources."[5] The idea was to provide a set of more formalized advisory services at relatively low fees—though at full cost recovery or better—to help other projects learn from JSTOR's experience. A number of JSTOR staff and board members, as well as outsiders, expressed enthusiasm mixed with concern that the project would become very complicated. At its November meeting, the board "was unanimous in encouraging JSTOR to move forward with [the] planning process. . . . JSTOR should play a role in helping to ensure that [other] efforts are not wasted and that the product of such efforts will be compatible with JSTOR."[6]

When growth in existing content and participants was on the agenda in February 1999, Guthrie made one thing clear. "While [consulting] may not be a central part of our mission, [advising others] is a problem for which we must find some solution, since it is already a drain on current resources."[7] The problem was that, as a nonprofit and a member of the community, JSTOR could not just say "no" when others came to it for

---

[5] Kevin Guthrie, "Meeting with Tom Nygren and Richard Quandt," email to William G. Bowen, Richard Quandt, Tom Nygren, Sarah Sully, and Gerard Aurigemma, October 6, 1998.

[6] Minutes of the JSTOR board of trustees meeting of November 4, 1998.

[7] Packet for the JSTOR board of trustees meeting of February 10, 1999.

advice. And yet, it should not just say "yes," for fear that it would become distracted from its central mission. In a small way here, one can see a clear advantage of a for-profit organizational model—fewer qualms would have existed about saying no. And while in the for-profit environment, some of JSTOR's staff might have split off to create a boutique consultancy, in the not-for-profit world it would be far more difficult for individuals to find funding for such an endeavor—not to mention that there would be less monetary incentive. So JSTOR itself was thinking of stepping in, even though consulting seemed to fall outside of its own mission. With major strategic decisions being made at that meeting on JSTOR's own mission-consistent growth (see below), the topic of consulting was tabled for the next meeting.[8] It would not, in fact, be taken up for another year, as we shall see in chapter 14.

ARTS & SCIENCES I PRODUCTION PROGRESS

At the end of 1998, more than sixty titles were available online. Since Fenton had taken charge of the Michigan production team in autumn 1997, production was fairly steady, averaging around 100,000 pages per month. Figure 13.1 shows this progress, measured as the number of pages accepted from the scanning vendor.[9]

With production under Fenton running smoothly, Guthrie presented the board, in conjunction with its meetings, with triennial updates on progress. This gave him the opportunity to note the average three or so journals that were released to library participants every month, steadily completing Arts & Sciences I. This regular progress, with routine monthly releases, must have been extremely reassuring both to library participants—who were seeing their risk in participating begin to pay off—and to the board.

Any number of factors caused this change. Fenton was an adept manager, able to coordinate many moving parts. In 1998, "as part of the effort to expand production at JSTOR's Michigan site," John Kiplinger was hired to fill the new position of production librarian. His responsibility was to obtain the full backfiles of the selected journal titles and to

---

[8] Minutes of the JSTOR board of trustees meeting of February 10, 1999.

[9] Although it is the simplest way to quantify production progress, this measure gives very little information about the cause of, say, a lowered rate of accepted pages. Such a lower rate could be caused by the vendor accumulating a backlog of unprocessed journals, the Michigan staff being unable to prepare sufficient materials for the process, or the publisher-relations group in New York being unable to sign sufficient titles. All of these problems have at times appeared. The "pages-received-per-month" statistic is used only with caution.

**Pages Accepted per
Month** (Thousands)

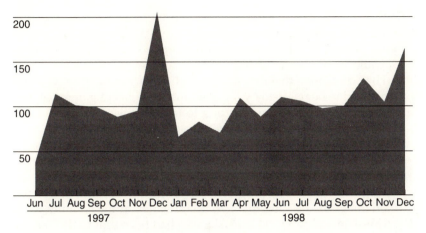

Figure 13.1. Arts & Sciences I Production: Thousands of Pages Accepted per Month, through December 1998

prepare the indexing guidelines for the scanning vendor, relieving Fenton of some of these tasks. Fenton, in turn, was able to concentrate more fully on the management and coordination of the Michigan production operation.[10] The growing professionalization of the operation, under dedicated full-time staff, was a significant factor in the steady output of digitized pages.

The regularity of production progress notwithstanding, it was becoming clear that the rate of production might not be sufficient. In September 1998, Guthrie wrote to the production management team, which consisted of Fenton and Bennett in addition to Sully and Aurigemma, to observe that JSTOR had only digitized twenty titles in the past nine months. The slow production, he hoped, could be accounted for by the unusual length of those twenty titles.

> We have quite a lot of work to do before the end of 1999. . . . I am getting increasingly worried that we are cutting our [Arts & Sciences I] promise *very* close. I must admit, I do not understand why it has taken us so long to get estimates of the page counts of the journals remaining to be digitized.

[10] Packet for the JSTOR board of trustees meeting, July 30, 1998.

Perhaps it is not clear just how important this is. We *cannot* fail to meet our promise to deliver [Arts & Sciences I] on time. If we do not know how much work is left to do we cannot possibly put the plans in place to get the work done.[11]

Guthrie's concern about the progress of production led to several discussions with Fenton about exactly what the Arts & Sciences I promise entailed. Since JSTOR had promised one hundred journals by the end of 1999, could it release the additional seventeen journals after the deadline? They concluded that the entire collection, including the additional journals, had to be released by the deadline, thus meeting or exceeding all expectations rather than resorting to technicalities.[12] This decision helped to lead Guthrie to a more active role in production management, making sure that Fenton had sufficient authority for the successful completion of Arts & Sciences I.

In one specific case, Fenton needed some additional leverage.[13] Even while regular production progress was ongoing, Fenton had become worried about the backlog that had accumulated at the scanning vendor. Approximately 750,000 journal pages had been sent to the vendor in the past two years without being scanned, and this backlog represented more than half of the pages remaining to be digitized for the Arts & Sciences I Collection. The backlog had to be eliminated, the datasets checked, and the pages loaded into JSTOR, if the deadline were to be met. Fenton and Guthrie were together able to deploy a combination of carrots and sticks, including the threat to send pages to a second vendor. As a result, the existing vendor assigned numerous additional staff to eliminate the backlog, and Guthrie reported to the board that "we are confident that we will reach our targets."[14] With this strategy in place, by March 1999 the vendor was delivering approximately 250,000 pages per month acceptable to JSTOR (see figure 13.2). At this rate, JSTOR added one million pages in four months, a volume that previously would have taken nearly a year.

While urging the scanning vendor to address its backlog, Fenton and Guthrie planned the expansion of Michigan's production capacity as permitted by the grant for the Ecology & Botany Collection. Once the new office was completed, Fenton added and trained staff, bolstering production capacity. When the vendor finally produced a glut of digitized

---

[11]Kevin Guthrie, "RE: Science Page Count," email to Elizabeth Bennett and Eileen Gifford Fenton, September 22, 1998.

[12]Kevin Guthrie, personal communication, January 10, 2002.

[13]Eileen G. Fenton, interview with the author, October 11, 2001.

[14]Packet for the JSTOR board of trustees meeting of November 4, 1998.

**Pages Accepted per
Month, 1999** (Thousands)

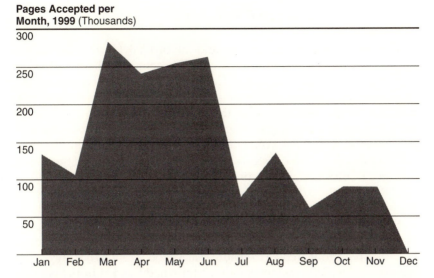

Figure 13.2. Arts & Sciences I Production: Thousands of Pages Accepted per Month, 1999

pages from backlogged journals, Fenton redeployed the Michigan staff from longer-term projects to the immediate task of receiving and accepting the pages. Without the added capacity at Michigan or Fenton's excellent management, delays might have ensued.

With the backlog beginning to be eliminated by early 1999, Guthrie was guardedly optimistic that JSTOR would meet its promise. By the summer of 1999, with a million more pages added to JSTOR and the vendor backlog completely eliminated, it was fairly clear that Arts & Sciences I would be completed on time. Indeed, as figure 13.2 shows, there was not enough Arts & Sciences I digitization to keep the Michigan staff occupied for the latter half of the year. As we will see in chapter 14, it had moved on to other tasks.

After the major push that digitized one million pages in four months, Arts & Sciences I required less than 100,000 pages per month for the last six months. Its final release, consisting of the *Journal of the Royal Anthropological Institute of Great Britain and Ireland, Monumenta Nipponica,* and the *American Journal of Mathematics,* was made available on November 23, 1999. Arts & Sciences I was finished five weeks ahead of schedule. The impact of this achievement on JSTOR's library relations—the rapid growth in participants and usage—is described in chapter 14.

STRATEGIZING FOR FUTURE EXPANSION

We have seen that in the summer and fall of 1998, Guthrie brought to the board plans for creating what would become the Business Collection and the Arts and Sciences II Collection. To ensure the optimal use of production capacity, all of the business titles would have to be signed and their backruns secured for the production process by November 1999. Perhaps in part because of greater attention directed at production, late 1998 and early 1999 would not be taken up principally with signing the Business Collection. Instead, with the near-completion of the Arts & Sciences I Collection in mid-1999 and concurrent library participation, JSTOR and its board took the opportunity to think strategically about the future.

JSTOR had struggled, with general success, to balance its need to compete vigorously in a rapidly changing market sector with its responsibility as a nonprofit archive to ensure that a good idea was not only good, but also viable. This was the lesson Guthrie had learned from his study of the New-York Historical Society—that more (good) analysis, rather than less, was desirable in setting future directions, especially for organizations without a surfeit of risk capital. And so, while the original plans had been for this period to be focused on signing the Business Collection, and though Arts & Sciences II could have been undertaken without such careful board-level planning, the risk of proceeding without careful board oversight, not to mention sufficient funding, seemed unacceptable. This decision would, as we shall see in chapter 14, have some negative consequences, including the inadequate provision of signed journals to the production group in 2000. But an incrementally growing organization could not (and should not) be turned into an enthusiastic expansionist over night. As we will see, JSTOR's leaders attempted to move forward as rapidly as possible without abandoning their commitment to careful analysis of the costs and benefits of each step.

JSTOR's first two new collections, General Science and Ecology & Botany, were selected somewhat serendipitously. The interest of the AAAS and of Bill Robertson, respectively, were both fortuitous and compelling. But while serendipity should be accepted when it manifests itself, it is a poor long-term strategy. Guthrie always looked toward careful planning and in this spirit undertook some extremely important conversations with the board in the first half of 1999.

The February 1999 board meeting was very similar to the one in July 1997, with Guthrie presenting several options for growth. First, JSTOR could add more libraries for its existing collections, which of course it had been doing already, especially by focusing on non-American and nonacademic libraries (see chapters 12 and 14). Second, it could more aggressively add new content. And third, it could move into other lines of work, such as providing consulting services for other digitization projects. With JSTOR already moving to expand its base of library participants, Guthrie's report to the board focused on the second area, adding more content.

Guthrie stressed that, based on previous and ongoing board conversations, capping growth with the two scientific collections "is not acceptable; there has been clear consensus that we should capitalize on the momentum we have established and continue to grow—perhaps aggressively."[15] It seems that "aggressive" growth would not necessarily mean expansion beyond JSTOR's existing production capacity. At that point, it had not yet been demonstrated that both Princeton and Michigan could work together to deliver this rate of production on a sustained basis—indeed, Princeton was not yet operating. So whether by "aggressive" he meant continuing to use the upcoming capacity or adding to it, clearly Guthrie was eager for JSTOR to build new collections. He was responding in part to publishers who felt they had to have their backfiles digitized—and if JSTOR would not do it, they would do it themselves. Perhaps even more important as a pressure toward aggressive growth was the dot.com explosion that was accompanied for JSTOR by steadily increasing library participation.

Guthrie's enthusiasm before the board was genuine, but he did not want to be headstrong. Keeping in mind the example of the New-York Historical Society, he reminded the board that "our initial success has been due in large measure to the fact that we set realistic, achievable goals and we made sure we had the resources in place to pursue those goals."[16] It was to the task of setting goals beyond Arts & Sciences I and the two scientific collections, and putting in place the resources to meet these goals, that Guthrie asked the board to turn.

Guthrie sent these thoughts to the board while finishing a survey of future directions for content development. The survey was a complicated and fairly arbitrary instrument, designed not to gauge opinion but to gather data on which academic disciplines should be prioritized by JSTOR. Although it sought objective data on the teaching and research interests in American higher education, JSTOR's main approach was to survey certain academic leaders to gain their impressions of the respective interests of research universities, teaching universities, and colleges, combining this impressionistic information with data on the concentration of journals in a field, the interaction of the field with Arts &

---

[15]Packet for the JSTOR board of trustees meeting, February 10, 1999.
[16]Ibid.

Sciences I, and expressed demand from participants and new markets. The survey was comprehensive, but somewhat more impressionistic than data-driven, which is not to say that its conclusions were incorrect. Among those who completed the survey were Richard Ekman and Harriet Zuckerman of the Mellon Foundation, JSTOR Board members Richard DeGennaro and Pat McPherson (then leaving Bryn Mawr to join the Mellon Foundation), Bowen, and Steven Stigler, a University of Chicago statistician who would subsequently join the JSTOR Board. This was an insider's survey. It was not aimed at obtaining broad opinion but at establishing a sound direction.

Guthrie's survey helped JSTOR reach several important conclusions about future directions for content development (see table 13.1). Before moving to these conclusions, it is instructive to summarize the survey's retrospective analysis of Arts & Sciences I. For each discipline, those surveyed offered their impression of its value to different sorts of academic institutions. For each institution, they ranked its value for archiving and access separately. A value of "high" was awarded two points, and so a discipline received four points for each institutional type that would highly value it. In virtually every case, those surveyed appear to have been unable to distinguish between the value of access and the value of archiving, so the survey in essence double-counted, a problem, if at all, of scale in the rankings rather than their ordinal results. Had this double-counting of access and archiving been eliminated, history would have received 14 out of 20 points (rather than 19 of 28). Economics, which in Guthrie's survey was a distant second at 14 points, would have in the single-counting system received 13 points, just one point shy of history and surely a more accurate relative measure.

For future disciplines, the survey's conclusions were of mixed utility. On the one hand, the survey confirmed JSTOR's interest in General Science and Ecology & Botany clusters, a useful exercise in itself. It suggested that there were several fairly compelling disciplines for JSTOR to tackle in the near-term future. Business in particular remained on JSTOR's horizon, and this survey confirmed business as an important new direction. Finally, it helped to demonstrate the value of area studies, art history, literature, medicine, psychology, and other disciplines.

The minutes of this meeting are unusually detailed and allow for a good understanding of how the board treated this important discussion on collection expansion. There was considerable discussion of the benefits and risks of individual fields. One trustee noted the very high appeal, by the survey's rankings, of several basic scientific disciplines, including biology and chemistry, but pointed out that a piecemeal approach would not work. Another spoke in favor of chemistry as being fairly unique among the sciences in the utility of its backfiles. But because

TABLE 13.1
JSTOR Disciplinary Rankings, February 1999

Discipline (Italics = Arts & Sciences I)	Score (out of 28)
History	19
Business/Finance	14
Economics	14
General Science	13
African Studies	12
Ecology & Botany	12
Art and Art History	11
Asian Studies	11
History of Science	11
Literature	11
Sociology	11
Archaeology	10
African American Studies	10
Biology	10
Chemistry	10
International Relations	10
Medicine	10
Psychology	10
Architecture	9
Mathematics	9
Philosophy	8
Physics	9
Anthropology	7
Education	7
Geology	7
Political Science	7
Population/Demography	7
Statistics	7
Ancient Studies	6
Linguistics	6
Performing Arts	6
Religion	4
Communications	1

of the commercial behavior of scientific publishers, the simply enormous number of journals in these fields, and the unusually high number of pages published per year per journal, "it was decided that JSTOR would not pursue the large [basic] scientific disciplines in any major way." Ruling out the further pursuit of basic science was a key conclusion. While it prevented JSTOR from leveraging its General Science and Ecology & Botany Collections in several obvious ways—by creating a complementary biology cluster, for example—it allowed JSTOR to focus its energies on fields that have value primarily for the ways in which they are useful to humanists and social scientists. In this sense, Ecology & Botany was critical for environmental studies (in addition to ecology specifically) and General Science for the history and sociology of science.

It was only at this point, in early 1999, that JSTOR began to differentiate clearly between those clusters that would make sense as stand-alones and those that would gain from being brought together in a bigger bundle. Bowen honed in on this as a subject of interest, his purpose being to distinguish, out of the many additional fields, those that might make the most sense on their own.[17] Under what he called his "taxonomy," his criteria were fairly straightforward. One key factor was "whether the fields are represented by separate schools at the graduate or professional level, or whether they are likely to be 'merely' departments or divisions in basic arts and sciences faculties." Bowen was clearly thinking about the way a univeristy was organized. Since graduate and professional school deans and libraries often have separate sources of funding, it might be possible to appeal to them separately, with more positive results. "Another criterion," he wrote, "is whether the potential clusters might be especially attractive to a new or broader market than the one we have reached to date." Participation trends would demonstrate, however, that while individual clusters might bring new libraries to JSTOR, these libraries rarely participated in the one cluster alone (see chapter 14).

Under these criteria, Bowen listed several disciplines that would become collections of their own, including General Science, Ecology & Botany, Business, Art History, and Literature, as well as several that to date have not, such as theology, education, and chemistry. But his purpose, more so than to identify specific stand-alones, was to develop a framework through which decisions could be made.

In addition to significant decisions about directions for further growth—avoiding the basic sciences and making use of discipline-specific bundles when appropriate—there was one major decision at

---

[17] William G. Bowen, "Thoughts about bunching and selling new content," memorandum to Kevin Guthrie, February 7, 1999.

this meeting. Whereas in the past there had been talk of offering some sort of interdisciplinary bundle that would "enhance" Arts & Sciences I, it was at this meeting that the board formally endorsed such a move. It would include disciplines such as classics, archaeology, and area studies, which would be "especially valuable when available as part of a larger collection" because of their interdisciplinarity.

The meeting concluded with a sense of direction for the organization. If anything, the board was frustrated that more progress had not already been achieved, and the minutes include an unusually crisp directive. "The position of the board was clear: JSTOR should take the steps necessary to capitalize on its early momentum and expand the organization as quickly as is practically feasible."[18]

With the planning exercise completed, JSTOR publisher-relations staff had new priorities. Sarah Sully left JSTOR in the spring of 1999, and McGregor took on the responsibility, working closely with Bowen and Guthrie. Specifically, she began to seek advice on each of the various disciplines that would make up Arts & Sciences II, speaking with faculty and organizing advisory committees. Identifying titles to target was a necessary but onerous preliminary. It was not possible for McGregor to begin contacting publishers until this exercise was completed.[19]

And other priorities arose. The Modern Language Association (MLA), a major scholarly society, was interested in digitizing important journal backfiles and using that work to help add retrospective indexing to its seminal bibliography of the field. It appealed to Mellon for funding, and after some consideration agreed to collaborate with JSTOR to create a Languages & Literature Collection.[20] Bowen stressed that this was "the big gap" in JSTOR's collections and that it should rise to the highest level of priority. Mellon would give a grant to the MLA, which would function similar to the ESA vis-à-vis Ecology & Botany. The MLA would use the Mellon funds to expand its indexing service retrospectively and secure journals for JSTOR. Guthrie, while not disagreeing with Bowen's sense of priorities, recognized that taking on another collection would impose a great deal of work on JSTOR—and specifically on McGregor. That said, he was "all for us being able to move forward on many fronts, since there are so many things people want us to do." It was just a question of what to do first.[21]

Bowen left not a bit of doubt about how he viewed JSTOR's need for the collection:

[18] Minutes of the JSTOR board of trustees meeting, February 10, 1999.

[19] Heidi McGregor, interview with the author, April 9, 2002.

[20] Ibid.

[21] Kevin Guthrie, "RE: MLA," email to William G. Bowen, April 20, 1999.

We do have to get this done, and get started getting it done, because otherwise these folks will go their own ways—and, in this area that would be a near-disaster. The language-lit[erature] area has so much overlap with other fields that we just cannot allow that. . . . If I am wrong and this takes staff time, then it does. This is vastly more important, for example, than signing up business journals, never mind education, etc etc.[22]

So in April, JSTOR added the development of a Languages & Literature Collection to its list of priorities. The Mellon Foundation awarded funds to the MLA in December 1999.[23]

With the board's direction and Bowen's ongoing enthusiasm, Guthrie dutifully rose to the challenge and began to plan for this massive expansion. He created a master business plan that forecast costs, pricing, take-up, and revenues for ten collections, including the three already underway (see table 13.2).[24] At some point, the proposal imagined, the JSTOR archive might contain the complete backfiles of about four hundred journals, or roughly nineteen million pages. For this, annual access fees would grow commensurately. Was this believable? Both libraries and publishers were calling for JSTOR to grow, but would journals participate? Would libraries pay?

At this May 1999 meeting, even while presenting this ambitious plan for growth, Guthrie reported that further progress was going to be challenging. Whereas for Arts & Sciences I, staff had almost three years to work with publishers to secure their titles—order in the production queue was not of concern—the smaller discipline-specific collections would present much more complexity. Even though existing publishers would likely contribute their titles with relatively little negotiation, reaching out to numerous scholarly societies would be a challenge. Guthrie therefore proposed to begin signing titles for Arts & Sciences II and discipline-specific collections concurrently. This approach meant that only later would JSTOR prioritize the many collections on its horizon.[25]

After this meeting, at which it became clear that the priorities were Arts & Sciences II, Languages & Literature, and Business—about 150 journals—another priority arose. The Mellon Foundation was beginning to consider creating a database of art images and collections, subsequently named ArtSTOR.[26] Bowen came to believe that having art history journals in JSTOR would bolster ArtSTOR and offer important

[22] William G. Bowen, "Re:RE: MLA," email to Kevin Guthrie, April 20, 1999.
[23] Mellon Grant #49900689.
[24] Packet for the JSTOR board of trustees meeting of May 27, 1999.
[25] Ibid.
[26] See *Report of the Andrew W. Mellon Foundation 1999* and *Report of the Andrew W. Mellon Foundation 2000*.

TABLE 13.2
Proposed Collections, May 1999

Collection	Number of Titles (est.)	Number of Pages (est.; millions)
Arts & Sciences I	117	4.8
Arts & Sciences II	114	4.5
Ecology & Botany	27	1
General Science	4	2
Business	30	0.7
Literature	30	1.2
History of Art	15	0.7
Medicine	5	1.8
Psychology	30	0.7
Education	10	0.4
History	30	1.2
Total	>400	19

opportunities for linking between the two. Again, Guthrie felt conservative. Noting that rapid growth was bringing risk, he wrote to Bowen and board member Pat McPherson, "I have no doubt that a core group of 100–150 institutions will pay whatever we choose to charge for whatever we [digitize]. But I imagine an increasing number of institutions that will opt out of paying more as our fees (and content) increase."[27] Guthrie was also worried about the complications posed by numerous art images in the pages of the journals. Yet once again, Bowen argued for putting a new collection on the queue:

> From my perspective (and there are of course other perspectives), digitizing the truly outstanding journals in the key fields of the humanities and social sciences falls into the "must do" category. And it does seem to me that art history is both a terribly important field in its own right and so closely associated (more and more, in terms of the way courses in other fields are taught) with history, literature, anthropology, area studies, and so on, that it is truly a "cross roads" field. This would be true even if there

[27]Kevin Guthrie, "FW: University of Wyoming backs off," email to William G. Bowen and Mary Patterson McPherson, July 7, 1999.

were no inclination to think about ArtSTOR—which only makes art history even more critical.[28]

And later in the conversation he outlined his sense of the dangers of delay:

> The danger is that impatience will drive one or more of the key journals to strike out on their own or to enter a partnership with another philanthropic funder [and fragment the arts and sciences]. We came within a hair, as you may recall, of having the Modern Language Association make this decision—which would have been a real mistake for them and for everyone. And they almost made it. . . . The general point is that non-profit, non-commercial entities in the fields that matter to us can cause a lot of trouble.[29]

Bowen's sense was that other entities could, with the best of intentions, develop projects that, taken together, were less efficient for scholarly research. He wanted to see all of the core arts and sciences fields covered in one location, to enable cross-searching that helps to encourage interdisciplinary work and to ensure archiving. A collection of art history journals was added to JSTOR's growing list of priorities.

As 1999 came to a close, it can only be said that publisher relations had an extensive agenda. About fifteen titles had been signed for Arts & Sciences II, three for Business. It was clear that the Business Collection, for one thing, was far behind Guthrie's prediction a year earlier that it would be ready to follow Arts & Sciences I in Michigan's production queue at the end of 1999. The implications of this are discussed in chapter 14. For Languages & Literature and Art History, conversations had begun with, respectively, the MLA and the College Art Association, a key scholarly society in that field. Medicine was also on the agenda. But there was a worrying development. "As publishers question more seriously the potential value of their historical content, our efforts to win the favor of journal editors and to provide benefits to publishers are becoming increasingly important."[30] This factor foreshadows a number of developments in the subsequent two years, covered in chapter 14.

SUMMATION

This chapter has witnessed the shift in growth strategy from cautious incrementalism to an almost boundless enthusiasm. Increased library

---

[28] William G. Bowen, "RE: University of Wyoming backs off," email to Kevin Guthrie, July 8, 1999.

[29] Ibid.

[30] Packet for the JSTOR board of trustees meeting of October 6, 1999.

participation was a foremost factor. This in turn was abetted, at least, by the on-time completion Arts & Sciences I. Although it may seem to have been only a small blip to cap this time period, fulfilling this obligation was a most important development: the major struggle of the past four years was completed. Having achieved its first major goal, JSTOR was poised for future growth.

On the other hand, the necessary planning efforts retarded more immediate progress. Whereas all the titles for the Business Collection should have been signed by 1999, they were delayed in part to allow the planning for more overall growth. While this delay may have prevented JSTOR's production capacity from being most efficiently used (see chapter 14), the planning it permitted gave JSTOR its growth priorities for about three years into the future. The board would not face strategic questions on collections growth again until 2002.

Challenges and Opportunities of Growth

JANUARY 2000–DECEMBER 2001

THE MILLENNIUM CELEBRATIONS were followed for JSTOR by two years of remarkable expansion and growth. At the same time, it both struggled to keep up with demand and considered branching out in other directions. The achievements in this period were many. New collections were digitized and released to acclaim. Institutional participation grew apace, especially among foreign and nonacademic libraries and in the newly released collections. Initiatives were undertaken to revamp the interface and to develop linking. And while all of this took place, JSTOR continued its thoughtful planning for future growth.

Yet amid this progress, a number of questions lingered. As several notable publishers—none of them JSTOR participants—began to digitize their own backfiles, should JSTOR continue to grow in essentially the same way, by adding collections and library participants? If it did continue in this fashion, could it grow rapidly enough to remain relevant in a field of tens of thousands of journals? Or should it instead leverage its experience and accomplishments to offer new services? In 2000 and 2001, JSTOR considered all of these options as it pursued growth.

PUBLISHER RELATIONS AND REVENUE SHARING

Following up on the planning that had taken place in 1999 (see chapter 13), JSTOR crafted a number of new collections on the same model as it had in the past. Among the collections under consideration were Business, Language & Literature, Law, and Medicine, in addition to Arts & Sciences II. Because several of these collections took JSTOR beyond its traditional arts and sciences focus, the publishers targeted were on balance less academically and more commercially oriented. Perhaps in part as a result, publisher agreements would eventually deliver more tangible benefits.

During the year 2000, Heidi McGregor negotiated with publishers to fill out much of Arts & Sciences II and Business. She spent a significant portion of the year working with the already invited publishers of these collections, explaining JSTOR's benefits and assuaging their concerns. By May, some forty titles were signed, a figure that rose to seventy by

October.[1] Invitations were sent to Language & Literature Collection publishers, and responses began to arrive back in the fall. JSTOR was assembling these collections as rapidly as possible.

Yet these efforts notwithstanding, indications were beginning to accumulate that signing new titles was becoming more challenging. At a board meeting in the fall of 2000, Guthrie and McGregor presented some of the new challenges:

> We are finding that publishers' transition to and deepening of their inventory of electronic journals puts pressure on our moving wall concept. Publishers also appear to be increasingly interested in capitalizing their content, including back issues, through services promising revenues. . . . And, many publishers are intent on creating their own digitization projects. Journals presenting the biggest challenges generally are published by commercial publishers or not-for-profit societies focused on the science, technical, medical, and business communities, professionally-oriented communities with markets broader than just academic researchers.[2]

As the topic was considered further, a significant part of the context was that other resources were beginning to digitize journal backfiles, with royalties promised.[3] EBSCO and ProQuest were among the most important players in this domain, and they paid royalties, although they did not as a rule digitize the full backruns and did not offer the same commitment to archiving.[4] In addition, individual publishers—and not only Elsevier, the largest—were beginning to digitize their own backfiles. These changes in the market led Guthrie and McGregor to conclude that JSTOR would have to provide more to publishers if it wanted to secure additional participation under curated conditions.

They questioned whether JSTOR should offer revenue sharing to all of its publisher participants once it began to do so for Arts & Sciences I titles. But even while presenting this as a topic of debate, they cautioned that much was in transition, including individual access and linking. And the list of participating libraries had been growing remarkably. With so much in flux, they seemed to be suggesting, immediate action was perhaps unwise. Although the board did not endorse broader

---

[1] In addition, funding had been secured from the Mellon and Niarchos foundations for a significant portion of Arts & Sciences II, in specific disciplines of interest.

[2] Minutes for the JSTOR board of trustees meeting of October 4, 2000.

[3] Packet for the JSTOR board of trustees meeting of October 4, 2000.

[4] Part of the problem was that these services had begun to offer current issues, and publishers therefore found them to present competition. Embargoes were thus introduced (along with, at least at the time, exclusive relationships). The embargoes seemed very similar to JSTOR's moving wall, making the royalty disparity all the more problematic. Heidi McGregor, interview with the author, May 18, 2001.

revenue sharing at this point, within a year it would be approved for all of JSTOR's journals.

Beyond revenue-sharing, JSTOR considered a number of other ways to provide more benefits for publishers. It was at this point that linking with current issues was jumpstarted. Furthermore, JSTOR began more clearly to articulate the benefits to publishers of having their entire back-file digitized and archived at no expense. Also, surveys of scholars were confirming the scholarly benefits of digitization. In sum, JSTOR made clear that publishers' participation should result from the nonroyalty benefits that it brought, with revenue-sharing expanded in 2002 as a modest sweetener.

By the close of 2001, JSTOR had made a great deal of progress with publishers, in terms of both policy and practice. The Business Collection was available online and Arts & Sciences II and Language & Literature were largely signed and in various stages of production. Music and Art History began to come into focus toward the end of 2001, as agreements were signed. Although publisher relations focused on curating collections rather than maximum (or even targeted) throughput, steady growth continued.[5]

PRODUCTION

A graceful handoff between McGregor, on the one hand, and Fenton and her staff, on the other, was necessary in order to keep the latter working at maximum potential. On balance, given that McGregor was tasked with curating collections and Fenton with steady production measured in pages, the success was remarkable. But all was not perfect. The delays that were observed in chapter 13 in licensing titles for the Business Collection left the production staff with less content than was expected in 2000. And as additional journals grew shorter in length, it took more publisher-relations successes to bring the same number of pages into the archive. Nevertheless, despite the complications of juggling two production offices, two scanning vendors, and multiple collections—each with its own challenges—millions of pages per year were added to the archive.

---

[5] This was yet another effect of JSTOR's curatorial mandate. McGregor "never approached collection development by saying 'I want 300,000 pages into production [per month]'. . . . You try to bring those things together, but I would never start from there." Heidi McGregor, interview with the author, April 9, 2002.

New Procedures

Elizabeth Bennett had joined JSTOR in mid-1998 to manage the Princeton production team. Guthrie's hope was that a sort of "friendly competition" would exist between Princeton and Michigan, a competition that would foster the development of new efficiencies and improve the quality of the JSTOR production operation. Adding a second scanning vendor would create competition for JSTOR's business that would hopefully reduce prices and improve digitization quality, while making JSTOR less dependent on a single vendor. Eventually, a second scanning bureau, Apex Data Services, Inc., was added to work, to begin with, on General Science through the Princeton office.[6]

Bringing on a second scanning vendor and production site provided an opportunity to rethink certain operating procedures, most critically the division of labor between JSTOR and its vendor. Since the pilot, JSTOR had considered, informally and irregularly, whether it could run its own OCR operation. By 1999, new technology permitted largely unmediated OCR and therefore eliminated most of the labor costs that had made it expensive.[7] JSTOR believed that it could thereby save money, and so the new vendor was asked to supply only scanned images and the indexing. At Princeton, the production process itself included OCR, in addition to the preparation and QC work. Michigan would gradually begin performing its own OCR, as well.[8]

[6] Packet for the JSTOR board of trustees meeting, July 30, 1998.

[7] Once JSTOR's first vendor, DIT, scanned and indexed journals, it ran the scanned page images through an OCR software "engine." Then, a human operator would spell-check the OCR'd text, attempting to fix any errors that "popped up." For a long time, this system of "pop-up" spelling correction provided the least expensive solution at high quality. But as OCR technology improved, it became possible to link together several different OCR software engines and allow them to "vote" among themselves, on a character-by-character basis, on the text. Although this voting software was more expensive than the software it replaced, it virtually eliminated labor costs. See Kenn Dahl, "OCR Trends and Implications," and John Price-Wilkin, "Access to Digital Image Collections: System Building and Image Processing," in Anne R. Kenney and Oya Y. Rieger, eds., *Moving Theory into Practice: Digital Imaging for Libraries and Archives* (Mountain View, CA: Research Libraries Group, 2000), 110–118.

[8] Although *Science* and the *PNAS* were prime candidates for this new OCR process, such was not the case for the Royal Society titles. Because the earliest volumes were so ancient, locating adequate source material presented unusual challenges. OCR would be challenging because of many serifs that had gone extinct and the ligatures on old s's that made them look like f's. The first hundred years of the Royal Society titles would not be amenable to standard OCR. Instead, at far greater expense, JSTOR's new vendor doublekeyed this text; that is, two typists each inputted the entire text, then the two files were compared and any differences between the two were addressed.

In addition to new OCR procedures, the General Science Collection also contained illustrations of greater complexity than JSTOR had previously encountered. The older Royal Society issues had delicate line drawings, while the late twentieth-century issues of some of the titles had elaborate computer-created graphics. The latter were heavily laden with color, a new development. JSTOR consulted an outside expert to help develop procedures to deal with these complications.[9]

Progress

Between these new processes, the new production office, and the new vendor, it came as no surprise that some of the ambitious goals were somewhat delayed. These factors, along with the fact that the organization measured success by collections rather than pages, are important for understanding this period.

In the fall of 1998, Bennett anticipated the completion of *Science* and *PNAS*—the Royal Society publications were not yet signed—by the summer of 1999. Had this goal been achieved, it is unclear what her staff would have tackled next—nothing was on the immediate horizon. This schedule was probably not realistic, and it was not achieved. JSTOR did not begin accepting pages from its new vendor for General Science until July of 1999—seven months later than had been called for by that early schedule.

The Princeton office cut its teeth on one title—the *Journal of Animal Ecology*—from Arts & Sciences I in the early summer of 1999 before moving on to the lengthier and more complex General Science titles. Other than that one title, the Princeton office did not assist with Arts & Sciences I. The General Science Collection had a deadline of its own, a promise to libraries that it would be completed by the end of 2000.

For about nine months, General Science production progressed more slowly than had been anticipated, largely because of vendor difficulties (see figure 14.1). The complicated collection, with its new procedures, was a challenge. It was not until April 2000—about eight months after production of the collection began—that the anticipated rate of about 100,000 pages per month was achieved on a regular basis.[10] (January was

---

[9]For an overview of the standards that were developed and implemented, see Elizabeth Z. Bennett, "Digitizing *Science:* JSTOR Faces New Challenges," in Kenney and Rieger, eds., *Moving Theory into Practice,* 26–27.

[10]As was noted in chapter 9, the statistic of pages accepted per month collapses the performance of JSTOR and its vendors. Often, the reason for declines in pages accepted was no fault of JSTOR's, although it impacted progress greatly.

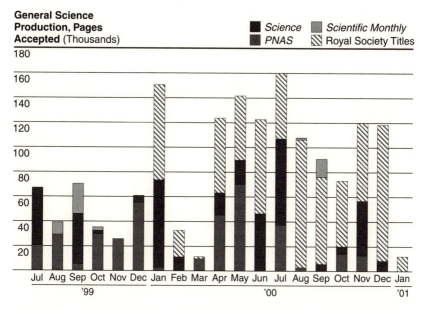

Figure 14.1. General Science Production: Pages Accepted per Month, by Title

anomalous, representing a glut of pages that had previously been rejected and had been reprocessed by the vendor; it was not, at that time, a sustainable achievement.) At this point, JSTOR was not yet able, organizationally, to control two discrete production processes concurrently. With Michigan working hard in 1999 to complete Arts & Sciences I, JSTOR's institutional focus was on that office and its work. It was not until Michigan completed Arts & Sciences I that the new Princeton office and the following collection—General Science—were able to achieve expected production rates.

Then, at the end of 1999 and in early 2000, Princeton and General Science were prioritized, and Michigan had a chance to breathe (see figure 14.2). With Business Collection titles only partially signed, its principal mandate was the Ecology & Botany Collection. As a result, in many months it received only about 60,000–90,000 pages from the vendor, out of a capacity of 150,000–200,000 pages per month. In terms of the Ecology & Botany Collection, April, May, and June of 2000 brought virtually no accepted digitized pages. Instead, staff focused on important retrospective projects not documented in these figures and worked on General Science during these months.

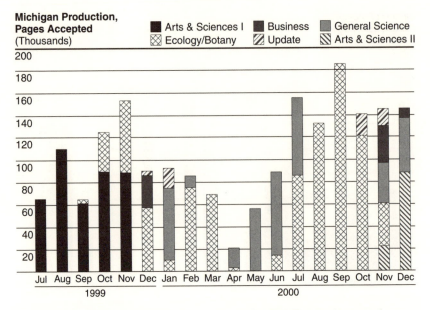

Figure 14.2. Michigan Production through 2000: Pages Accepted per Month, by Collection

Michigan's stasis allowed for these important retrospective projects to be completed, but it had not originally been planned. Rather, it was a natural if unfortunate result of the transition from Arts & Sciences I to future collections. In the first half of 1999, the pressure to complete Arts & Sciences I entailed the production librarians tracking down every issue of the backfiles and managing the preparation of the hard-copies for indexing. This focus was possible because it had been anticipated that a partner organization would obtain the complete hard-copy back-files of the Ecology & Botany titles. Unfortunately, this did not happen early enough for a perfectly smooth transition and delays cascaded through the process. The first half of 1999 was the period in which growth prospects were still somewhat uncertain (see chapter 11) and as a result JSTOR leaders may understandably not have pushed the organization and its vendor as hard as they might have otherwise. Such were the challenges of shifting priorities after the long and successful effort to complete Arts & Sciences I.[11]

As we are seeing, JSTOR had a great deal of trouble, often for reasons outside of its control, in making use of its expanded capacity in the most

[11]Eileen G. Fenton, interview with the author, October 11, 2001.

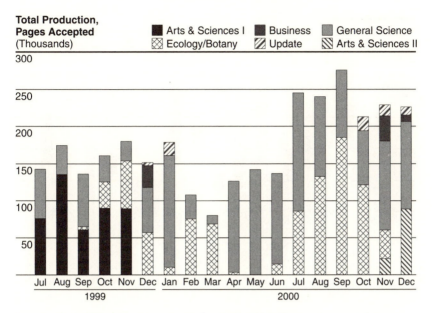

Figure 14.3. Total Production, July 1999–2000: Pages Accepted per Month, by Collection

efficient ways. In 2000, with one team at Princeton and one and a half teams at Michigan, and given adequate vendor support, capacity should have been about 250,000 pages per month. At this rate, JSTOR's production fell nearly 1.3 million pages short of its 3 million page capacity in the year-long period from July 1999–June 2000. As we have seen, sequencing collections in this period was a struggle, at the levels of board-level strategy, publisher relations, production, and the scanning vendor. Instead, retrospective projects were completed.

But after the first half of 2000, as figure 14.3 reveals, production was more steady. Several months of impressive figures in July through September transitioned fairly well in the late fall and early winter to Arts & Sciences II (see figure 14.4). When there was some extra capacity, Fenton's group took the opportunity to digitize the current issues so they would be ready for when the moving wall pushed them into the archive. The next year, 2001, was more erratic. Although a number of glut months were mixed with several months below 150,000 pages, the overall rate measured against capacity was about 90 percent. This relatively recent experience suggests that there is at times a longer start-up time to expanded production capacity than might have been expected, not necessarily in the production department but in the organization as a whole.

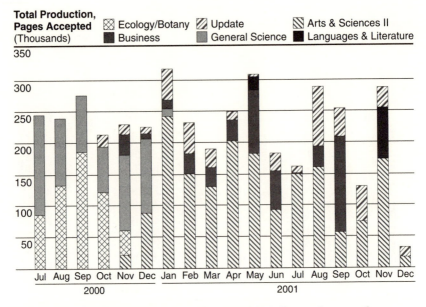

Figure 14.4. Total Production, July 2000–2001: Pages Accepted per Month, by Collection

JSTOR's broader experience with two offices developing different processes and discrete relationships was not altogether positive. It was at first difficult for one office to flexibly take up the slack from the other, or to put digitization work out to the other office's vendor when its vendor's backlog grew. Much was learned during this period about the difficulties of planning ahead for collections that have substantial lead times, while also managing the ongoing production work and keeping releases on schedule. Here is some additional evidence of the usefulness of the JSTOR organization—a body with clear mission and responsibility—as opposed to the preexisting Michigan grant structure.

Eventually, when Bennett left JSTOR-Princeton to take a position elsewhere, Eileen Fenton, the Michigan production coordinator, took on the overall oversight of the Princeton operation as well. Fenton brought greater standardization to the work of Princeton and Michigan, allowing much more flexibility between vendors. This brought great advantages in terms of efficiency. But the downside was apparent. Although JSTOR had multiple partially redundant production facilities, the skilled production librarians and coordinator were based only at Michigan. After Bennett's departure, the redundancy of key personnel was no longer in place for production. Evidently, JSTOR's relations with the University of Michigan had improved sufficiently to make this seem a reasonable risk, although only time will determine whether it was a wise risk to take.

INCREASING ACCESS AND PARTICIPATION

The period studied in this chapter was important because it was then that JSTOR's participant scale shifted from untenable in the long-term to fairly clearly self-sustainable. Had library participation been frozen at about six hundred JSTOR would have found self-sustainability far more elusive. At twelve hundred its success was unqualified. The factors that led to this rather rapid development are studied in this section.

Growth in Library Participation

Looking back retrospectively from the close of 2001, JSTOR's unabated growth in library participation is striking (see figure 14.5). The 750 U.S. participants foreseen by the business plan were not secured until May 2001—seventeen months later than projected. And yet by this time, international participation took the figure above 1,000. By the close of 2001, over 800 U.S. libraries participated for a total of about 1,200 worldwide.

Several factors conspired to enable increased library participation. Once Arts & Sciences I was completed toward the end of 1999, libraries no longer had to license a promise but now could immediately obtain the full collection. In addition, a remarkably large number of libraries outside of the United States participated under the new pricing plan that had been established for them. These factors combined with a broader development in higher education: more money was available for electronic resources.

This overall shift had two specific characteristics. First, favorable economic conditions led to a general loosening of budgetary constraints at many colleges and universities. Second, as the Internet was transformed from a novelty to a ubiquitous scholarly resource, the importance of electronic resources was increasingly recognized and reflected in budgets. Among the ARL libraries (a group that had significant overlap with the Research I universities), overall library expenditures increased by about one-third between 1994 and 1999. In addition, electronic resource expenditures, as a percentage of total materials expenditures, had grown from a median of 5.3 percent in 1994–1995 to 12.8 percent in 1999–2000 (and no doubt has continued to grow, though there is a lag in publishing

Library Participation
(Hundreds)

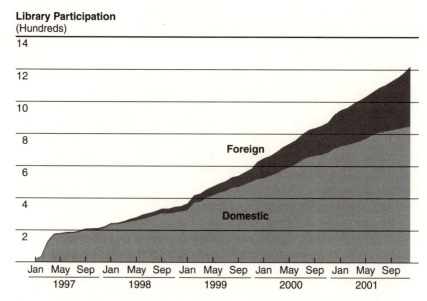

Figure 14.5. Library Participation in Any Collection, U.S. and Foreign

the statistics).[12] Similar trends toward adding electronic resources are observable in far broader groups of American academic libraries, though with an additional lag. Licensing electronic resources had become a significant part of the work of academic librarians.

For both the American and the non-U.S. libraries that participated in JSTOR for the first time during this period (see table 14.1 for a typical week), it is safe to say that the majority held less than half of the journals in hard-copy format. This was a critical factor in understanding why they chose to participate. For them, JSTOR participation was about collection building. They were much less typically concerned with archiving or accessing hard-copy backfiles that they already held. Rather, JSTOR participation was the only sensible way for them to add these titles to the collection, since adding the hardcopy or microfilm backfiles would be significantly more expensive yet offer markedly less powerful access. MacAdam estimates that by the close of 2001, only 10–15 percent of new participants did so principally for space-saving purposes. Most of the rest did so for collection-building or ease-of-access reasons.[13]

[12]Martha Kyrillidou and Mark Young, *ARL Supplementary Statistics 1999–2000* (Washington, DC: ARL, 2001), 9.

[13]Carol MacAdam, interview with the author, March 13, 2002.

TABLE 14.1
Library Participants New to JSTOR, Week of October 1–5, 2001

Participant	Country	Pricing Class
Institute of Policy Studies	Sri Lanka	Very Small
University of Turku	Finland	Large
University of San Francisco	U.S.	Medium
Economics Education & Research Consortium	Russia	Very Small
University of Massachusetts Medical School	U.S.	Special
University of Tennessee, Martin	U.S.	Medium
Universita Internazionale Degli Studi Sociali	Italy	Small

Source: Aimee Pyle, "RE: FW: New Licenses," email to author, March 28, 2002.

This factor was reflected in the source of institutional interest within the United States, which MacAdam believes to have switched unmistakably from librarians in 1998 and 1999 to faculty in 2000 and 2001. That is, librarians were more likely to be licensing JSTOR for their institutions in response to faculty requests (and sometimes pressure) rather than as a result of their own decisions, made independently. (It could not, of course, have been otherwise previously, since there had been relatively few journals digitized to elicit faculty attention.) As recent Ph.D.s from JSTOR-participating universities took up faculty positions at institutions across the United States and throughout the world, they spread demand for JSTOR to new places. This demand for access led to library participation.

Much international participation reflected a similar interest in collection building and ease of access. The typical foreign academic participant might have held less than one-third of the Arts & Sciences I titles, so there was relatively little space-saving to be had. Collection building was most important.[14] The first contact from a foreign school often came from a faculty member asking JSTOR about participation. Dawn Tomassi would use this communication to initiate contacts with librarians, allowing JSTOR to demonstrate tangibly that faculty were interested in it. Internationally, JSTOR was more exclusively responsive than it was in the United States. There was very little systemic data, on the order of the Carnegie *Classification,* on international libraries or

[14]Dawn Tomassi, interview with the author, April 30, 2002.

educational institutions. Barring such data, JSTOR had no ready means by which to target its broad international outreach. Better, perhaps, simply to respond to all expressed interest, at least while there seemed to be such a great deal of it.[15]

A significant proportion of foreign participation, perhaps one-third, came from nonacademic institutions like think tanks and national banks. For many of them, the economics and business journals were probably of greatest relevance. Most of these nonacademic institutions participated on their own, rather than in partnership with others. It was not unusual for the national bank to be the sole participant from a given country.

For the academic institutions, expressions of interest came in many cases from a national consortium, a national library, or a funder with a specific regional interest. Even funders and consortia were not pre-identified and targeted. They found JSTOR from peers via serendipity. These partners were able to help JSTOR develop more targeted lists of institutions likely to be relevant. National libraries or formal consortia played a valuable role in such situations, allowing JSTOR to funnel some amount of its interactions through one source rather than several. This approach was also helpful in surmounting language barriers and cultural differences. The negotiator for a national library or a consortium has generally been fluent in English and familiar with American resource-providers, allowing for easier interactions. As a result, real savings in time and money were achieved by dealing with international consortia, savings that were far less likely to accrue through American consortia. Nationwide groups in Israel, Finland, Taiwan, and elsewhere brought dozens of participants. Sometimes, these license agreements were signed by the individual libraries, sometimes by the consortium on their behalf, but either way JSTOR strived to maintain relations with each participating library. Language differences proved to be surmountable in negotiating these agreements, which were always written in English.

In Russia, the John D. and Catherine T. MacArthur Foundation offered support to seventeen pre-identified university libraries that wished to participate in JSTOR.[16] The idea was to offer support to the new private research universities that were growing up in the former Soviet Union, in addition to several Russian state universities.[17] This $300,000 grant

---

[15] And indeed, between early 2000 and early 2002, the amount of interest had only increased as libraries became more familiar with what JSTOR had to offer. Dawn Tomassi, interview with the author, April 30, 2002.

[16] Jonathan Fanton, letter to Kevin Guthrie, January 29, 2001.

[17] "Foundation Grants Extend JSTOR Access to International Scholars," *JSTORNEWS* 3, no. 1 (March 2001): 2.

would allow these libraries to participate in JSTOR without paying the one-time fee and without paying the annual fee for the first three years.[18] By the close of 2001, at least ten libraries were participating through this program, with several others expected thereafter. The MacArthur Foundation was also interested in supporting JSTOR access to some of its university grantees in Nigeria, but in the words of Mac-Arthur President Jonathan Fanton, "given Nigeria's lack of reliable high-speed internet access, not to mention problems with assuring a regular supply of electricity, I expect that this . . . must remain a longer-term goal."[19]

In South Africa, with the end of apartheid and the transition to democracy, the Mellon Foundation had perceived a special opportunity to help strengthen higher education.[20] Academic libraries soon became one of the program's foci. The availability of JSTOR would greatly augment what was, for many, inadequate scholarly resources. Yet not only were most South African universities too poor to participate, but their Internet connectivity was abysmal. The Mellon Foundation was willing, even eager, to subsidize JSTOR access for South African academia, but first several organizations (including the foundation) had to team up to radically improve connectivity for South African higher education. After prolonged negotiations, connectivity was improved.[21] Working through a consortium called Sabinet, Mellon subsidized JSTOR access to South African higher education as it had for the ACA and HBCU schools (see chapter 10).[22] In 2001, JSTOR was beginning to sign license agreements with these universities, whose connectivity had now improved markedly.

---

[18] [Kevin Guthrie,] "Proposal to the MacArthur Foundation: Extending JSTOR Access to Russia," November 9, 2000.

[19] Jonathan Fanton, letter to William G. Bowen, August 10, 2000.

[20] Under apartheid, numerous disciplines—one example was population studies—had become impossibly politicized. Much the same had happened, for a somewhat different set of disciplines, in the Soviet Union and Communist Eastern Europe.

[21] The story is too complicated for this book, and might indeed be an interesting case study for those interested in the worldwide development of the Internet. Before 2000, South African universities had network connectivity, but the highest speeds were prohibitively expensive because of the monopolistic behavior of telecommunications providers. South African library consortia, telecommunications providers, and universities worked with support from the Mellon Foundation and another foundation that opted to remain anonymous to bring low-cost, high-speed network connectivity to South African higher education for the first time. Even if this would have seemed a compelling project for Mellon in any case, the foundation's interests in JSTOR surely underscored the value of a connectivity initiative in South Africa. Thus the JSTOR and connectivity projects can be viewed synergistically. Thomas I. Nygren, interview with the author, May 23, 2001.

[22] Mellon Grant #20000750.

·

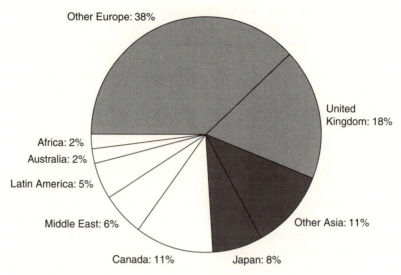

Figure 14.6. Foreign Library Participation, by Region, as of
December 2001

A number of foundations awarded grants in 2000 to provide access
to JSTOR in specific countries.[23] The Stavros S. Niarchos Foundation
awarded a grant to subsidize the participation of Greek universities
(in addition to offering funding for archaeology and classics journals in
Arts & Sciences II; see chapter 11). The Mellon Foundation awarded
funds to help Eastern European universities participate.[24] Two anonymous foundations awarded funds to abet Irish and Israeli participation.
The Asia Foundation, the Eurasia Foundation, and other grantmakers
assisted in individual cases.

The internationalization of JSTOR was remarkable, far more so than
had ever been anticipated. Figure 14.6 shows the breakdown by con-
tinent of non-U.S. participation at the close of 2001. This masks the
diversity of the fifty-two countries it included, which are reflected in
table 14.2. The worldwide demand for the most prestigious academic
journals in the arts and sciences was substantial. Moreover, the mechanism of distribution worked. JSTOR had three mirror sites, two in the
United States and one in the United Kingdom, but no more. Originally
intended to "miniaturize" journals on CD-ROM and then finding that
the Internet had obviated CD-ROMs and saved a huge amount of money,

[23] "Foundation Grants Extend JSTOR Access to International Scholars," *JSTORNEWS*
3, no. 1 (March 2001): 2.
[24] Mellon Grant #19800697.

TABLE 14.2
Countries of JSTOR's International Participants, as of December 2001

Country	Number of Participants	Country	Number of Participants
UK	65	Brazil	2
Canada	39	Hungary	2
Japan	25	India	2
Finland	19	Malaysia	2
Taiwan	18	New Zealand	2
Italy	14	Slovakia	2
Switzerland	12	Thailand	2
Denmark	11	United Arab Emirates	2
Israel	11	Uruguay	2
Russia	11	Belarus	1
Germany	10	Belgium	1
Hong Kong	8	Bulgaria	1
Netherlands	8	Chile	1
Ireland	7	Costa Rica	1
Norway	7	Cyprus	1
South Africa	7	Egypt	1
Australia	6	El Salvador	1
France	6	Estonia	1
Mexico	6	Indonesia	1
Argentina	5	Luxembourg	1
Greece	5	Macau	1
Spain	5	Nicaragua	1
Sweden	5	Pakistan	1
Turkey	5	Saudi Arabia	1
Czech Republic	4	South Korea	1
China	3	Sri Lanka	1
		Total	369

JSTOR had seen the need for mirror sites largely obviated, as worldwide connectivity improved beyond anyone's expectations. The lower cost of international distribution allowed JSTOR to price its database accordingly, thereby increasing participation.

Setting Fees for Subsequent Collections

In 1999, JSTOR offered only the Arts & Sciences I Collection, but in 2000, it released two additional collections, General Science and Ecology & Botany. Because it would implement almost precisely the same pricing plan for the collections released in 2001, Arts & Sciences II and Business are also discussed in this section. Just as managing multiple collections put pressure on JSTOR's publisher relations and production staffs, so, too, did it change the dynamics of the library-relations group. For the first time, JSTOR had more than one "product" it was offering in the marketplace.

Guthrie had planned by mid-1998 to continue making use of the general pricing scheme that had been adopted for Arts & Sciences I—the combination of one-time and annual fees (see chapter 8).[25] The system worked well in part because it was not too confusing for librarians, and it had the advantage of combining the ongoing annuity stream with a one-time capital charge that could be directed toward the creation of an endowment for archiving. The main innovation was differential pricing, based on whether a library participated in Arts & Sciences I. One important cosmetic change was renaming the Database Development Fee (DDF) the Archive Capital Fee (ACF). This nominal change was necessary because the two new collections were digitized with funds provided by foundation sources. So, rather than principally funding digitization, the smaller one-time fees would instead be directed almost exclusively toward building an endowment for JSTOR.[26]

In terms of the pricing structure, evidence continued to indicate that the pricing plan for Arts & Sciences I remained flawed in that the differential between the larger and smaller pricing classes was too small. JSTOR believed that for future collections, the Very Large participants should pay a higher share of the costs.[27] In setting these new prices, JSTOR did not assume, as it had in 1996, that its value came principally from space-saving. This significant departure from the Arts & Sciences I model resulted from a more refined understanding of the library participants

---

[25] Minutes of the board of trustees meeting, July 30, 1998.

[26] Packet for the JSTOR board of trustees meeting of May 27, 1999.

[27] Kevin Guthrie, interview with the author, October 20, 2001.

TABLE 14.3
Fees for Participation in Subsequent Collections, as of 2001

JSTOR Classification	Ecology & Botany		General Science		Arts & Sciences II		Business	
	ACF	*AAF*	*ACF*	*AAF*	*ACF*	*AAF*	*ACF*	*AAF*
Very Large	$4,800	$4,800	$7,500	$7,500	$20,000	$8,000	$6,000	$2,400
Large	$3,200	$3,200	$5,250	$5,250	$12,000	$5,000	$4,800	$1,280
Medium	$2,000	$2,000	$3,750	$3,750	$8,000	$2,000	$2,800	$880
Small	$1,200	$1,200	$2,250	$2,250	$5,000	$1,250	$1,600	$600
Very Small	$600	$600	$750	$750	$2,000	$1,000	$800	$400

over the past three years. Table 14.3 shows the fees set for the subsequent collections.[28]

Recognizing that nearly all of the Large and Very Large participants would elect to participate in subsequent collections, Guthrie believed pricing for them could be designed to help to correct for the original value-based flaws that we have seen. Table 14.4 illustrates the combined

TABLE 14.4
Annual Price (AAF) for U.S. Participants in All Collections

JSTOR Classification	End of 2000[i]	End of 2001[ii]
Very Large	$17,800	$27,700
Large	$13,200	$19,730
Medium	$9,000	$11,630
Small	$6,200	$7,300
Very Small	$3,600	$4,750
Ratio of Very Large / Very Small	4.9	5.8

[i]Includes Art & Sciences I, General Science, and Ecology & Botany
[ii]Includes Art & Sciences I, General Science, Ecology & Botany, Arts & Sciences II, and Business.

[28] It would be the case that virtually all library participants selected Arts & Sciences I. It would also be the case that very few libraries would select Business without also Arts & Sciences II. Because participation in Arts & Sciences I affected fees for subsequent collections and participation in Arts & Sciences II affected fees for the Business Collection, the prices listed here assume participation in both Arts & Sciences collections.

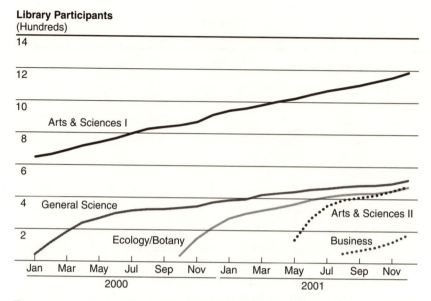

Figure 14.7. Library Participants, by Collection

pricing of all available collections, by pricing class. The upshot was that, while libraries could opt to select only one or two collections, JSTOR designed pricing on the assumption that many libraries would participate in all three. In the wake of these changes, the Large and Very Large participants contributed a greater share of JSTOR's revenues than they had in the 1997–1999 period. This is illustrated most clearly in the fee ratio of Very Large to Very Small, which after the repricing was 2.5 for Arts & Sciences I, but for all collections grew to 4.9 in 2001 and 5.8 in 2002.

Participation in New Collections

As striking as the growth in new participants was the number of participants, both existing and new, U.S. and foreign, signing up for multiple collections.[29] All of the four new collections achieved four hundred library participants within a year, compared with two and a half years for Arts & Sciences I (see figure 14.7). Building on a base of preexisting participants, already convinced of JSTOR's value, was significantly easier than starting from scratch! Table 14.5 illustrates the collection participation data for a fairly typical week in 2001.

[29] The relationships between new collections and new participants is complicated, because the new collections had a great deal to do with motivating new participants.

TABLE 14.5
Collection Participation in JSTOR, Week of October 1–5, 2001

Participant	Country	New Participant?	Collections Added
Aalborg University	Denmark	No	Business
Det Kongelige Bibliotek	Denmark	No	Business
Economics Education & Research Consortium	Russia	Yes	Arts & Sciences I
Georgia College and State University	U.S.	No	Arts & Sciences II
Handelshojskolens Bibliotek, Syddansk	Denmark	No	Business
Handelshojskolens Bibliotek, Kobenhavn	Denmark	No	Business
Institute of Policy Studies	Sri Lanka	Yes	Arts & Sciences I
Princeton Theological Seminary	U.S.	No	Arts & Sciences II
Roskilde Universitetsbibliotek	Denmark	No	Business
South Danish University	Denmark	No	Business
Universita Internazionale Degli Studi Sociali	Italy	Yes	Arts & Sciences I
Universite Laval	Canada	No	Business
University of Manitoba	Canada	No	General Science
University of Massachusetts, Medical School	U.S.	Yes	Arts & Sciences I Arts & Sciences II General Science Ecology & Botany Business
University of Nebraska, Lincoln	U.S.	No	Business
University of North Alabama	U.S.	No	Business
University of San Francisco	U.S.	Yes	Arts & Sciences I
University of Tennessee, Martin	U.S.	Yes	Arts & Sciences I
University of Turku	Finland	Yes	Arts & Sciences I
Vassar College	U.S.	No	Business
Worcester Polytechnic Institute	U.S.	No	Arts & Sciences II

Source: Aimee Pyle, "RE: FW: New Licenses," email to author, March 28, 2002.

It is important to note that, to the user, JSTOR's collections were indistinguishable. That is, at a library that participated in both Arts & Sciences I and General Science, a scholar would not realize that the collections are separate; he or she simply would have access to more journals. Titles were organized by academic discipline and not by collection, allowing a user to search across all journals in all collections to which his or her library participated. As a result, the synergies that came from a bundle of journals were magnified at libraries that participated in numerous JSTOR collections.

Marketing subsequent collections was therefore far easier than marketing the original Arts & Sciences I Collection. Simply by emailing existing participants and inviting them to mail back an agreement, JSTOR netted a large number of participants. Whereas only nine libraries signed on to Arts & Sciences I when it was first released, General Science had 36 advance participants, Ecology & Botany had 39, Arts & Sciences II had 100, and Business had 111. The transaction costs of these agreements were extraordinarily modest, since libraries could piggyback onto the existing license via a simple rider, rather than having to come to terms with an altogether new agreement.

In addition, JSTOR had developed ongoing relationships with its many participants. At every semi-annual meeting of the American Library Association, JSTOR held information meetings for participants, showing them its latest work on, for example, remote access to the database or the dangers and opportunities associated with the commercialization of library resources. When another collection was being developed, these information meetings were perfect venues at which to introduce the collection to libraries without subjecting them to a sales pitch. User-services staff held similar meetings in countries that had a significant number of participants, and Tomassi sometimes attended these meetings to meet local nonparticipants and discuss new collections.

Also, whenever a student or faculty member from a participant emailed to ask why a certain journal was not available, JSTOR took action. MacAdam or her assistant sent a personal email to a library contact, informing him or her that there was campus interest in another collection. MacAdam marvels at the "many times" that appreciative librarians licensed the additional collection and only wished that researchers had thought to speak with them directly.[30] For state university librarians experiencing budget cuts, this phenomenon was not altogether positive. One reported that "We've become sort of addicted to it now. It is so popular that we might not be able to say 'no'" to future collections.[31]

[30] Carol MacAdam, interview with the author, March 13, 2002.
[31] Bill Potter, interview with the author, April 26, 2002.

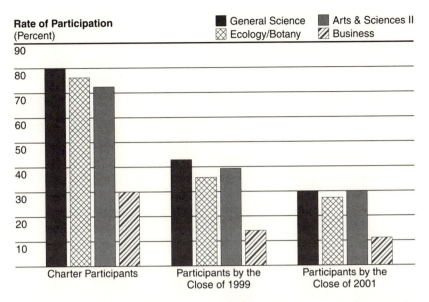

Figure 14.8. Rate of Participation, by Collection and Date of Original Participation in JSTOR, as of December 2001.

Finally, existing participants paid less for most collections (though not for Arts & Sciences II), and charter participants less for all. Where available, the nondiscounted rates were rarely relevant: only 3 percent of participating libraries selected subsequent collections without first (or concurrently) participating in Arts & Sciences I. In part, this was because the pricing made the combination more attractive than simply licensing one of the new clusters alone. More significantly, the Arts & Sciences I titles were of significant enough importance to attract massive participation on their own; there were few libraries that would want the new clusters, which were in allied arts and sciences fields, that did not already participate in Arts & Sciences I. So while some libraries, such as that at the NASA Goddard Space Flight Center, were interested only in the science clusters, many libraries saw the growth of JSTOR's database as proof of its value and good reason to combine their participation in several collections to receive a discount.

Perhaps the most important variable in determining which libraries signed on to additional collections was when they first participated in JSTOR, as figure 14.8 illustrates. Charter libraries participated at a stunning rate in new collections, not least because of the generous discounts they received. But in addition, those libraries that participated after the

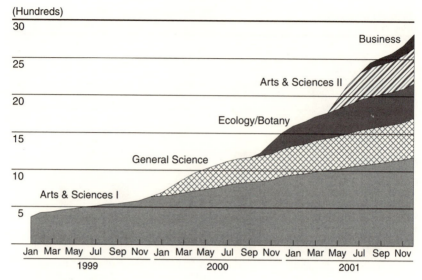

Figure 14.9. Collection-Participants

close of the charter period but before the end of 1999 participated at markedly, though not extravagantly, higher rates than those libraries that first gained access in 2000 and 2001. Part of the explanation for this may have been the increasingly international base of new participants in 2000 and 2001, many of which had less access to immediate funds. Also, the earlier participants had more experience with JSTOR.

The importance of these new collections and their levels of participation cannot be overstressed. Figure 14.9 illustrates the growth in what are termed "collection-participants," which is to say the number of participants in each of the available collections. The steep slope in this figure has been the key to JSTOR's move toward self-sustainability.

Library Distribution at the Close of 2001

The distribution of American and non-American libraries by pricing class is strikingly different. As Figure 14.10 illustrates, non-American participants were far more likely to be Large, while far less likely to be Very Large. This reflected, in part, the paucity of university-based research libraries outside of the United States that had materials budgets as large, and serials subscriptions as numerous, as the American ARL libraries.

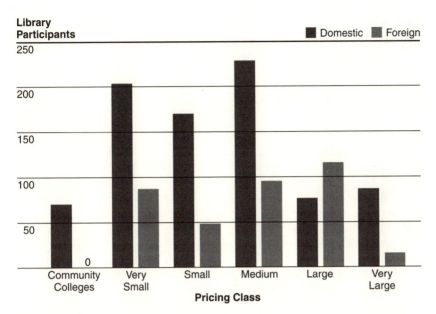

Figure 14.10. Library Participants, December 2001, by Country and Pricing Class

Most of the largest non-American libraries were more like the libraries at American Doctoral I and Research II universities.

In the case of U.S. libraries, it is possible to further break down these figures by Carnegie classification, as in figure 14.11. One effect of their wealth and the good value that they received from JSTOR's pricing was that all eighty-eight of the Research I universities (the Very Larges) elected to participate. The Research II and Doctoral I universities (Large) participated at a rate above 80 percent, with JSTOR staff expressing optimism that most of the remainder would join in a matter of time. And the Baccalaureate Is, the private, selective, liberal arts colleges that accounted for most of the Small pricing class, also joined at a significant rate, as did the Doctoral IIs.

Two factors have undoubtedly affected these relative participation rates: the pricing readjustment of 1998 and the fees that were set for new collections. In chapter 12, it was observed that between the readjustment and the close of 1999, the percentage increase in participation was highest for those schools that were targeted by it. In looking at the rates of growth in 2000 and 2001 (see figure 14.12), it is clear that the Baccalaureate schools had particularly strong growth rates, probably due to the multiple-collection pricing.

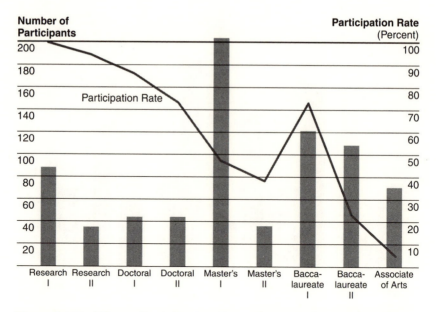

Figure 14.11. Library Participation, December 2001, by Carnegie *Classification* Groupings

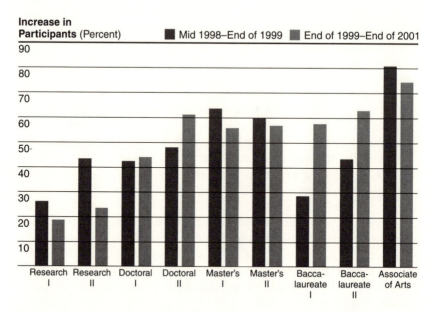

Figure 14.12. Increase in Participants, by Carnegie *Classification* Groupings

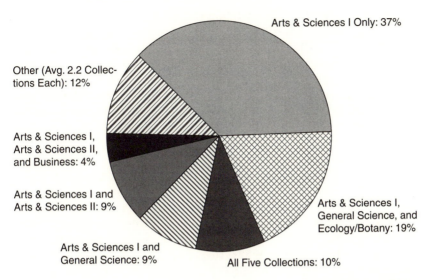

Arts & Sciences I Only: 37%

Other (Avg. 2.2 Collec-
tions Each): 12%

Arts & Sciences I,
Arts & Sciences II,
and Business: 4%

Arts & Sciences I and
Arts & Sciences II: 9%

Arts & Sciences I and
General Science: 9%

All Five Collections: 10%

Arts & Sciences I,
General Science, and
Ecology/Botany: 19%

Figure 14.13. Library Participants, by Collections, December 31, 2001

Circling back to figure 14.11, it remains the case that Master's I, Master's II, and Baccalaureate II schools participated in JSTOR's Arts &
Sciences I Collection, and indeed in all collections, at much lower rates
than any of the other four-year institutions. There was clearly a natural
break between the value these schools placed in JSTOR, even at the revised pricing level, compared with other academic libraries. Participation rates were lowest in the Master's II and Baccalaureate II groupings.
Pricing for these schools, which fall into the Small and Very Small classes
respectively, continued to exceed the value that many of them place on
the Arts & Sciences I Collection. It is difficult to be certain whether there
would have been any price low enough for them: evidence indicates
that the arts and sciences subject matter of JSTOR's collections may have
had relatively little relevance to their interests, one reason among many
that JSTOR created the Business Collection.

Examining the collections selected by American participants, it is clear
that there are several very common profiles (see figure 14.13). Nearly
40 percent participate in Arts & Sciences I alone, while only about 25 percent participated in three or more collections. The most common two-
collection combinations were Arts & Sciences I with either Arts &
Sciences II or General Science. It will be interesting to see how these
patterns evolve with additional time.

As JSTOR expanded its efforts to broaden its participant base, it hired
additional library-relations staff. In 2000, Bruce Heterick joined JSTOR

to oversee the growing library-relations group. His experience working for subscription agents and other academic vendors brought a different background to further strengthen an already successful group. (Part of the reason for expanding the staff in this direction was to expand JSTOR's audience from academia alone to other scholars and students.) Still, at the end of 2001, JSTOR had a total of three library-relations professionals (and three other staff), a very small group compared with the typical vendor to academic libraries.

ENABLING LINKS TO OTHER RESOURCES

The advantages of linking JSTOR's backfiles with other content were not unknown when staff began working on these issues in earnest in 2000. As abstracting and indexing services began to include some amount of article text, it became clear that system-wide costs would be reduced if they could link directly to a fulltext resource like JSTOR, rather than attempting to duplicate its efforts.[32] Moreover, from a user's perspective, linking was one of the key advantages of the online world, making research significantly more efficient and effective.[33] Librarians were eager for these links to be enabled (and in some cases dismayed that linking out from JSTOR journals' footnotes might be prohibitively expensive due to the page-image format).[34] But not only the indexing services were interested—faculty and librarians were eager to provide electronic syllabi that would allow them to post a link on a website taking a student directly to an article in JSTOR. But though aware of the community's interest in linking into JSTOR, it was not until 1999 that the organization began to think seriously about whether—and if so, how—to enable such access.[35] Its consideration of linking is a key depiction of how JSTOR adressed the growing needs of its community while giving sustained attention to strategic concerns.

In the first paper he wrote for the board on the topic in early 1999, Guthrie was clearly concerned about the implications of linking for

---

[32]For a brief overview of this topic, see Pricilla Caplan, "Reference Linking for Journal Articles: Promise, Progress and Perils," *portal: Libraries and the Academy* 1, no. 3 (2001): 351–56.

[33]Services like SFX and Encompass existed to make these links significantly easier.

[34]Dale Flecker, interview with the author, April 2, 2002; Michael Keller, interview with the author, May 21, 2002.

[35]There also exists the potential to link forward from an article, taking a researcher to the places where it was later cited. This was believed to be a significantly more complicated undertaking and was not seriously considered.

JSTOR.[36] Bibliographic links offered one-click redirection of a user from an indexing database like MathSciNet, PCI, EconLit, or EBSCO to JSTOR's article page images. Although Guthrie recognized the advantages to scholarship inherent in a well-linked research environment, he was concerned about the strategic implications.

He had two concerns. First, he believed that because of JSTOR's great mass of archival materials, a horizontal linker would receive an incredible amount of value by enabling links to JSTOR. He was less convinced that there was significant value to JSTOR from receiving links under such an arrangement. Second, and perhaps even more important, he was concerned that horizontal links might tend to reduce the perception, and the value, of JSTOR as a curated collection of journals. Concerned that in-linking organizations would receive a great deal of value while JSTOR received little—or perhaps even lost value—Guthrie at first mused about ways in which JSTOR could charge horizontal linkers or mandate that they give a rebate to JSTOR participants.[37]

The board shared Guthrie's concerns, and it reached only a very tentative conclusion at this point. "It was agreed that JSTOR should cooperate in linking its database to other electronic resources, provided these arrangements will not put JSTOR's viability at risk." The board agreed to pursue a pilot project with the nonprofit MathSciNet, which contained indices to a number of JSTOR's mathematics titles, to explore linking into the JSTOR archives.[38] For the moment, that would be all; the technical hurdles were significant, and until the strategic picture was clearer, there was no reason to prioritize the great amount of work involved.

In late 1999 the links from MathSciNet were enabled for a relatively small number of titles, and in 2000 the partnership grew to cover all of the titles common to both. In 2000, links brought MathSciNet users directly to JSTOR articles some 61,000 times.[39] It is probably impossible to know if linking such as this contributed to additional use of JSTOR, or whether it simply made such use easier for researchers, but it is generally believed that both were the case.

---

[36] Packet for the JSTOR board of trustees meeting of February 10, 1999.

[37] Although in retrospect the notion of charging for in-linking may seem contrary to the character of the Internet, it should be kept in mind that at this time there was a significant amount of legal tussling about linking. One example is *Ticketmaster Corp. v. Tickets.com Inc.*, 2000 U.S. Dist. LEXIS 4553 (C.D. Cal. 2000), aff'd, 248 F.3d 1173 (9th Cir. 2001). While JSTOR never attempted to charge for in-linking, Guthrie's thoughts are illustrative of the broad uncertainties in this domain at the time.

[38] Minutes of the JSTOR board of trustees meeting of February 10, 1999.

[39] "Technical Development Linking, Searching and Authentication," attachment to Gerard Aurigemma, letter to Ms. Gassman, March 30, 2001.

When the experiment with the nonprofit MathSciNet was getting underway, Guthrie was not yet an enthusiast. "From a strategic standpoint," he explained, "enabling links to [JSTOR] at the article level is not an easy call and not without risk." He remained concerned that, by allowing direct access to JSTOR content without the JSTOR "experience," users would derive less value from the collection. As a result, JSTOR would become less compelling to publishers asked in the future to participate. In the last analysis, Guthrie believed firmly that, in a linking environment, the depth of JSTOR's backfiles offered far more opportunities for in-linking than for out-linking. And this, he thought, raised questions as to whether linking was in JSTOR's best interests.[40]

The board considered this topic carefully. One trustee favored reference linking—the process by which a scholar follows a footnote to its source—but he noted that bibliographic linking, from an indexing database to JSTOR's articles, was different. He expressed concern that JSTOR should pay attention to its mission and be sure that its library and publisher participants, and not merely commercial database-providers, stood to benefit.[41]

Another trustee offered a solution to these concerns that endorsed many of Guthrie's views. He believed that if value was being exchanged as a result of linking, then in-linking entities should provide some recognition of this to JSTOR. He believed that the for-profit concerns would in essence view links to JSTOR as a tool by which to maximize profit. Thus participating libraries, he feared, might end up paying higher fees to for-profit in-linkers precisely as a result of the value of the links. He recommended a charge for in-linking that could be rebated, either directly or via lowered fees, to participating libraries.

With all of this in mind, JSTOR had applied for a grant from the Alfred P. Sloan Foundation—awarded in January 2000—to develop software and other tools necessary for linking.[42] These funds allowed programmers to focus intently on standardizing naming protocols and crafting a user-friendly interface in conjunction with user-services librarians. Developing the infrastructure was, in this case, a step made independently of a conclusion on strategy.

Realizing the challenges it faced, JSTOR made a useful distinction in thinking about the bibliographic linking partners with which to first work: "JSTOR has prioritized linking agreements that benefit its institutional constituencies" of both libraries and publishers. Among other

---

[40] Packet for the JSTOR board of trustees meeting of February 11, 2000.

[41] Minutes of the JSTOR board of trustees meeting of February 11, 2000.

[42] Stewart F. Campbell, letter to Gerard Aurigemma, January 10, 2000 re: Mellon Grant #99126.

things, this meant insuring a high-quality user experience. Only later, once it had developed "technical experience and broad-based strategic understanding"—which came in part by creating the software—would JSTOR consider "linking opportunities outside the JSTOR 'family.'"[43] But it should be noted that publishers as a group also favored linking, since they wanted the maximum exposure to their journals.[44]

By February 2001, most of the technical challenges to enable large-scale bibliographic and reference linking had been resolved, and there was a major shift in JSTOR's approach. For one thing, Guthrie couched the discussion as a strategic choice about levels of risk—as JSTOR grew more successful, were there opportunities, or indeed obligations, to take risks that could benefit its constituencies? He also presented the positive and negative cases for linking, noting that reasonable people might disagree on the degree of risk. Finally, he noted that if JSTOR were viewed by the library community as an archive, rather than principally as an access resource, linking could not be viewed as threatening in any way. On balance, Guthrie believed that linking was an example of the type of risk for which JSTOR should have an increased appetite, and the board was asked for advice.[45] There was "a brief discussion during which the board reaffirmed its support for enabling links between JSTOR and other resources."[46]

And so within a few months, JSTOR deployed a public interface to announce and to automate the creation of links. It decided to enable two types of links concurrently, perhaps since both used essentially the same technology.[47] First, faculty members, librarians, and others interested in creating electronic bibliographies and syllabi were able to find a stable URL that they could use. Second, major bibliographic linkers, such as indexing services, but also publishers whose current issues might have footnote reference-linking to JSTOR, were offered automated tools to create links to articles at no cost. While the first type of link was easily available, for the second type JSTOR signed a license agreement specifying among other things the quality of the outside links necessary in order for it to enable them.[48]

JSTOR was soon able to report that, with regard to both types of linking, "the enthusiasm for linking into JSTOR on the part of our participants

---

[43] Packet of the JSTOR board of trustees meeting of May 17, 2000.

[44] Heidi McGregor, interview with the author, April 9, 2002.

[45] Packet for the JSTOR board of trustees meeting of February 7, 2001.

[46] Minutes of the JSTOR board of trustees meeting of February 7, 2001.

[47] In both cases, the links combined bibliographic information about the article into a SICI code, which could be created automatically and directed the web browser directly to the relevant article in JSTOR.

[48] Packet for the JSTOR board of trustees meeting of June 20, 2001.

has been obvious and immediate. . . . Response from libraries to this announcement [about the second type of linking] has been consistently enthusiastic."[49] All of the enthusiasm was creating a great deal of un-anticipated work for the user-services group, testing links and fixing them when there was a problem, but JSTOR was undeterred. The number of bibliographic partners was being expanded from PCI, SFX, and ABC-CLIO to include OCLC FirstSearch, Gale, EBSCOhost, and more.

Of course, enthusiasm and expansion did not in and of themselves serve to moot the strategic concerns. It was too soon to know whether these had been applicable. The detailed and thoughtful consideration of strategy, in which risk was identified and accepted, indicates, however, the ways in which a new method of research facilitation—so important to JSTOR's mission—was evaluated.

Bibliographic linking also introduced a number of ongoing questions for JSTOR, in particular how to deal with researchers who had access to the in-linking resource but not to JSTOR itself. One option that was considered and ultimately rejected would have made individual articles available for a fee. In 2001 and afterwards, JSTOR began to make its archive available to high school and public libraries. In this way, linking seemed to have the potential to bring JSTOR a wider user-base.

LINKING CURRENT ISSUES AND ARCHIVING THEM

Combining the backfiles with current issues led JSTOR to pursue the latter itself, as was seen in chapter 6. Ever since JSTOR came to the conclusion that it would not be involved in bringing current issues on-line, it had intended to link its archive to current issues. This goal was supplanted by late 1996 with an effort—stated but not yet undertaken—"to develop technical linkages" between each journal's current issues and its backfile.[50] In a sense the separation between the previous section on outside linking and the present one on current issues is an artificial one, since the board often considered the two together, perhaps only due to nomenclature and not really to strategy. And the two were developed somewhat concurrently, in part because, as was seen in chapter 6, publishers were initially hesitant to provide current issues online. The movement to publish current issues of humanities and social science journals online en masse did not develop for some time. But as more of

---

[49] Packet for the JSTOR board of trustees meeting of October 11, 2001.
[50] Minutes of the JSTOR board of trustees meeting of October 29, 1996.

JSTOR's titles went online, it began in 1999 and 2000 to develop plans for linkages.[51] These plans took it in ambitious new directions.

JSTOR's caution on horizontal linking was juxtaposed against enthusiasm for linking current issues. Some 30 percent of its journals had current issues available online in early 2000, and the advantages of linking these to the backfile seemed straightforward: "Making entire journal runs as 'seamless' as possible will promote the purchase of both JSTOR and the current issues by librarians, will signify that JSTOR is part of a complete archiving solution, and will provide the user with enhanced functionality and convenience."[52] In a pilot project with the ESA's journals, JSTOR was going to first make available at its website the tables of contents of current issues, allowing researchers to link to them directly.

From McGregor's conversations with publishers about current issues, it had become clear that they were "very excited. . . . They're excited about users being able to search the complete run of a journal. . . . They are equally, if not more so, excited about JSTOR pointing users to their current issues."[53] The more current issues the better, yet readers rarely knew where to go for current issues published by a university press or a commercial house. And where access was denied as a result of the link from JSTOR, it might encourage the individual or the library to subscribe.

At the end of 2001, a number of pilot projects were underway. While the final system had not been determined, it seemed likely that the development of current issues linking offered an opportunity to begin archiving the electronic versions of current issues in addition to the hard-copy versions. This new development, if implemented, would impose significant additional costs but would contribute to the transition towards electronic-only journals.[54]

---

[51] There were good strategic reasons to link with current issues, as well. Some observers have suggested that without somehow incorporating current issues, JSTOR would be perceived as less useful. The moving wall was perhaps not enough. This would be the case to an even greater extent as current issues were being published online. Once online, current issues should not, it was thought, be retrieved from a different interface from the archive. And as multiple years of the journal accumulated at the current issues' website, JSTOR would lose some of its uniqueness. Dale Flecker, interview with the author, April 2, 2002.

[52] Packet for the JSTOR board of trustees meeting of February 11, 2000.

[53] Heidi McGregor, interview with the author, April 9, 2002.

[54] A number of libraries, including that of the University of Chicago, were "ahead" of the community in moving away from hard-copy journals. In the sciences, the electronic journal was often "perfect"—including color graphics and earlier availability. Even when obtaining the paper and electronic together would cost only $10 more, Chicago often opted to spend $1,000 for the electronic alone. Frank Conaway noted the simple reasoning: "We

CONSULTING

In 1998 and 1999, JSTOR began to consider the idea of franchising or consulting services as an outlet for pressure to grow (see chapter 11). In 2000 and 2001, amid all of the very real growth we have observed in this chapter, JSTOR continued to consider, and began to act on, the creation of such a service. But the vision of consulting as near to, but just outside of, JSTOR's core mission prevented an early and enthusiastic launch.

In early 2000, in response to the interest of the board, Guthrie considered the demand for, and advantages of, a consulting group. In February, he presented some plans to the trustees, in which he was clear about one key proviso: "We are not prepared to draw from either the capital or human resources supporting our core mission to manage this initiative." Self-sustainability could not be threatened. With such a strong statement about where consulting fit into JSTOR's priorities, Guthrie noted that a foundation might be interested in funding the startup capital. He imagined a small group of dedicated staff that could assist ten to fifteen other projects per year, or one per month, charging approximately $75,000 for each project.[55] The board was sufficiently enthusiastic that it requested a formal recommendation at its next meeting.[56]

At this point, planning accelerated. Guthrie developed a set of proposals for the enterprise, which on balance he strongly endorsed. Most importantly, he noted that at their last meeting, the trustees had agreed that consulting services constituted a "direct extension of our mission . . . so long as it does not distract staff from their primary responsibility or drain resources from our mission." He outlined some of the specific projects and organizations that JSTOR could assist. He showed how the enterprise could support itself without foundation funding, but he noted that there would be risk to this approach, since any shortfalls would have to be covered by JSTOR.[57]

He also mentioned that there was a likelihood of being able to secure some foundation funding (from one of its existing anonymous supporters) that would reduce the risk substantially, and the trustees as a group were adamant that such funding was a prerequisite. There was

---

don't want to be bothered with [print]—don't want to be bothered with binding it, processing it, checking it in, and so forth." Interview with the author, March 22, 2002. The development of appropriate archiving mechanisms would, if implemented successfully by JSTOR or others, play a key role in discontinuing hard-copies.

[55] Packet for the JSTOR board of trustees meeting of February 11, 2000.

[56] Minutes of the JSTOR board of trustees meeting of February 11, 2000.

[57] Packet for the JSTOR board of trustees meeting of May 17, 2000.

some discussion of whether a consulting enterprise would end up fostering competition with JSTOR for the journals it most wanted, but they concluded that JSTOR's system-wide perspective was exactly what had led it to consider such an enterprise to begin with. The conclusion at this meeting was typical of all we have seen so far: "While voicing its support, the board unanimously urged caution, advising that we take care not to draw resources from the pursuit of our core mission. . . . The activities in which we engage on this front must support our mission."[58]

Guthrie and Bowen continued to negotiate with the anonymous foundation on the form of a grant. The details were complicated and took some time to arrange, and JSTOR did not receive the first portion of the award until early March 2001.[59] The consulting initiative was thus only really tentatively established in 2001.

PRESSURES FOR COLLECTIONS GROWTH

Amid the movement in new directions, including two kinds of linking, archiving online editions, and consulting, one thing that could not be doubted was the continuing din of demands for more journals. These pressures came from some, but not all, librarians, researchers, and publishers. Each had a different genesis, but it was clear that a significant proportion of the community was ready for the large-scale digitization of journals. The question was what role JSTOR would play. Although the marketplace was glutted with unwanted online information, the slow growth that seemed not undesirable for JSTOR in 1998 and early 1999 meant that participants' wants in 2001 were not being satisfied.

Librarians and researchers appreciated the value of JSTOR's much-improved access to the backfiles and they wanted more. Librarians were growing increasingly concerned that, in the transition to online resources, information available only in hard-copy form was becoming increasingly marginalized. Although JSTOR offered the "seductive" feature of fulltext, according to Frank Conaway of the University of Chicago, there were thousands of journals relevant for American history, very few of which were available through JSTOR. Conaway looked forward to a day when "JSTOR has, if this ever should occur, instead of a few hundred [journals], a few thousand."[60] Describing JSTOR as

---

[58] Minutes of the JSTOR board of trustees meeting of May 17, 2000.

[59] Packets for the JSTOR board of trustees meetings of October 4, 2000, February 7, 2001, and June 20, 2001.

[60] Frank Conaway, interview with the author, March 22, 2002.

"tiny" in its scope, Dale Flecker of Harvard observed that "Harvard takes 4000 electronic journals and 100,000 journals in paper right now, and so 200 is a small, small number." Although in general the more the better, he would stop counting the number of journals as a shortcoming "were it in the thousands instead of the hundreds."[61]

While the major research libraries wanted both more breadth and depth, the smaller participants tended to favor breadth. They wanted JSTOR to broaden its scope to additional disciplines, although there were also some calls for additional depth in existing disciplines.[62] The JSTOR Board tried to address both of these issues by planning new discipline-specific collections as well as Arts & Sciences II.

Although all five collections that had been released were successful, estimating demand for future collections was tricky. Even when librarians expressed unbridled enthusiasm, it was never possible to be certain that their ardent calls for expansion could be translated into a regular stream of annual payments. Would librarian enthusiasm translate into a willingness to pay?

When questioned, librarians expressed a degree of commitment toward an expanded JSTOR. Conaway of Chicago stated unequivocally that "cost is not an issue. If the product were increased ten-fold [and prices commensurately], I think it would still be a bargain." Of course, the University of Chicago had one of the most important research libraries in the world. If Chicago had been unwilling to license additional journals at additional cost, no school would have done so. And yet librarians at smaller universities and colleges were also enthusiastic about paying for an expanded JSTOR.[63] These limited anecdotes, while indicative of some measure of demand, would not have been sufficient for business planning.

Of course, the enthusiasm of librarians would be relatively worthless without the complementary enthusiasm of publishers, and among the latter there was significant variation. In early 2000, a number of significant not-for-profit publishers were less than enthusiastic about contributing additional journals to JSTOR. Even one of the most significant journal publishers in the arts and sciences had reservations. And yet

---

[61]Dale Flecker, interview with the author, April 2, 2002.

[62]Michael LaCroix, interview with the author, May 3, 2002.

[63]Asked how his library could continue to participate in further collections, the librarian of Creighton University says, "We believe in JSTOR. We find it valuable." Michael LaCroix, interview with the author, May 3, 2002.

the publishers that contributed the greatest numbers of journals—for example, Blackwell's and Johns Hopkins—were at least somewhat frustrated that more of their titles could not be included. These latter presses were not digitizing their backfiles, and so were eager for JSTOR to include an ever greater share of their titles.[64]

Economically speaking, then, there was some demand for an expanded JSTOR and some amount of supply of the necessary "raw materials." But the pressures to grow by an order of magnitude or more would have had serious consequences that deserve attention. These consequences allow us to speculate about the value of JSTOR's curatorial function.

A number of librarians believe that after the core journals in each discipline are identified—the group that JSTOR had targeted up to this point—the value of carefully curating the next groups of titles in those disciplines is significantly lower.[65] When adding journals in a given discipline, then, JSTOR staff could have applied fairly mechanical criteria—more than X institutional subscriptions and more than Y years of backfiles—and done an effective job identifying the next 3,000 most important journals to digitize. In addition, they could have attempted to "vacuum" up all of the relevant journals published by scholarly societies and university presses in the United States. Hesitant publishers would not be courted at any length; only those who were eager would have been included. This type of approach, which seems to follow naturally from the calls for order-of-magnitude growth, would have the added benefit of being both cheaper and faster than hand-crafted curation.

It seems fairly clear that if JSTOR and its participants were purely focused on saving space, such an uncurated growth strategy would have been appropriate. And yet, as we also saw in chapter 2, there was a conviction that ensuring the inclusion of the most important titles was critical. Moreover, it is exceptionally difficult to market collections of randomly agglomerated scholarly materials. JSTOR did not in this period pursue radical approaches to collections growth.

---

[64] In the competitive world of publishing journals on behalf of sponsors, houses like Blackwell's would be at a competitive advantage if their services included backfiles digitization. Thus, if JSTOR could ever reach a blanket agreement with a publisher for all of its titles, and any yet to come, the publishers might be glad not to take on the expense themselves. But JSTOR's curatorial policies meant that it was not possible to sign such a blanket agreement involving hundreds or thousands of titles.

[65] Dale Flecker, interview with the author, April 2, 2002.

SUMMATION

During the two years covered in this chapter, JSTOR was transformed from a provider of a small, if important, resource, to a major provider of digital scholarly materials. In both perception and goals, it was a growing force, with hundreds of new participants and journals; with linkages to numerous other resources; with a more mature relationship with publishers. At the same time, as an escape valve for the pressures to grow, JSTOR was beginning to move in the other direction, thinking about how to benefit the community, via consulting services or other growth, beyond what it could do simply as an archive of journals. It remains too early to know whether the latter direction will in the end become as important a contribution as JSTOR's archived journals.

A Self-Sustaining Organization

INTERNATIONAL AND U.S. LIBRARIES continued to participate, while many libraries elected to take new collections as they were introduced. And the pressures to grow continued unabated. This chapter, which has four distinct components, considers JSTOR's accomplishments and its future. First, it reflects on the context within which JSTOR matured, giving some indication of JSTOR's unique place in the broader information industry. Second, it explores definitions of archival self-sustainability and then examines revenues and expenses to see if JSTOR has achieved self-sustainability. Third, it considers some of the broader economic and organizational ramifications of JSTOR as an archive. Finally, it evaluates JSTOR against its original mission of space-saving, which is an important component of its ability to grow further. As a coherent whole, this chapter poses the questions of whether JSTOR's model has succeeded and if it is poised for further growth.

THE LARGER CONTEXT

In the period covered by this study, the Internet became a major social and economic force in American life. In parallel, and partially as a result, an important shift occurred (and is at the time of this writing still underway) in the scholarly communications "industry." We have seen evidence of this interspersed throughout JSTOR's history, but it is useful to consider how this might affect definitions of success and self-sustainability and how, for an entity doing business with academic customers, this period was unusual.

As a result of the lower costs of distribution and the new methods of accessing information that the Internet permitted, numerous academic resources moved to the web during the late 1990s: from high-energy physics datasets to rare books and even papyri. It was in response to these many new possibilities that the larger research libraries increased the share of their materials budgets devoted to electronic resources to nearly 13 percent by 2000 (from 5 percent in 1995). The shift online also permitted new business models and pricing structures that allowed both smaller and poorer libraries to increase vastly their offerings, at relatively modest prices.

Electronic resources markedly improved research efficiency, and, in at least some disciplines, effectiveness. Where their libraries licensed them, students and scholars had desktop access to current issues of journals, recent editions of virtually all reference works, and an increasing selection of monographs. All of this information was fully searchable with a few keystrokes, at all hours of the day and night, lessening the need for afternoon and evening research trips to the campus library. Researchers were able to identify sources that could never before have been located.

In chapter 14, the complementary concern was raised: the view emerging among undergraduates (and perhaps even among some scholars) that if a resource were not online, it was not worth consulting. This point of view was problematic for two reasons. First, with the exception of JSTOR and a few other resources, online information was heavily biased toward more recent publications. Second, online collections were rarely "complete" in any sense, bundled not by discipline but by publisher. All of the major commercial science publishers released current issues online, but through proprietary interfaces. Major university presses such as Chicago and Johns Hopkins did so, as well. Abstracting and indexing services like EBSCO and ProQuest included article fulltext through their own proprietary systems. A key question had become, through which interface would a given journal be found? The answer to this question was both confusing and mutable, so new resources like jake would in time grow up to answer it, and many began to view linking as not only desirable, but indeed almost mandatory.[1] (The proprietary publisher interfaces had characteristics of what would come to be called the "dark web," that portion of the Internet that was nearly invisible.) With current issues of journals on multiple publisher-bundled websites that were largely agnostic to discipline, searching in a way that was useful for scholarship required a great deal of effort.[2] JSTOR was different from almost all online publishing in that it focused on the retrospective and cut across publishers to create curated collections.

The shift online affected nonacademic information, too. In that domain, a smaller number of firms were able to create unusually broad resources ("portals"), obviating some of the problems faced by academia. Accompanying this, however, was the bubble economy, which briefly threatened to push the value of information asymptotically toward infinity.

As the stock market boomed in the late 1990s, academia found itself awash in a sea of donations, with endowments performing so well that

---

[1] See *http://jake.med.yale.edu/*.

[2] As a result, developments like the Open Archives Initiative (OAI) tried to provide a common way to link together such resources, though it is unclear how many commercial providers will in the end be willing to adopt it.

spendable income from them grew at staggering rates. As a general rule, libraries had more money for resources; provosts had enough to fund library expansions. Although this meant that libraries had enough funds with which to participate in JSTOR, it also meant that they were not nearly so interested as they would otherwise have been in space-savings. Rather, JSTOR was lauded largely for the access it provided. For higher education, this was all to the good, at least in the short run.

But the economy also threatened to commodify higher education itself, as administrators and scholars at some universities seemed ready to discard values built over the centuries to cash in on the "new economy." For-profit subsidiaries were created to provide distance education.[3] Faculty fought for control of their intellectual property. Measures of both opportunity and fear could be found on campuses.

Well-capitalized digital library startups, such as Questia and Net-Library, were established, in part to take advantage of the distance education that seemed poised to replace residential education. But they failed as for-profits in part because they were incautious in their expectations of short-term demand for a new resource. In just these two startups, venture capitalists invested (and seem largely to have lost) approximately $200 million.

These examples were part of a broader trend to commercialize non-profit segments of academia. This trend has had standout successes, most prominently the University of Phoenix. But it also led to a dynamic that in retrospect seems bizarre. JSTOR itself received a number of inquiries about purchasing its database at a substantial "profit" over the cost of creating it.[4] This offer was spurned as being entirely incompatible with mission.

Amid the waves of enthusiasts, there were voices of caution. Bowen delivered an important speech at Oxford on the dangers that were accompanying the commercialization of learning and scholarship.[5] And as the bubble burst, new realities set in. When NetLibrary filed for bankruptcy, OCLC—a nonprofit—purchased its e-book assets to ensure their preservation.[6] OCLC's chance of success cannot be known at the time

---

[3] For a retrospective focusing on the efforts of Columbia and NYU, see Katie Hafner, "Lessons Learned at Dot-Com U.," *New York Times*, May 2, 2002, G1. For analysis of developments on both sides of the Atlantic, see Donald MacLeod, "Economic downturn is not the only problem facing e-learning programmes," *Guardian* (London), April 2, 2002, 20.

[4] *Building and Sustaining Digital Collections: Models for Libraries and Museums* (Washington, DC: Council on Library and Information Resources, 2001), 5.

[5] William G. Bowen, "At a Slight Angle to the Universe: The University in a Digitized, Commercialized Age," The Romanes Lecture for 2000, delivered before the University of Oxford on October 17, 2000 (Princeton University Press, 2001).

[6] Jeffrey R. Young, "Judge Approves Sale of netLibrary's E-Books to Nonprofit Library Group," *Chronicle of Higher Education* 48, no. 20 (January 25, 2002), A31.

of this writing, but it is clear that, at least in the short term, commercial players failed in the academic market for electronic books.[7]

It is against this backdrop of omnivorous digitization, some of which was invaluable and some just omnivorous, that JSTOR's maturation must be seen. We saw in chapter 14 that library expectations for JSTOR's eventual size had increased substantially. While it did not digitize as many journals nearly as rapidly as some would have liked, JSTOR achieved other ends. Given the scarce resources it believed to characterize the budgets of academic libraries, it carefully curated collections without regard to publishers, so that the most useful titles would be included whenever possible. It also successfully ignored the "build now—sell later" pathology that infected even nonprofit academia. JSTOR not only reached self-sustainability while expanding at a moderate rate, but it also set aside reserves for the future.

A SELF-SUSTAINING ORGANIZATION

When Guthrie and the board crafted the business plan, they had no foreknowledge of the financial health that lay ahead for American academe. The business plan was for a resource designed to eke out savings in capital costs. When they projected costs and revenues for three years, through the close of 1999, they did not anticipate operational self-sustainability. Rather, the Strategic and Operating Plan envisioned a deficit of $1 million when scanning expenses and DDF revenues were excluded. It was known that other revenue sources—international participation and new collections are two that come to mind—would have to be developed to reach true self-sustainability. Consequently, there will be no attempt here to evaluate the success of the Strategic and Operating Plan, which was soon superseded. Instead, we will consider the goal of self-sufficiency, evaluating it as a criterion of success and JSTOR's drive to achieve it.

Archiving: The Definition of Sustainability

Initially, JSTOR planned for a self-sustainability that would, even if it ceased to add new journals or collections, allow it to meet its ongoing

---

[7] The questions of why commercial players were not successful, how NetLibrary gave way to OCLC, and whether a nonprofit can succeed where a commercial firm did not, deserve careful study. They may help to better explain the structure of the market for scholarly communications.

responsibilities to libraries into the indefinite future. To some, this would have seemed ambitious. Other organizations maintained that by depositing their data with a third party, they met their responsibilities to ensure the existence of an archive. This was in essence what took place when NetLibrary's assets were transferred to OCLC, but it was not what JSTOR planned for itself.

JSTOR's definition of archiving had for years been different in a number of ways. First, it included updating the archive to take account of the moving wall. As a retrospective resource, it had long recognized that it would have to add journal issues prospectively. The moving wall was a real commitment to both publishers and libraries; it meant that "preserving" the archive involved an ongoing "building" task. No other digital resource has ever made such an ambitious archiving commitment.

Second, it went beyond preserving the data itself. In the paper-based world, archiving and access are similar services—to archive a journal, for example, a library need only not throw it away; to provide access to that journal, a library need only allow readers to see it. Some observers began to suggest that, in the digital environment, archiving could be ensured by depositing essentially inaccessible copies, thus bifurcating the responsibilities of access and archiving. But from an early point in JSTOR's planning, Guthrie came to believe that, while the two features were conceptually separable, they could not be successfully decoupled. That is to say, he believed that in an era when readers expected their resources to be available online, a resource that was not online—for instance, an archive that was not accessible—was for all purposes useless. Without an effective online presence, a digital archive would be useless for most all users and, from a practical standpoint, nonexistent.

As a result, keeping the data preserved was, in JSTOR's vision, only a small part of "archiving," since it also must keep the archive updated and accessible. Beyond ongoing production costs, there was what JSTOR Director of Finance and Administration Gerard Aurigemma defines as "support and services to users."[8] This was a much more ambitious, and expensive, long-term promise than ensuring data preservation, or even just guaranteeing to pass the data off to a third party in the event of failure. And "support and services" was a moving target—as JSTOR's financial base became more secure, its users' calls for various services, such as reference linking, current issues linking, and so forth, became more pressing.

If the archiving promise were not reflected in financial planning, it would be meaningless, and in JSTOR's case this promise was at the core

---

[8] Gerard Aurigemma, interview with the author, October 18, 2001.

of its projections. JSTOR planned that so long as demand continued, it would have the resources, in the form of AAF payments, to deliver its collections online. This task included annual production work due to the moving wall, user services and technologists to keep the database accessible online, and minimal general administration. As new collections brought new sources of AAFs, user needs for new types of services could be addressed. In this way, the presence of new collections brought a shift in the definition of self-sustainability, since it would be difficult, if it ever became necessary, to pull back from many of the new features that had been made available.

JSTOR planned furthermore that, even if demand were to drop so precipitously that AAF revenue nearly disappeared, it would have the resources to maintain a "dark," offline archive. Dark archives have generally been viewed with disdain, since, as public goods, it is almost impossible to develop revenue streams to support them. An endowment might therefore overcome this problem, possibly functioning as a "dowry" to encourage another organization to take over JSTOR's stewardship responsibilities. In either case, the endowment is intended to serve as a fail-safe method to preserve the archive. While it is probably impossible to estimate with any great accuracy the resources required for this purpose, JSTOR has planned for an endowment that would generate on the order of $1 million in annual spendable income. Until such time as this income is required for archival purposes, it can be used to lower, in effect, the fees to libraries. This in turn should help to forestall the need to fund a dark-only archive. But in such an event, JSTOR will have what is essentially insurance, that, by funding the necessary infrastructure, migration, and staff, the "dark" archive never expires. By design, even if every library participant were to cancel its JSTOR access, the collections would not be lost. JSTOR was one of the few scholarly resources to have made such plans.[9]

In sum, to "archive" was first a question of business planning, to ensure the financial resources necessary to maintain the collections prospectively in the presence of demand for them.[10] Beyond the business-model, of course, throughout the history we have seen attention to archiv-

---

[9] In the Strategic and Operating Plan, Guthrie allotted approximately $800,000 to these costs.

[10] Guthrie's broad definition of archiving noted that it meant "to preserve and provide access to a collection of journal literature over time, without regard for how frequently these materials are being read or used," but not necessarily in the absence of *demand*. Kevin Guthrie, "Challenges and Opportunities Presented by Archiving in the Electronic Era," *portal: Libraries and the Academy* 1, no. 2 (2001): 121–28.

ing.[11] But the necessary archiving work was predicated on having the resources to pay for it.

Probably no other academic resource provider has developed a business model that seeks to guarantee its own ability to preserve its database even if demand disappears. Certainly none have sought to define archiving as a prospective formulation that includes an ongoing building commitment. In JSTOR's model, access pays for archiving; the link between the two is essential. Thus every improvement in access—linking, current issues, and so forth—contributes toward the viability of the prospective and retrospective archive.

JSTOR's business-model obsession with archiving has proved to be a significant draw for librarians, who have viewed JSTOR as far more a part of the academic community than the typical library vendor. And yet the very fact that archiving and access are so intertwined impedes our ability to determine quantitatively whether JSTOR is self-sustainable. It is certainly self-sustainable if that means providing the type of access that it did in 1997. First, we shall consider costs, which have increased since then as ambitions have grown. Then, we shall in turn examine the build-up of the endowment and the extent of AAF revenue, which represent the revenue side of the ledger.

Costs

The biggest surprise of Guthrie's initial Strategic and Operating Plan is how closely it resembled the actual expense side of the ledger. Expenses in 1997 and 1998 were within 15 percent of plans, with the principal variance occurring in production costs.[12] Guthrie developed a realistic financial plan that was rigorously followed—quite an achievement for a newborn organization with a novel approach. In 1999, JSTOR's expenses

[11] The license agreements with publishers and librarians were developed to include unusual termination agreements to ensure perpetual access. Consultations with outside experts had sought to identify standards for scanning images, and JSTOR continued to move the software and database infrastructure toward widely accepted standards. The entire archive was mirrored in a number of locations in politically stable countries on two continents (in addition to several offline locations). As necessary, migration would have the chance to follow so long as the resources were in place.

[12] The Andrews-Landis process redesign (see chapter 9) led to significantly increased costs for the Michigan production operation, but the most significant cause for the increase lay not with costs per page. Rather, JSTOR digitized one million pages more for Arts & Sciences I than it had originally planned, as journals proved to be larger than expected and it included more journals than originally anticipated. Consequently, the 1999 figure for Arts & Sciences I scanning proved to be about twice as high as the anticipated $600,000.

rose well beyond the expectations of the Strategic and Operating Plan, as it began to work on the General Science and Ecology & Botany Collections. What costs would remain if JSTOR were to cease adding new collections, going into "archive-only" mode?

Although, under Guthrie's leadership, JSTOR was generally conservative about spending money, there was never a hesitation to spend in order to improve quality or service to users. Even though the web reduced the number of user-services staff necessary—since there was a standard piece of software—increased ambitions have led to a substantially increased technology and user-services staff. The cost of this technology and interface development group can be viewed in part as variable— some retrenchment might be expected in this area if library demand fell. But so long as JSTOR actively markets new collections, and appeals to new libraries, it will be critical that it provide the most advanced features possible. This might entail, in addition to linking to JSTOR articles from outside of the database, linking within JSTOR, so that footnotes can lead directly to their sources and articles can link forward to where they are cited. Or it might entail prospective archiving of both hard-copy and online editions, a duplicative proposition. Identifying which part of these activities would be optional, and which mandatory, may be somewhat subjective, and in the end the choice would effectively be made by library-participant demand.

In every year, JSTOR's recurring costs increased over the previous year. This was due mostly to raised expectations, rather than costs rising in a "steady-state" environment. While steady-state recurring costs were probably as low as $3 million, it is clear that this sum would not fund many of the new initiatives that JSTOR undertook. Under increased expectations, in 2001 JSTOR's recurring costs may have been as high as $7 million, and they would have been expected to grow in the future, if new collections were added and new libraries elected to participate. The upshot is that recurring costs in 2001 were more than $3 million and less than $7 million, but a more refined breakdown is purely subjective.

Annual Access Revenues

AAF revenues grew in every year, with new participants and new collections. Table 15.1 shows AAF revenues from 2001. The annualized 2001 revenues were themselves about $6 million, since late-year participation, including in the two new collections, led to prorated fees. AAF revenues should continue to grow in a way that benefits the bottom line, since each additional collection-participant contributes to the fixed costs of the operation.

TABLE 15.1
Recurring Revenues by Collection

Collection	2001–Actual
Arts & Sciences I	$2,880,000
General Sciences	$1,310,000
Ecology of Botany	$730,000
Arts & Sciences II	—
Business	—
Total	$4,920,000

The Endowment

By the terms of the Strategic and Operating Plan, by the close of 1999 JSTOR had hoped to accumulate a cumulative surplus of approximately $20 million from the DDFs. Instead, at that time, its cash balance was only $4 million. Why so little? JSTOR overestimated the speed with which it could sign libraries to participate and reduced prices for participants. These challenges notwithstanding, JSTOR nevertheless has built an endowment.

During the pricing readjustment of mid-1998, many libraries were reclassified to smaller (that is, less expensive) sizes, while the one-time fees were reduced for several of the pricing classes. Most important, however, has been the length of time before libraries participated. Because libraries did not participate as rapidly as had been expected between mid-1997 and mid-1999, JSTOR generated a smaller amount of AAF revenue than it had anticipated. In the absence of this AAF revenue, one-time revenues could not be set aside for the endowment but rather were used to pay for a greater share of ongoing operations than originally intended.

Because of the creation of several additional collections, and the licensing of all of its collections abroad, JSTOR was able to build its surplus fund nearly to the level Guthrie had initially planned. By the close of 2001, it contained approximately $16 million, and it continued to grow as new collection-participants contributed additional ACF revenues. The fund itself generated $700,000 in income in 2001. Had the initial business plan proven accurate in all regards, JSTOR could have created a larger endowment fund today, closer to the $26 million of one-time revenues it accumulated. A larger endowment would have meant greater independence from the pressures of the market, allowing JSTOR to do what it wished, even if demand were to decrease. But the pressure to provide more services to more libraries brings what economists might consider to be a social good: valuable information reaches more scholars and students.

The Balance

JSTOR's decision to take on the mission of archiving has meant that it has worked hard over several years to guarantee, financially, its ability to continue long-term operations. Of course achieving balance in one year does not guarantee the future. New collections that do not attract grant funding—such as Business—will prove to be significant risks if they fail to attract sufficient participants. And no one can be certain of the expenses of a data migration in the future.

Fundamentally, the cycle of increasing revenues yielding increasing expectations that leads to additional library participation and thereby pays for archiving, complicates the analysis. If access and archiving are linked, as the business plan insists, then investing in access will lead to long-term preservation. By 2001, the success of this strategy was evident. Recurring costs approximated $3 million in the steady state, and perhaps $7 million under increased expectations. Recurring AAF revenues, on an annualized basis, approximated $6 million. The endowment contributed about $700,000. In other words, JSTOR's budgets reached a point at which virtually no retrenchment would be necessary if it were to cease adding new collections. Financially, the archive seemed secure so long as library demand did not decline. The business plan's primary goal was, at least in the most recent year, achieved.

THE RAMIFICATIONS OF ARCHIVING

But JSTOR's planning may have unitentionally made a contribution even more important than achieving self-sustainability. In the hard-copy world, there appears to have been a significant market failure in the apportionment of responsibility for archiving. It would be a brilliant outcome of the transition to online resources if this market failure were repaired. Experience from JSTOR suggests that, under the appropriate circumstances, this may be possible.

Generally speaking, archiving of printed materials was a responsibility assumed by only the wealthiest libraries. In the United States, there were perhaps two hundred libraries that counted archiving as a core aspect of their mission. These libraries acquired not only those materials that were valuable in the present, but also those that they foresaw being valuable in the future. Because of this long view, they invested substantially in preserving their collections.[13]

Beyond this group, interest in, or even understanding of, archiving was uneven at best. Of course non-archiving "working" libraries felt obligations for specialized collections that they held uniquely, but, as a rule, the overwhelming majority of academic, public, and corporate libraries did not contribute, financially or otherwise, toward the perpetual storage and preservation of humanity's cultural and intellectual heritage. Rather, these libraries were "free-riders" in a system in which a public good—archiving—was supported by only a small number of the beneficiaries. That is, the beneficiaries of archiving extended far beyond those that paid for it. For example, a researcher at the library of a small Baccalaureate II college can usually gain access to the collections of an archiving research library via interlibrary loan (ILL); yet he or she will pay at most the direct cost of the loan and none of the costs of archiving. Since someone else was willing to pay for archiving, there was no reason (or organized way) for the vast majority of libraries to direct resources for that purpose themselves. The working libraries were free-riders, taking the benefits that were available but paying none of the costs.

As large multilibrary catalogs like those of OCLC and RLG made interlibrary loans far easier, the problem grew in the 1970s and thereafter.[14] Libraries no longer faced the dilemma that if they did not acquire an item, it would not be available to their readers. Rather, they undertook cost-benefit analysis to see what portion of their collections they should "store remotely," by not purchasing and then archiving but merely borrowing on demand. Since there was no mechanism by which the working libraries could (or had to) contribute to the ongoing cost that continued to face the largest archiving libraries, the savings that

---

[13] One of the features that marks a research library, according to one author, is that "the average frequency of use per title may be as low as one use in fifty years or more." Herman H. Fussler, *Research Libraries and Technology* (Chicago: University of Chicago Press, 1973), 23.

[14] Data indicate that 2.1 million lending requests in 1969–1970 increased to 21 million requests by 1981 and 28 million in 1993, as OCLC and RLIN enabled a great deal more lending, however the compatibility of these figures is unclear. Vernon E. Palmour, Edward C. Bryant, Nancy W. Caldwell, and Lucy M. Gray (compilers), *A Study of the Characteristics, Costs, and Magnitude of Interlibrary Loans in Academic Libraries* (Washington, DC: Association of Research Libraries, 1972); Gillian Page, Robert Campbell, and Jack Meadows, *Journal publishing* (Cambridge: Cambridge University Press, 1997).

resulted were not shared system-wide.[15] While total system-wide expenses for archiving were reduced, the distribution of these costs almost certainly became more skewed.[16] Even in the cases where a group of libraries apportioned responsibility for collecting and then turned to one another for ILL, the effects were deleterious.[17]

In developing JSTOR's business plan, there had been some initial consideration of offering a "lease" option for those libraries that were uninterested in JSTOR's commitment to archiving (see chapter 8). Under such an approach, JSTOR would offer a hypothetical library annual access for $2,000, or access and archiving for $3,000. It is difficult to imagine almost any library agreeing to take the latter. It is certainly the case that very few of JSTOR's nearly 1,500 participants would have chosen to do so. And yet all of these participants contribute towards the archiving of the journals in JSTOR, because Bowen, Guthrie, and the other trustees decided not to offer the option of leasing the database (two-year colleges are, however, given the lease option). This is a critical feature of the library community that JSTOR has built—all four-year academic libraries that access it also contribute towards its archiving. In this regard, Guthrie has described JSTOR's work as selling access but delivering archiving. JSTOR's experience demonstrates that, while few libraries were willing to pay for archiving alone, they were willing to pay for access, collection-building, and space-savings.

Is it appropriate to link access with archiving? All of this suggests that by refusing to provide one without the other—a condition made

---

[15] Fussler notes that "some libraries believe that in some circumstances partial compensation should be paid to the owning library for the initial costs of acquisition and processing of the desired material, especially in those cases when the materials are rare, costly, or unusual." Fussler, *Research Libraries and Technology*, 41.

[16] One prominent librarian, Graham R. Hill, has noted that "the proposition that there is a symbiotic relationship between the two activities of developing research collections and using them as resources held in common needs careful probing. . . . The idea of sharing implies not only the notion of reciprocal benefit, but also the prerequisite that each institution doing the sharing has something worth sharing." "Funding, Buying, and Sharing: Natural Sequence or Unnatural Acts," in Association for Research Libraries, *Minutes of the Meetings: Collections: Their Development, Management, and Sharing*, 76. In that same volume, University of Chicago Librarian Martin D. Runkle noted that "no library should be in the position of sharing its collections without a fair return. . . . Altruism has no place in the equation" (128). Runkle, however, noted his belief that the development of the OCLC catalog actually mitigated the problem for research libraries, since other libraries had exposed their collections for potential ILL.

[17] In such a case, the cancellations would have contributed in the long term to increased prices for books and journals for those that retained broad commitments to collecting and archiving.

impossible for hard copies by the existence of ILL—it can be possible for all beneficiaries to pay for both services. Consequently, the JSTOR model may be of significant relevance to any broader debate on electronic archiving. Bundling forms of access with archiving offers one plausible solution to lessening the free-rider problem, making the archiving system more fair and, in the long run, more effective for all.

SPACE-SAVING AND THE DILEMMA OF FURTHER GROWTH

Now, if every participant pays for archiving, how do they afford to do so? JSTOR's twofold mandate has been to allow libraries to save costs even while providing journals in ways that improve access. If libraries save by participating in JSTOR—that is, if participation costs them less than the alternative—then they should, out of self-interest, participate. And for a library that held the hard-copies of the journals from the five collections, space valued at $300,000 could be saved.[18] JSTOR's dilemma has been that library demand for its collections seems to derive principally from access rather than space-saving, even at the many libraries that could benefit from both. Further expansion of JSTOR's collections will be most sensible if librarians perceive that real costs are saved.

From the earliest collections-development decisions, the JSTOR project was on a dual path. In originally identifying those journals that had the greatest scholarly value, rather than those with the most linear feet of backfiles, Mellon selected many of the most important journals in their disciplines for the JSTOR project. These were, in turn, the paper backfiles that librarians were least likely to move off-campus or deaccession. Following its independence, JSTOR continued with a more refined version of essentially the same policy. As a result of having this lineup of initial collections, however, librarians have tended to view JSTOR more as an access tool to important journal backfiles than as a space-saver for titles of less interest.

---

[18]At the end of 2001, JSTOR's collections included approximately nine million pages, or on the order of twelve thousand volumes. Calculate ten volumes per square foot and $250 in construction costs per square foot, according to Jay Lucker.

Beyond space-savings, there are real savings to be found in operating costs, according to Paul Gherman of Vanderbilt University. In 1996, that university reshelved 2,700 volumes of JSTOR titles, which he estimated would save $2,700 in student wages, a significant proportion of the JSTOR annual fee. "Can the Electronic Revolution Save Us Money?" *Moveable Type: The Newsletter of the Mark O. Hatfield Library* 5, no. 1 (Fall 1997): 8.

In addition, saving space turned out to be relatively less appealing than JSTOR (and, earlier, Mellon) had at one point believed it to be. First, the roughly 1,200 square feet occupied by JSTOR's collections are relatively insignificant compared with the size of most library expansions. Consequently, while participating in JSTOR might allow many libraries to delay or scale down their expansion projects, the amount would have been a relatively small percentage.[19] Of course, this is a matter of scale, rather than concept, and as more journal backfiles are digitized by JSTOR and others, the scale will become less of a barrier. As more books, slides, and other scholarly materials are digitized, the possibility for space-saving will increase even more dramatically. But in the short-term there has been no way to capitalize on JSTOR's potential savings.[20]

Another important factor at work here is budgeting. Academic libraries have never really had to pay for the capital costs of constructing, and keeping in good repair, a library building.[21] These costs are almost always paid from a central administrative budget. Even if these costs were reduced or eliminated, no library funds would be saved. Especially at state schools, these costs may not be fungible. Asking libraries to spend in order to save, when the spending came from their budgets but the savings did not accrue there, was unrealistic. This was Gilbert Whitaker's concern in 1995 when presented with Bowen's initial thoughts on a business model. Of course, a provost and a library could develop an internal system to recognize that the library's expense brought savings to the larger institution. The provost might pay the JSTOR fees directly or alternatively might "repay" the library with any identifiable savings down the line. But such arrangements have not often come to fruition.

---

[19] And there was a significant disincentive to removing the volumes when any space remained available. The rankings of American research libraries—extremely important for many libraries in making the case that they deserved additional funding—counted the total number of physical volumes as a key factor. Thus, even though JSTOR brought the equivalent of tens of thousands of physical volumes, often in fact adding to library collections, those libraries competing in the rankings might well have chosen to retain the physical volumes.

[20] Moreover, there are other sources of savings that accompany JSTOR, which may help in changing perceptions. Many libraries ceased binding new volumes of JSTOR journals, which saved some libraries nearly the cost of their AAFs. And if current issues become available exclusively online and no longer in hard-copy—a shift seen by many as inevitable—system-wide savings could be expected to be substantial, not least in changing the nature of JSTOR's ongoing production work.

[21] See, for example, the discussion of space costs being ignored at pages 138–41 of Brian L. Hawkins, "The Unsustainability of the Traditional Library and the Threat to Higher Education," in Brian L. Hawkins and Patricia Battin, eds., *The Mirage of Continuity: Reconfiguring Academic Information for the 21st Century* (Washington, DC: Council on Library and Information Resources, 1998).

Only if institutional accounting allows the benefits and the costs to be shared could JSTOR have an adequate opportunity to be valued for its cost-saving potential. In other words, JSTOR is perceived by some to be an access resource because there is no easy way to recognize and reward a space-saving resource.

Whereas placing responsibility for archiving involves strategic thinking at the institutional level, it is easy for libraries to buy into access. Luckily for JSTOR, in recognition of the value of all sorts of electronic resources, librarians reallocated their materials budgets.[22] Most of their new electronic resources offered little opportunity for savings but significantly improved access. Participating in JSTOR for access alone was therefore not unusual.

It is a related, but altogether rhetorical, question whether JSTOR, built without access features but only to save space, would have been of interest to libraries. A JSTOR distributed on CD-ROM, containing page images only and no searchable fulltext, and without in-linking, might well have been such a resource.[23] But the desire to enhance access wherever possible was precisely what led Mellon to develop its JSTOR project not for CD-ROM distribution but for the Internet and with searchable fulltext included; it is precisely what led JSTOR itself to develop in-linking. Microfilm is extremely relevant in this regard. Offering potential savings of space with unimproved, if not impeded, access, microfilm was rarely used by librarians to save space.[24] JSTOR, as a resource that not only could save costs but also provide improved access, had more than one source of value. It was as a result of a number of key decisions, many made when JSTOR was a Mellon-Michigan project and others since, that the database was positioned for this exigency.

The upshot is that, between the great demand for access to these journals and the problems with space-saving, most participants selected JSTOR principally for collection building and access.[25] While both access and space-saving are components of the algorithm of many libraries'

---

[22] Guthrie recognized the importance of JSTOR's access value in "Archiving in the Digital Age: There's a Will, but Is There a Way?" *EDUCAUSE Review* 36, no. 6 (November/December 2001), 56–65.

[23] Librarians themselves are not unanimous in what access features they value. For example, Bill Potter of the University of Georgia is highly enthusiastic about fulltext searching, while Dale Flecker of Harvard is not certain that this feature is cost-effective. Interviews with the author, April 26, 2002 and April 2, 2002, respectively.

[24] And when they did, disasters at times ensued. See Nicholson Baker, *Double Fold: Libraries and the Assault on Paper* (New York: Random House, 2001).

[25] Bruce Heterick, interview with the author, February 4, 2002; Carol MacAdam, interview with the author, March 13, 2002.

demand, independent research, although anecdotal, tends to confirm the preponderance of access.

But even if space-saving was only one of several sources of demand for JSTOR, the number of libraries that have made use of the space-saving option has clearly been growing. As of 2000 it was clear that the majority of participants had not done so.[26] JSTOR's own surveys indicate that 34 percent of 138 responding libraries have moved at least some JSTOR titles to remote storage, while 22 percent have discarded titles.[27] The small number of responding libraries indicates the possibility of response bias, with those responding probably more likely to have deaccessioned backfiles or moved them off-campus. In addition, some librarians would like to move titles off-campus or discard them altogether but feel compelled not to do so because of faculty resistance that should eventually decrease.[28] The upshot is that half or more of JSTOR's participants may already have realized some amount of space-saving due to participation.

Independent research in 2001 and 2002, although anecdotal, confirms that while space-saving is only one of several sources of demand, librarians are frequently making use of this feature, or plan to do so. Most librarians, when asked, assert that their libraries participate in JSTOR for access or collection building. And yet a surprisingly high number of them—but far from all—confirm that they have already realized space-savings from JSTOR, or will soon.

David Shi, the president of Furman University, reports that "the most attractive feature is the ability to search through backfiles of journal articles to retrieve full-image articles. As for saving on capital costs . . . , we have estimated that [Arts & Sciences I] would save us several hundred square feet in our new library wing, a modest space savings. However, because JSTOR is such a trusted organization, we believe we can remove the bound journals with a high level of confidence that digital access will be provided in perpetuity."[29]

When asked about the experiences of the Appalachian College Association (ACA) schools, Carson-Newman's outgoing library dean states that their interest in JSTOR was not principally for space-savings, but rather for collection building. Nevertheless, in some of the ACA libraries, including Carson-Newman's, JSTOR has unequivocally brought savings. "Put it this way, at Carson-Newman we pulled them all. Frankly

---

[26] Scott Carlson, "JSTOR's Journal-Archiving Service Makes Fans of Librarians and Scholars," *Chronicle of Higher Education*, July 27, 2001.

[27] *2000 Bound Volume Survey*; available online at *http://www.jstor.org/about/bvs2000.html*.

[28] Charles E. Phelps, interview with the author, April 22, 2002.

[29] David Shi, "Re: History of JSTOR," email to the author, April 23, 2002.

it made room for another computer lab. . . . So we went ahead and did away with them. . . . I think a lot of us have gotten rid of all or most of the JSTOR titles."[30]

Creighton University maintains a working collection, and so it provides access but does not maintain collections in perpetuity. Initially, it participated because of JSTOR's access features. Michael LaCroix, the director of the main campus library, recalls that, after first participating in 2000, when space became scarce in 2000, "we pulled every bound journal volume that was covered by JSTOR, we moved them out of the building." Not only did Creighton make use of the space-saving option, it reports that the access features of the JSTOR electronic versions make the hard-copies obsolete: "Since we've [participated in] JSTOR, we've not had a single request for them. So our goal . . . is to sell them or give them away."[31]

Frank Conaway of the University of Chicago was far less enthusiastic. He says that space-saving has "never been our justification for participating, or even a high interest on our part. . . . It's truly a marginal feature for most of us at this time. Especially because right now [JSTOR] only [has] about 300 titles anyway." But Conaway is nevertheless a strong supporter of JSTOR, because it helps to address "the obviously widespread desire for fulltext on your desktop . . . and we know there's a strong demand for that. We know faculty want it. We know students want it. Everyone wants it. I want it."[32]

Dale Flecker of Harvard reports that the libraries there have not deaccessioned JSTOR titles or moved them off campus, but this had to do with the decentralized nature of the library system there. Since each campus library pays for its own space in the off-campus depository library, the first to move JSTOR titles there would pay for their storage perpetually, while the other libraries might simply discard their own copies, creating another free-rider problem. Each library being unwilling to be "cheated" by the others, stasis ensues. Flecker predicts that a system to address these concerns will be enacted, allowing at least one copy of the journals to be moved off-campus for perpetual safeguarding. "Every little bit [of on-campus space freed] helps, so it's worth doing."[33]

Note that all of this anecdotal evidence that JSTOR is valued for access, and yet nevertheless allows space to be saved, does not in any way undermine JSTOR's long-term potential to offer significant cost savings

---

[30] Tony Krug, interview with the author, March 26, 2002.
[31] Michael Creighton, interview with the author, May 3, 2002.
[32] Frank Conaway, interview with the author, March 22, 2002.
[33] Dale Flecker, interview with the author, April 2, 2002.

as a component of archiving. If anything, it confirms that the decision to bundle the two was most appropriate.

Nevertheless, there are significant advantages to JSTOR if librarians and administrators perceive it as a potential space-saver, and it has therefore encouraged this perception. The most prominent effort has been to seek provostial recognition of its work. This has come in a number of forms, including Bowen's numerous conversations with provosts and presidents, and Guthrie's speech before provosts at the AAU. Heterick identifies this effort as one of the biggest library-relations challenges that JSTOR faces.[34] Although it is unclear that any definite action has resulted, there is a clear advantage to JSTOR in such outreach.

SUMMATION

These concerns come together in the question of how JSTOR should have responded to the pressures to grow. While JSTOR attracted a significant number of participants to its first five collections—focusing on core, important titles with generally lengthy backruns—a move to build an archive of thousands of journals would involve a number of compromises. Some of these were addressed in chapter 14, not least the likelihood that JSTOR's role would become less curatorial. A tenfold increase in titles would result in the inclusion of journals that were both less core and of lower quality. This would be fine—even the less-core, lower-quality titles publish important articles and count numerous libraries as their subscribers. But the library overlap is smaller. And it must be obvious that the number of libraries that have demand for the backfiles of these titles will be lower than the number that manifested demand for the existing collections. Increasing the pricing differential, as we saw in chapter 14, might have some impact, but quite a number of libraries might well have no demand.[35]

As subsequent collections attract a presumably smaller number of academic library participants, how should JSTOR recover its costs? It is Guthrie's vision that JSTOR's best chance to grow is to allow universities

[34] Bruce Heterick, interview with the author, February 4, 2002.

[35] Tom Sanville of OhioLINK seems to believe as much. He has expressed concern that a continual stream of additional JSTOR collections may "end up bumping into more primary and current information needs." From this alone, it is clear that he does not expect space-savings to generate significant cost savings for his member libraries. Interview with the author, October 29, 2001.

and colleges to view JSTOR as a cost savings, rather than as an expense. The archiving libraries already store all the journals that JSTOR might consider including. They could be virtually guaranteed to participate if comparable realizable savings balanced the AAFs. If real savings resulted from JSTOR participation, then better access could be provided to existing materials. This twofold good would, in turn, allow JSTOR to provide an evergrowing research resource for smaller libraries around the world that have some demand but that have heretofore not had such resources available. Librarians of both large and small institutions seem to agree that a greater price differential among them would be desirable. JSTOR, in this model, would bring system-wide savings, as well as other benefits, every time it digitized additional materials. This is the optimistic view.

In the period we have studied, the financial health of higher education combined with JSTOR's decision to first build collections of core titles to obviate concerns about why libraries participate. But ever changing economic circumstances will likely bring a time in which librarians and their institutions experience heightened resource constraints, while JSTOR digitizes journals that are substantially less core. In such cases, will the major libraries continue to view the archive JSTOR provides as being appealing? Will smaller libraries that never collected such journals in the hard-copy format view collection building via JSTOR as necessary? And will fully searchable, desktop-accessible journals, for all of their appeal, be worth paying for, perhaps at the expense of another, perhaps more current, resource? In other words, in the long term, will the archive remain accessible?

The proponents of JSTOR acted with the conviction that scholarly resources could be moved online without negative consequences, that libraries could continue to safeguard those resources without taking up space locally. Without their willingness, and that of others like them, to take a leap, "projects" and "experiments" might have continued without progress. And JSTOR, in particular, offers evidence that through the application of appropriate business models, technology can deliver system-wide improvements to academia. One is left hopeful that a better and cheaper way has been created by which to maintain scholarly resources for generations to come.

Lessons Learned

AT THE TIME of this writing, about eight years after the germinal ideas for JSTOR's creation were first heard at Denison University, there is no question but that JSTOR represents a remarkable achievement. An organization and mission virtually without precedent, JSTOR has digitized more material, and distributed it more broadly, than anyone's wildest expectations. In this epilogue, we shall step back from the details of JSTOR's development to try to understand what broader lessons can be learned.

LESSONS FOR GRANTMAKERS

A Pilot Project Requires Sources of Leverage and Funding

Bowen was able to use Mellon's bully pulpit to win a place on the agenda of potential publishers and to win the ear of potential test sites. With a number of the pilot publishers having been past grantees—or recognizing that they might become so in the future—Bowen had enormous leverage to encourage their participation. Nevertheless, he tried not to be heavy-handed, offering instead the chance for experimentation. The JSTOR-B compromise was crafted to satisfy one set of objections, and there was a general commitment to "make things right" if the pilot resulted in unforeseen disaster. While it might have been possible for an independent JSTOR to have gotten underway without this preexisting work, the momentum was unquestionably helpful. The seed funding was critical. In addition, Mellon made a number of decisions, for example about scanning resolution, that might have been viewed by another organization as prohibitively expensive.

Foundations Have Severe Limitations
When It Comes to Carrying Out a Project Such as JSTOR

The work of actually managing a project as complex as JSTOR could not be done (or at any rate not done very well) within the structure of an entity that has a fundamentally different mission. The Mellon Foundation was not in a position to manage the project on an ongoing basis. Releasing JSTOR, while continuing to support it with grants and influence, was clearly the right decision.

Even with the Most Trusted of Partners, Grant Terms Require Careful Advance Consideration

When Mellon and Michigan developed terms for the 1994 grants, both organizational and intellectual property issues were not carefully considered. Divisions of labor, the locus of project management, the vision of the future, and deadlines were all obscured. Since then, based in part on the JSTOR experience, Mellon has developed a formal policy on intellectual property to govern its grants. It has also grown at least somewhat more cautious about setting other terms and expectations in advance. There may, however, be a natural tendency to minimize these efforts with trusted grantees.

LESSONS FOR LIBRARIES AND PUBLISHERS

The Development of Digital Archiving Requires Compromises among Both Publishers and Libraries

Librarians and scholars would have preferred that JSTOR include the full run of each title. Publishers were hesitant to cede any of their intellectual property, and certainly not current issues, in 1995 and 1996. The moving wall was therefore created, a compromise that was workable only because both publishers and libraries agreed to it (through their participation). Perfection cannot be allowed to prevent progress.

Savings and Archiving Are Hard to Sell on Their Own

Library demand has focused on the value of access and collection building in the period we have studied. The 1994 decision to pursue important core journals rather than more narrowly focused titles was a key sign that the project was to enhance access in addition to seeking to save costs, but JSTOR's core titles have made it more difficult for cost savings to be realized than if JSTOR archived obscure journals. JSTOR's pricing has been adjusted to recognize at least in some measure that libraries value access over cost savings, but it has counterbalanced this with attempts to convince the highest administrative echelons of the importance of cost savings. Only time will tell whether JSTOR's twofold mission will be validated by libraries and administrators, or whether it will be seen as just another vendor.

By Bundling Access and Archiving,
Digital Archives Can Reduce the Free-Rider Problem

Many libraries have long been free-riders when it comes to archiving, with a set of research libraries footing virtually the entire bill for the country. By selling access but providing archiving—and steadfastly refusing to unbundle these two features—JSTOR has substantially mitigated this problem. At the close of 2001, JSTOR's archiving costs were spread across some nine hundred American libraries, rather than the one hundred or so that share the burdens of archiving print resources. As more scholarly information shifts online, there will be important opportunities for the higher education system to spread archiving costs more evenly.

For Scholarly Purposes,
Journals Have Significant Value in Digital Form

Two factors related to ease of access are most important. First, online they can be "physically" accessed from home or office, twenty-four hours per day, and they are never "checked out." Second, searchable fulltext and complete indexing information dramatically increase the ease of bibliographic access, as is indicated by the high percentage of use that comes from searching. It was the access value of JSTOR's digitized backfiles that led to the remarkable levels of library participation. This in turn demonstrated that arts and sciences backfiles have significantly greater value than was expected, which caused JSTOR to increase publisher remuneration.

To Work Effectively with Nonprofits,
Library Consortia Must Be More than Mere Buying Cooperatives

Some consortia failed to understand how JSTOR was different from traditional library vendors. In the course of looking out for the best interests of their member libraries, these consortia failed to consider the system-wide advantages of supporting JSTOR and the savings that it promised. Instead, they demanded pricing that would have threatened to undermine not only JSTOR's self-sustainability, but perhaps even its very viability. Self-interest can prove unnecessarily costly in the long run. For their own sake, consortia must recognize their broader role in the system of scholarly communications.

Bundled Information Goods
Offer Both Economic and Scholarly Benefits

There were important scale effects from the number of titles bundled together in the Arts & Sciences I Collection, reducing transaction costs and offering an appealing collection for cross-searching. Similar effects can be seen via the new collections that have subsequently been created. But these bundles are not easy, or inexpensive, to create.

Branding by Publishers May
Cut against the Needs of Scholars

Publishers were inclined to aggregate their own journals (as Johns Hopkins University Press initially did with Muse and Elsevier did with ScienceDirect), and service providers (such as HighWire) were often able to accomodate this desire. But by selling to libraries, JSTOR was able to meet scholars' desire to have multiple core titles available from one interface. This allowed them to search content by subject matter, without regard for the identity of the publisher. The early decision to create "clusters" of content, organized by discipline, was a critically important strategic choice.

LESSONS OF MISSION

Mission Is Critical for Startup Nonprofits

Never in JSTOR's conception and development was technology treated as a "field of dreams." As a project of the Mellon Foundation, its mission could be summarized as "to pursue system-wide benefits by digitizing and distributing journal backfiles." The demand for such a service was tested before any serious development began. During these earliest days, the focus on mission was seen virtually everywhere. It explained the composition of the advisory committee, the focus on the arts and sciences, the partnership with Michigan, and the decision to digitize a "faithful replication" of journal pages.

This well-defined mission allowed Mellon to "spin off" JSTOR as a separate not-for-profit entity and to choose appropriate leadership. Although with independence the mission was defined more broadly ("to help the scholarly community benefit from advances in information technology"), allowing for future developments, in terms of operations JSTOR never really strayed from its original course. The exploration, and subsequent putting aside, of current issues left JSTOR focused on journal backfiles, although accessibility and collection building had joined system-wide savings as its raison d'être. Finally, reference to mission made possible a number of operating decisions, such as the extent to which JSTOR would enable large-scale linking. The only time that the mission was exanded for operating purposes was in considering a consulting enterprise.

The Mission Must Not Be So Tightly Defined That It Precludes Addressing the Needs of the "Ultimate Consumer"—the Student and Scholar

Although "cheaper" was JSTOR's earliest goal, its leadership never became exclusively obsessed with expenses. JSTOR made major efforts to understand the needs of the ultimate user and to meet them. It provided the database in a way that permitted remote access to it, encouraging libraries to offer such access. It allowed interlibrary loans. It updated the interface. It provided a wide array of printing options. And it permitted in-linking and reciprocal linking with current issues. By willingly spending money in pursuit of quality, JSTOR created a resource that truly was better.

Nonprofit Missions Should, in Some Cases, Encompass System-Wide Effects

Even though neither publishers nor libraries were viewed as ends in and of themselves, JSTOR recognized the importance of appealing to both. JSTOR was decidedly not trying to undermine the preexisting system of scholarly communications (as was the goal of some actors in this time period). Rather, JSTOR recognized that publishers had to view participation as appealing. Guthrie and Bowen crafted terms that would encourage the owners of the content to contribute their journals. This included everything from free digitization of journal backfiles to the downside guarantee and the publisher pool for revenue sharing. Without publisher participation, JSTOR could not have been created. In the absence of an organization like JSTOR, there would have been no way to provide the benefits of, and in exchange to receive payments to cover, the digitization of journal backfiles in the arts and sciences, most particularly for smaller and midsize publishers.

The Needs of Different Types of Libraries Pose Complications for Online Resources

Finding the right balance between meeting the needs of the largest research libraries and all other libraries may not be simple. The former value both breadth and depth, demand archival commitments, and envision thousands of titles of journal backfiles. The latter generally value breadth over depth and demand access or collection building but rarely archiving. If scale-effects are required, finding the appropriate balance is critical.

LESSONS OF ORGANIZATION

While Being Part of a Larger Organization Can Obscure Costs, Independence Brings a Clearer Attention to Self-Sustainability

Numerous examples exist of units of larger entities obscuring costs and the bottom line. JSTOR benefited enormously from the discipline of having to plan for a day when revenues from users would cover its running costs. This pressure to operate economically led JSTOR to produce a "product" that would be so valuable to the scholarly community that libraries would pay license fees to have access to it. Not every not-for-profit should be expected to reach operating self-sustainability. In other cases, there is an understood relationship between the contributions made by users of the resource and philanthropies that underwrite the activity because of its intrinsic merit— the model of private universities and other major not-for-profits, such as museums and orchestras. But regardless of whether long-term subvention is necessary, organizations do not reach self-sustainability by pursuing their mission without any sense of who will pay for it—as Guthrie himself demonstrated in his book on the New-York Historical Society.

There Are Key Advantages to
Being Organized as a Public Charity

The fact that JSTOR existed not to make money, but to serve educational and scholarly purposes, was crucial in persuading publishers to contribute their journals without royalty payments. It also helped explain the pricing plan: "value-based" pricing was designed to permit small colleges to participate, alongside large universities. The not-for-profit orientation also contributed to JSTOR's commitment to transparency and "fairness" in pricing, and its hesitation to "do deals" to encourage more participation. Nonprofit status, combined with JSTOR's strong foundation and academic ties, encouraged universities such as Michigan to provide technical and other support at cost. Also, it allowed JSTOR to receive foundation grants, which were important to build collections at low enough cost that they could be made available to colleges on an affordable basis. None of this would have been possible if JSTOR had been a for-profit.

Partnering with For-Profit Corporations for Mission-Driven
Purposes Should Only Be Contemplated with Extreme Caution

In several cases, corporations seemed to have assets that would be valuable in launching the JSTOR project, including UMI for scanning and Chadwyck-Healy for metadata. In both cases, the attempts to create partnerships failed. On the other hand, the competitive bidding processes that resulted in scanning vendors, rather than partners, were largely successful. Asking a for-profit corporation to pursue mission-driven ends is of questionable value; but purchasing its services can result in useful arrangements.

Having an Internal Staff Capacity
Brings Key Advantages over Grantee Mechanisms

By developing an "internal" capacity at Michigan and Princeton, Guthrie was able to interact more effectively with staff and to manage the enterprise with much greater care. Universities are dedicated to teaching and research, and, in general, are not organized to manage complex projects with business-like needs. They are also not designed to take a system-wide perspective. Some operating subsidiaries (such as HighWire) have achieved great success. These successes require a high degree of institutional commitment and specific organizational structures, and they are uncommon. A grant awarded within the standard organization of a university cannot result in the nimbleness needed for an entity such as JSTOR and might well result in a dilution of the project's mission.

That said, academia is a valuable partner when building resources to serve it. The expertise and preexisting work contributed by the initial Michigan staff allowed the JSTOR project to get off the ground more rapidly than would have otherwise been possible. And being based at the university allowed JSTOR to draw on a talented supply of librarians, information technologists, and consultants. Finally, the affiliations with Michigan, Princeton, and the JISC were reputationally most useful. Parterning with, rather than vending to, academia can offer key advantages.

Small Size Allows for Nimbleness

JSTOR had to make decisions promptly, most especially on collections development. It identified the core journals in a field, with only the advice and consultation necessary, and then wooed the publishers. It also has had to be quick in correcting its errors, for example adjusting its pricing. If JSTOR had been part of a larger entity, it might never have succeeded in capturing sufficient high-level attention to make these decisions rapidly. JSTOR made its share of errors, but it was able to correct them, to redirect itself as needed, and to adapt.

LESSONS OF OPERATIONS

Associations with Outsiders
Can Allow a Startup to Accumulate Credibility

Mellon's long interest in libraries, scholarly communication, and higher education made its backing of JSTOR especially valuable. By partnering with the university library and the School of Information at Michigan, Mellon added another important source of credibility (and skill) for its JSTOR project. The JSTOR Board of Trustees could not have been assembled without these affiliations. Mellon, Michigan, and the former's trustees were important in building trust throughout the scholarly community. Specifically, they were important in dealing with university presses, scholarly societies, and libraries (especially when the libraries were asked to be "charter" participants and pay a substantial one-time charge for access to a collection yet to be developed).

Strong Management Is Critical

While this work has not been a detailed study in leadership, there can be no doubt but that JSTOR's early (and ongoing) success was a direct result of Guthrie's personal style. The excellent partnership between Guthrie and Bowen, in which the latter was constantly pushing for aggressive growth while the former worked for more careful planning and the achievement of goals, was a key division of labor. Yet while Guthrie focused on policy and strategy and tried to avoid becoming mired in the daily ebb and flow, he was not perched exclusively on high. He was able to maintain this balance by learning to "speak the language" of the various teams of librarians and programmers. He tried to delegate responsibilities, even while staying actively informed about the progress of work. When the digitization was not acceptable, he asked if certain improvements could be made. When determinations had to be made about which disciplines to pursue, he spoke to scholars and librarians to determine needs. When a business plan had to be written, he wrote it. A leader who was not only able, but also willing, to do all of this work, and to keep the long hours necessary to do so, was the only way in which JSTOR could progress as much as it did between mid-1995 (at independence) and mid-1997 (when its archive was available to much of academia).

Of course, Guthrie was only able to do this because he had the full confidence of the trustees and the sole responsibility for making JSTOR a success. There was no dilution in responsibility, or authority, whatsoever. Bowen and the board delegated to Guthrie the authority to make JSTOR happen, while in turn he felt responsible for its development. Soon after Guthrie's appointment, many of the Mellon staff members who had been involved in JSTOR's development began to recede and Guthrie took over their tasks. At Michigan, while the process took longer, Frank and Lougee receded while Guthrie took on increasing authority and in turn delegated responsibility to full-time JSTOR staff in Ann Arbor. A combination of Guthrie's style and the undiluted responsibility vested in him was a critical factor in JSTOR's development.

A Strong Financial Base Is Necessary in Order to Take the Long View

Especially before Arts & Sciences I was released, this backing allowed JSTOR to make commitments and assume risks, knowing that its support came from an entity that itself took the long view and was not expecting immediate returns. JSTOR never felt pressured to find the cheapest short-term solution or the approach that would meet next week's payroll. Also, the backing of the foundation meant that JSTOR did not have to devote time and attention in its early days to fundraising or advertising itself. It had the luxury of being able to concentrate on building its substance for the long run. JSTOR's resource-base and its foundation-backing permitted it to take the long view and to make firm commitments to staff members, to vendors digitizing content at a high level of quality, to university partners such as Michigan, to publishers who were asked to give JSTOR "perpetual" rights, and to libraries who were asked to sign on to an initial Arts & Sciences I Collection that was only a concept and then to contemplate relocating journals and taking other irrevocable steps.

The Mission Must Be Matched with Marketplace-Driven Operating Principles and the Leadership to Implement Them

The decision to write a formal business plan setting out precisely what JSTOR would do, and how, and when, allowed staff to avoid other "compelling" projects that came along, such as (at first) *Science* magazine, which clearly fell outside of the Arts & Sciences I mandate. No matter how appealing *Science* may have been, JSTOR wanted to succeed at its first collection before becoming distracted by additional work. The same caution against overextension was evidenced in the long delays in choosing to pursue consulting and in the prudent rate of growth that prevented JSTOR's expenditures from increasing faster than demand.

Many of JSTOR's trustees were recruited from the educational world, including Bowen, Ira Fuchs, and Pat McPherson. Gilbert Whitaker was both an academic administrator and an experienced director of for-profit corporations. DeGennaro was able to think about the institutional needs of libraries and reach out effectively to them. Elton White balanced business skills with scholarly sensitivity, and his exhortations to "let's be sure the dog will eat the dog food" before embarking on anything significant were key. Charles Ellis (chairman and CEO of John Wiley) provided important direction and discipline. The board in turn selected an entrepreneur who was extremely sensitive to scholarly needs, Kevin Guthrie, as chief executive. His experience in studying the troubled history of the New-York Historical Society was directly relevant. Because of its ability to combine marketplace and scholarly concerns, JSTOR's leadership was able to resolve effectively a number of thorny issues—including the ongoing concerns about optimal pricing.

Curating Collections Brings Far Higher Value to Libraries, but Far More Challenges

It is clear that libraries valued the decision only to include the most important, well-regarded journals. Yet this has prevented JSTOR from operating opportunistically or from reaching blanket deals with publishers. Instead, publisher-relations staff had to develop terms that satisfied not only the smallest scholarly societies, but also major university presses and even commercial publishing houses. The need to offer consistent terms to all participating publishers helped to sink the publication of current issues; while it mandated a stream of compromises from JSTOR-B and the downside guarantee to the publisher pool that eventually became revenue-sharing.

Scale Effects Can Be Key to Self-Sustainability

The surprising number of libraries that chose to participate once access value had been demonstrated, and once international participation was encouraged, dramatically improved JSTOR's bottom line. The rapid growth in collection-participants in 2000 and 2001 led to self-sustainability. Although the assumptions that marginal costs are minimal in the online environment has not been fully borne out, by providing hundreds of journals to well over one thousand libraries, JSTOR is able to provide a wealth of reformatted information at a low average cost. Without such scale-effects, success might not have been possible.

The Importance of Having the Right Timing Should Never Be Forgotten

First and most importantly, the Internet and the web—without which JSTOR could not have succeeded—became viable on a large scale. At the same time, relatively inexpensive scanning and OCR was available. Also significantly, the worldwide economic expansion that accompanied it played at least two roles. It swelled the endowments of college and universities, allowing them to invest more in all of their resources, including libraries, than had been possible for many years. In addition, it swelled the endowments of foundations like Mellon, Howard Hughes, Macy, and so forth, allowing each of these to invest in new programs and support the ongoing work of JSTOR in ways that might otherwise not have been possible.

For a Small Organization, the Balance between Strategic Planning and Operations Is Critical, but Difficult to Perfect

Some organizations begin to plot long-term strategy before near-term goals are achievable; it is an appealing distraction. But it is time-consuming and, in the end, not useful. JSTOR managed to avoid this tantalizing option. On the other hand, it is most important to recognize the significant lead-times between planning and execution. In a few isolated cases (related to the transitions between collections), more lead-time might have been beneficial. While it may be impossible to achieve the perfect balance, an awareness of the trade-offs between operations and planning is desirable.

All Journals in JSTOR, by Collection

Accurate as of December 31, 2001
Updated information available at
http://www.jstor.org/about/.
Many journals appear in multiple collections.

Arts & Sciences I

African American Review
American Economic Review
American Historical Review
American Journal of International
   Law
American Journal of Mathematics
American Journal of Political Science
American Journal of Sociology
American Literature
American Mathematical Monthly
American Political Science Review
American Quarterly
American Sociological Review
Annals of Applied Probability
Annals of Mathematical Statistics
Annals of Mathematics
Annals of Probability
Annals of Statistics
Annual Review of Anthropology
Annual Review of Ecology and
   Systematics
Annual Review of Sociology
Anthropology Today
Applied Statistics
Biometrika
Callaloo
China Journal
Contemporary Sociology
Current Anthropology
Demography
Ecological Applications
Ecological Monographs

Ecology
Econometrica
Economic Journal
Eighteenth-Century Studies
ELH (English Literary History)
Ethics
Family Planning Perspectives
Harvard Journal of Asiatic Studies
International Family Planning
   Perspectives
International Organization
Journal of American History
Journal of Animal Ecology
Journal of Applied Econometrics
Journal of Asian Studies
Journal of Black Studies
Journal of Blacks in Higher Education
Journal of Business
Journal of Ecology
Journal of Economic History
Journal of Economic Literature
Journal of Economic Perspectives
Journal of Finance
Journal of Financial and Quantitative
   Analysis
Journal of Health and Social Behavior
Journal of Higher Education
Journal of Industrial Economics
Journal of Military History
Journal of Modern History
Journal of Money, Credit and
   Banking

Journal of Negro Education
Journal of Negro History
Journal of Philosophy
Journal of Political Economy
Journal of Politics
Journal of Southern History
Journal of Symbolic Logic
Journal of the American
  Mathematical Society
Journal of the American Statistical
  Association
Journal of the History of Ideas
Journal of the Royal Anthropological
  Institute of Great Britain and
  Ireland
Journal of the Royal Anthropological
  Institute/Man
Journal of the Royal Statistical Society:
  Series A (Statistics in Society)
Journal of the Royal Statistical
  Society: Series B, Statistical
  Methodology
Mathematics of Computation
Mind
MLN
Monumenta Nipponica
Nineteenth-Century Literature
Noûs
Pacific Affairs
Philosophical Perspectives
Philosophical Quarterly
The Philosophical Review
Philosophy and Phenomenological
  Research
Philosophy and Public Affairs
Political Science Quarterly
Population and Development Review

Population Index
Population Studies
Population: An English Selection
Proceedings of the American
  Mathematical Society
Proceedings of the American Political
  Science Association
Proceedings of the Royal
  Anthropological Institute of Great
  Britain and Ireland
Public Opinion Quarterly
Quarterly Journal of Economics
Renaissance Quarterly
Representations
Review of Economic Studies
Review of Economics and Statistics
Review of Financial Studies
Reviews in American History
Shakespeare Quarterly
SIAM Journal on Applied
  Mathematics
SIAM Journal on Numerical
  Analysis
SIAM Review
Social Psychology Quarterly
Sociology of Education
Speculum
Statistical Science
Statistician
Studies in Family Planning
Studies in the Renaissance
Transactions of the American
  Mathematical Society
Transition
William and Mary Quarterly
World Politics
Yale French Studies

General Science

Philosophical Transactions:
  Biological Sciences
Philosophical Transactions:
  Mathematical, Physical and
  Engineering Sciences
Proceedings: Biological
  Sciences

Proceedings: Mathematical, Physical
  and Engineering Sciences
Proceedings of the National Academy
  of Sciences of the United States of
  America
Science
Scientific Monthly

Ecology & Botany

American Journal of Botany
American Midland Naturalist
American Naturalist
Annals of the Missouri Botanical
   Garden
Annual Review of Ecology and
   Systematics
Biotropica
Brittonia
Conservation Biology
Diversity and Distributions
Ecological Applications
Ecological Monographs
Ecology
Evolution
Functional Ecology
Global Ecology and Biogeography

International Journal of Plant
   Sciences
Journal of Animal Ecology
Journal of Applied Ecology
Journal of Biogeography
Journal of Ecology
Journal of the Torrey Botanical
   Society
Journal of Tropical Ecology
Limnology and Oceanography
Missouri Botanical Garden Annual
   Report
New Phytologist
Paleobiology
Quarterly Review of Biology
Systematic Biology
Systematic Botany

Arts & Sciences II

American Antiquity
American Journal of Philology
Annals of the Association of
   American Geographers
Asian Survey
Biometrics
British Journal of Middle Eastern
   Studies
British Journal of Political Science
Brookings Papers on Economic
   Activity
Brookings Papers on Economic
   Activity: Microeconomics
Bulletin of Symbolic Logic
Canadian Journal of Economics
Classical Philology
Comparative Politics
Comparative Studies in Society
   and History
Economic Geography
Economica
Economic History Review
Europe-Asia Studies
French Historical Studies
Gender and Society

Geographical Review
Harvard Studies in Classical
   Philology
Hesperia
Hispanic American Historical
   Review
Historical Journal
History and Theory
History of Education Quarterly
International Affairs
International Economic Review
International Journal of African
   Historical Studies
International Journal of Middle East
   Studies
International Migration Review
International Security
International Studies Quarterly
Isis
Journal of Aesthetics and Art
   Criticism
Journal of African History
Journal of British Studies
Journal of Conflict Resolution
Journal of Contemporary History

Journal of Interdisciplinary History
Journal of Japanese Studies
Journal of Labor Economics
Journal of Latin American Studies
Journal of Marriage and the Family
Journal of Modern African
  Studies
Journal of Palestine Studies
Journal of Peace Research
Journal of Roman Studies
Journal of Southern African Studies
Latin American Perspectives
Latin American Politics and Society
Latin American Research Review
Mershon International Studies
  Review
Middle East Report
Modern Asian Studies
Modern China
Oxford Economic Papers

Pakistan Forum
Philosophy of Science
Phylon
Political Theory
PS: Political Science and Politics
PSA: Proceedings of the Biennial
  Meeting of the Philosophy of
  Science Association
RAND Journal of Economics
Russian Review
Sixteenth Century Journal
Slavic and East European Journal
Slavic Review
Social Forces
Social Studies of Science
Sociological Methodology
Sociological Theory
Transactions of the American
  Philological Association
World Archaeology

Business

Academy of Management
  Journal
Academy of Management
  Review
Accounting Review
Administrative Science Quarterly
American Economic Review
Brookings Papers on Economic
  Activity
Brookings Papers on Economic
  Activity: Microeconomics
Canadian Journal of Economics
Econometrica
Economic History Review
Economic Journal
Economica
Industrial and Labor Relations
  Review
International Economic Review
Journal of Accounting Research
Journal of Applied Econometrics
Journal of Business
Journal of Consumer Research

Journal of Economic History
Journal of Economic Literature
Journal of Economic Perspectives
Journal of Finance
Journal of Financial and Quantitative
  Analysis
Journal of Human Resources
Journal of Industrial Economics
Journal of International Business
  Studies
Journal of Labor Economics
Journal of Money, Credit and
  Banking
Journal of Organizational Behavior
Journal of Political Economy
Journal of Risk and Insurance
Journal of the Operational Research
  Society
Management Science
Management Technology
Managerial and Decision Economics
Marketing Science
MIS Quarterly

Operations Research
Organization Science
Oxford Economic Papers
Quarterly Journal of Economics
RAND Journal of Economics

Review of Economic Studies
Review of Economics and
   Statistics
Review of Financial Studies
Strategic Management Journal

Bibliography

Archives

JSTOR
The Andrew W. Mellon Foundation

Interviews

Ken Alexander
  June 14, 2001, by telephone

Sherry Aschenbrenner
  May 30, 2001, Ann Arbor

Daniel Atkins
  May 31, 2001, Ann Arbor

Gerard J. Aurigemma
  October 18, 2001, New York

Mary Barber
  September 20, 2001, Washington

Elizabeth Barry
  May 30, 2001, Ann Arbor

William G. Bowen
  October 31, 2000, New York
  November 20, 2000, New York
  January 17, 2001, New York
  June 26, 2001, New York

Nancy Cantor
  May 29, 2001, Ann Arbor

David Cook
  April 13, 2001, New York

Frank Conaway
  March 22, 2002, by telephone

Sue Corbett
  August 20, 2001, by telephone

Richard DeGennaro
  March 30, 20001, by telephone

Henry Drewry
  May 23, 2001, Princeton

Richard Ekman
  February 28, 2001, Washington
  April 16, 2001, by telephone

Alice F. Emerson
  June 15, 2001, New York

Ray English
  May 3, 2002, by telephone

Eileen G. Fenton
  May 29, 2001, Ann Arbor
  May 31, 2001, New York
  June 19, 2001, New York
  October 11, 2001, New York

Dale Flecker
  April 2, 2002, by telephone

Randy Frank
  July 10, 2001, by telephone

Ira H. Fuchs
  November 2, 2000, New York
  November 22, 2000, New York
  December 21, 2000, New York
  July 19, 2001, New York

Kristen Garlock
    May 25, 2001, Ann Arbor
    August 14, 2001, New York

Marvin Guilfoyle
    May 7, 2002, by telephone

Kevin M. Guthrie
    December 13, 2000, New York
    February 1, 2001, New York
    February 20, 2001, New York
    April 11, 2001, New York
    July 23, 2001, New York
    October 30, 2001, New York
    December 6, 2001, New York
    March 25, 2002, New York

Bruce Heterick
    February 4, 2002, New York
    April 30, 2002, New York

Karen Hunter
    September 5, 2001, New York

Arnita Jones
    September 20, 2001, Washington

Robert Kasdin
    May 29, 2001, Ann Arbor

Michael A. Keller
    May 21, 2002, by telephone

Amy J. Kirchhoff
    December 21, 2001, Princeton
    May 2, 2002, Princeton

Tony Krug
    March 26, 2002, by telephone

Michael LaCroix
    May 3, 2002, by telephone

Wendy Lougee
    May 30, 2001, Ann Arbor
    May 31, 2001, Ann Arbor
    December 13, 2001, by telephone

Clifford Lynch
    October 25, 2001, New York

Carol MacAdam
    March 13, 2002, New York
    April 30, 2002, New York

Katherine McCarter
    September 20, 2001, Washington

Heidi McGregor
    May 18, 2001, New York
    June 5, 2001, New York

Thomas I. Nygren
    May 23, 2001, Princeton

Charles E Phelps
    April 22, 2002, by telephone

David M. Pilachowski
    June 22, 2001, Williamstown,
        Massachusetts

William G. Potter
    April 26, 2002, by telephone

James Roemer
    September 26, 2001, by telephone

Tom Sanville
    October 29, 2001, by telephone

Spencer Thomas
    May 29, 2001, Ann Arbor

Dawn Tomassi
    April 30, 2002, New York

Gilbert Whitaker
    December 4, 2000, Houston

Elton R. White
    February 6, 2001, New York

Katherine Willis
    March 7, 2002, by telephone

Books, Journal Articles, and Other Sources

Alderman, John. *Sonic Boom: Napster, MP3, and the New Pioneers of Music* (New York: Perseus, 2001).

Alexander, Adrian W. "Towards the 'Perfection of Work': Library Consortia in the Digital Age." *Journal of Library Administration* 28, no. 2 (1999): 1–14.

Altbach, Philip G. "The Role and Nurturing of Journals in the Third World." In Philip G. Altbach and Damtew Teferra, eds., *Knowledge Dissemination in Africa: The Role of Scholarly Journals* (Chesnutt Hill, MA: Bellagio Publishing Network, 1998), 5–11.

Andrew W. Mellon Foundation. The Explanatory Statement on the Andrew W. Mellon Foundation's Intellectual Property Policy for Digital Products Developed with Foundation Funds. Available online at *http://www.mellon.org/ip.policy.2.pdf.*

Ashby, Peter and Robert Campbell. *Microform Publishing* (London: Butterworths, 1979).

Association of Research Libraries. *Meeting (113th: 1988: York, England) Collections: their development, management, preservation, and sharing : papers from the Joint Meeting of the Association of Research Libraries and the Standing Conference of National and University Libraries, University of York, September 19–22, 1988* (Washington, DC: Association of Research Libraries, 1989).

Baker, Nicholson. "Discards." *New Yorker,* April 4, 1994.

———. *Double Fold: Libraries and the Assault on Paper* (New York: Random House, 2001).

Bakos, Yannis, and Erik Brynjolfsson. "Bundling Information Goods: Pricing, Profits, and Efficiency." *Management Science* 45, no. 12 (December 1999): 1613.

Bakos, Yannis, Erik Brynjolfsson, and Yu (Jeffrey) Hu. "Site Licensing Information Goods." Unpublished paper, May 2002.

Ballard, Terry. "JSTOR Reaches Critical Mass." *Information Today* 17, no. 2 (February 2000): 38–39.

Barber, Peggy. "Look up and look out—librarians are not alone." *American Libraries* 27, no. 4 (April 1996): p. 65.

Baumol, William J., and Matityahu Marcus. *Economics of Academic Libraries* (Washington, DC: American Council on Education, 1973).

———. *On the Economics of Library Operations* (Princeton, NJ: Mathematica, for the National Advisory Commission on Libraries, 1967).

Baumol, William J., and Sue Anne Batey Blackmun. "Electronics, the Cost Disease, and the Operation of Libraries." *Journal of the American Society for Information Science* 34, no. 3 (1983): 181–91.

Baumol, William J., and William G. Bowen. *Performing Arts—The Economic Dilemma: A Study of Problems Common to Theater, Opera, Music and Dance* (New York: Twentieth Century Fund, 1966).

Bennett, Elizabeth Z. "Digitizing Science: JSTOR Faces New Challenges." In Anne R. Kenney and Oya Y. Rieger, eds., *Moving Theory into Practice: Digital Imaging for Libraries and Archives* (Mountain View, CA: Research Libraries Group, 2000).

[Bennett, Scott]. *Report on the Conoco Project in German Literature and Geology* (Stanford, CA: Research Libraries Group, 1987).

Bergman, Jed I. *Managing Change in the Nonprofit Sector: Lessons from the Evolution of Five Independent Research Libraries* (San Francisco: Jossey-Bass Publishers, 1996).

Bonn, Maria S., and Jeffrey K. MacKie-Mason. "A Report on the PEAK Experiment: Context and Design." *D-Lib Magazine* 5, no. 6 (June 1999).

Borgman, Christine L. "What Are Digital Libraries? Competing Visions." *Information Processing and Management* 35 (May 1999), 227–43.

Bowen, William G. "At a Slight Angle to the Universe: The University in a Digitized, Commercialized Age." The Romanes Lecture for 2000, Delivered before the University of Oxford on October 17, 2000 (Princeton: Princeton University Press, 2001).

———. "How Libraries Can Help to Pay Their Way in the Future," *Logos* 7, no. 3 (1996): 237–41.

———. "JSTOR and the Economics of Scholarly Communication," *Journal of Library Administration* 26, nos. 1–2 (1998): 27–44.

———. "JSTOR and the Economics of Scholarly Communications." Speech to the Council on Library and Information Resources, Washington, DC, September 18, 1995. Revised version online at *www.Mellon.org/jsesc.html.*

———. "The Foundation's Journal Storage Project (JSTOR)." In *Report of the Andrew W. Mellon Foundation 1994,* (New York: Andrew W. Mellon Foundation, 1995).

———. *Inside the Boardroom: Governance by Directors and Trustees* (New York: John Wiley and Sons, 1994).

———. "The Princeton Library: Report of the President March 1986." In *Ever the Teacher: William G. Bowen's Writings as President of Princeton* (Princeton: Princeton University Press, 1987).

Bowen, William G., Thomas I. Nygren, Sarah E. Turner, and Elizabeth A. Duffy. *The Charitable Non-Profits: An Analysis of Institutional Dynamics and Characteristics* (San Francisco: Jossey-Bass Publishers, 1994).

Bremer, Joseph P. *Guide to Database Distribution: Second Edition* (Philadelphia: National Federation of Abstracting and Information Services, 1994).

Brindley, Lynne, and Kevin M. Guthrie. "JSTOR and the Joint Information Systems Committee: An International Collaboration." *Serials* 11, no. 1 (March 1998): 41.

Brint, Steven, and Jerome Karabel. *The Diverted Dream: Community Colleges and the Promise of Educational Opportunity in America, 1900–1985* (New York: Oxford University Press, 1989).

Brockman, William S., Laura Neumann, Carole L. Palmer, and Tonyia Tidline. *Scholarly Work in the Humanities and the Evolving Information Environment* (Washington, DC: Digital Library Federation, 2001).

Bronner, Ethan. "You Can Look It Up, Hopefully." *New York Times,* January 10, 1999: Section 4, 4.

Bryan, Harrison. "American Automation in Action." *Library Journal,* January 15, 1967, 189–96.

Building and Sustaining Digital Collections: Models for Libraries and Museums (Washington, DC: Council on Library and Information Resources, 2001).

Buruma, Ian. "The Road to Babel." *New York Review of Books,* May 31, 2001, 23.

Caplan, Priscilla. "Reference Linking for Journal Articles: Promise, Progress and Perils." *portal: Libraries and the Academy* 1, no. 3, (2001): 351–56.

Carlson, Scott. "JSTOR's Journal-Archiving Service Makes Fans of Librarians and Scholars." *Chronicle of Higher Education,* July 27, 2001.

Cetto, Ana María, and Octavio Alonso-Gambosa. "Scientific and Scholarly Journals in Latin American and the Caribbean." In Philip G. Altbach and Damtew Teferra, eds., *Knowledge Dissemination in Africa: The Role of Scholarly Journals* (Chesnutt Hill, MA: Bellagio Publishing Network, 1998), 102.

Chapman, Karen. "An Examination of the Usefulness of JSTOR to Researchers in Finance." *Behavioral & Social Sciences Librarian* 19, no. 2 (2001): 39–47.

Chepesiuk, Ron. "JSTOR and Electronic Archiving." *American Libraries* 31, no. 11 (December 2000): 46–48.

———. "JSTOR: a non-profit working to redefine access to the scholarly journal." *Against the Grain* 9 (April 1997): 29–30.

A Classification of Institutions of Higher Education: 1994 Edition. Princeton, NJ: The Carnegie Foundation for the Advancement of Teaching, 1994.

Coffey, James R., ed. *Operational Costs in Acquisitions* (New York: Haworth Press, 1991).

Computer Applications in Libraries: Part 1. *IEEE Annals of the History of Computing* 24, no. 2 (April–June 2002).

Computer Applications in Libraries: Part 2. *IEEE Annals of the History of Computing* 24, no. 3 (July–September 2002).

Cox, John E. "Publisher/Library Relationships in the Digital Environment." Commissioned by the STM Library Relations Committee, April 1999.

———. "Model Generic Licenses: Cooperation and Competition." *Serials Review* 26, no. 1 (2000): 3.

Cressanthis, George A., and June D. Cressanthis. "Publisher Monopoly Power and Third-Degree Price Discrimination of Scholarly Journals," *Technical Services Quarterly* 11(2): 13–36.

Cummings, Anthony M., Marcia L. Witte, William G. Bowen, Laura O. Lazarus, and Richard H. Ekman. *University Libraries and Scholarly Communications* (Washington, DC: Association of Research Libraries for the Andrew W. Mellon Foundation, November, 1992).

Dahl, Kenn. "OCR Trends and Implications." In Anne R. Kenney and Oya Y. Rieger, eds., *Moving Theory into Practice: Digital Imaging for Libraries and Archives* (Mountain View, CA: Research Libraries Group, 2000), 111–12.

DeGennaro, Richard. "JSTOR: Building an Internet Accessible Digital Archive of Retrospective Journals." *INSPEL* 32, no. 2 (1998): 88–92.

DeLoughery, Thomas J. "Journal Articles Dating Back 100 Years Are Being Put on Line." *Chronicle of Higher Education* 43, no. 15 (December 6, 1996): A30, A32.

———. "Humanists and Computers." *Chronicle of Higher Education,* April 20, 1993.

———. "Scholarly Journals Via the Computer." *Chronicle of Higher Education,* March 9, 1994.

Dementi, Margit. "Access and Archiving as a New Paradigm." *Journal of Electronic Publishing* 3, no. 3 (March 1998).

Dowd, Sheila T. "Fee, Fie, Foe, Fum: Will the Serials Giant Eat Us?" In Sul H. Lee, ed., *The Impact of Rising Costs of Serials and Monographs on Library Services and Programs* (Binghamton, NY: Haworth Press, 1989), 17–38.

Downs, Antonie B. "JSTOR: Building an Electronic Archive of Scholarly Journals." *SLA Social Science Division Bulletin* 39, no. 1 (October 1997): 14–16.

Drewry, Henry N., and Humphrey Doermann. *Stand and Prosper: Private Black Colleges and Their Students* (Princeton: Princeton University Press, 2001).

Ekman, Richard, and Richard E. Quandt, eds. *Technology and Scholarly Communications* (Berkeley: University of California Press, 1999).

———. "Scholarly communication, academic libraries, and technology." *Change* 27, no. 1 (January 1995): p. 34–44.

———. "Potential Uses of Technology in Scholarly Publishing and Research Libraries." Discussion Paper Presented to the Trustees of the Andrew W. Mellon Foundation, December 13, 1993 (unpublished).

Elsevier Science. *TULIP Final Report.* (New York: Elsevier, 1996).

Fordahl, Matthew. "Market Glut May Hurt Fiber Carriers." *AP Online,* February 7, 2002.

Foundation Center. *Foundation Grants Index* [database].

"Foundation Grants Extend JSTOR Access to International Scholars." *JSTOR-NEWS* 3, no. 1 (March 2001): 2.

Fowler, Tom. "Online college library and research firm slows pace, reduces staff by almost half." *Houston Chronicle,* May 9, 2001.

———. "Questia again cuts its workforce 50% on low growth rate." *Houston Chronicle,* November 30, 2001.

Fussler, Herman H. *Research Libraries and Technology* (Chicago: University of Chicago Press, 1973).

Garlock, Kristen L., William E. Landis, and Sherry Piontek. "Redefining Access to Scholarly Journals: A Progress Report on JSTOR." *Serials Review* 23 (Spring 1997): 1–8.

Gherman, Paul M, "Can the Electronic Revolution Save Us Money?: A Response to Thomas G. Kirk." *Moveable Type: The Newsletter of the Mark O. Hatfield Library* 5, no. 1 (Fall 1997): 8.

Gordon, Helen A. "*Online* Interviews Rowland Brown of OCLC." *Online* 11, no. 3 (May 1987): 38–44.

Gore, Daniel, ed. *Farewell to Alexandria: Solutions to space, growth, and performance problems of libraries* (Westport, CT: Greenwood Press, 1976), 4.

Grassmuck, Karen. "Columbia U. to Phase Out Library School; Officials Hope to Move It to Another Campus." *Chronicle of Higher Education,* June 20, 1990.

———. "Questioning a Commitment: Columbia Treads Carefully as It Considers Closing the School of Library Service, the Last of Its Kind." *Chronicle of Higher Education,* April 25, 1990.

Guthrie, Kevin M. "Archiving in the Digital Age: There's a Will, But Is There a Way?" *EDUCAUSE Review* 36, no. 6 (November–December 2001), 56–65.

———. "Challenges and Opportunities Presented by Archiving in the Electronic Era," *portal: Libraries and the Academy,* 1:2 (2001), 121–128.

———. "The Development of a Cost-Driven, Value-Based Pricing Model." In Richard Ekman and Richard E. Quandt, eds., *Technology and Scholarly Communications* (Berkeley: University of California Press, 1999).

————. "JSTOR and the University of Michigan: An Evolving Collaboration." *Library Hi Tech* 16, no. 1 (1998) 9–14, 36.

————. "JSTOR: From Project to Independent Organization." *D-Lib Magazine* July–August 1997. Available online at: *http://www.dlib.org/dlib/july97/07guthrie.html.*

————. *The New-York Historical Society: Lessons from One Nonprofit's Long Struggle for Survival* (San Francisco: Jossey-Bass Publishers, 1996).

Guthrie, Kevin M., and Wendy P. Lougee. "The JSTOR Solution: Accessing and Preserving the Past." *Library Journal*, February 1, 1997: 42–44.

Gwinn, Nancy E., and Paul H. Mosher. "Coordinating Collection Development: The RLG Conspectus." *College & Research Libraries* 44 (March 1983): 128–40.

Gyeszly, Suzanne, and Elka Tenner. "JSTOR: the Economic Realities of Building a Core Electronic Library." *Journal of Business & Finance Librarianship* 4, no. 4 (1999): 3–17.

Hachigian, Nina. "China's Cyber Strategy." *Foreign Affairs* March–April 2001, 121.

Hafner, Katie. "Lessons Learned at Dot-Com U." *New York Times,* May 2, 2002, G1.

————. "A New Way of Verifying Old and Familiar Sayings." *New York Times,* February 1, 2001, G8.

Hamlin, Arthur T. *The University Library in the United States: Its Origin and Development* (Philadelphia: University of Pennsylvania Press, 1981).

Hane, Paula J. "*IT Interview:* Questia Provides Digital Library, Research Tools: Company president and CEO Troy Williams discusses details of the new research service." *Information Today*, 18, no. 2 (February 2001).

Hardesty, Larry, ed. *Books Bytes and Bridges: Libraries and Computer Centers in Academic Institutions* (Chicago: American Library Association, 2000).

Hawkins, Brian L. "The Unsustainability of the Traditional Library and the Threat to Higher Education." In Brian L. Hawkins and Patricia Battin, eds., *The Mirage of Continuity* (Washington, DC: Council on Library and Information Resources and Association of American Universities, 1998).

Hawkins, Brian L., and Patricia Battin, eds. *The Mirage of Continuity* (Washington, DC: Council on Library and Information Resources and Association of American Universities, 1998).

Haworth, Karla. "Many 2-Year Colleges Impose Tougher Academic Standards." *Chronicle of Higher Education,* January 22, 1999.

Henderson, Albert. "The Growth of Printed Literature in the Twentieth Century." In Richard E. Abel and Lyman W. Newlin, eds., *Scholarly Publishing: Books, Journals, Publishers, and Libraries in the Twentieth Century* (New York: John Wiley and Sons, 2002), 6–7.

Henthorne, Eileen. "Digitization and the Creation of Virtual Libraries: The Princeton University Image Card Catalog—Reaping the Benefits of Imaging." *Information Technology and Libraries* 14, no. 1 (March 1995), 38.

Holland, Mary. "IEEE/IEE on CD-ROM: a review from a beta test," *CD-ROM Librarian* 5, no. 2 (February, 1990), 34.

Hopkins, Bruce R., and Jody Blazek. *Private Foundations: Tax Law and Compliance* (New York: John Wiley and Sons, 1997).

Hughes, Thomas Parke. *Networks of Power: Electrification in Western Society, 1880–1930* (Baltimore: Johns Hopkins University Press), 29.

Hunter, Karen. "PEAK and Elsevier Science." In Wendy Lougee and Jeffrey Mackie-Mason, eds., *Bits and Bucks: Economics and Usage of Digital Collections* (Cambridge, MA: MIT Press, forthcoming).

———. "Publishing for a Digital Library—What Did TULIP Teach Us?" *Journal of Academic Librarianship,* May 1996, 209–11.

———. "Sleepless Nights Redux." *Against The Grain,* February 1998, 29.

———. "Things That Keep Me Awake At Night." *Against the Grain,* February 1997, 40–42.

———. "TULIP—The University Licensing Project." *Journal of Interlibrary Loan, Document Delivery, and Information Supply* 4, nos. 3 and 4, 1994: 19.

International Coalition of Library Consortia. "Guidelines for Statistical Measures of Usage of Web-Based Indexed, Abstracted, and Full Text Resources." *http://www.library.yale.edu/consortia/webstats.html.*

"Internet EDGAR snatched from death!" *Searcher* 3, no. 9 (October 1995), 18.

Joint Funding Councils' Libraries Review Group. *Report* (Bristol, England: External Relations Department, HEFCE, 1993).

Kahin, Brian, and Hal R. Varian, eds. *Internet Publishing and Beyond: The Economics of Digital Information and Intellectual Property* (Cambridge, MA: MIT Press, 2000).

Kalin, Sari. "Deregulation; Foreign Internet access costs soar above United States." *InfoWorld* October 28, 1996, p. TW/2.

Kaplan, Philip J. *F'd Companies: Spectacular Dot-Com Flameouts* (New York: Simon & Schuster, 2002).

Kenney, Anne R. "Digital Benchmarking for Conversion and Access," 28–29. In Anne R. Kenney and Oya Y. Rieger, *Moving Theory into Practice: Digital Imaging for Libraries and Archives* (Mountain View, CA: Research Libraries Group, 2000), 24–60.

———. "Digital Image Quality: From Conversion to Preservation and Beyond." In Richard Ekman and Richard E. Quandt, eds., *Technology and Scholarly Communication* (Berkeley: University of California Press, 1999).

———. "Digital Resolution Requirements for Replacing Text-Based Materials: Methods for Benchmarking Image Quality." The Commission on Preservation and Access, April 1995.

Kenney, Anne R. and Oya Y. Rieger. *Moving Theory into Practice: Digital Imaging for Libraries and Archives* (Mountain View, CA: Research Libraries Group, 2000).

Kernan, Alvin. *In Plato's Cave* (New Haven: Yale University Press, 1999).

Kingma, Bruce R. "The Economics of Access versus Ownership: The Costs and Benefits of Access to Scholarly Articles via Interlibrary Loan and Journal Subscriptions." In Meredith A. Butler and Bruce R. Kingma, eds., *The Economics of Information in the Networked Environment* (Washington, DC: Association of Research Libraries, 1996).

Kohl, David F. "Cheaper by the (Almost Half) Dozen: The Ohio State-Wide Remote Storage System." In Danuta A. Nitecki and Curtis L. Kendrick, eds., *Library Off-Site Shelving: Guide for High-Density Facilities* (Englewood, CO: Libraries Unlimited, 2001).

Kyrillidou, Martha, and Mark Young. *ARL Supplementary Statistics 1999–2000* (Washington, DC: ARL, 2001).

Lemberg, William Richard. "A Life-Cycle Cost Analysis for the Creation, Storage and Dissemination of a Digitized Document Collection." Ph.D. dissertation, Berkeley, 1995.

Liblicense discussion list. Available at *http://www.library.yale.edu/~llicense/ListArchives/*.

"Library Space Use." Unsigned memorandum, December 22, 1993, Denison University librarian's office.

Line, Maurice. "Access as a substitute for holdings: false ideal or costly reality?" *Interlending & Document Supply* 23, no. 2 (1995): 28–30.

Lougee, Wendy, and Jeffrey Mackie-Mason, eds., *Bits and Bucks: Economics and Usage of Digital Collections* (Cambridge, MA: MIT Press, forthcoming).

Lowry, Charles B. "Resource Sharing of Cost Shifting?—The Unequal Burden of Cooperative Cataloging and ILL in Network." *College & Research Libraries,* 51, no. 1 (January 1990): 11–19.

Lynch, Clifford A. "The Battle to Define the Future of the Book in the Digital World," *First Monday.* Available at *http://www.firstmonday.dk/issues/issue6_6/lynch/index.html*.

———. "The TULIP Project: context, history, and perspective." *Library Hi Tech* 13, no. 4 (1995): 8–24.

Machlup, Fritz. "Publishing Scholarly Books and Journals: Is It Economically Viable?" *Journal of Political Economy,* 85, no. 1 (February 1977): 217–25.

Maciuszko, Kathleen L. *OCLC: A Decade of Development* (Littleton, CO: Libraries Unlimited, 1984).

Mackey, Terry. "Interlibrary loan: an acceptable alternative to purchase." *Wilson Library Bulletin,* 63 (January 1989): 54–6.

MacLeod, Donald. "Economic downturn is not the only problem facing e-learning programmes." *Guardian,* April 2, 2002, 20.

Marcum, Deanna B. "Transforming the curriculum; transforming the profession." *American Libraries,* 28, no. 1 (January 1997): 35.

Martin, Thomas H. *A Feature Analysis of Interactive Retrieval Systems* (Springfield, VA: National Technical Information Service, 1974).

Maruskin, Albert R. *OCLC: Its Governance, Function, Financing, and Technology* (New York: Marcel Dekker, 1980).

McGowan, Frank M. "The Association of Research Libraries 1932–1962." Ph.D. dissertation, University of Pittsburgh, 1972.

Mostert, Paul. "TULIP at Elsevier Science." *Library Hi Tech* 13, no. 4 (1995): 25–30.

Nakamura, Cara C. *Wealth Disparities* (Princeton, NJ: Andrew W. Mellon Foundation, 2001, [unpublished]).

Needleman, Mark. "TULIP and the University of California, Part I: Implementation and the Lessons Learned." *Library Hi Tech* 13, no. 4 (1995): 69–72.

"New bibliographic product from Chadwyck-Healy." *CD-ROM World* 8, no. 1 (January 1993): 19.

Nitecki, Danuta A., and Curtis L. Kendrick. *Library Off-Site Shelving: Guide for High-Density Facilities* (Englewood, CO: Libraries Unlimited, 2001).

Noll, Roger, and W. Edward Steinmuller. "An Economic Analysis of Scientific Journal Prices: Preliminary Results." *Serials Review* 18, nos. 1–2 (Spring and Summer 1992): 32–37.

Ogburn, Joyce. "A Look Back at Licensing." *Against the Grain* 13, no. 4 (September 2001).

Okerson, Ann. "Are We There Yet? Online E-Resources Ten Years After," *Library Trends* 48, no. 4 (March 22, 2000): 671.

———. *Of Making Many Books There Is No End: Report on Serial Prices for the Association of Research Libraries.* 1989.

———. "The Transition to Electronic Content Licensing: The Institutional Context in 1997." In Richard Ekman and Richard E. Quandt, eds., *Technology and Scholarly Communication* (Berkeley: University of California Press, 1999): 53–70.

———. "What Academic Libraries Need in Electronic Content Licenses." Presentation to the STM Library Relations Committee, October 1, 1996. Available online at *http://www.library.yale.edu/~okerson/stm.html.*

Page, Gillian, Robert Campbell, and Jack Meadows, eds. *Journal Publishing* (Cambridge: Cambridge University Press, 1997).

Palmour, Vernon E., Edward C. Bryant, Nancy W. Caldwell, and Lucy M. Gray (compilers). *A Study of the Characteristics, Costs, and Magnitude of Interlibrary Loans in Academic Libraries* (Washington, DC: Association of Research Libraries, 1972).

Pasteur, Louis. *Œuvres,* Vallery-Radot, ed., (Paris, 1922–1939), volume 7, 131.

Pavelsek, Mary Jean. "Guidelines for Evaluating E-journal Providers with Applications to JSTOR and Project Muse." *Advances in Librarianship,* 22 (1998): 39–58.

Payne, Valerie J., and Mary Burke. "A cost-effectiveness study of ownership versus access." *Serials Librarian* 32, no. 3–4 (1997): 139–152.

Petroski, Henry. *The Book on the Bookshelf* (New York: Vintage Books, 1999).

Pinto-Duschinsky, Michael. "Selling the Past." *The Times Literary Supplement,* October 23, 1998.

Price-Wilkin, John. "Access to Digital Image Collections: System Building and Image Processing. In Anne R. Kenney and Oya Y. Rieger, eds., *Moving Theory into Practice: Digital Imaging for Libraries and Archives* (Mountain View, CA: Research Libraries Group, 2000): 101–118.

"Printed Back Volumes and Issues: A Thing of the Past?" In P. Michelle Fiander, Joseph C. Harmon, and Jonathan David Makepeace, eds., *From Carnegie to Internet2: Forging the Serials Future* (New York: Haworth Press, 2000): 237–41.

"Proceedings of the Annual Meeting of the Medieval Academy of America." *Speculum,* 70, no. 3 (July, 1995): 718–30.

"Project to Digitize Back Issues of Scientific Journals Gains Support." *Chronicle of Higher Education,* October 23, 1998, A23.

Quandt, Richard E. *The Changing Landscape in Eastern Europe: A Personal Perspective on Philanthropy and Technology Transfer* (New York: Oxford University Press, 2002).

———. "Electronic Publishing and Virtual Libraries: Issues and an Agenda for the Andrew W. Mellon Foundation." *Serials Review* 22 (Summer 1996): 9–24.

———. "Simulation Model for Journal Subscription by Libraries." *Journal of the American Society for Information Science* 47, no. 8 (1996): 66–67.

Quint, Barbara. "The Database Connection: Full of text; Difficulties of Full-text databases." *Document Delivery World* 9, no. 3 (April, 1993): 34.

Regier, Willis. "Electronic Publishing Is Cheaper." In Richard Ekman and Richard E. Quandt, eds., *Technology and Scholarly Communication* (Berkeley: University of California Press, 1999).

Report of the Andrew W. Mellon Foundation (New York: Andrew W. Mellon Foundation, 1985–2000).

"The RLG Conspectus and the National Shelflist Count." In Thomas E. Nisonger, *Collection Evaluation in Academic Libraries: A Literature Guide and Annotated Bibliography* (Englewood, CO: Libraries Unlimited, 1992).

Salmon, Stephen R. "User Resistance to Microforms in the Research Library." *Microform Review* 3, no. 3 (July 1974).

Scholarly Communication: The Report of the National Enquiry (Baltimore: Johns Hopkins University Press, 1979).

"Scholars in 39 Developing Countries Benefit from Database Project." *Chronicle of Higher Education,* December 15, 2000, A47.

Schwartz, Laura, and Sarah Covington. "Renaissance Society of America Council Meeting." *Renaissance Quarterly* 49, no. 4 (Winter 1996): 918.

"'Science' to Appear in Journal Archive on the Web." *Chronicle of Higher Education,* July 24, 1998, A17.

Shapiro, Carl, and Hal R. Varian. *Information Rules: A Strategic Guide to the Information Economy* (Cambridge, MA: Harvard Business School Press, 1999).

Smith, K. Wayne, ed. *OCLC 1967–1997: Thirty Years of Furthering Access to the World's Information* (New York: Haworth Press, 1998).

Strauch, Katina P. "A Conversation with Kevin Guthrie, Executive Director, JSTOR." *Against the Grain,* 9 (April 1997): 31.

Sully, Sarah E. "JSTOR: An IP Practitioner's Perspective." *D-Lib,* January 1997, available online at *http://www.dlib.org/dlib/january97/01sully.html.*

———. "JSTOR—an update on content." *Education Libraries,* 21, no. 3 (1997): 13–15.

Tenopir, Carol, and Donald W. King. "Setting the Record Straight on Journal Publishing: Myth vs. Reality." *Library Journal,* 121 (March 15, 1996): 32–35.

Thomas, Spencer W., Ken Alexander, and Kevin M. Guthrie. "Technology Choices for the JSTOR Online Archive." *Computer,* 32, no. 2 (1999): 60–65.

Thornton, Glenda A. "Impact of Electronic Resources on Collection Development, the Roles of Librarians, and Library Consortia." *Library Trends,* 48, no. 4 (Spring 2000):, 842–56.

Varian, Hal R. "The AEA's Electronic Publishing Plans: A Progress Report." *Journal of Economic Perspectives,* 11, no. 3 (Summer 1997): 95–104.

———. "Differential Pricing and Efficiency." *First Monday,* 2 (1996). Available online at *http://www.firstmonday.dk/issues/issue2/different.*

"VTLS Inc. teams with Princeton University to create database." *Information Today,* 10, no. 6 (June 1993): 50.

Wanat, Camille. "TULIP and the University of California, Part II: The Berkeley Experience and a View Beyond." *Library Hi Tech,* 13, no. 4 (1995): 73–74.

Warro, Edward A. "What Have We Been Signing? A Look at Database Licensing Agreements." *Library Administration & Management* 8, no. 3 (Summer 1994): 173–77.

Waters, Donald, and John Garrett. *Preserving Digital Information: Report of the Task Force on Archiving of Digital Information* (Washington, DC: Commission on Preservation and Access, 1996).

Watkins, Beverly T. "New Era for Library Schools: They strive to overhaul curricula to reflect the explosion in information technology." *Chronicle of Higher Education*, May 18, 1994.

Weber, David C. "A Century of Cooperative Programs Among Academic Libraries." *College & Research Libraries*, May 1976: 205–221.

What the OCLC Online Union Catalog Means to Me (Dublin, OH: OCLC, 1997).

Willis, Katherine. "TULIP at the University of Michigan." *Library Hi Tech*, 13, no. 4 (1995): 65–68.

Wilson, David L. "Major Scholarly Publisher to Test Journals by Computer." *Chronicle of Higher Education*, June 3, 1992.

Young, Jeffrey R. "Judge Approves Sale of netLibrary's E-Books to Nonprofit Library Group," *Chronicle of Higher Education*, 48, no. 20 (January 25, 2002): A31.

Index